D0230926

CREDIT DERIVATIVES

Applications for Risk Management, Investment and Portfolio Optimisation

CREDIT DERIVATIVES

Applications for Risk Management, Investment and Portfolio Optimisation

Published by Risk Books, a specialist division of Risk Publications.

Haymarket House

28–29 Haymarket

London SW1Y 4RX

©Financial Engineering Ltd 1998

ISBN 1 899332 56 1 (hardback)

ISBN 1 899332 61 8 (softback)

British Library Cataloguing in Publication Data

A catalogue record for this book is available from the British Library

Risk Books Commissioning Editor: Robert Jameson

Typesetter: Miles Smith-Morris

Printed and bound in Great Britain by Selwood Printing Ltd. West Sussex

Conditions of sale

All rights reserved. No part of this publication may be reproduced in any material form whether by photocopying or storing in any medium by electronic means whether or not transiently or incidentally to some other use for this publication without the prior written consent of the copyright owner except in accordance with the provisions of the Copyright, Designs and Patents Act 1988 or under the terms of a licence issued by the Copyright Licensing Agency Limited of 90, Tottenham Court Road, London W1P 0LP.

Warning: the doing of any unauthorised act in relation to this work may result in both civil and criminal liability.

Every effort has been made to ensure the accuracy of the text at the time of publication. However, no responsibility for loss occasioned to any person acting or refraining from acting as a result of the material contained in this publication will be accepted by Financial Engineering Ltd.

Many of the product names contained in this publication are registered trade marks, and Risk Books has made every effort to print them with the capitalisation and punctuation used by the trademark owner. For reasons of textual clarity, it is not our house style to use symbols such as TM, ®, etc. However, the absence of such symbols should not be taken to indicate absence of trademark protection; anyone wishing to use product names in the public domain should first clear such use with the product owner.

PREFACE

The emergence of a market in credit risk derivatives is one of the most exciting recent developments in investment banking and risk management. An alluring feature of these instruments is that they offer bankers a new way to establish themselves as intermediaries in the credit market. Using financial engineering techniques imported from other derivative markets, bankers are busily transforming some readily definable blocks of credit risk into the kind of standardised credit-linked securities that investors demand.

Yet this is simply the icing. The cake itself is the more intractable wedge of credit risk submerged in the loan and derivative portfolios of banks, financial institutions and large corporations around the world. This "tied" credit risk is the most fundamental of the risks borne by the financial industry, yet over the last two decades it has stood firm while interest rate risks, equity risks and even commodity risks have liquefied around it.

Why is this? One reason is that while all bankers know the value of credit, no-one knows its price. A rash of new pricing models is being promoted in the credit market, but like all models these depend on inputs. They tend to assume either that the probability of default of any given credit reference is known, or that the difference between a credit-risky and a credit-riskless interest rate (such as the rate offered by US government debt) is solely dependent upon the price of the credit risk trapped in the risky security. These assumptions are more convenient than true.

Model-watchers know this, but observers outside the loop seem to be hoping that the credit market will one day discover its own "real" model. After all, the discovery of the Black–Scholes model gave birth to the other derivatives markets, did it not? It did not. Markets in options have existed since the 18th century at least, and the Chicago Board Options Exchange opened just *before* the Black–Scholes paper was published. Black–Scholes was fundamental to the development of the modern derivatives market because it showed mathematically how *existing* prices could be converted into an "implied volatility", which could then be backed out to give the value of an option and of all sorts of related instruments of various tenors. It was a way of leveraging price information across markets and instrument structures, not a magical source of price discovery.

Herein lies the problem. In the credit markets today, there is very little basic information about the price of naked credit risk. This is why the new credit models are necessary but not sufficient. They need to be fed with prices free of distortions caused by market inefficiencies, arbitrary investor preferences, tax strategies and government regulations. Paradoxically, this means that growth in the market for credit derivatives may depend upon ... growth in the market for credit derivatives. At a certain stage, not yet reached, the market in various kinds of agreements that offer naked credit risk will attain a critical informational mass. At that point, models already developed will suddenly multiply in practical relevance and power. Pools of liquidity will grow and start to flow into each other, spilling information back into the "dirty" credit markets we know today.

As this happens, there will be a bonanza for those who master the instruments that measure, price, slice, and transfer portfolio credit risk, whether the risk is pushed towards the securities markets or traded and swapped over the counter. Provided that risk managers can prevent credit derivatives turning into the financial industry's equivalent of "smoke and mirrors", there will also be a wider industry gain in terms of safer and more efficient portfolio management.

To realise this promise, leading banks are setting in train a series of changes in the way they organise themselves and how they are regulated. The most daunting aspect of these changes is the extent to which they are interrelated; it is difficult to tackle them sequentially. Likewise, readers of the diverse writings in this book will find themselves moving backwards and forwards between discussions of instrument structure, applied risk management, credit modelling, bank structure, regulatory trends, taxation and many other theoretical and practical concerns.

This oscillation, rather than the sophistication of the derivative structures, seems to be a defining feature of the new credit market. As well as offering clear explanations of the family of contracts that have come to be known as credit derivatives, we hope this book captures some of that dynamic. And that it helps explain why credit derivatives are likely to have such a profound effect on the financial institutions of the future.

CONTENTS

REGULATORY TRENDS AND ISSUES
IN TAXATION

APPLYING CREDIT DERIVATIVES
KEY THEMES AND EXAMPLES

Throughout this book special panels introduce key themes and offer illustrative examples:

CONTRIBUTORS

W. Robert Allen is Head of Global Investments at Westpac Banking Corporation in Sydney. Robert has been associated with credit portfolio management and the evolution of the credit derivatives markets both in his present role and in previous roles in credit and market risk management areas. Robert's exposure to related global credit and financial markets activity spans 28 years, taking in most of the world's major international financial centres, firstly with Bankers Trust and then with Westpac. Robert holds a Bachelor of Economics degree from the University of Sydney and an MBA from the Wharton School of the University of Pennsylvania.

Elliot Asarnow is a managing director and co-founder of ING Capital Advisors, Inc, an investment management firm that specialises in managing portfolios of floating rate, senior secured corporate bank loans and packaging them to provide investors with a wide spectrum of risk/return alternatives. Prior to joining ING in 1995, Elliot was a managing director at Citibank, NA, where he had directed the activity of the bank's North American Global Finance portfolio strategies group since 1987.

Karen E. Becker is the Director of Treasury Documentation for the Toronto-Dominion Bank in London. Previously, Karen worked in New York specialising in Emerging Markets and Derivatives.

She has served on various working groups for the Emerging Markets Traders Association and ISDA, and was awarded a Masters Degree in International Relations in 1987.

Richard B. Buy is a senior vice president in Enron with specific responsibility for identifying, quantifying and controlling risks in both Enron's trading activities and investment opportunities. Additionally, Rick is responsible for managing the overall portfolio of Enron investments with the goal of tracking investment returns and controlling exposures to various risks at the portfolio level. These activities are administered from the Risk Assessment and Control Division of Enron, which reports to the Office of the Chairman of Enron, and is outside of any of the operating groups or profit centres. Rick is also president and principal at Enron Capital & Trade Resources (ECT) Broker/Dealer firm, ECT Securities Inc., which gives ECT the legal capabilities of selling securities, and is a board member of Mariner Energy and CGAS Production Company. Prior to joining Enron in April 1994, Rick was a vice president at Bankers Trust in New York and Houston where he was involved in various facets of the energy lending and trading businesses. He has a BS in Mechanical Engineering and an MBA in Finance from Rensselaer Polytechnic Institute and an MS in Petroleum Engineering from the University of Houston. Rick also holds series 7,

16 and 24 licenses from the NASD and is a Registered Professional Engineer.

Arturo Cifuentes is a senior vice-president within the Structured Finance group of Moody's Investors Service. His major responsibilities are in the area of collateralised debt obligations, asset-backed securities, structured notes, credit-linked notes and emerging markets. Before switching to the financial arena, Arturo worked as a scientist and engineer, first at The MacNeal-Schwendler Corporation in Los Angeles, California, and then at the IBM Research Division in Yorktown Heights, New York, specialising in earthquake engineering, finite elements and numerical methods. He also held faculty positions at the University of Chile, the University of Southern California and the California State University. Arturo holds a degree in Civil Engineering from the University of Chile; an MS in Civil Engineering, and a PhD in Applied Mechanics from the California Institute of Technology; and an MBA in Finance from New York University.

Robert DeSantes is Head of Corporate Banking for CRT in the United States. In addition to overseeing the bank's corporate activities in the US, he is also responsible for the bank's credit derivative activities. During the past two years CRT has transacted over

$1 billion in default and total return swaps. During his 25 years or so as a banker, Bob has gained experience in trade finance, aircraft leasing and general corporate banking. He has a BBA in Finance and Economics and has performed graduate work at the University of Chicago and the Darden School of Business at the University of Virginia.

Isaac Efrat is a vice-president with Moody's Investors Service's Structured Finance group, where he is primarily involved with credit derivatives, structured notes and catastrophe-linked bonds. He has previously held positions as a derivative analyst and marketer and as a foreign exchange trader. He holds a PhD in mathematics and has served on the faculties of MIT and Columbia.

Matthew Elderfield is ISDA's Director of European Policy and head of the Association's London-based European Office. In addition to directing ISDA's overall activities in Europe, he has lead responsibility for ISDA's work on EMU, risk management, capital adequacy and European Union legislation. Matthew has worked previously for the British Bankers' Association and the London Investment Banking Association, and has held brief secondments with the Bank of England and the Securities and Futures Authority.

David Geen is a partner in the Banking & Finance group of Baker & McKenzie's London office. His practice covers a wide range of international financing transactions and he specialises in derivatives and derivatives-related financings. In particular, he is involved with structured products and with advising financial institutions and end-users on their OTC derivatives documentation and other aspects of their derivatives activities,

including with respect to credit derivatives. He is a participant in various industry working groups on derivatives documentation and regularly speaks at conferences on issues relating to derivatives.

Mark Gheerbrant is Head of Credit Trading & Structuring and the Global Product Manager for Credit Derivatives for Rabobank International, London. After graduating from Bristol University with a degree in Mechanical Engineering, Mark joined Arthur Andersen in London, where he qualified as a Chartered Accountant. Since then he has spent 12 years in investment banking in various roles, primarily in derivatives trading and structured finance with Swiss Bank Corporation, IBJ and, for the last two years, Rabobank International.

Jeremy A. Gluck is currently managing director in the Structured Derivative Products Group at Moody's Investors Service, New York. The group is responsible for ratings of collateralised bond and loan obligations, derivative product companies, structured notes, insurance-linked notes etc. Previously, Jeremy was a vice-president and money market economist at Mitsubishi Bank, New York. Prior to working in the corporate sector, Jeremy was a senior economist at the Federal Reserve Bank of New York. He holds a PhD in Economics from Stanford University.

Walter Gontarek is a managing director of TD Securities, the investment-banking arm of the Toronto-Dominion Bank in London. He joined TD in February 1997 to contribute to the establishment of its first Global Credit Derivatives Group and concentrated on issues relating to credit policy, marketing and documentation. He has since executed $15 billion in credit default swaps, total return

swaps, credit spread options and other credit derivative transactions. He has also worked in a similar position with CIBC Wood Gundy in New York and executed several of its early credit derivative transactions. Walt previously served as a bank privatisation consultant in eastern Europe and as a president of a retail bank subsidiary in the US. He has a BBA from Loyola College, an MBA in Finance from New York University, and a certificate from ISA at the HEC Graduate School of Management in France.

Schuyler K. Henderson is a partner of the international law firm of Baker & McKenzie. Since moving to London in 1977, he has worked closely with many international financial institutions in creating, developing and documenting swaps, related derivatives products and derivatives-driven financings, and advising with respect to enforcement, regulatory, tax and capacity issues. He has published extensively on a number of financial topics and is a frequent speaker at conferences on financial law. Schuyler obtained his undergraduate degree from Princeton University in 1967 and his law degree (JD) and business degree (MBA) from the University of Chicago in 1971 and is a member of the New York and Illinois bars.

Jessica James is in the Strategic Risk Management Advisory group of the First National Bank of Chicago. Jessica started life as a physicist and completed her DPhil in Theoretical Atomic and Nuclear Physics at Christ Church, Oxford. After a year as a college lecturer at Trinity, Oxford, she began work at the First National Bank of Chicago.

Vincent Kaminski is a vice president and head of research in Enron Risk Management and Trading, a unit of Enron Capital & Trade Resources (ECT), based in

Houston, Texas. Vince is responsible for developing analytical tools for pricing commodity options and other commodity transactions, hedging strategies and the optimisation of financial and physical transactions. He joined Enron in June 1992, having previously been vice president in the research department of Salomon Brothers in New York (Bond Portfolio Analysis Group) and a manager in AT&T Communications. Vince holds an MS degree in international economics and a PhD degree in mathematical economics from the Main School of Planning and Statistics in Warsaw, Poland and an MBA from Fordham University in New York.

Samantha Kappagoda is an economist at Caxton Corporation, a New York-based macro hedge fund. Ms Kappagoda joined Caxton after completing an MBA in Finance at the Graduate School of Business, University of Chicago. Prior to her MBA, she worked as an economist at the World Bank in Washington, DC. She also holds a Masters degree in Economics from the University of Toronto, and a Bachelor of Science (Honors) degree in Mathematics from Imperial College of Science and Technology, University of London.

Steven L. Kopp is a senior tax associate at Orrick, Herrington & Sutcliffe LLP working principally in the areas of structured finance and derivative products. He has helped structure a wide variety of innovative financial products and has previously written for the *Journal of Taxation* on the subject of credit derivatives. He received both his JD and LLM (in taxation) from New York University and his BA from the University of Pennsylvania. Steven was previously an associate at Weil, Gotshal & Manges.

David Lando is an associate professor of mathematical finance at

the University of Copenhagen, Department of Operations Research. He holds a PhD in statistics from Cornell University and a degree in mathematics and economics from the University of Copenhagen. His main area of research is the modelling of credit risk. He works as a consultant for Den Danske Bank and SimCorp A/S.

Tom McNerney currently heads TD Securities Market Risk Management Group in London. He previously worked on exotic interest rate derivatives and credit derivatives at TD, being responsible in particular for the development of TD's systems and models for credit derivatives. His trading experience in derivatives includes several years spent at both BZW and SG Warburg. He has a first class honours degree in Mathematics from Cambridge and an MSc in Operational Research from Lancaster.

David K. A. Mordecai is a director in the Commercial Asset Backed Group at Fitch IBCA, Inc., where he participates in rating emerging asset-class securitisations, including credit derivative and swap-dependent structures, franchise loan securitisations and catastrophic risk bonds. As the lead analyst for Fitch IBCA's synthetic securities, structured note and repackaged assets rating effort, David's responsibilities include note rating transactions and developing rating analytics for equity-, commodity-, asset swap-, and credit-linked notes. He is currently working on a PhD at the University of Chicago Graduate School of Business, for which his research involves credit arbitrage and the intermediation of credit risk. He joined Fitch upon completion of PhD coursework in finance, economics, probability, and statistical decision theory.

Since 1984, he has been employed as a capital markets professional for various financial institutions in New York. David has worked as an Assistant Vice President at WestLB, a Vice President at an investment bank, and as a consultant to senior management of a Fortune 100 company. He is also an MBA (1987) graduate in finance from the New York University, Stern Graduate School of Business.

Eileen Murphy is a managing director in the Structured Derivative Products Group at Moody's Investors Service, New York. The group is responsible for ratings of collateralised bond and loan obligations, derivative product companies, structured notes, insurance-linked notes etc. Prior to working at Moody's, Eileen was an associate at the New York law firm of Seward & Kissel, working in the areas of corporate finance and bankruptcy law. She holds a JD degree from the University of North Carolina at Chapel Hill.

David Z. Nirenberg is a partner at Orrick, Herrington & Sutcliffe LLP where he is the Chair of the firm's New York Office Tax Practice Group. He has played a significant role in the structuring of a wide variety of innovative domestic and cross-border financial products in both the structured finance and derivative products markets. David also advises real estate investment funds and regulated investment companies. He has written and lectured extensively in the area of financial products. He received his JD from Columbia University, an MBA from Boston University and a BS from Cornell University. David was previously of counsel at Weil, Gotshal & Manges and an associate at Cleary, Gottlieb, Steen & Hamilton.

Krishnarao Pinnamaneni is a risk manager in the research group at Enron Corp., based in Houston, Texas. His research interests are in the areas of commodity finance, valuation of assets and contracts as real options, and application of optimisation methods for trading and risk management. He received a Bachelors degree in Mechanical Engineering from the Indian Institute of Technology at Madras, a Masters degree in Statistics from Rensselaer Polytechnic Institute and a PhD in Operations Research from Stanford University.

Richard Quinn is a director of the British Bankers' Association (BBA), covering financial regulation and supervision of the wholesale markets in the Markets and Regulation team. Current areas of activity include the reform of the regulatory structure, the implementation of CAD2 and Basle and credit derivatives. Between 1986 and 1996 he worked at the Bank of England. Between 1990 and 1994, he was seconded by the Bank to the Office of the UK Permanent Representative to the EU in Brussels, where he represented the UK in negotiations on financial services.

Robert Reoch is Managing Director and Global Head of Credit Derivatives at Bank of America, based in San Francisco. Before joining Bank of America in 1997, he was a Director at Nomura International plc in London, where he was responsible for building Nomura's credit derivative business. Prior to Nomura, Robert spent 10 years at JP Morgan. From 1988 to 1993 he was based in Hong Kong and worked in the M&A Group covering the Philippines and Indonesia. His last year in Hong Kong was spent on the team advising on the new Hong Kong airport. On his return to London in 1993, he joined the Investor Derivatives Marketing

Group where he was responsible for setting up JP Morgan's European credit derivatives business. Robert holds a degree in Chinese and Law from the University of Cambridge.

David M. Rowe is a senior vice president at Bank of America in charge of the Risk Management Information Group within Trading Exposure Control and Compliance. His primary responsibility is the design and deployment of global systems for monitoring credit and market risk on trading activities (especially derivatives, foreign exchange and securities trading) and development of aggregate management reporting on such exposures. David holds a PhD in Econometrics and Finance from the University of Pennsylvania in addition to an MBA in Finance from the Wharton Graduate School and a BA in Economics from Carleton College.

Vasant Shanbhogue is a director of research at Enron Corp. Vasant is responsible for developing analytical tools for credit risk management and commodity price risk management, and works closely with the Treasury, Credit and Risk Control Groups. Vasant joined Enron in May 1995 after getting an MBA in Analytic Finance from the University of Chicago. Vasant also holds a PhD in Computer Science from Cornell University and a BTech in Computer Science from the Indian Institute of Technology, Kanpur.

Richard K. Skora is the founder of Skora & Company Incorporated, a credit risk management consulting firm offering products and services to structure, model, trade and manage credit risky products. This includes traditional products such as loans and bonds as well as non-traditional products such as

over-the-counter financial and commodity derivatives. Richard has worked in the field of credit risk management since 1992. He has developed numerous products and models for portfolio risk management, and has traded exotic credit derivatives including default swaps, default options and basket swaps. Richard has held academic positions at The Institute for Advanced Study in Princeton, and at Columbia University in New York. He received a BS in Mathematics from the University of Illinois in Champaign-Urban and a Phd in Mathematics from the University of Texas in Austin.

Jamie Storrow is the British Bankers' Association Markets and Regulations Analyst. He is responsible for analysing and researching various methods of improving the efficiency of the financial markets, including the area of credit derivatives where he produced the BBA's 1997/98 Credit Derivatives Report. Before joining the BBA in 1997, he worked in equity research for Pacific International Securities. Jamie holds a BA in Economics from the University of Western Ontario and an MSc in Economics from the University of London.

Phyllis S. Thomas is a managing director with The First National Bank of Chicago, where she is Manager of Marketing for First Chicago NBD's Global Risk Management Products. She has been responsible for developing and delivering interest rate, currency rate, commodity, equity and credit risk linked derivative products to corporations, asset managers, financial institutions and regulated entities in the Western Hemisphere. Phyllis earned her MS from Duke University and has an MBA from the University of Chicago in Finance and Accounting.

DEFAULT PROTECTION AND CREDIT PORTFOLIO MANAGEMENT

1

Approaches to Bank Credit Portfolio Diversification

Credit Derivatives and the Alternatives

W. Robert Allen

Westpac Banking Corporation

We are all familiar with the old adage, "don't put all your eggs in one basket."[1] In other words – diversify. But what does it actually achieve? Other chapters in this book also discuss the theoretical basis for portfolio diversification, but if I can be permitted to sum up in layman's words, portfolio diversification offers the next best thing to a "free lunch" that the laws of economics have to offer. For a given expected outcome it can significantly reduce the likelihood of an undesirable unexpected outcome occurring or, turning it around the other way, for a given likelihood of an undesirable unexpected outcome occurring, it can provide a significantly improved expected outcome. For expected outcome, read "return". For the likelihood of an undesirable unexpected outcome occurring, read "risk". Less risk for a given return, or more return for a given level of risk. Of course, this "free lunch" is not entirely free. There may be costs associated with the diversification process.

The key to the "free lunch" is the correlation that exists between the possible returns from each pair of assets or, more particularly, the less than perfect positive correlation that generally exists between most asset returns. Correlation measures the extent to which pairs of numbers tend to move together. In the credit context, it is the extent to which a default on one loan makes it more or less likely that a default will occur on another. As Chapter 9 discusses in more detail, the more the success or failure of the respective borrowers is linked to the same economic drivers – geography, industry, and so on – the more highly correlated their likelihood of default will be.

The worst case, from a diversification per- spective, is where two investment returns are perfectly positively correlated. Their returns move in lock-step, as if they were effectively identical investments. This achieves no diversification whatsoever. The best case from a risk reduction point of view is where the returns are perfectly negatively correlated and the perfectly offsetting gains and losses eliminate risk entirely, though usually any potential upside is eliminated in the process. However, this still leaves the entire range of possible correlations in between perfect positive and perfect negative where the risk of the combination of any pair is still always less than the sum of the individual risks of the pair. The mathematical proof of this basic proposition is robust; Panel 1 overleaf further illustrates the point.

The limit to the risk-reducing potential of diversification is the point where only that risk remains which is common to the entire investment universe. This is the so-called "systematic" risk deriving from changes in the basic social, political, economic, technological and physical environment that affect everybody and everything. All the so-called "idiosyncratic" risk relating to the impact of specific changes on specific economic units can – in theory – be diversified away.

Relative to other financial assets such as equities, the correlations between the default-driven risks on debt instruments are very low. Consequently, the reduction in risk that can be achieved through further diversification of debt portfolios continues well beyond the point where further diversification of equity portfolios would suffer diminishing returns.

Another argument in favour of the broad diversification of credit portfolios is the highly

PANEL 1

CORRELATION, RISK AGGREGATION AND DIVERSIFICATION

The effect of correlation on risk aggregation can be shown diagrammatically. Imagine we hold an investment A with risk equal to 10 units. We have the opportunity to invest in another investment B, also with risk equal to 10 units. The figure shows how the risks of the two investments combine under different correlation assumptions.

As correlation falls from +1.0 to –1.0, the angle at which the two individual risks combine to determine the risk of the portfolio declines from 180° to 0°.

The improvement in the return for risk through diversification arises because the expected income from the combination of any two assets is the simple sum of their individual expected incomes. But as we have seen, unless the two risks are perfectly correlated the risk of the combination is always less than the simple addition of the two risks in isolation.

Assume that the expected income from each of investment A and investment B is equal at 2.5 units, giving a total portfolio income of 5 units. The table below shows how the risk-reducing potential of correlation illustrated in the figure translates into improved returns for risk for the combined portfolio.

Effect of correlation on risk aggregation

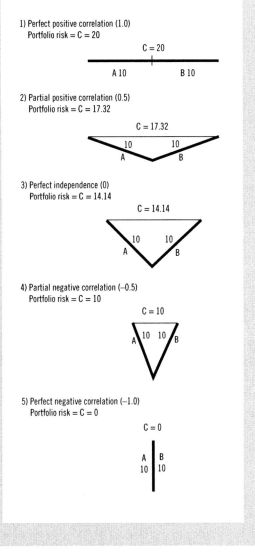

1) Perfect positive correlation (1.0)
   Portfolio risk = C = 20

2) Partial positive correlation (0.5)
   Portfolio risk = C = 17.32

3) Perfect independence (0)
   Portfolio risk = C = 14.14

4) Partial negative correlation (–0.5)
   Portfolio risk = C = 10

5) Perfect negative correlation (–1.0)
   Portfolio risk = C = 0

Risk reduction through diversification

Correlation	1.0	0.5	0	–0.5	–1.0
Combined risk reduction (%)	0	13.4	29.3	50.0	100
Combined risk	20.0	17.32	14.14	10.00	0
Combined income	5	5	5	5	5
Combined return on risk (%)	25	28.9	35.4	50.0	∞

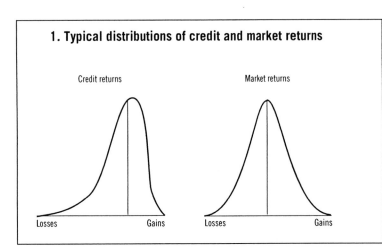

1. Typical distributions of credit and market returns

Credit returns   Market returns

Losses   Gains   Losses   Gains

skewed shape of the distribution of possible returns on each of the credits making up the portfolio. Unlike the typical normal distribution of asset returns, where gains or losses of equal magnitude are of equal probability, with credit instruments the upside is truncated: it is limited to the contractually agreed rate of interest, whereas the downside may lead to the loss of all principal. Probabilities aside, possible losses far exceed possible gains (Figure 1). In a highly concentrated credit portfolio, the probability of default and hence the "expected" loss may well be very low, but most likely so also would be the interest return. While it may appear remote, if it did occur, a single "unexpected" default could be large enough to be fatal. Obviously, the smaller the size of the individual credits in a portfolio, the less damage any single default can inflict. The less correlated those individual credits are with one another, the lower the likelihood of multiple defaults inflicting major damage.

For any given tolerance for risk of loss, a rational investor should always seek to maximise his expected return or, alternatively, for any given desired expected return, to minimise the risk. This should be so regardless of the particular risk appetite of the investor – or banker – concerned. For a given level of risk, more return is always better than less. For a given expected return, less risk is always better than more.

As indicated earlier, risk can be viewed as the likelihood of an unexpected undesirable outcome occurring. However, in the credit context it is important to distinguish between the admittedly undesirable but nonetheless "expected" loss on a portfolio and the possibility of further "unexpected" losses. Only the "unexpected" element constitutes real risk. The "expected" element is the mean, or average, of the possible loss distribution for the particular credit or portfolio in question, which is generally estimated or inferred from historic data. The "expected" element should be recognised as an unavoidable cost of engaging in the credit extension business: it should be an "unexpected" pleasant surprise if it does not occur. "Expected loss" should therefore be charged directly to Profit and Loss and written off; it has very direct implications for the pricing of credit risky instruments, as Chapter 8 of this book explains. On the other hand, the potential for further "unexpected" loss means that the bank must also hold a capital buffer or cushion so that it can weather any "unexpected" events.

The discussion to follow is restricted to the diversification of credit risk. While the overall risk exposure of a bank may in fact be reduced by diversification across other broad risk types, such as interest rate risk, which are less than perfectly correlated with credit risk, that discussion falls outside the scope of this chapter. Also, I will not address the use of corporate mergers and acquisitions as a means of achieving credit risk diversification because the end result of such initiatives may well be overwhelmed by the impact on other, potentially more dominant, business risks. Needless to say, opportunities for credit portfolio diversification through mergers and

acquisitions do still exist. Finally, I have assumed that it is an appropriate prerogative of bank managements to diversify credit risk at the individual bank level. I do not believe it is economically feasible to leave the job of credit risk diversification to end-investors through their selection of diversified portfolios of bank stocks with individually concentrated underlying loan portfolios.

The remainder of the chapter will first review the "portfolio concentration limit" (as distinct from "portfolio optimisation") approach to credit portfolio diversification, and examine the conditions that make credit portfolio optimisation achievable. We then move on to assess the effectiveness of the whole range of transactional tools available to banks to pursue the diversification of their credit portfolios. The conclusion provides a brief assessment of where we currently are on the road towards the ideal of credit portfolio optimisation, and of the possible implications for the structure of banking institutions of further moves in that direction.

Concentration limits

In the past, most bank managements and regulators have not sought to optimise the risk/return balance of credit portfolios through diversification, but rather to limit risk in absolute terms through the imposition of constraints, or limits, on portfolio concentration. These limits generally apply to individual borrowers, industries and geographies. Little, if any, attention was paid to return, and hence return for risk, in setting these limits. The focus was almost exclusively on risk in isolation – the risk that a default by a single borrower, or a downturn in the financial fortunes of a particular geographic region or industry, could threaten the survival of the bank. This is a legitimate concern – it just does not go far enough.

Regulatory single-borrower concentration limits are usually set at some arbitrary percentage of bank capital without reference to the risk of the particular exposure or the overall portfolio within which it resides. Up until quite recently, internally imposed bank limits on single borrowers, industries, or geographic regions, were equally non-discriminatory. Such "one size fits all" limits inevitably mean that new value-creating business in some segments will be rejected, while new value-diluting business in others will be permitted.

More recently, banks have at least sought to establish limits which reflect the relative riskiness of the particular borrowers or segments,

PANEL 2

INDUSTRY CONCENTRATION LIMITS AT WESTPAC

Westpac recently revamped its methodology for setting industry concentration limits to reflect the portfolio effects of correlations between the modelled sensitivities of each industry grouping to a series of assumed economic shocks (as opposed to the relative sensitivities of each industry grouping when viewed in isolation).

The bank's total tolerable portfolio risk limit is set with reference to both the bank's available capital and the required statistical confidence level for the adequacy of that capital buffer to absorb credit losses in the face of extremely adverse economic conditions. The total risk figure is allocated in equal shares to each industry grouping. The asset portfolio limit for each industry grouping is then calculated such that its contri-

bution to the risk of the total portfolio, taking correlation into account, equals its allocated share of the total.

While this new approach represents a major advance on the former non-correlation based methodology, it falls well short of the ideal. It remains exclusively "risk" driven, rather than "return on risk" driven – as would be required for portfolio optimisation. As each industry grouping's risk contribution is set the same, the portfolio would only be optimal if each industry grouping's profit contribution was also the same – a highly unlikely occurrence. As a practical matter, it will be some time before data and modelling capabilities permit banks such as Westpac to progress to an approach based on true portfolio optimisation.

though these still treat the risk in isolation and do not account for the impact on the risk of the combined portfolio. Some more progressive banks are now endeavouring to take the next step forward, and are establishing limits that take account of the historic correlations of credit default experience across industry and geographic segments (see Panel 2). However, an enormous gulf exists between establishing rational, correlation-based segment limit constraints on the possible shape of a bank's credit portfolio, and designing optimal credit portfolios. The data and market efficiency requirements needed to take that final step are daunting.

It is interesting to note that if the necessary conditions for portfolio optimisation were to be met, risk concentration limits would be unnecessary. All that would be necessary is a single minimum return on (risk) capital "hurdle rate". All deals would be evaluated on the basis of their expected income and their incremental contribution to the risk (capital requirement) of the entire portfolio, taking correlation into account. As the concentration of particular risk exposures increased, correlation between further transactions with those same risk characteristics and the rest of the portfolio would increase and consequently so would the marginal increment to total portfolio risk (capital requirements). Ultimately, marginal deals would be declined simply because the expected incremental income failed to achieve the hurdle rate of return on the incremental capital requirement.

Requirements for credit portfolio optimisation

The goal of credit portfolio diversification should be portfolio optimisation, ie to seek to move the portfolio in the direction of the maximum achievable expected return for a given level of risk, or the minimum achievable level of risk for a desired expected return. In an optimal portfolio of any given size, assets are selected from within the available universe and weighted such that, at the margin, their expected income return on their incremental contribution to the risk of the portfolio does not reduce the expected income return on the total risk of the portfolio. The critical factor is the marginal impact of an asset on the risk of the total portfolio – as distinct from the risk of the asset when viewed in isolation.

To construct and maintain a truly optimal credit portfolio in an ideal world, three ingredients are needed:
1) complete knowledge of the available returns, default probabilities and potential loss recoveries of each credit and their correlations with every other credit;
2) the computational capacity to derive the optimal portfolio from among the total universe of opportunities; and
3) the ability to trade freely and efficiently in every form of credit exposure.

While the increasing pace of deregulation in financial markets in recent years and the rapid development of financial and information technology are combining to create an environment in which both the benefits of credit portfolio diversification are becoming more evident, and the opportunities to achieve it more varied and accessible, we are still a very long way from 1) and 3) above becoming a reality. For 2) we are probably already there in terms of the optimisation methodology, if not quite in terms of the amount of computer processing power required.

Transactional tools for credit portfolio diversification

Table 1 summarises the range of transactional tools now available to banks to diversify their credit portfolios. In this section, we look at the merits of each tool in more detail.

CUSTOMER RELATIONSHIP LENDING – THE BANKER'S PARADOX

Lending to customers is an obvious place to start building a loan portfolio. It is unlikely to lead to optimal portfolio diversification, however. On the contrary, it is quite likely to lead to high levels of portfolio concentration. This is due to the aptly named "banker's paradox". In seeking to maximise the efficiency of their loan origination and related customer-servicing activities, banks focus their efforts on areas where they believe they have a competitive marketing advantage. This leads to relative strategic marketing concentrations by geography, industry, demographics and other market characteristics; in turn, these translate into credit concentrations in the composition of the loan portfolios that result.

Thus, there is a conflict between optimisation in terms of loan origination efficiency on the one hand, and optimisation in terms of the risk/return efficiency achievable from a more diversified loan portfolio (requiring a less cost-effective, more diffused origination strategy), on the other. The lesser the geographic reach and the narrower the demographic, industry and product focus of the bank in question, the more acutely this conflict is likely to apply. The multi-product nature of customer banking relationships reduces further banks' ability to control the types of loan assets originated from the perspective of loan portfolio optimisation.

Lending decisions are often reactive, and driven by the need to support the sale of other banking services, rather than pro-active (ie driven by the attractiveness of the loans themselves in terms of optimising the bank portfolio). Multi-product customer relationships act as an even greater constraint on the disposal of existing customer loan assets in search of optimisation. Customer lending is therefore more likely to create the need for other means of loan portfolio diversification than to provide a mechanism for achieving optimal portfolio diversification.

PRIMARY MARKET LOAN SYNDICATION

Loan syndication has been around for a long time and it remains one of the most common means employed by banks to satisfy customer needs for borrowings that are much larger than the individual bank's appetite for exposure to the particular borrower. Under a standard loan syndication, one bank, or possibly a small group of banks, is granted a mandate by the borrower to arrange the required amount of financing on agreed terms. Nowadays, the lead banks usually agree to underwrite the transaction, which provides the borrower with certainty that the funds will become available, though sometimes the arrangement is on the basis of "best efforts" only.

The lead managers then invite other banks, often at the suggestion of the borrower, to participate as lenders in the transaction. Generally the larger the commitment the higher the rate of fee

Table 1. Transactional tools for bank credit portfolio diversification

	ADD EXPOSURE	REMOVE EXPOSURE
Customer relationship lending	Solicit new customer borrowings	Terminate existing customer borrowing relationships
Primary market loan syndication	Participate in other banks' customer loan syndications	Syndicate customer loans to other banks
Secondary market loan trading	Buy assignments of, or participations in, other banks' customer loans	Sell assignments of, or participations in, customer loans to other banks
Debt securities trading	Buy debt securities issued by individual target borrowers	Sell (short) debt securities issued by individual target borrowers
Securitised loan dealing	Buy debt securities representing securitised diversified portfolios of loans	Securitise and sell portfolios of customer loans
Credit derivatives dealing	Buy credit derivatives such as default swaps and total return swaps, on owned or target credits	Sell credit derivatives such as default swaps and total return swaps, on owned or target credits
Credit-linked structured securities dealing	Buy structured debt securities with embedded credit derivatives	Issue/sell structured debt securities with embedded credit derivatives

APPROACHES TO
BANK CREDIT
PORTFOLIO
DIVERSIFICATION

participation and the higher the seniority status in the syndicate. Each participating bank becomes a direct lender to the borrower for the amount of its participation, but one of the lead banks assumes the ongoing responsibility as agent for the syndicate, to monitor compliance by the borrower with the agreed terms of the transaction and generally to represent the interests of the syndicate with the borrower.

Compared to "large ticket" bilateral lending, primary loan syndication clearly has advantages in terms of portfolio diversification. It is a somewhat inflexible tool, however. The lead managers rarely have free rein to structure the syndicate in order to achieve optimum levels of participation for their own portfolios. Customer relationship considerations remain important to borrower and lenders alike. The borrower may want its lead banks to demonstrate their commitment to their broader banking relationships by taking larger participations than they would otherwise wish for. The borrower may also have reasons for wanting to exclude other potential lenders from the syndicate. Nowadays, there is less of this "relationship interference", but it is unlikely ever to disappear completely.

While loan syndication has long been an important part of the banking landscape, up until the late 1980s activity was overwhelmingly concentrated in sovereign and very large corporate credits. Since then, however, a number of factors have come together to extend the loan syndication universe into sub-investment grade US corporate credits. Of particular significance here is the increasing demand for higher yielding short duration debt assets in the US, and the emergence of new players in syndicated loan origination (serving to increase the supply of new deals).

The new demand is coming from US retail investors through mutual funds dedicated to the sub-investment grade corporate loan asset class, as well as US and international insurance company and other non-bank institutional portfolios. On the supply side, the new players are the major US investment banks who, now that US financial market deregulation is blurring the historic distinctions between financial institutions, are seeking to provide one-stop shopping in competition with the traditional lending banks for borrower clients wishing to access both the public issue securities and syndicated bank loan markets.

Figure 2 shows how sub-investment grade bank loan syndication volume in the US has increased almost ten-fold over the past few years, thereby vastly improving the ability of banks to achieve appropriately diversified portfolios within this attractive asset class.

The infrastructural and capital requirements that are needed to underwrite large corporate and sovereign credits make the origination side of the loan syndication business a game for the bigger banks, but the participation side is open to all.

SECONDARY MARKET LOAN TRADING

The secondary market purchase and sale of loans might seem at first sight to be the most logical way for banks to diversify their loan portfolios. In practice this has not been so, however. Up until the end of the 1980s, even in the US, the volumes of secondary market loans traded was minuscule, and that which was traded was almost all "distressed", meaning in default. Customer relationship considerations have tended to act as a constraint on secondary market trading as well as primary loan syndication.

The legal form of the lending arrangements has traditionally also been highly constraining. Loans are often not assignable to other lenders without the permission of the borrower, or sometimes under any circumstances. Where such restrictions apply, the only way to transfer an interest in a loan is likely to be by way of participation, which does not effect a clean transfer. The original lender remains the lender of record to the borrower. The purchaser of the participation is therefore exposed to the risk that the seller may not meet its obligations under the participation, in addition to the risk that the borrower itself may default.

Other necessary but lacking conditions for a liquid secondary market in loans have been the lack of standardised documentation, the lack of standardised trading and settlement conventions,

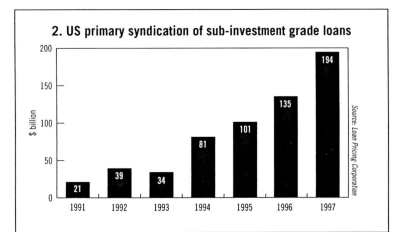

2. US primary syndication of sub-investment grade loans

Source: Loan Pricing Corporation

Year	$ billion
1991	21
1992	39
1993	34
1994	81
1995	101
1996	135
1997	194

the lack of sufficient price makers and quoted market price coverage, the lack of standardised credit ratings, and the lack of sufficient historic data on market prices and credit default and recovery experience. Fortunately, all of these shortcomings are now being addressed.

The Loan Syndication & Trading Association (LSTA) was formed in New York at the end of 1995 and its membership is growing rapidly, now including representation from the institutional investor camp as well as banks. Considerable progress has been made by LSTA in developing and agreeing standard trading documentation and settlement procedures. On behalf of LSTA, a major consultancy has begun collecting and tabulating loan price data on an initial universe of 300 borrowers. The US LSTA initiative has now been followed in Europe by the formation of the Loan Market Association in London. The US Loan Pricing Corporation (LPC) continues to expand the depth and breadth of its loan data collection, analysis and publication efforts, and is seeking ways to play an even more direct role in the facilitation of secondary market loan trading. All of the major US credit rating agencies have now expanded their coverage to include bank loans as well as publicly-issued debt securities.

Figure 3 shows the rapid growth in secondary trading in sub-investment grade US corporate loans from almost zero at the beginning of the decade – an advance spawned by the developments listed above.

DEBT SECURITIES TRADING

In countries where broad, liquid bond markets exist, such as the US, debt securities can represent an extremely useful addition to the credit risk diversification armoury. A large universe of credit exposures can be accessed in this way, ranging from upper-middle-market corporates all the way up to the top investment-grade names. Desired credit exposures can be acquired and disposed of relatively quickly and efficiently without the need for disclosure to or permission from the borrower. In more liquid markets, the ability to short-sell can be an invaluable tool for hedging undesirable or excess loan and counterparty credit exposures where direct exposure reduction is precluded by customer relationship or operational considerations.

One practical difficulty that arises in using traded debt securities as hedges for bank loans is the determination of the appropriate hedge ratio. Usually the bank loans will be the most senior secured obligations of the borrower, with a much

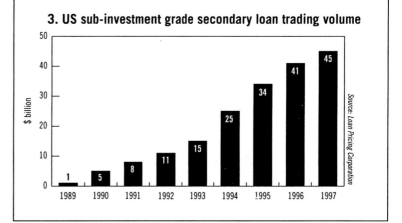

3. US sub-investment grade secondary loan trading volume

Source: Loan Pricing Corporation

higher expected recovery rate in the event of default than the generally more junior unsecured publicly issued securities. Because of the lower expected loss on the loans, generally a lesser amount of bonds would need to be shorted to hedge a given amount of bank loan exposure. Unfortunately, calculating the correct hedge ratio requires the exact relative recovery rates in the event of default, which is unknown (see Panel 3).

Another complication in dealing with bonds is that they are usually fixed interest rate obligations, whereas the bank loans they are hedging are usually floating rate. While most of the interest rate risk can be hedged out using interest rate derivatives, usually some sort of prepayment risk remains.

Banks with the infrastructure and market familiarity that comes with an active involvement in the debt securities markets on behalf of customers or as proprietary traders clearly are better positioned than others to employ traded debt securities for credit portfolio diversification and hedging purposes.

SECURITISATION

The idea of securitisation is to transform pools of assets that are relatively unmarketable in their original form into new forms which are tailored to be attractive, and therefore more marketable, to targeted groups of investors. The underlying assets are sold into a special purpose vehicle (SPV) which then funds the purchase by the sale of its own obligations with characteristics desired by the investors. Over and above the diversification provided by the pooling of the underlying assets, the credit quality of the securitised obligations may be enhanced relative to that of the underlying assets through over-collateralisation, credit insurance and various other techniques. The securitised obligations may take the form of conventional bond-type instruments, pay-

PANEL 3

BOND/BANK LOAN HEDGE RATIO CALCULATION

The expected loss on any credit exposure is a function of the probability of the borrower defaulting and the expected severity of the default, should it occur. Severity is measured in terms of the proportion of the amount defaulted that is actually lost, net of any amounts recovered. The probability of default relates to the entire borrower, rather than just to a particular class of debt instrument, and is therefore the same for all obligations of a particular borrower. The expected severity of the default, however, will vary with the seniority of the particular claim within the borrower's capital structure. For example, senior secured claims rank ahead of senior unsecured claims, which in turn rank ahead of subordinated claims.

The figure below, based on recent research by Moody's, indicates average recovery rates for the respective classes of corporate debt.

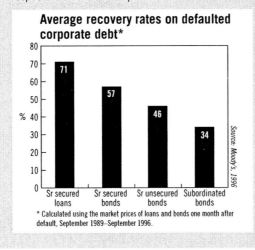

Average recovery rates on defaulted corporate debt*

Source: Moody's, 1996

* Calculated using the market prices of loans and bonds one month after default, September 1989–September 1996.

Based on this data, an average hedge ratio for hedging a senior secured bank loan exposure with a short sale of a senior unsecured bond can be calculated as follows:

Percentage of senior unsecured short sale required
= (1 – expected recovery rate on senior secured bank loans)/(1 – expected recovery rate on senior unsecured bonds)
= (1 – 0.71)/(1 – 0.46)
= 0.29/0.51
= 57%

A short sale of approximately $570,000 of senior unsecured bonds could be employed to hedge a $1 million senior secured loan exposure.

While use of these "average" hedge ratios should produce acceptable results over a very large portfolio of hedges, in practice large portfolios of hedges are unlikely to arise. On a one-off basis, the average hedge ratio could vary from the actual required ratio by a very large margin. This is due to the tremendous dispersion in the range of actual recoveries experienced. The 71% average for senior secured bank loans, for example, results from a distribution ranging from 15% to 98%, with a standard deviation of 21%. Unfortunately, this means that selection of the appropriate hedge ratio on a case-by-case basis cannot be much better than educated guesswork.

ing a fixed income return, with the underlying assets simply pledged as collateral security for the bond-holders. Alternatively, the securities issued may provide for direct flow-through to the investors of the cashflows generated by the underlying assets. There are many possible variations on these themes.

In the context of diversifying bank credit portfolios, securitisation simply expands the range of opportunities open to banks to dispose of assets which are over-weighted relative to the optimal portfolio and to acquire assets in which they are underweight. On the sell side, in particular, it provides another useful tool for addressing the "banker's paradox". It can largely eliminate the optimal portfolio constraint on the volume of a particular asset class that can be originated and serviced on an ongoing basis. In the knowledge

that it can securitise and sell any excess portfolio exposure that it generates, the bank is free to exploit its price- and quality-based competitive advantages in the origination and servicing of particular asset classes in particular markets.

Potentially, the types of assets that can be securitised are almost limitless. As a practical matter, however, the less standardised the contractual form of the asset class, the less reliable historic data there is available on default and pre-payment experience in the asset class; also, the larger the unit size of the asset class, the more difficult it is to structure securitised debt instruments with broad investor appeal. For these reasons, the most commonly securitised asset classes to date have been residential mortgage loans, credit card receivables, auto loans and other kinds of retail customer exposures. One of the most interesting consumer receivable securitisation innovations in recent years took place in Australia where a Westpac vehicle has securitised the margin financing receivables of a share-broker customer, tapping the US commercial paper market for the funding.

Banks and other securitisers are continuously seeking to expand the limits of the securitisable asset universe, and some of the most notable developments in recent years have involved moves into the domain of larger-sized wholesale business lending. Commercial mortgages were a logical first step in this direction and these have now been followed by securitised pools of sub-investment grade corporate bonds, known as collateral bond obligations (or CBOs) and, of greater interest to banks, by securitised diversified pools of interests in sub-investment grade corporate loans, known as collateralised loan obligations (or CLOs). As Chapter 8 explains in more detail, CLOs provide banks with another opportunity to sell excess corporate loan exposures and also to acquire already diversified sub-portfolios of asset classes which the banks are competitively or infrastructurally ill-equipped to originate and service themselves.

The "ROSE" CLO transaction, completed in 1996 by one of the UK clearing banks, provided an early example of a large and complex wholesale loan securitisation exercise. This transaction involved a portfolio of $5 billion of the bank's "wholesale" loans. Aside from its size, this transaction broke much new ground in that it had to contend with the problems of large and widely varying unit size, credit quality and legal form, in the underlying corporate loan exposures. "ROSE" opened the floodgates on a series of large corporate loan portfolio securitising CLOs by other major international banks, several involving further significant innovations, such as the securitisation of credit-linked notes linked to the underlying assets via credit derivatives, rather than securitising the underlying assets themselves.

CREDIT DERIVATIVES
As with their interest rate and currency relatives, credit derivatives provide banks with potentially the most flexible and efficient tools for constructing and modifying portfolios of risk. This is primarily because credit derivatives, as distinct from physical transactions, are almost totally invisible to the parties whose credit exposures are being traded. No permission is required; no disclosure is required. Thus credit exposure can be sold without jeopardising relationships with borrower customers, and can be acquired without having to establish a relationship where one does not already exist. A unique feature of credit derivatives is that the required characteristics of the credit exposure to be traded, such as the amount of notional principal, the tenor and seniority, can be agreed between the contracting parties without the need for underlying debt instruments with those same precise characteristics to even exist. A further important advantage over physical transactions is that the notional principal values of the derivatives do not clog up the balance sheet.

While the range of types of credit derivative is potentially infinite, two basic types currently dominate the market and are likely to do so for the foreseeable future. These are credit default swaps (sometimes referred to as credit default options) and total return credit swaps.

Under the credit default swap (Figure 4a), the credit protection buyer effectively pays a fee to the protection seller in return for the protection seller undertaking to reimburse the buyer for any loss that the buyer may suffer as a consequence of a default on the protected exposure. In substance, a credit default swap is little different from a credit guarantee, but treatment as a swap can have significant advantages in terms of documentation, accounting and tax treatment. The key variables in a credit default swap are the agreed events of default, including some measure of materiality, and the basis for calculating loss in the event of default. This may be linked to the decline in value of some reference security

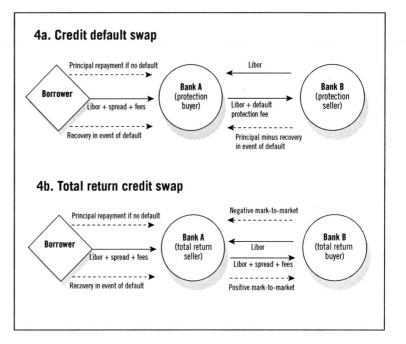

4a. Credit default swap

Principal repayment if no default

Borrower — Libor + spread + fees → Bank A (protection buyer) ← Libor — Bank B (protection seller)

Libor + default protection fee →

Recovery in event of default

Principal minus recovery in event of default

4b. Total return credit swap

Principal repayment if no default

Negative mark-to-market

Borrower — Libor + spread + fees → Bank A (total return seller) ← Libor — Bank B (total return buyer)

Libor + spread + fees →

Recovery in event of default

Positive mark-to-market

issued by the same borrower, or some pre-set percentage of the gross exposure. Alternatively, the swap may grant the right to the protection buyer to assign or participate some of its defaulted underlying loan exposure to the seller at book value. Many variations are possible.

The pricing of credit default swaps is conceptually no different from the pricing of guarantees, or any other credit exposures for that matter. The fee receivable by the protection seller should cover the expected loss on the protected credit plus a margin to cover costs, and provide a satisfactory return on the risk capital required to support both the risk that the loss on the protected credit will be higher than expected, and the risk that the protection seller may also default if called upon to perform on its protection payment obligation.

Total return credit swaps (Figure 4b) go beyond the transfer of pure default exposure to provide for the transfer of a reflection of the entire economic interest in a particular credit exposure or portfolio of exposures. The seller of the total return (equivalent to the protection buyer in the case of a default swap) agrees to pay net amounts to the buyer at set intervals equal to all fees and interest margin on the underlying exposure plus any increase in the capital value of the exposure, or minus any reduction in the capital value of the exposure. If a reduction in the capital value occurs which exceeds the interest and fees receivable by the total return buyer, the flow reverses and there is a net payment from the buyer to the seller. Generally, the capital value at each interval is calculated by marking-to-market but this is not always the case.

In addition to being used to transfer credit exposures between counterparties, total return credit swaps are now also being used within securitisation structures as a means of transferring the economic interest in portfolios of underlying assets into a securitisation vehicle without having to transfer the assets physically.

Again, the pricing and valuation of total return credit swaps is no different conceptually from the pricing and valuation of the underlying exposures. As explained in more detail in Chapter 7, it is a function of expected credit loss and the shape of the distribution of possible unexpected loss and, in the portfolio context, its correlation with the distribution of possible portfolio credit loss.

As the credit derivative markets develop and become more liquid, they will help to make credit prices more transparent, but in and of themselves credit derivatives will not provide any magic formulae. If there are difficulties in correctly assessing an underlying exposure, by definition those same difficulties flow through to its derivative.

The potential for the use of credit derivatives as flexible and efficient tools for credit portfolio management has been widely understood and significant volumes are now being transacted among banks in the upper-middle to upper levels of the sophistication spectrum. Even among these institutions, however, the real potential remains largely untapped. While much progress has been made in terms of "how to transact" with credit derivatives, much less progress has been achieved in terms of "what to transact". This question underlies the technical discussion of portfolio analysis in Chapter 4, and brings us back to the issue of portfolio optimisation.

Recognising the enormous benefits that credit derivatives offer for portfolio diversification, one major US-based global wholesale financial institution devoted much time and effort to trying to organise pool diversifying credit swap arrangements. The idea was to bring groups of banks together, with each bank contributing via credit swaps a given amount of a given number of its large credit exposures and receiving back, also via credit swaps, its proportionate share of the exposures contributed by each other member of the pool. The organising bank was to assist in selecting acceptable exposures, setting pricing, and acting as the counterparty to each pool bank on both sides of the swap. My understanding is that this idea never come to fruition, at least in its original form. There were a number of technical problems and the cost of compensating the organiser for its efforts and counterparty credit exposure was also an issue. However, far and away the most problematic issue was the selection of the appropriate exposures to swap out of and into. How could the swaps be shown to be fair to all parties? How could the natural tendency for all involved to try to get rid of their worst assets and get the best back in return be overcome?

The answer, in theory, is to select impartially that combination of inward and outward swaps which, subject to whatever practical constraints apply, jointly optimises the portfolios of the participating pool members. But can this be done in practice? It is probably still some time before a multilateral pool solution will be feasible, but technology already exists that could determine the jointly optimal solution for a bilateral exchange, at least for top-end corporate credit portfolios.[2] The key to this technology is the derivation of debt default probabilities, and most importantly correlations, by inference from equity price behaviour using options pricing theory. The joint optimisation procedure starts with each bank's current portfolio available for swapping, which represents the universe of potential new exposures available to the other bank. Using independently-sourced data on current market credit yields, default probabilities and default correlations, the optimiser iteratively constructs new portfolios for each bank by switching exposures between them to the point where no further exchange can be made, which both improves the Sharpe Ratio of one bank's portfolio and does not reduce that of the other. The Sharpe Ratio is the ratio of the current portfolio return minus the risk free rate (the risk premium) to the standard deviation of portfolio returns (the risk) – a standardised measure of return for risk.

My understanding is that this technology has yet to be proven in an actual transaction, but it holds enormous promise. Portfolio optimisation aside, its impartial and systematic approach to selection of the exposures to be swapped overcomes perhaps the greatest obstacle to any bilateral or multilateral credit swapping initiative.

CREDIT-LINKED STRUCTURED DEBT INSTRUMENTS

Credit-linked structured notes (or other debt instruments) are really members of the extended credit derivatives family. As in Figure 5, a straight debt instrument can be combined with, say, a credit default swap to return to the investor at maturity the original principal less any net amount payable to the protection buyer under the embedded default swap, should the protected exposure default. The interest rate payable to the investor should be higher than the rate normally payable by the issuer on its straight unstructured debt by an amount approximately equal to the default protection fee receivable under the embedded default swap. The risk to the investor is a function of the default risk of both the issuer of the instrument and the linked credit on which protection has been sold. If either defaults, the investor will suffer. The way in which these two risks combine will again be determined by the extent to which their default probabilities are correlated.

Given the advantages of dealing in derivatives over comparable physical transactions, there might seem little reason for banks to complicate their lives by using credit-linked structured physical instruments as a diversification tool when they could transact the required embedded derivatives directly, and avoid cluttering up their balance sheets. However, most of the demand for credit-linked structured debt does not come from other banks but from other types of investors who, for a variety of reasons, are constrained from dealing in derivatives directly. They may have no choice but to deal in physical instruments with the desired derivative features embedded.

An example would be where a bank was unprepared to transact a credit swap directly with an investor because of its concern about the investor's ability to meet its obligations under the swap if it suffered significant losses from the default of the swapped credit. Also, in some cases the credit-linked note might provide the investor a convenient way of killing two birds with one stone – employing a single investment instrument to take positions on both interest

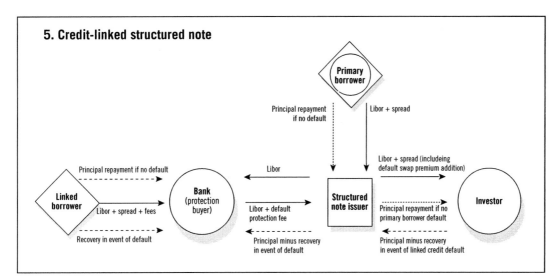

5. Credit-linked structured note

PANEL 4

QUASI-SECURITISATION STRUCTURES

Debt instruments linked to credit derivatives are now being employed in quasi-securitisation structures to reap the principal benefits of securitisation – ie shifting credit risk while tapping new funding sources – without necessitating the removal of the underlying assets from the balance sheet. One way of doing this is to create separate credit-linked notes for each underlying loan via credit derivatives, and then to sell the portfolio of linked notes into a securitisation vehicle. The credit linkage may be by way of default swaps, producing fixed coupon instruments carrying only the underlying credit default risk, or total return swaps, creating instruments which carry both the upside and the downside of credit-induced market price movements in the underlying exposures as well.

An alternative approach is to dispense with the securitisation vehicle and create a single credit instrument linked to the entire portfolio of underlying exposures via credit swaps, either individually or as one or more baskets. It is also possible to introduce leverage into these structures by transacting credit swaps for an underlying asset value of some multiple of the principal value of the linked debt instrument.
See also discussion in Chapter 8.

---

rates and credit. Consequently, most banks cannot afford to omit issuance of credit-linked structured debt instruments from their armoury of diversification weapons. Given the complexity involved in the structuring and risk management of these instruments, however, only the largest and most sophisticated wholesale institutions are equipped to cope with them.

Which tools to use?

It is difficult to be prescriptive about the most appropriate choices among these various portfolio diversification tools for different types of banking institution operating in different market environments. Choices involve trade-offs in terms of the extent of each tool's availability in the particular market, its relative cost, and the operational and financial capacity of the user bank. All of the tools described in this chapter have a place, though credit derivatives offer the greatest all-round flexibility, and therefore the greatest potential for general use in the longer term.

The narrower a particular bank's customer business origination focus – geographically, by industry or product type – in theory the greater its need for the non-customer-origination tools described here. In practice, however, the complexity and cost of gearing up to structure and trade sophisticated credit derivatives and securitised and credit-linked debt instruments, for example, may be beyond a bank's reach. At the top end of the market, all of the tools described above are likely to prove necessary; at the bottom end, as a practical matter the choices may be quite limited.

The way forward

To recap, the necessary conditions for bank credit portfolio optimisation are:
1) complete knowledge of the available returns, default probabilities and potential loss recoveries of each credit and its correlations with every other credit;
2) the computational capacity to derive the optimal portfolio from among the total universe of opportunities; and
3) the ability to trade freely and efficiently in every form of credit exposure.

While this is an ideal, considerable progress has been made in all three areas in recent years, and the pace of that progress is accelerating. However, there is also a critical fourth ingredient:
4) the acceptance by bank managements that credit portfolio optimisation is essential in order to maximise overall stockholder value.

Unfortunately, it is still not clear that most bank managements see credit portfolio optimisation as a necessary goal. There may be a "free lunch" out there, but many do not yet appear to be hungry. They are preoccupied with what they perceive to be more evident, urgent and potentially rewarding priorities – such as better satisfying customer demands for improved products and service, and improving cost efficiency.

What can be done to increase the awareness of bank managements of the potential for increased shareholder value through credit portfolio optimisation? Higher share prices, achieved through increasing earnings without increasing risk, or lower earnings capitalisation rates (and higher price/earnings multiples) achieved through reducing risk, are the ultimate test – though proving cause and effect to a sceptical audience may be difficult. Bank stock analysts and credit ratings agencies have a role to play here. The banking regulators could also help by rewarding banks with less risky, more diversified credit portfolios with concessions on their minimum regulatory capital requirements. There is certainly plenty of room for improvement in the current primitive Basle Accord approach to calculating banks' minimum credit risk capital requirements; these are based on a few very undiscriminating risk categories and do not recognise diversification benefits at all.

Another key practical issue is the question of how banks should structure themselves organisationally to pursue credit portfolio optimisation and deal with the conflicting priorities of the "banker's paradox"? As Chapter 6 describes, given the conflict noted earlier between credit origination cost efficiency on the one hand, and credit portfolio risk efficiency on the other, perhaps the only truly effective solution would be to make non-customer-driven discretionary credit portfolio management a quite separate business from the customer-driven loan origination, distribution, and servicing activities. By virtue of their common ownership, the origination and portfolio businesses could still maintain a "preferred counterparty" relationship, but the portfolio unit would need to have total discretion as to which of the assets offered to it by the origination unit it would accept.

This might be achieved by way of individually determined offers and bids between the origination and portfolio units on a deal-by-deal basis, or alternatively by way of relatively fixed pre-established credit transfer pricing grids based on credit quality, tenor, amount, and industry and other relevant portfolio concentrations. While somewhat more inflexible, the latter would provide more certainty to the originators as to their ability to place any particular loan internally with the portfolio unit. The portfolio unit would still need to be free to source the other credit exposures it needed to optimise its portfolio from the market at large. The volume of customer origination activity that could be supported would

Table 2. US BB/B rated senior secured corporate loans

	Basis point returns over Libor per annum 1990-95		
	Average	Standard deviation	Sharpe Ratio
Citibank BB/B Loan Index	175	110	1.6
Composite of five loan mutual funds	362	41	8.8

become extremely dependent on the ability of the distribution function to syndicate, securitise, and otherwise trade out of excess credit exposures, given that it could no longer rely upon the portfolio unit to absorb whatever was originated.

An illustration of the potential for performance improvement achievable by non-customer-driven active discretionary credit portfolio management, relative to banks' traditionally more customer-driven passive credit portfolio accumulation, is shown in Table 2. This compares the performance of a composite of five mutual funds investing exclusively in sub-investment grade (BB/B) senior secured US corporate bank loans with that of an index representing the average performance of all bank lenders and others investing in the same BB/B grade senior secured US corporate bank loan asset class. The figures show the average returns, the standard deviations (a measure of the variability or risk associated with the returns) and the Sharpe Ratios (a measure of return relative to risk). Over the six years 1990-95, the hard-nosed, non-customer-relationship based, active discretionary portfolio management approach (represented by the mutual funds) generated returns more than double those of the overall market (dominated by the banks) and with significantly less risk.

The dismemberment of banks as we know them, as suggested above, would be a somewhat radical solution. Large numbers of banks – or their successor financial services providers – will not implement these ideas overnight. Even so, the development of financial and information technology and infrastructure continues apace, making the benefits of better, if not yet optimally, diversified credit portfolios both more evident and more accessible to all.

APPROACHES TO BANK CREDIT PORTFOLIO DIVERSIFICATION

1 *This chapter is based upon a paper given at a conference on Credit Risk in Banking that took place at H.C. Coombs Centre for Financial Studies, Sydney, 1–2 May 1997. The chapter is a revised and extended version of an article published in the proceedings of the conference by the Bank Supervision Department, Reserve Bank of Australia, eds B. Gray and C. Cassidy.*

2 *The technology has been developed by the KMV Corporation in San Francisco as an extension of the default probability estimation and single entity portfolio optimisation technology for which this firm is already well known.*

2

Hedging with Credit Derivatives

Practical Applications and Considerations

Walter Gontarek[1]
TD Securities

articipants in the financial markets look to their treasury units to manage the traditional market risks associated with interest rates, currencies, equities and commodities. Shareholders and rating agencies clearly reward firms that reduce cashflow volatility by hedging these risks. Yet one irony is that for many credit-granting institutions, the single largest source of earnings (and earnings volatility) is associated not with market risks but with *credit risk*.

As Chapter 1 described, the traditional means to deal with credit risk include underwriting guidelines, loan covenants, collateral, concentration limits (eg with regard to single names, industries or geographic regions) and loan sales. However, these measures often impair client relationships.

At the same time, derivatives-based technologies were slow to migrate to the credit markets. The absence of supporting infrastructure, including internal measurement systems, standardised transaction documentation, and regulatory guidance has retarded market development.

However, progress in credit default modelling, advances in regulatory treatment of credit derivative products, the application of securitisation technology and the growth in credit trading activities (Panel 1), all support the view that credit derivatives will increasingly augment traditional credit risk management practices. Indeed, credit derivatives provide a means to apply modern portfolio theory to bank credit portfolios, fuelling a transition from an accrual accounting environment towards one of mark-to-market credit origination and dynamic credit hedging.[2]

Banks are not the only beneficiaries of these developments (Table 1). Leasing contracts, vendor-related financings, derivatives portfolios, investment portfolios and corporate treasury centres all have embedded credit exposures. Thus corporations, insurance companies, government agencies and investors can also now turn to credit derivatives to manage credit exposures without incurring relationship, tax or accounting implications.

This chapter first describes the different types of credit derivative products and then shows how each can be employed to mitigate credit concentrations, provide opportunities for defensive credit hedging and promote effective capital management. We will also discuss how demand for these new instruments has grown with the emergence of credit portfolio management techniques, increased credit markets volatility, and the unprecedented focus on risk and return in the investment community.

Credit derivatives defined

A credit derivative is an over-the-counter bilateral contract between two or more counterparties, the value of which is derived from a credit instrument. Most credit derivatives segregate credit risk from other forms of market risk (ie interest rate, currency, commodity or equity risks) and provide a risk transference mechanism from hedger to investor using an ISDA-defined frame-

Table 1. Credit hedging: who, what and why

Who	What	Why
Commercial banks	Single loans	Credit concentrations
	Loan portfolios	Capital management
	Sovereign credit risk	Credit line management
Investment banks	Securities and bonds	Short-term hedging
	Economic and industry sectors	Index management
Agencies	Derivatives exposures	Credit line management
	Sovereign credit risk	Credit concentrations
Corporates	Vendor-related financing	Beyond purview of business
	Long-term supply contracts	Credit concentration
Non-bank financial institutions	Leasing contracts	Defensive hedging
Pension plans	Deferred compensation plans	Defensive hedging
Investors	Securities and loans	Rating migration

PANEL 1

A GROWING MARKET: THE 1998 BBA SURVEY

Richard Quinn and Jamie Storrow
British Bankers' Association

The global credit derivatives market had reached an estimated $180 billion at the end of 1997, according to the 1998 survey by the British Bankers' Association (see Table). Projected growth rates for the credit derivatives market are extremely high: the London market is set to grow to $380 billion by the end of the year 2000, while the global market is set to grow to $740 billion.

London and New York continue to be the dominant centres, with most of the institutions surveyed stating that London had the largest market share. London was predicted to increase its market share by the year 2000, primarily due to its strategic position in the European timezone as the European secondary loan market develops.

Banks represent the largest buyers and sellers of credit protection using credit derivatives, currently accounting for about two thirds of the buyers of credit protection, and a little over half of the sellers of credit protection. The dominance of the banking sector is expected to be somewhat eroded by the end of the year 2000 as a broader spectrum of firms enter the market, but banks are still expected to account for just over half the buyers of protection, and around 40% of the sellers. Market professionals anticipate that the technical sophistication of insurance companies will lead them to rival securities firms as the second largest sellers of credit protection in the industry by the year 2000.

Credit default products (swaps and options) remain the most used credit derivative instrument, accounting for just over half of transactions at the end of 1997. This is expected to fall over the next two years as more firms begin to use second-generation products. Credit spread products in particular are expected to become more widely used, as banks and other financial firms look to protect themselves against movements in credit spreads, as opposed to specific credit events.

Our survey results indicate that credit derivatives will be increasingly written on corporate reference credits; the breadth of the corporate asset market, the search for higher returns, and improvements in data on corporate assets were all cited as reasons for this predicted increase.

Credit derivatives are increasingly being written on loans, or loans and bonds combined, as opposed to bonds, and this trend is expected to continue. The size of the loan market, the better recovery rates on loans as opposed to bonds, and an increased standardisation of loan transactions were seen as the principal reasons for this change.

The infrastructure of the market has been much improved. ISDA's recently published confirmation for non-sovereign OTC credit swap transactions has been widely applauded. All of the interviewed institutions used the ISDA confirmation as a template for their credit swap documentation, which in some cases amounted to as much as 80% of their total credit derivative transactions. Also, consultation between banks, trade associations, and regulators has recently produced new regulatory guidance for credit derivatives in both Europe and North America that rewards prudent credit risk management.

But more remains to be done. Despite the new ISDA confirmation, surveyed institutions still cited a lack of standard documentation, along with regulatory environment and market liquidity, as the largest constraints to the growth of the credit derivatives market.

Perhaps the greatest development since the first BBA survey has been the proving of the market in action. The Asian crisis brought credit derivatives to the fore in late 1997 and allowed the market to demonstrate its maturity and worth. At times, credit derivatives proved to be more liquid than the underlying assets (see Chapters 3 and 9 for further discussion).

Summary of the key survey statistics

	1997	1998	2000
London market size ($bn)	70	170	380
Global market size ($bn)	180	350	740
London's % of global market	39	49	51

	1997	2000
Banks' % of protection buyers market	64	51
Securities houses' % of protection buyers market	18	15
Banks' % of protection sellers market	54	43
Securities houses' % of protection sellers market	22	19
Market share of credit default products	52	38
Market share of credit spread products	13	21
Market share of sovereign assets	35	29
Market share of corporate assets	35	44
Percentage of bond based transactions	53	29
Percentage of loan based transactions	30	36

Source: 1997/1998 BBA Credit Derivatives Survey

work. Financial guarantees, credit insurance and letters of credit may be similar to credit derivatives, but they do not offer the same flexibility, liquidity and regulatory benefits. Only credit derivatives bridge the gaps between the loan, securities and derivatives markets, thus contributing to the liquidity of credit markets.

In the credit derivatives market, the basic "building blocks" are credit default swaps and total return swaps. These two products also take the lion's share in terms of volumes traded. Other credit derivative products include credit-linked notes, credit spread options, credit basket and index swaps, and collateralised debt obligations (CDOs).

CREDIT DEFAULT SWAPS
A credit default swap is a transaction in which a credit hedger (fixed rate payer) pays a periodic fee to an investor (contingent payer) in return for protection against a credit event experienced by a reference party (ie the underlying credit that is being hedged). According to the British Bankers' Association (BBA), credit default swaps comprise 52% of the total estimated London credit derivatives market in 1997.[3]

Credit events include failure-to-pay, bankruptcy or insolvency, adverse debt rescheduling, cross acceleration and cross-default and debt repudiation. Credit default swap reference obligations can include debt securities and loans to investment grade, high yield and emerging market entities such as corporations, banks and sovereigns. Common reference assets include senior and subordinated Eurobonds, Brady Bonds, widely syndicated or bilateral term loans and revolving credits, vendor-related financings, leasing contracts and obligations documented under ISDA agreements.

Once a credit default swap has been transacted, there are two possible outcomes during the life of the transaction. The first is that the specified credit event does not occur, in which case the (hedging) fixed rate payer pays all required premiums and upon maturity the swap would mature with no other cashflows. Alternatively, a credit event does occur, at which point the calculation agent generates a credit event notice and evidence of publicly available information and the hedger is compensated by the investor for the decline in value of the reference obligation.

This compensation can be accomplished via physical or cash settlement. Physical settlement is the most common (see Panel 3). It entails the

fixed rate payer physically putting, assigning, or selling the reference obligation to the contingent payer in return for receiving par (100%) of the notional amount of the swap. Cash settlement involves the calculation agent determining the post-default cash value (bid, mid or offer price) of the reference obligation from cash market dealers. Then the difference between par and this price is used to calculate the cash settlement value. A hybrid of the cash settlement method includes binary payouts (a payment of a pre-determined fixed sum) or formula-linked payments.

TOTAL RETURN SWAPS
A total return swap represents an off-balance sheet replication of a financial asset such as a loan or bond. Whereas credit default swaps capture only credit risk, total return swaps involve the transfer of the total economic return of the asset (ie both credit and market risks). The BBA estimates that total return swaps comprised 16% of the London market in 1997.[4]

Most total return swaps provide for the payment of the total return of an asset versus payment of a variable rate of interest (such as Libor) plus or minus a pre-determined spread. The total return can be measured in arrears as the total accrued cashflows (ie accrued interest, coupons, amortisation and pre-payments) plus the price change of the reference obligation during the swap tenor. The reasons for entering into total return swaps are quite different to those associated with credit default swaps. For asset hedgers, they provide a *complete economic hedge* and a short position in a security where a liquid repo market may be limited (or simply fails to exist). Total return swaps capture even modest reductions in the price of an asset due to market or credit quality changes, unlike credit default swaps.

Total return swap reference obligations include many of the same reference obligations as credit default swaps, but lend themselves particularly well to hedging the credit and market risks of amortising, pre-payable and fixed-rate assets. The settlement mechanisms for total return swaps normally involve netting three separate calculations during the swap tenor:

Total return payer payments =
reference obligation cashflows and
accrued interest
− total return swap financing leg and spread
+ absolute value of reference obligation price
change during swap tenor

THE CREDIT HEDGING TEAM

Walter Gontarek
TD Securities

The first challenge of credit derivatives is appreciating the potential cultural and business implications for the firm. Product accountability and "ownership" can be thorny issues. Successful credit hedging teams include representatives from many areas of the firm.[1] For commercial and investment banks, these are likely to include relationship managers, credit portfolio professionals and the credit derivative traders, with support provided by quantitative analysis, back-office areas, and legal and documentation professionals.

Relationship managers (RMs) are the link between the bank and the customer and are responsible for originating transaction opportunities. Increasingly, RMs and their portfolios are being evaluated on a return-on-capital basis. Given the tight pricing found in the bank loan market, RMs are constantly being asked to substantiate (or exit from) low return relationships. RMs have proven to be advocates of credit derivatives as these products allow them to continue to originate transactions and offer the scope to improve returns-on-capital. In the credit derivatives hedging process, RMs (and loan syndication desks) help identify candidates for hedging and educate other transaction partners in the process as to pricing trends and market developments. "The client-relations side of commercial banking has undoubtedly been a major driving factor behind credit derivatives. Commercial bankers, however, are also in the perfect position to analyse and price loan risk, thus gaining information on how much they should pay for a credit derivative."[2]

Credit portfolio managers also play a critical part of the credit derivatives hedging process. Banks assign overall responsibility for implementing credit policy and risk management issues, portfolio diversification objectives and return to portfolio management. Ultimate responsibility for originating credit hedging requirements (driven by concentration management needs, defensive credit hedging requirements and capital management requirements) resides with these professionals.

The *credit derivatives trading desk* has ultimate transaction responsibility once the decision to hedge is taken by the credit portfolio function. A good credit derivatives desk can advise its partners on investor preferences, pricing and capital implications of different hedging vehicles. Thus their contribution is measured in terms of effective transaction structuring, pricing, and distribution to end-investors.

Other important partners in the credit hedging process include *quantitative analysts*. They collect and analyse data such as credit and counterparty correlations, credit recovery rate estimates, default rates and before and after transaction return-on-capital rates. The *back-office* provides critical product assistance in terms of post-transaction support such as booking, credit risk monitoring, reference obligation tracking, capturing and reflecting credit positions (long and short) in the bank's exposure systems, mark-to-market functions, accounting systems and P&L estimates.

Legal support is yet another area that supports the front-line hedging team. These professionals first prove their worth when the credit derivatives trading desk is establishing its infrastructure – the time when legal and regulatory issues can be most prevalent. They can also serve as a liaison with the appropriate bank regulator to address on-going regulatory capital treatment and advise of changes in prudential regulations. Their help in addressing issues relating to product suitability, potential insurance issues, and netting questions is invaluable. Lastly, an important member of the credit hedging team is the *credit derivatives documentation group*. Given the wide array of applications and the many reasons for entering into credit derivatives, documentation support is indispensable in minimising documentation risks for dealers and end-users alike. A successful credit derivatives documentation function balances commercial needs with documentation integrity.

Because credit derivatives represent an organisational dilemma for many banks and affect so many parts of the firm, a successful credit derivatives business must have the support of all of the above groups plus sponsorship by the organisation's senior management. Without internal partners, a credit derivatives trading team operates in a vacuum and has a limited chance of sustained success.

1 For a discussion on the organisational issues associated with where to place a credit derivatives function, see *Credit Derivatives: An Organisational Dilemma*, Rick Nasson, Christine Cromarty and Stevan Maglic, Sponsorship Statement, Credit Risk Supplement to *Risk*, March 1998.
2 Theodore Kim, "A Hundred Ways to Slice Up Credit", *Euromoney*, March 1998, p. 97.

PANEL 3

PHYSICAL DELIVERY UNDER CREDIT DEFAULT TRANSACTIONS

David Geen and Schuyler K. Henderson[1]
Baker & McKenzie

One of the major issues in the documentation of credit default products is physical settlement. The ISDA standard form of Confirmation for OTC Credit Swap Transaction (Single Reference Entity, Non-Sovereign) – the "ISDA Confirmation" – allows for either physical or cash settlement, or elements of both.

Where physical settlement applies, or might apply at one party's option or as a fall-back to cash settlement, consideration must be given to the mechanics of delivery. This important issue should be considered in the context of both the normal course of events and of situations in which delivery in the expected manner is impossible or impracticable, for whatever reason.

Some key issues

Definition of "Deliver" The ISDA Confirmation contains a satisfactory definition of "deliver". This definition is, however, drafted in rather general terms. If the terms of a particular transaction contemplate delivery of a specific asset (particularly a bilateral contract such as a loan or a derivative contract, or assets that are held in a particular jurisdiction that imposes particular formalities on transfer), users should review the wording of the definition in the ISDA Confirmation to ensure that it covers the manner (including in relation to timing) in which that particular asset will be transferred. This is perhaps especially relevant in structured transactions in which all of these mechanical issues are likely to be particularly critical.

Definition of "Deliverable Obligations" The protection buyer will not necessarily be restricted to delivering the Reference Obligation(s). "Deliverable Obligations" are the different obligations – loans, bonds, etc – that the protection buyer is required, or entitled, to deliver. Users of the ISDA Confirmation should carefully review this definition to ensure that it is appropriate in the context of their proposed transaction and that they are not disadvantaged by a definition that is too broad or too narrow for their particular hedging needs or risk appetite.

Delivery of Obligations other than G7 bonds Obligations other than routinely-traded bonds can

CREDIT-LINKED NOTES

A credit-linked note is simply a securitised form of a credit default swap. In other words, they are debt instruments with an embedded credit derivative. Credit-linked notes represented 14% of the credit derivatives market in 1997.[5] The credit risk delivered to a credit-linked note investor is a dual risk, that of the credit-linked note issuer (normally highly rated) and the reference obligation of the embedded credit derivative. Like credit default swaps, credit-linked notes pay an enhanced coupon and mature as scheduled unless a credit event occurs. If such a credit event does occur, the credit-linked note will typically be redeemed by the issuer at a price linked to the value of the reference obligation.

From a dealer perspective, credit-linked notes are simply an alternative product delivery vehicle. They allow the risk to be distributed to a much broader market of investors than would unsecuritised credit default swaps and total return swaps. Credit-linked notes are fully collateralised and thus provide transaction opportunities with clients to whom credit lines are limited or unavailable. Finally, they may also provide the hedger with preferential capital treatment due to the high credit quality of collateralised transactions.

CREDIT SPREAD OPTIONS

Credit spread options enable credit hedgers to acquire protection from an unfavourable movement or "migration" of an asset, as measured by a widening of its credit spread. Credit spread options transfer credit spread risk from the credit spread hedger to an investor, in return for an upfront or periodic payment of premium. Credit spread options represented 13% of the global credit derivatives market in 1997. This share is expected to grow to 21% by the year 2000 as credit traders become more sophisticated in measuring credit spread changes, and the rise of a single European currency heightens relative value credit trading over a single Euro Libor curve.[6]

Credit spread options may be for a specified period exercisable in American, European or give rise to issues requiring particular care. For example, emerging markets assets – even bonds – are likely to require careful due diligence, both in relation to the terms of the asset itself and in terms of any local clearing systems. Due diligence will also be important where the asset to be delivered is a loan. Although the wording of the ISDA Confirmation is likely to be broad enough to cover the manner in which most loans are transferred, it is advisable to review the terms of specific loans that may be transferred pursuant to physical settlement of a credit default transaction in order to ensure that their terms permit transfer in a manner compatible with the settlement provisions of the transaction in question.

Consequences of inability to deliver or take delivery The ISDA Confirmation provides that if a party is unable to deliver the Portfolio (ie the required amount of Deliverable Obligations), it will deliver that part that it can deliver; if that party cannot then deliver the remainder of the Portfolio within 30 days, an Early Termination Date will occur with the delivering party as the Affected Party. A similar provision applies to the party that is intended to take delivery if it is unable to do so. Users should consider whether this is the outcome that they require in a particular transaction. Alternatives might be:

❏ reverting to cash settlement for the portion that

cannot be delivered;

❏ closing-out transaction with no payments or deliveries by either party.

The broader the universe of Deliverable Obligations, the less likely this is to be an issue.

Timing issues Users should consider carefully whether they will, in fact, be able to make or take deliveries on the days specified in the Confirmation. For example, the ISDA Confirmation provides for the Physical Settlement Date to fall a specified number of Business Days following the satisfaction of all conditions to payment. Depending on how it is defined, "Business Days" might not take account of days on which the obligations in question may be delivered.

Does an obligation have to be "impossible" to deliver in order to trigger the alternatives? Documentation used by different institutions in the market tends to use various standards. Some, including the ISDA Confirmation, require that an obligation be "impossible to deliver"; others only that it is "impracticable". It should be noted that, at least as a matter of English law, "impossibility" is a very high standard and would require efforts well beyond those generally regarded as commercially reasonable.

1 This discussion does not constitute legal advice and does not purport to be exhaustive. Specific legal and other appropriate professional advice should be taken in relation to specific situations. © 1998 David P. Geen and Schuyler K. Henderson. All rights reserved.

Bermudan style at a pre-set strike quoted in cash price or Libor spread terms. The option may be cash settled or physically settled into an asset swap. Later in this chapter we look at examples of physically settled credit spread options such as puttable asset swaps and synthetic revolving agreements.

CREDIT BASKET AND INDEX SWAPS

Credit basket and index swaps are credit derivatives that are based on more than one reference issuer. The payout of a credit basket swap is linked to an itemised group or "basket" of credit references. If any one of the credits in a first-to-default basket experience a credit event, the investor would compensate the hedger for this first-to-default loss, but the remaining names in the basket would then be considered unhedged. As might be expected, pricing credit basket swaps is more complex than with basic credit derivative structures, and relies on the default correlation of the reference assets. Investors must conduct a thorough due diligence on all the

names in the basket, as the first to experience a credit event will require a contingent payout. For investors, credit basket swaps are basically a means to leverage an investment view, as they typically receive enhanced premium for the multi-name credit exposure embedded in the transaction.

Index swaps allow hedgers and investors alike to express views across entire investment classes, industries or economies. For example, index swaps make it possible to invest in or hedge investment grade, high yield, or emerging market, and government bond indexes. Credit indexes are also a useful tracking mechanism for credit investment managers for the purposes of comparing investment performance.[7]

CDOS (COLLATERALISED DEBT OBLIGATIONS)

CDOs include both collateralised loan obligations (CLOs) and collateralised bond obligations (CBOs), which are respectively securitised pools of commercial loans and bonds. Since banks are more interested in hedging their loan portfolios, we will focus on CLOs, but the same principles apply to CBOs. Perhaps the most attractive feature of CLO structures for banks is that, while preserving the origination of new lending opportunities, CLOs offer banks the opportunity to remove high quality (and low yielding) assets from the balance sheet by securitising the credit risk into a tradable security – and thus potentially freeing up regulatory capital.

The collateral for the CLO (the underlying loans) usually resides in an SPV (special purpose vehicle) which in turn issues several levels of debt such as senior, mezzanine, and subordinated tranches (as explained further in Chapter 8). The cashflows generated from the collateral are dedicated to paying each debt tranche in order of seniority. Most senior CLO tranches can withstand high levels of default because of this cashflow prioritisation and as a result senior CLO pieces are high quality assets (and rated as such) with mezzanine and subordinated tranches rated accordingly.

CLOs differ from credit-linked notes in several ways. A CLO will provide credit exposure to a diverse pool of credits (up to 200 or more) whereas most credit-linked notes are linked to a single credit. CLOs may provide a true transfer of ownership of underlying assets, whereas credit-linked notes typically do not provide such a transfer. Thus true sale CLOs may enjoy a higher credit rating than that of the originating institution whereas the rating of credit-linked notes are effectively capped to the issuer level. Credit derivative structures have been used within CLO transactions as a means to transfer credit risk or market risk between the originator and the SPV issuer.

Credit hedging applications

A revolution is under way in the field of credit hedging. First, with advances in credit portfolio management techniques, bankers can finally begin to identify credit concentrations across all business lines, including their lending, securities and derivatives books. Second, the volatility experienced in the credit markets in 1994/95 (the Mexican credit crisis) and again in 1997/98 (the Asian and Russian credit debacles) has heightened investor awareness of defensive credit hedging. Lastly, credit hedging is gaining support from bank regulators. Regulators in at least four countries have established eligibility criteria for the provision of regulatory capital treatment of credit derivatives, and further advances in this area are anticipated.

At the same time, many banks with significant trading activities have deployed proprietary economic capital models in-house, and have acquired regulatory approval for these. They have also made advances in considering how to tackle the difficult problem of pricing credit risk (see Panel 4 overleaf).

These trends have accelerated the use of credit hedging in three key strategic areas: concentration management, defensive credit hedging and capital management.

CONCENTRATION MANAGEMENT

A popular phrase today in credit risk management circles is "the credit paradox". The phrase highlights the conflict of interest between bank relationship managers, who are responsible for originating client business, and credit portfolio managers, who are tasked with overall portfolio performance. Just as an institution gains expertise in originating and structuring financings with a borrower, portfolio managers impose concentration limits (in terms of single names, geographic or industry subsets) that hinder further transaction opportunities. "Without credit derivatives, a commercial bank would eventually reach a ceiling beyond which it could no longer lend."[8]

As described in the following examples, credit derivatives provide an effective tool for resolving the credit paradox. The relationship manager can continue originating business, while the portfolio function can hedge credit risk dynamically. To accomplish this, banks are increasingly shifting away from making traditional decisions about credit and toward RAROC (risk-adjusted return on capital) lending, which demands a higher RAROC performance for each additional unit of credit exposure (Figure 1).[9]

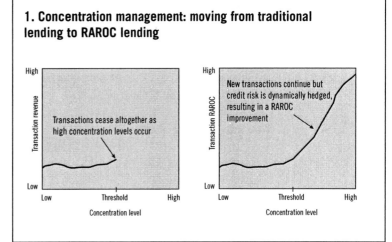

1. Concentration management: moving from traditional lending to RAROC lending

Transactions cease altogether as high concentration levels occur

New transactions continue but credit risk is dynamically hedged, resulting in a RAROC improvement

MODELS FOR DEFAULT AND CREDIT DEFAULT SWAPS:
DIFFERENT APPROACHES AND DIFFERENT APPLICATIONS

Walter Gontarek and Tom McNerney

TD Securities

Unlike traditional derivative markets, which enjoy a range of pricing and risk management systems, technology providers have yet to respond fully to the development of the credit derivatives market. While the methodologies used in the calculation of yield curves and volatilities have migrated from the general world of derivatives, credit risk itself presents several challenges from a pricing and risk management perspective. As the art of pricing credit risk slowly evolves into a science, three basic approaches to modelling default risk and pricing default swaps are developing.

The *empirical approach* relies on the credit rating agencies' record and analysis of credit rating migration among different rating categories (also known as transition matrices), default rates and recovery rates. Examples of the empirical modelling approach might include JP Morgan's CreditMetrics, CSFP's CreditRisk+, and McKinsey's CreditPortfolio View. CreditMetrics simulates the behaviour of a credit portfolio over a series of credit rating changes and CreditRisk+ considers the average credit default rate with each credit rating notch. Both are obviously heavily dependent upon published credit rating data. However, macro-economic variables also have a considerable impact upon future default rates. McKinsey's approach links economic variables and default risk via the use of regression variables.

The advantage of the empirical approach is that it makes use of advances in measuring expected and unexpected credit losses, and can promote effective credit pricing and calculation of the level of capital required to support a credit portfolio. The disadvantage of this approach is two-fold. The first limitation is the lack of rating data available concerning non-US credits. For analysts looking toward continental Europe and Asia, obtaining credit rating data below the sovereign level can be difficult. Secondly, historical data has its limitations: past experience does not guarantee future performance in terms of predicting default rates and recovery rates.

The *obligor asset approach* represents a second way of modelling default. It draws on Merton's seminal ideas about modelling an asset value as a random walk, with defaults occurring when obligor's asset value falls below its liabilities. KMV, the credit portfolio management firm, has refined this approach in combination with a correlation model that is also based on obligor assets and which seeks to identify credit concentrations and economic capital requirements. The advantages of the obligor asset approach are its intellectual attractiveness and its applicability in markets where credit ratings are less readily available, such as in continental Europe. The disadvantages of the approach lie in the fact that it cannot be applied to sovereign credits, and in the difficulty of calibrating the model to bond market prices and spreads.

The third approach is the *arbitrage-free credit spread model*. This approach is based on the practical notion that most risky credit assets provide a positive credit spread (versus some risk-free benchmark such as Libor) that rewards investors for credit, liquidity and other risks. For example, if the one-year risk free rate is 5%, a risky one-year credit asset yields 6%, and the expected recovery rate is 50%, the implied probability of default is approximately 2% per annum. More sophisticated approaches include the construction of tree technology to map out the effect of different recovery rate and other post-default scenarios.[1] The advantage of the arbitrage-free credit spread approach is its practicality: credit derivatives are priced in a context that relates directly to how hedgeable the credit positions are. For example, a dealer funding at Libor flat might quote 50 basis points when asked to offer a credit default swap on a credit if he is certain that he can hedge it with a credit-linked note that is paying 43bp. The disadvantage of this approach is that it provides the user with a market-determined credit level without explaining how that valuation was determined, or the underlying assumptions.

1 Jarrow, R.A., D. Lando and S.M. Turnbull, 1997, "A Markov Model of the Term Structure of Credit Spreads", *Review of Financial Studies*; Jarrow, R.A., and S.M. Turnbull, 1995, "Pricing Derivatives on Financial Securities Subject to Credit Risk", *Journal of Finance* 50(1), pp. 53–85.

Example 1: Hedging loan concentrations

Imagine that a bank has a long-standing relationship with a retailer. The retailer now requires a loan in order to refurbish stores recently acquired in a corporate acquisition. The loan terms call for a $50 million, 5-year bilateral term loan that is pre-payable by the borrower. As a BB+ rated borrower, the retailer borrows in the loan market at Libor + 180bp. The bank cannot extend the loan because, after a long period of profitable financings, the new exposure would exceed bank limitations to any single non-investment grade client.

Solution The bank can extend the loan and arrange a total return swap with a hedge fund investor that cannot easily access the loan market (Figure 2). The total return of the loan, paid on a periodic basis, includes all fees, interest received, amortisation and any pre-payments.

The *advantages* of this approach include:
❏ Economic risk of the loan has been hedged.
❏ Assuming the transaction meets regulatory capital criteria, the bank may achieve a reduction of the amount of regulatory capital that it is required to hold against a hedged position.
❏ It overcomes an "investors' paradox": while investment managers have targeted the loan asset class for their investment appeal and attractive recovery rates, they face significant barriers of entry into the loan market.
❏ All loan administration is completed by the bank hedger.
❏ The investor may enjoy higher returns depending upon the degree of collateral posted, as shown in Table 2.

The *disadvantages* in using this approach include:
❏ The monitoring associated with marking-to-market the loan, and the administration associated with collateral postings.
❏ The inability of the investment manager to trade in and out of the position.

Example 2: Transferring default risk

Imagine that an A-rated oil company is planning to arrange a fully drawn one-year revolving credit (R/C) for $2 billion and has invited its relationship banks into the deal. The facility pricing is Libor + 20bp. Due to the firm's corporate policy of restricting its banking groups to a small number, it prices the commitment fee according to the notional amount of the draw-down commitment (Table 3).

The relationship manager in the house bank

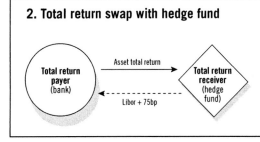

2. Total return swap with hedge fund

Total return payer (bank) — Asset total return → Total return receiver (hedge fund); ← Libor + 75bp

Table 2. Comparison of cash versus synthetic returns for hedge fund investment in loan (Example 1)

Cash investment	
Capital investment	$50 million
Annual return	$3.65 million
Return-on-capital	7.3%
Synthetic investment	
Capital investment[1]	$5 million
Annual return[2]	$800,000
Return-on-capital	16%

Assumptions:
Libor = 5.5%
[1] 10% initial margin posting; [2] Includes synthetic loan accrual + interest income on margin accrued at Libor

would like to commit to $600 million, but the bank's credit portfolio management team has placed a limit of $200 million; they are concerned about the bank's significant overall exposure to the oil company stemming from extensive loans and highly credit-intensive commodity swap transactions.

Solution The house bank can commit to the total financing and arrange a credit default swap with another bank for the difference. Good credit risk originators can approach foreign or regional banks that are at a credit risk origination disadvantage and transfer the credit risk of the revolving credit without transferring the loan itself (Figure 3).

Table 3. Commitment fee structure (Example 2)

Notional commitment	Up-front fee
$0–250 million	6 bp
$250–500 million	8 bp
$500 million and more	12 bp

3. Transferring default risk

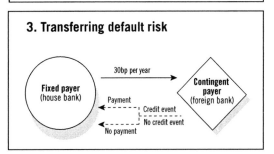

Fixed payer (house bank) — 30bp per year → Contingent payer (foreign bank); Payment · · · Credit event; · · · No credit event / No payment

The *advantages* of this approach include:
❏ The bank-client relationship is preserved and the bank can extend the maximum level of commitment.
❏ Alternative strategies, such as sale in the secondary markets or participation, may have adverse consequences for the bank-client relationship.
❏ The bank enjoys the more generous fee structure associated with the higher commitment level.
❏ The hedging bank has significantly diversified its risk, only experiencing a default if *both* the oil company and counterparty bank fail jointly and concurrently to perform. This joint probability of default is likely to be quite low, assuming their default correlations are not high.
❏ The return on capital of the hedged position can be significantly higher than an unhedged position, subject to meeting regulatory requirements.

Issues to *consider* include:
❏ Potential basis risks between the credit exposure and the reference obligation on the credit default swap, if these are not the same.
❏ The credit default swap offers a limited degree of liquidity, and may have to be terminated early due to repayment of the reference asset.

Example 3: Revenue neutral diversification
Credit losses can increase due to an overly concentrated credit exposure to a single company, industry or geographic region (concentration risk). The expected loss is greater as the correlation of the credits in any bank portfolio is greater (Figure 4). The level of correlation is expressed by the correlation coefficient – a statistical measure of the extent to which two or more variables move together – and is measured on a scale of +1 (perfect positive correlation of returns) to –1 (a perfect offsetting relationship).

Conversely, adding securities to a portfolio can reduce portfolio variance provided the assets are less correlated with one another than the assets in the existing portfolio. Although there are practical problems associated with extending this concept to credit intensive assets (such as obtaining data on credit correlations and default rates), let us show the hedging potential of credit derivatives in a portfolio context.

We begin by defining a simple two-asset bank credit portfolio in terms of a given risk level (ie standard deviation). Using credit derivatives, the bank can increase the diversity of the portfolio by adding a third asset that is less positively correlated and maintain portfolio return. Let us assume that a simple credit portfolio of a European bank is comprised of loans (one to an Italian corporation and one to a Greek bank) and can be defined in terms of risk (Table 4).

Now let us assume that the European bank increases its degree of diversification by adding assets in a way that is neutral in terms of revenue and capital. One way to achieve this portfolio reallocation or credit switch is to buy credit protection from a highly rated (and not highly correlated) bank counterparty on one-half of the notional of the two original assets. The premium for this credit default swap may be funded by the sale of protection on other credit assets that are less positively related to the original portfolio, for example an A+ rated Canadian municipality, and which may reduce portfolio co-variance.

Given a credit spread for the third asset that is at least equivalent to either assets 1 and 2, and assuming no other transaction costs, we can demonstrate that the portfolio risk defined as the standard deviation is reduced while portfolio

4. The effect of correlation on portfolio return

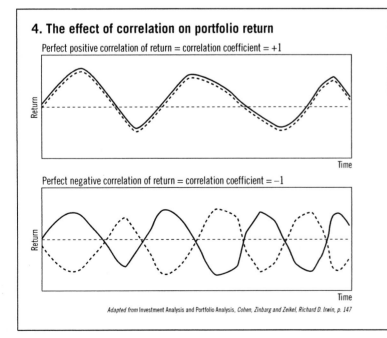

Perfect positive correlation of return = correlation coefficient = +1

Return / Time

Perfect negative correlation of return = correlation coefficient = –1

Return / Time

Adapted from Investment Analysis and Portfolio Analysis, Cohen, Zinbarg and Zeikel, Richard D. Irwin, p. 147

Table 4. Simple two-asset portfolio (Example 3)

	Asset 1	Asset 2
Tenor	2 years	2 years
Rating	AA–	A–
Spread	X bp	Y bp
Asset weighting	0.50	0.50
Standard deviation	0.30	0.40
Portfolio standard deviation	31.4% *	

Assumes:
Correlation coefficient = + .6
* See Table 5b

Table 5a. Simple three-asset portfolio

	Asset 1	Asset 2	Asset 3
Tenor	2-years	2-years	2-years
Rating	AA-	A-	A+
Spread	X bp	Y bp	Y bp
Weighting	0.333	0.333	0.333
Std dev	0.30	0.40	0.40
Portfolio standard deviation	21.6%*		

Assumes:
Correlation coefficient = + .4
* See Table 5b

Table 5b. A typical risk calculation using standard deviation

A typical proxy for risk is the portfolio standard deviation:

$$\text{Risk} = \text{Std}(p) = \sqrt{\left(\sum_{\text{Assets } 1-n}^{(w^2 * \text{Std}^2)}\right) + n * w_1 * w_2 * \ldots w_n * \text{Cov}_n}$$

where w = asset weighting, n = number of assets in portfolio, Std(x) is standard deviation of x, and Cov_n is the covariance of a portfolio of n assets = (correlation coefficient of the portfolio of n assets * Std (asset[1]) * Std (asset[2]) * ... Std (asset[3])).

Thus for the simple n = 2-asset portfolio we have:

$$\text{Risk} = \text{Std}(p) = \sqrt{\left(w_1^2 * \text{Std}_1^2\right) + \left(w_2^2 * \text{Std}_2^2\right) + \left(n * w_1 * w_2 * \text{Cov}_n\right)}$$
$$= \sqrt{(0.25 * 0.09) + (0.25 * 0.16) + (2 * 0.5 * 0.5 * 0.072)}$$
$$= 31.4\%$$

Thus for the simple n = 3-asset portfolio we have:

$$\text{Risk} = \text{Std}(p) = \sqrt{\left(w_1^2 * \text{Std}_1^2\right) + \left(w_2^2 * \text{Std}_2^2\right) + \left(w_3^2 * \text{Std}_3^2\right) + \left(n * w_1 * w_2 * w_3 * \text{Cov}_n\right)}$$
$$= \sqrt{(0.0098) + (0.01742) + (0.01742) + (3 * 0.33 * 0.33 * 0.33 * 0.0192)}$$
$$= 21.6\%$$

revenue remains neutral (Tables 5a–b).

The *advantages* of the strategy shown in this simple example include:

❏ A reduction in credit concentration as the portfolio allocation is increased from a two-asset portfolio to a three-asset portfolio.

❏ No reduction in portfolio return.

The *challenges* are:

❏ Practical difficulties in applying standard deviation and correlation coefficients in a credit portfolio context.

❏ The example assumes there are no other transactions costs.

Example 4: Sovereign risk credit hedging

Concentration challenges also occur with regard to sovereign credit lines. Transaction opportunities in loan, project finance, trade finance, and derivatives activities can exceed available country line limits. Assume an investment bank engages in profitable trade finance activities of up to 18 months with Israeli counterparties but is nearing its country line limits. Further assume that most State of Israel credit risk is priced at Libor + 5bp, and that the shortest alternative tenors are securities of a three-year tenor.

Solution The investment bank can structure and place with investors a credit-linked note linked to the State of Israel. By embedding a credit default swap paying 12.5bp into a Libor-flat medium-term note (MTN), the investment bank can solve its concentration challenge. Table 6 presents a sample term sheet of the transaction.

The *advantages* of this approach include:

❏ The bank acquires the country line it requires.

❏ No credit lines to the credit-linked note buyer are required (ie the transaction is fully collateralised).

❏ The hedger may realise capital benefits as the credit exposure to a non-OECD sovereign is being replaced by a collateralised hedge.

❏ Alternatives such as PRI (political risk insurance) may result in basis risks between political events and an actual default.

❏ Investors that desire State of Israel risk for short tenors cannot locate attractively priced product "inside" of three years, thus this credit-linked noted creates a new investment class with good relative value.

The potential *disadvantages* include:

❏ Sourcing the investors.

❏ The delivery of dual risk of credit-linked note issuer and the State of Israel.

❏ The relative illiquidity of credit-linked notes.

Example 5: Hedging counterparty risk

Credit risk management for derivatives counterparty exposures can be somewhat complex, as explained in more detail in Chapter 5.[10] Credit exposures embedded in derivatives contracts are dynamic (ie can change over the tenor of the transaction). Unlike loans, two measures of

Table 6. Credit-linked note – indicative terms and conditions (Example 4)

Note buyer	Investor
Note issuer	Investment bank
Reference credit	State of Israel
Reference asset	X% FRN due XX-XX-XX
Price	Par, no accrued interest
Maturity date	18 months, unless subject to early redemption
Maturity value	Par, unless subject to early redemption
Coupon	Libor + 12.5bp
Early redemption	The note will be redeemed by the issuer at the credit event price after the occurrence of a credit event
Credit event price	The mid price of the reference asset quoted in percent terms
Credit event	Failure to pay, cross acceleration, repudiation

potential exposure must be considered: expected exposure and maximum exposure. Expected exposure reflects the anticipated amount of credit exposure stemming from a derivative contract. Maximum exposure is the highest anticipated amount of credit exposure stemming from a derivatives contract at a specified probability level (the true exposure level is stochastic or subject to a process of randomly-generated prices).

Imagine a situation in which a lower-rated corporation has borrowed from a bank but presently faces financial distress. It would like to hedge $100 million notional of its floating-rate interest rate exposure on its Libor-based loans but is unable to obtain a derivatives trading line and cannot post collateral at this time. The bank feels it is in its own interest to provide a trading line subject to an event trigger, such as a further downgrade, but its credit risk management group will not extend the credit exposure.

Solution The bank can provide the interest rate swap and price into the transaction the cost of providing default protection for itself (using a credit default swap). The bank may use its ISDA agreement, or its loans, as the reference obligation. The credit default swap notional may be a binary amount related to a conservative calculation of the maximum credit exposure stemming from the transaction, not less than the expected exposure (Figure 5).

The *advantages* of this approach include:
❑ The bank provides an interest rate swap product to its borrower and assists its client in its liability management requirements.
❑ The interest rate swap reduces the market risk embedded in the loan, thus potentially dampen-

ing the earnings volatility of the corporation and reducing its financial distress.
❑ The administrative burdens associated with the mark-to-market provisions of collateral agreements, assignments, unwinds or third-party supports may be avoided.

Issues to *consider* include:
❑ The potential difficulty of sourcing a provider of binary credit default protection referenced to the corporation.
❑ Managing basis risks between the true credit exposure originating from the interest rate swap and credit hedge (that is, the bank is likely to be over- or under-hedged subject to its probability estimates and volatility in market rates).

Example 6: Hedging vendor credit risks
Certain corporations have emerged as sophisticated users of credit derivatives in order to address the risks that they incur in their everyday commercial activities. For example, many firms provide financing for sales contracts. Leasing agreements and long-term supply contracts also generate sizeable credit risks for corporations.

Suppose that a multinational engineering company is involved in building a power station in Mexico. The construction contract is awarded on condition that the company provides a $50 million loan over five years to finance the construction costs during the build, operate and transfer (BOT) phase of the contract. The loan, arranged for the project and fully guaranteed by the sovereign for repayment of principal and interest, is pre-payable and amortises on each anniversary date. Commencing at a price of par, the loan carries a fixed interest rate of US Treasuries + 250bp. Although compelled to extend the financing, the engineering firm is uneasy about the economic and political risks associated with the region and would like to hedge the total economic risk immediately – and confidentially.

Solution The engineering company can hedge the total economic risk of the private placement by paying the total return to a credit derivatives dealer (Figure 6). In paying the total return on the reference obligation, the engineering firm can mitigate both credit and market risks in one transaction. For the life of the swap, the total return payer pays all cashflows associated with the instrument including coupons, amortisation and any pre-payment versus receipt of a Libor-adjusted payment. The dealer can now do what dealers do best: strip out complex credit and

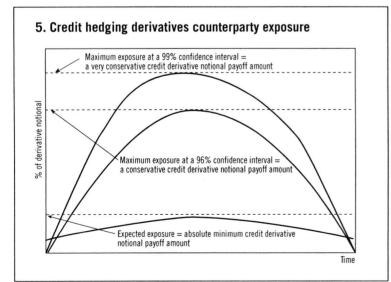

5. Credit hedging derivatives counterparty exposure

% of derivative notional

Maximum exposure at a 99% confidence interval = a very conservative credit derivative notional payoff amount

Maximum exposure at a 96% confidence interval = a conservative credit derivative notional payoff amount

Expected exposure = absolute minimum credit derivative notional payoff amount

Time

market risks and place the various legs with the best risk taker.

Assuming par as a starting price, the dealer can first hedge the market risk of this fixed rate instrument by paying fixed in the swap market – for example, a rate set at US Treasuries + 30bp. Now that the market risk has been mitigated, the dealer is left with a pure credit position. Next, if the dealer can source a taker of the credit risk (via a credit default swap or a credit-linked note) at 210bp, it can preserve an attractive profit for itself. Assume that another bank funding at or above Libor is attracted by Mexican credit risk priced at Libor + 210bp, but does not want to deal with settlement complexities associated with peso-denominated securities. A credit default swap can offer a suitable replacement. Both swaps can be structured on an amortising sum.

The *advantages* of this structure include:
❑ The provision of a full asset hedge for the engineering firm, hedging both credit risks and market risks (as well as any pre-payment and amortisation).
❑ The provision of pure Mexican credit risk to the investing bank in an unfunded transaction with no administration or securities settlement.
❑ No hedge basis risks for the engineering company.
❑ The generation of 30bp in revenue for the dealer in return for transaction and hedge origination, and managing the resultant credit, basis and timing risks of the transaction.

The *considerations* include:
❑ The degree of counterparty credit risks between the various swap legs.
❑ Transaction illiquidity and difficulties associated with early termination.

Yet another potential solution would be for the engineering firm to pay the total return versus a credit index, such as an emerging market index or investment grade index. In effect, this approach substitutes one credit risk for another index of risks, and whether it is attractive depends upon the credit view and the relative hedge costs.

Defensive credit hedging

Investors, banks and corporations with significant default and credit spread exposures can employ credit derivatives to protect themselves from adverse changes in credit quality. The use of credit derivatives as defensive hedges has been boosted by the recent volatility witnessed in global credit markets. During a month-long period in late 1997, over $800 million in credit

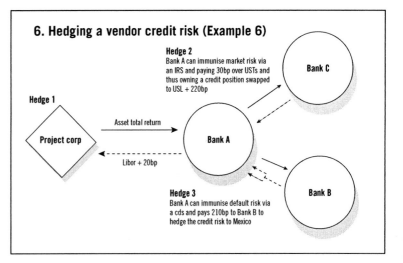

6. Hedging a vendor credit risk (Example 6)

derivatives are believed to have been executed on South Korean and Thai credits alone.[11]

Example 7: Hedging illiquid bonds
One useful aspect of credit derivatives is their ability to mitigate illiquid credit and market risks. We have already noted that illiquidity can be caused by relationship, accounting or tax factors. Another source of illiquidity arises from the tender process of puttable bonds. Many investors have invested in securities issued by the Korea Development Bank and the Industrial Finance Corporation of Thailand that were puttable upon a given credit event, such as a credit downgrade. In late 1997, with the downgrade provisions met in the market turmoil of the Asia crisis, many investors exercised their put options on these securities. These options are exercisable at par and the securities are tendered for good value in 30 days' time. However, many investors, having tendered the securities, became concerned that the distressed issuers might be unable to honour the put. We can explore a solution to this problem. Let us assume that the security is trading at 97% of par at the time of tender; due to the high risk of issuer default given its liquidity squeeze, our investor would like to create a price floor at 97% and give up the opportunity of participating in any appreciation to par.

Solution Pay the total return on the security to a credit derivatives dealer, creating a 97% price floor on the investment. By paying the total return for the period leading up to the put value date (ie in 30 days), the investor is immunised against any further fall in price below the total return swap starting level of 97%.

Note that a short-term credit default swap (for the 30 days) would largely achieve the same objective, in return for the swap premium.

Example 8: Hedging credit spread risk

Some credit hedgers are less concerned with credit default risk *per se*, but instead are exposed to the risk of a credit spread widening (due to either a decline in the creditworthiness of the reference credit or to an overall widening of credit spreads). Syndication desks, security portfolios, asset swap trading desks, loan portfolio managers (exposed to legal and/or regulatory threats), and issuers themselves are all exposed to a widening of credit spreads.

Imagine that an investment bank syndication desk is asked to bid on a five-year $500 million bond issue for a single-A rated corporation that has significant interests in the tobacco industry. The syndication desk is prepared to underwrite the bond issue at a spread equivalent to Libor + 35bp and is confident that it can profitably distribute $400 million of the issue immediately, but will subsequently require more time to sell the remaining $100 million. The credit risk management function is not keen to increase its exposure to the tobacco industry even though it concedes that default is unlikely. Thus, it has authorised the syndication desk to hold up to $100 million of the issue for a maximum of one year, subject to a requirement that any spread widening beyond Libor + 60bp will be hedged. Each basis point of spread widening costs the syndication desk approximately $40,000, thus it must be able to cap the amount of potential loss due to spread migration.

Solution Structure and execute a credit spread option with an investor that is attracted to the single-A tobacco credit risk but (due to its investment yield criteria or its own funding limitations) must realise a wider spread to Libor than that offered in the cash markets. One means to accomplish this is via a synthetic revolver, as illustrated in Table 7.

A synthetic revolver is an option to "put" an asset swap (with a loan or security as the reference asset) to a counterparty at a pre-determined (and usually out-of-the-money) spread to Libor in return for an up-front fee. Thus, in many ways, these structures represent a synthetic form of revolving credit agreements in which investors are paid an up-front commitment fee in order to stand by and lend for a given tenor and for a given spread. Synthetic revolvers are usually unfunded until (or if) the option is exercised by the hedger.

The *advantages* of this approach include:
❑ The hedger is capping the potential losses due to credit spread widening at Libor + 60 bp.
❑ The investor has the opportunity to access the credit risk that it finds attractive at its required spread to Libor, and receives an up-front fee for its commitment to perform under the terms of the structure.

The *disadvantages* of this approach include:
❑ Difficulty in determining and managing credit exposure on the part of the investor (ie will the option be exercised?)
❑ Potential capital and credit allocation uncertainty.

An alternative is to execute a double-up asset swap. A double-up asset swap is the placement of a traditional asset swap and the simultaneous purchase of the right to execute more of the same placement at a later date and effectively double (or triple) the notional of the initial placement in return for an enhanced Libor spread on the package. Double-up asset swaps can be likened to a traditional asset swap with an embedded credit spread. They are funded for the initial amount, unlike synthetic revolvers.

Example 9: Credit enhancement and wrapping

Some portfolio investors are mandated with strict investment guidelines as to issuer risk weighting, credit rating and geographic origin. Yet these investors often find it difficult to source sufficient quantities of credit products with adequate yield. Credit derivatives can be combined with traditional cash products in order to create a new class of securities.

Suppose that a floating rate investor owns a portfolio of high quality floating-rate assets. To be included in the portfolio, the debt must (1) have been issued by a leading commercial bank from an OECD country (2) carry a rating of at least single-A and (3) pay a spread of Libor +

Table 7. Synthetic revolver – indicative terms and conditions

Underlying

Issuer	ABC Tobacco Co.
Security	X% Eurobond due XX-XX-XX
Tenor	5 years
Swap level	$ Libor + 60bp
Price	Par, no accrued interest
Notional	TBD

Option

Type	Put option, American style
Option tenor	1 year
Underlying	As noted above
Option buyer	Investment bank name
Option seller	Investor name
Premium	8bp paid up front on notional

12.5bp for a maximum tenor of seven years. The investor's problem is that most market spreads are less than Libor + 5bp.

Solution To enhance, via a credit wrap, securities of high-quality banks that are domiciled in OECD countries but that would not otherwise qualify for the investment portfolio. For example, commercial banks domiciled in Greece, Poland, Hungary and Mexico qualify as OECD-area issuers but fail to meet the credit rating requirements for the portfolio, notwithstanding their attractive yields. However, senior debt securities can be credit wrapped via a credit default swap with a commercial bank or via a monoline insurer. This can raise the effective credit rating of the securities from BBB to that of the bank or insurance counterparty, while still potentially achieving the Libor + 12.5bp yield requirement.

This credit-wrapping approach, known as two-party pay (TPP), has long been recognised as a means of enhancing the credit profile of lower rated assets. Certain rating agencies are beginning to accept that a third-party guarantee of a credit may achieve a rating which is greater than that of the underlying credit or guarantor.

The *advantages* of this approach include:
❑ The creation of a new and very high-quality asset class for the portfolio.
❑ The satisfaction of the portfolio yield criteria.
Issues to *consider* include:
❑ The difficulty of sourcing the credit wrap at an attractive price.
❑ The fact that two credit lines may be needed for the transaction (the underlying credit and the wrapper).
❑ Investment illiquidity.
❑ Honouring an out-of-the-money interest rate swap if a credit event occurs and the securities are swapped with an external swap counterparty.

Capital management applications

In the last few years, the investment community has focused on return to an unprecedented extent. While there are many measures of return, return-on-capital is perhaps the most widely employed by investors. Return-on-capital attempts to determine a level of return per unit of capital.

REGULATORY CAPITAL APPROACH
Commercial banks, for example, have long been required to follow regulatory capital standards laid down by their regulators and inspired by the Bank for International Settlements (BIS). These standards, although an improvement over the previous regime of a simple "percentage of assets" calculation, attempt to attach low capital requirements to (what are perceived to be) low risk assets. For example, OECD government debt requires a zero percent charge, while higher capital charges exist for other categories (such as 20%, 50% and 100% of 8% for OECD banks, mortgages and all others including corporations, respectively). Increasingly, these rules are regarded as inadequate by investors, bankers and the regulators themselves. "Capital requirements are crude protection at best... the international standard forcing banks to set aside capital equal to at least 8% of the value of their loan portfolios has come to look hopelessly outdated... Privately, they (bank regulators) admit that the current approach is badly flawed."[12]

Yet, for the moment, these standards are used to judge the capital requirement of most banks. Credit derivatives can increase the returns on capital, because credit positions that are sufficiently credit hedged (and meet regulatory guidelines) require significantly less capital support. This makes intuitive sense as the overall risk stemming from a credit exposure can be reduced significantly using credit derivatives.

Example 10: Increasing returns on capital
Imagine a bank with a credit portfolio comprised of investment grade assets that offers an unsatisfactory return-on-regulatory capital. The bank also has a problem avoiding credit concentrations when transacting with its regular clients. The bank would like to know what effect a thorough credit hedge would have on its return-on-regulatory capital, assuming the transaction met the relevant regulatory requirements.

First solution Consider the portfolio comprised of three corporate borrowers whose specifications are given in Table 8a. Assume that the bank executes a series of three separate credit default swaps, as given in Table 8b overleaf.

The *advantages* of this approach include:
❑ An increase in the overall credit portfolio qual-

Table 8a. Simple three-asset portfolio

	Asset 1	Asset 2	Asset 3
Tenor	2 years	2 years	2 years
Rating	AA–	A–	A+
Spread	10bp	20bp	15bp
Weighting	0.333	0.333	0.333
Notional	$10m	$10m	$10m
Capital	$800,000	$800,000	$800,000

Table 8b. Comparison of portfolio regulatory returns before and after credit hedge

	Before hedge	After hedge
Revenue	$1,695,000	$1,695,000
Liability	$1,462,800	$1,564,560
Hedge	n/a	$45,000
Net revenue	$232,200	$85,440
Capital	$2.4 million	$480,000
Return	9.675%	17.71%

Assumptions
Libor = 5.5%
Bank funding at Libor −20 bp
Credit hedge costs the full Libor coupon on the assets hedged.
After hedge return does not include any effect of earnings on capital saved.
Bank meets all regulatory criteria

ity and an accompanying increase in return-on-regulatory capital (post credit hedge).
❏ Client relationships are preserved notwithstanding the credit hedge.
❏ Any credit concentrations are reduced for the two-year period.

The *disadvantages* of this approach include:
❏ Absolute levels of revenue drop due to the cost of the hedge.
❏ Managing the hedge transaction process.

Second solution Alternatively, the bank could arrange a CLO transaction backed by credit-linked notes for a diverse pool of credits in the portfolio (Figure 7). Under this type of structure, the issuer neither sells nor transfers the loans to the special purpose vehicle (SPV) involved in the transaction. Instead, the SPV purchases a credit-linked note(s) from the issuing bank, which represents an obligation(s) to pay principal plus accrued interest on the relevant reference credits as long as no credit event occurs. This type of structure has been employed by various banks.

The *advantages* of this structure include:
❏ As before, client relationships are preserved and credit concentrations may be reduced.
❏ It diversifies the funding sources for the bank.
❏ Although not true sales, a CLO transaction using credit-linked notes will generally obtain regulatory capital relief for the issuer as the credit exposures are fully hedged.
❏ Unlike the credit default example, a CLO transaction does not require counterparty credit lines to exist between the bank hedger and the transaction end-investor.
❏ End-investors often find the credit rating and spread on CLO transactions attractive, as they are highly rated and demonstrate a high degree of diversification.

The *disadvantages* of this approach include:
❏ CLO transactions are complex transactions requiring a significant amount of structuring, regulatory and internal co-ordination.

SELF-MODELLING CAPITAL APPROACH
Another approach to bank capital determination is the employment of economic capital models that self-determine the amount of economic capital support, subject to regulatory approval of the model:

> ISDA European Policy Director Matthew Elderfield said at the organisation's annual meeting in Rome that the standardised capital-calculation method employed by the BIS is out of date and doesn't encourage good risk management policies within banks.... ISDA said this ruling (the current standards) doesn't reward competent risk management techniques such as portfolio diversification or the hedging of outstanding positions.[13]

In particular, the credit derivatives market has in part been fuelled by the growing popularity of a measurement called "risk-adjusted return on capital", or RAROC. "RAROC models measure the amount of economic capital needed to support business lines and help banks more accurately correlate risks and returns in those businesses."[14] Let us examine each of the elements in a typical RAROC calculation (Table 9) to understand the measure's

7. A typical simple credit-linked note CLO transaction

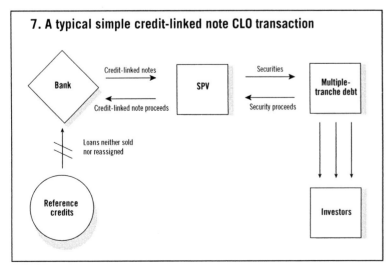

Table 9. A typical RAROC formula

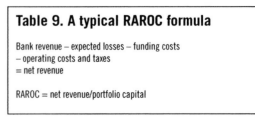

Bank revenue − expected losses − funding costs
− operating costs and taxes
= net revenue

RAROC = net revenue/portfolio capital

REGULATORY CAPITAL VERSUS MODELS-BASED CAPITAL: GIVING CREDIT TO NEW APPROACHES

Walter Gontarek and Charles Colbourne
TD Securities

For years, credit derivatives traders justified to a doubting majority, bank regulators, and their superiors alike the attraction of a derivatives market to transfer credit risk. Now, with the doubters in retreat and more users entering into credit derivative transactions, the same traders have found a new cause célèbre: the reformation of the bank capital regime for credit risk.

Until late 1996, credit derivatives lacked any regulatory recognition that rewarded the use of credit derivatives. Then, first in North America and shortly after in Europe, leading regulators responded to calls for the recognition of the benefits of prudent credit derivatives usage and issued preliminary guidance. Having achieved this, dealers and end-users alike again lobbied the regulators to address the limitations of this preliminary treatment, including limited recognition of partial hedges and transactions with non-bank or non-collateralised counterparties.

This in turn has lead to industry calls (with support from ISDA, the International Swap and Derivatives Association) for a complete reform of regulatory bank capital.[1] The debate revolves around the inadequacy of the 1988 Basle Capital Accord (which sets current bank regulatory capital guidelines) and proposes the application of internal models to calculate the appropriate amount of risk capital in a credit portfolio context.

Regulatory capital currently differentiates credit risk into categories which originate from issuers such as OECD (Organisation of Economic Cooperation and Development) governments, OECD banks, and all corporates (regardless of rating or domicile). Credit risk arising from these issuers require 0%, 1.6%, and 8% capital requirements respectively. The requirements do not look to the creditworthiness (as defined by credit rating) of the counterparty or position, and are summed in order to obtain a portfolio capital requirement. Thus, for example, a funded loan of $100 to a B-rated Turkish bank (a bank domiciled in an OECD area) would require $1.6 in regulatory capital. Alternatively, a portfolio of 100 funded loans of $1 each to AAA-rated North American and European corporates would require $8 in regulatory capital, or five times more

(notwithstanding the arguably higher credit quality and portfolio diversity of this second set of transactions).

The pillars of the risk capital modelling approach include the use of VAR (value at risk) models, which estimate the probability distribution of worst case credit losses at some confidence interval (say 99%) for a given time horizon or liquidation period. While reserves address expected losses, risk capital is held against this VAR model calculation (which reflects the magnitude of reference asset exposure) minus any collateral posted. Thus, to the extent that collateral level is equivalent to the VAR calculation, transactions may require minimal if any risk capital.

Another tenet of the internal modelling approach is the recognition of concentration risks to single names and the benefits of portfolio diversification. The internal modelling approach also promotes dynamic capital charges that reflect the realities of the macro-economic cycle, default estimates and recovery rates rather than static assumptions of 0%, 1.6% and 8%. Unlike regulatory capital, the internal modelling approach implicitly recognises the effects of term structure upon default probabilities and acknowledges the positive impact of limited offsets, or risk mitigating transactions (such as "long" cash assets and "long" credit derivative hedges) that provide significant if not perfect risk reduction.

Undoubtedly, the challenges associated with the adoption of internal modelling are many and some smaller financial institutions may be slow to recognise these benefits. Moreover, several practical issues surrounding the implementation of this approach remain outstanding, including their administrative and quantitative complexity, model validation, and establishing backtesting horizons and confidence intervals.

Nevertheless, many industry observers believe that some form of internal modelling is now justified and indeed prudent given advances in credit risk methodologies and the development of the credit derivatives market.

---

1 For an articulate discussion of this subject, see "Credit Risk and Regulatory Capital", ISDA, March 1998, and Chapter 12 of the present volume.

CREDIT DERIVATIVES: AN END-USER INVESTOR PERSPECTIVE

Robert DeSantes

Banca CRT

Much of this chapter discusses the benefits of hedging using credit derivatives. But what motivates the end-users who invest in the products? Take, for example, a non-domestic bank whose performance is measured in terms of the level of overall portfolio asset quality and revenue production within a given time period.

This bank might have a $100 million unfunded commitment available as follows:

❏ one third for 364 days at 5bp pa; and

❏ the remainder for five years at 8bp pa.

This would return $70,000 in fee income. And yet a three-year default swap for the same name would be priced at 16bp pa or $160,000 in fee income.

Essentially, credit default swaps remove the "relationship costs" from the syndication process, which is particularly useful for smaller banks that employ fewer relationship managers.

Secondly, as a protection seller an end-user can use its relationships with major credit derivatives dealers and loan syndication teams and take up excess capacity from the credit markets. For the investor, this can prove a cost-effective means of originating credit risk. Investors using credit derivatives do not require ancillary business units across the treasury, risk management and loan products spectrum. Such a credit investor can remain focused and limit its involvement to a credit decision and acceptance of default risk, acting solely as a portfolio manager.

Many medium-sized domestic and foreign banks use credit derivatives to acquire the credit risk of high-quality corporations at attractive prices. Using relationships within the credit derivatives markets, they structure transactions with rating, tenor and funding profiles that they could never originate directly in the syndication markets, thus benefiting bank portfolio return, revenue and diversification targets.

Total return swaps offer an additional source of business. Buyers of counterparty risk can rent their balance sheets to a dealer, finance loan or security inventory, and achieve a yield on the counterparty risk that again looks attractive compared to traditional credit-line products such as the interbank money markets.

---

importance to the credit derivative markets.

Bank revenue is a function of investment income and other fees generated. Investment revenue can be increased by investing using credit derivatives. For the first time hedge fund investors can access the loan asset class (Example 1, above), investment managers can locate credit investment opportunities that do not exist within their tenor constraints (Example 3), and bank portfolios can enhance credits so as to meet investment guidelines (Example 8).

Expected losses are equivalent to the mean value of the loss distribution of a given credit portfolio. They are an intuitive measure of credit risk and represent numerically the expected probability of default (for a given tenor) multiplied by the loss given default (or, 1 – recovery rate percentage) multiplied by the expected exposure amount. For certain asset classes such as US loans or bonds, rating agencies have provided default probabilities and recovery rates, although more rigorous quantitative work is required for a robust expected loss calculation for a global credit portfolio. A capital cushion for expected losses is provided by bank provisioning policies. The level of these reserves are directly linked to credit pricing issues, and portfolio managers seek to price new exposures to cover their contribution to portfolio expected losses. The higher (lower) the expected loss calculation, the greater (lower) level of reserves required to support the new credit exposure.

Funding costs can be proactively managed using credit derivatives. In a non-synthetic (ie non-credit derivative) world, investors who face high funding costs would be limited to higher risk assets that generate a sufficient spread over their funding levels. Higher quality assets would be the strict domain of lower cost funders (ie banks that fund below Libor), as only a lower cost funder can earn a positive spread over low yielding assets. With the emergence of the credit derivatives market, high-cost funders have a comparative advantage in investing in very high quality credit default swaps, while low cost funders are proving to be the most active originators and hedgers of credit risk. Credit derivatives will serve as an intermediary technology between credit hedger and investor, benefiting both sides of a credit derivative transaction.

Effectively, high-cost funders will remain on Markowitz's efficient frontier (Figure 8), but will increase their allocation of high quality assets and, most likely, increase the overall portfolio quality and diversity. Markowitz also applied a capital market line to his efficient frontier and argued that firms which can leverage at a given risk-free rate may be able to jump off the efficient frontier on to segment M–A of the capital market line as illustrated on the figure.

Credit derivatives do not provide financing at the risk-free rate, thus they seem unlikely to facilitate such a transition. But they do provide effective leverage to investors. In short, the effect of credit derivatives upon funding costs is that credit risk can be redistributed more widely to more takers of credit risk, and all investors can now migrate along the efficient frontier and invest in a broader array of assets.

Operating and transactions costs plus taxes also play a role in changing the distribution of risk. High operating costs and low client profitability have required many lenders to exit from long-standing bank relationships. RAROC lending (as discussed earlier) encourages lenders to demand an increase in transaction RAROC in return for additional credit exposure. Hedging with credit derivatives is one way of overcoming the need to exit from longstanding relationships, and is clearly one reason for the growth in the CLO market.

Different tax treatment and the effect of withholding tax can lead to security illiquidity and distortions. Credit derivatives provide a synthetic risk transference mechanism that is tax neutral, and thus not affected by these credit market distortions.

Portfolio or risk capital is the amount of capital held to cushion against *unexpected losses* (Figure 9). Whereas credit reserves address expected losses, unexpected losses are calculated using simulation technology (such as value-at-risk) and are expressed at given confidence intervals. Unexpected loss results from the stochastic process governing defaults originating from abnormally large losses, or volatility in asset portfolio valuation.

The higher the confidence interval employed in the simulation, the more economic capital is

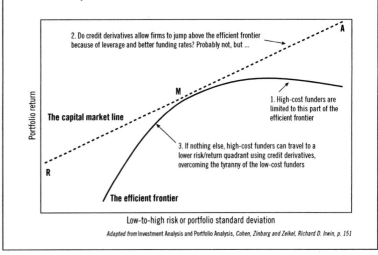

8. The capital market line and the efficient frontier

2. Do credit derivatives allow firms to jump above the efficient frontier because of leverage and better funding rates? Probably not, but ...

Portfolio return

The capital market line

M

A

1. High-cost funders are limited to this part of the efficient frontier

3. If nothing else, high-cost funders can travel to a lower risk/return quadrant using credit derivatives, overcoming the tyranny of the low-cost funders

R

The efficient frontier

Low-to-high risk or portfolio standard deviation

Adapted from Investment Analysis and Portfolio Analysis, Cohen, Zinbarg and Zeikel, Richard D. Irwin, p. 151

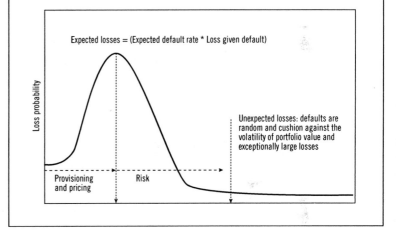

9. Economic capital: the defence against unexpected losses

Expected losses = (Expected default rate * Loss given default)

Loss probability

Provisioning and pricing

Risk

Unexpected losses: defaults are random and cushion against the volatility of portfolio value and exceptionally large losses

required as a cushion against unexpected losses. But as this capital requirement rises, fewer and fewer transactions meet RAROC hurdles. As already demonstrated, credit derivatives can reduce the risk of losses and are thus consistent with the RAROC approach to lending.

Hedging pitfalls in practice

Potential hedging pitfalls tend to occur in one of three steps of the credit derivatives transaction process: transaction origination, structuring, or documentation.

Transaction origination is the first point of contact between the potential hedger and the taker of risk. Successful credit derivatives dealers endeavour to:
❑ establish client/product suitability;
❑ identify and fully appreciate end-user motivations and portfolio;
❑ appreciate the needs of investors in term of gaining approval for transactions, procedural constraints and "credit culture";

PANEL 7

PITFALLS IN DOCUMENTATION

Karen Becker

The Toronto-Dominion Bank, London branch

Although documentation for credit derivatives continues to improve, new and more complex products and trades constantly emerge. In order to keep up with the market, documentation must constantly be modified to accommodate these variations.

In order for the documentation process to be effective, documenting trades in a vacuum must be avoided. Credit derivatives documentation specialists should receive as much information as possible regarding the transactions contemplated. This information should include the basics such as a term sheet, trade ticket and credit approvals as well as more complex information such as the motivation for the trade (from both the end-user and dealer perspective), the hedging strategy and regulatory implications. Providing quality informa-

tion to documentation specialists will enable the trade to be structured as intended by the users.

Another important link in the documentation process is the ISDA Master Agreement between two parties and the credit derivative confirmations. One example of this relates to the schedule to the ISDA document which usually contains a threshold amount for the purpose of determining cross default based on the credit strength of the counterparty. In a credit default swap parties have the option of including a "threshold", or default requirement relating to the assets that comprise the trade. This requirement must be met before payout occurs. The default requirement can be set independently and is not likely to be related to the threshold amount set in the schedule.

❑ provide clients with a constant flow of product, regulatory, and documentation support and information;

❑ address documentation issues early in the hedging process, especially in the case of first-time counterparties.

End-users will generally need to:

❑ provide useful feedback and help manage expectations about the timing of transactions;

❑ understand that transaction terms are generally indicative and not firm;

❑ appreciate that dealers may have limits on their appetite for certain credits; and

❑ appreciate the limitations and liquidity restraints of the developing credit derivatives market.

Transaction structuring occurs once a credit derivatives transaction has been originated and the major terms and conditions are set out. Issues to confirm at this stage include that:

❑ All settlement methods are agreed and market disruption clauses have been considered.

❑ The hedging strategy employed is the most efficient vehicle in terms of funding, relationship issues and capital treatment.

❑ If the reference asset and the underlying credit risk are one and the same, no residual basis risk remains (or, if it does, is identified and priced accordingly). In addition, a thorough check of the reference asset is required to iden-

tify any risk of pre-payment, extension, sinking fund or call features.

❑ The assignability of the unvetted underlying assets is established (otherwise alternative settlement techniques need to be established).

❑ The parties have a thorough understanding of any materiality tests requirements, especially in the case of non-investment grade credits.

❑ If a credit-linked note is being issued by a funder, it must confirm that credit events in the credit default swap confirmation are mirrored in the credit-linked note pricing supplement.

❑ Credit events are appropriate for the situation, such as determining if repudiation is required for sovereign credit derivatives transactions.

Transaction documentation includes the preparation of the transaction facsimile as presented by the credit derivatives desk to the documentation support function, and is the last stage prior to execution. As such, all transaction structuring issues must be resolved prior to documentation. As discussed in Panel 7, a successful documentation process includes:

❑ Presentation by credit derivatives trading to documentation of a transaction term sheet setting out terms and conditions.

❑ Good communication between all members of the credit hedging team.

❑ An appreciation of transaction objectives and goals.

❏ Problem-solving approach with the credit derivatives trading desk, the end-users and other internal partners.

❏ A well thought-out transaction template or use of ISDA-sponsored transaction confirmation.

Conclusion

The versatility of credit derivatives has been demonstrated in a wide array of concentration management, defensive hedging and capital man-agement applications. Credit derivatives, when combined with portfolio management tech-niques, default modelling, securitisation technol-ogy, and a robust credit trading platform, enhance traditional credit risk management prac-tices. Given their role in enhancing portfolio diversification and increasing return-on-capital, and the accelerating liquidity in the credit mar-kets, the revolution in credit derivatives is certain to continue in the years ahead.

1 *Walter Gontarek is a managing director of global credit derivatives with TD Securities. The views expressed in this chapter are those of the author and do not necessarily repre-sent the views of TD Securities. "TD Securities" represents TD Securities Inc., TD Securities (USA) Inc. and certain invest-ment activities of The Toronto-Dominion Bank. TD Securities is a trademark of The Toronto-Dominion Bank. Issued and approved by The Toronto-Dominion Bank, regu-lated by the SFA.*

The author wishes to acknowledge the efforts of associ-ates at Toronto-Dominion Bank and TD Securities, notably Trevor Bull, Ann-Marie Cerio, Charles Colbourne, Lucile de Carbonnieres, Joseph Hegener, Tom McNerney, Chris Pinkney, Emma Vassallo, and Hugh Whittle. Outside of TD, many thanks to Robert DeSantes of Banca CRT, Susan Hooker of Capital Re Corp, Sumit Paul-Choudhury and Rob Jameson of Risk Publications, Janet Tavakoli of First Chicago Corp, Nels Anderson of Moody's Investors Service Ltd, Jamie Storrow of the British Bankers' Association, and David Geen of Baker & McKenzie.

2 *For more information on credit risk practices, see "Learning to Play Around with Loans", Euromoney, pp. 123-6, May 1998.*

3 The BBA Credit Derivatives Report 1998, *data for all houses, July 1998.*

4 The BBA Credit Derivatives Report 1998, *data for all houses, July 1998.*

5 The BBA Credit Derivatives Report 1998, *data for all houses, July 1998.*

6 The BBA Credit Derivatives Report 1998, *data for all houses, July 1998.*

7 *For further uses of these products, see "What are Credit Derivatives?", Ronit Ghose,* Credit Derivatives: Key Issues, BBA, *March 1997, pp. 10-11.*

8 *"A Hundred Ways to Slice Up Credit", Theodore Kim,* Euromoney, *March 1998. p. 97.*

9 *See "Learning to Play Around With Loans",* Euromoney, *May 1998, pp. 123-6.*

10 *For more information on understanding derivatives exposures, see* Managing Financial Risk: A Guide to Derivative Products, Financial Engineering and Value Maximisation, *Charles W. Smithson and Clifford W. Smith, Jr. with D. Sykes Wilford (Chicago, 1995) Chapter 17.*

11 *See* Financial Times, *January 11, 1998.*

12 *"When Borrowers Go Bad",* The Economist, *February 28, 1998, p. 97.*

13 *Adam Bradbery, "Derivatives Body Aims to Urge BIS to Amend its Capital Rules",* Wall Street Journal Europe, *March 26, 1998, p. 8.*

14 *"You Ain't Seen Nothin' Yet",* Euromoney, *December, 1997, p. 70.*

3

Managing Country Risk using Credit Derivatives

Mark Gheerbrant
Rabobank International

Country risk is, quite literally, all around us. Any company with international ambitions, whether involved in manufacturing or financial services, will face the problem of having to manage country risk exposures. Furthermore, for a company seeking to expand internationally, the best opportunities will usually exist in the developing countries where the credit risks and volatilities are often the greatest.

At the time of writing, we are in the midst of an "Asian crisis" caused by severe currency devaluations, stock market crashes and high loan losses in the local banks. South Korea, for example, has seen its long-term debt rating fall from A1- to Ba1 (Moody's rating for the Korea Development Bank) – a fall of six notches in the space of 24 days. During that period the spreads on its international debt widened from 25 basis points to as much as 1000 bps (Figure 1).

This turmoil, however, has not been confined to South Korea. Thailand, Malaysia and Indonesia have also been badly affected and in Japan, whilst the country itself remains sound, many of the major local banks and corporations are facing severe problems.

Whilst Asia is currently the focus of attention, one does not need too long a memory to recall credit crises in Latin America (most recently the problems with the Mexican peso in 1994/95) and in Eastern Europe.

Traditionally, the country risk manager has had a fairly limited arsenal of weapons with which to tackle these problems. Export guarantees and credit insurance have been around for many years but are inflexible and are generally related to specific transactions or projects. It has

therefore been very difficult for companies to hedge general economic exposures to countries or regions, short of pulling out of an area (which is often impractical, or attempted too late).

The growth in credit derivatives in recent years provides the risk manager with another and more flexible tool for managing a company's country exposures. Credit derivatives are not a panacea, however. In particular, users need to pay attention to how credit events are defined and to the procedures and financial consequences of one or more of these events occurring. This chapter, therefore, aims to help the reader understand both the applications and the limitations of using credit derivatives for managing country risk.

Types of country risk

Not all country risks are the same in nature. The first step in deciding when and how to use credit derivatives (Figure 2 overleaf) involves understanding the types of risk that are involved. These can be sub-divided into the three main categories described below.

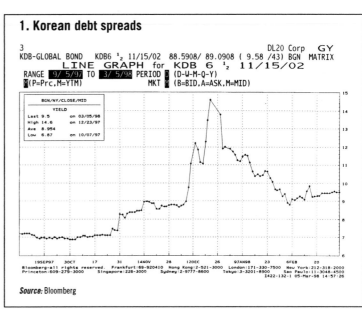

1. Korean debt spreads

Source: Bloomberg

The material contained in this chapter is not intended to provide specific advice on any matter and is not intended to be comprehensive. No responsibility for any loss occasioned to any person relying on material contained in this chapter will be accepted by the author, his employer or the publishers.

2. Checklist: hedging country risk with credit derivatives

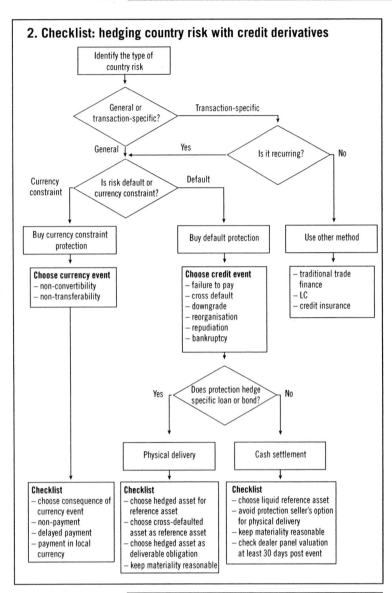

Table 1. Comparison of local currency and foreign currency ratings

Standard & Poor's long-term sovereign debt ratings for Latin America

	Foreign currency	Local currency
Argentina	BB	BBB–
Brazil	BB–	BB
Colombia	BBB–	A+
El Salvador	BB	BBB+
Paraguay	BB–	BBB+
Peru	BB	BBB–
Uruguay	BBB–	BBB+

Source: Standard & Poor's

SOVEREIGN COUNTERPARTY RISK

Counterparty risk in general is a function of an entity's ability to honour its obligations as they fall due. This, in the longer term, is itself a function of the balance between the entity's revenues and its costs (for a sovereign entity, essentially its balance of payments), but in the shorter term it is also a function of liquidity. It is almost always a lack of cash that causes an entity, whether sovereign or corporate, to default on its debt obligations.

This is a particularly important point in relation to country risk. A country rarely has liquidity problems in its local currency (since it has the ability to manage its domestic financial system), but emerging countries quite often face a shortage of hard currency. A clear distinction must therefore be drawn between sovereign risks denominated in local currency and those denominated in hard currency. This difference is demonstrated by the difference in the credit ratings assigned to the two types of obligations (Table 1). This brings us on to the second type of country risk.

CURRENCY CONTROLS: CONVERTIBILITY AND NON-TRANSFERABILITY

Currencies become "inconvertible" when restrictions are imposed by the country on the exchange of local currency for foreign currency. This can either take the form of prohibitions on any currency exchange transactions or, more likely, the fixing of an artificial exchange rate at which all transactions must take place. Currencies become "non-transferable" when restrictions are imposed by the country on the amount of hard currency that can be transferred out of the country.

The reason for introducing these measures is often to safeguard precious hard currency reserves.

There is clearly a link between currency restrictions and counterparty default. Most emerging countries rely heavily on investments from overseas, often in the form of debt issues in hard currency in the international capital markets. Any default, or even indication of intention to default, on these obligations severely affects a country's ability to raise finance in these markets – and raises its financing costs. The imposition of currency controls is therefore often an indication that a country with a worsening economic situation is trying to safeguard dwindling supplies of hard currency in order to service its international debt. In this sense, it can be seen as a precursor to sovereign default.

POLITICAL RISK

Political risk is the risk that the value of assets in a country will be reduced or lost altogether through acts of war, revolution or insurrection, nationalisation, expropriation, confiscation or requisition.

Whilst this chapter is concerned primarily with country risk, and not individual counterparty risk, the two are clearly inextricably linked. As stated earlier, counterparty risk is a function of an entity's ability to source sufficient liquidity to meet its obligations. Regardless of the strength of an individual company, it will not be able to meet its hard currency obligations overseas if currency controls are imposed. Since, as we have seen, currency controls are themselves an indication of rising country risk, then clearly any exposures within a country, even if not directly linked to the sovereign, are subject to sovereign country risk.

This is reflected in counterparty ratings. Except in exceptional circumstances, counterparty ratings are given a ceiling by the major ratings agencies that reflects the credit rating of the country within which they are domiciled.

Sources of country risk

Before examining hedging methods in more detail, it is worth considering the various ways in which country risk exposures can arise. The most obvious example is investment in overseas loans, bonds or equities. These investments are generally made by financial institutions such as banks or investment funds. Various permutations are possible between investments in sovereign issues or corporate issues or equities, denominated in either hard currency or local currency. The risks, however, are similar in each case. Whilst a corporation may be financially sound, it is unlikely to be in a position to service its obligations if the country in which it is based is in default. Similarly, although debt denominated in local currency is more likely to be repaid, the money received will be of little value to an overseas investor if it cannot be exchanged for their functional currency.

Take, for example, the case of a bank lending to an overseas corporation in US dollars. The bank will perform the usual credit analysis of that company and only extend the loan provided it is convinced of its financial viability. The company's ability to repay the bank, however, will be entirely dependent upon its ability to obtain US dollars. Here the bank has no direct exposure to the country but it does have a currency convertibility/transferability risk. The distinction may seem fine, but since it is possible to hedge each of these risks separately with credit derivatives the difference is important.

Another way that country risk can arise is from investment in overseas operations such as subsidiaries, branches, joint ventures, etc. Here a distinction must be drawn between overseas operations providing goods or services for the local market, and those which are primarily producing goods for export. In the former case, the

cash and revenues would be in local currency and the risk would be to the net profit that would be expected to be repatriated to the parent company. In the latter case, the costs will be in local currency but the revenues may well be in hard currency. In both cases, complications may arise if materials need to be imported which may require hard currency. A company's entire investment in an overseas operation will of course be subject to political risk.

A third source of country risk lies in an institution's participation in major overseas projects. These are very common in developing countries, particularly for infrastructure projects such as road building, power stations, etc (see Chapter 2 for an illustrative example). The participation might take the form of a loan or equity investment, or the provision of expertise or services. In each case the risks will be similar to those described in the two scenarios above.

Finally, all cross-border transactions generate various kinds of country risk, depending upon the type of transaction involved. When importing, the supplier is mainly exposed to performance risk. There are clearly elements of country risk here, but these are probably best hedged through good business practice (eg avoiding over-reliance on particular suppliers). Exporters are exposed to a greater degree of country risk, as the buyer is generally required to pay in hard currency. Trade finance is commonly used in such situations but since it is sometimes provided by local banks it may not mitigate the country risk exposure.

In general, therefore, for non-financial companies with overseas operations the largest exposure is likely to arise from political risk – which could potentially lead to the confiscation of an entire operation. There is no direct sovereign counterparty risk (with the exception of some infrastructure projects) and currency constraints can often be avoided if the parent company has access to hard currency. Overseas operations are normally continuing businesses and the investors do not usually have a firm date planned on which they might exit the market.

By contrast, investors in bonds or loans to overseas companies or sovereigns generally invest for a specific time period (ie the maturity of the bond) and are therefore reliant upon a country being solvent, or there being no currency constraints, at a particular point in time. For this reason financial institutions face a higher level of exposure to country risk and are therefore likely to be the greater users of credit derivatives.

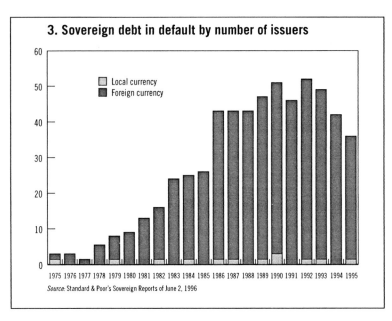

3. Sovereign debt in default by number of issuers

Local currency
Foreign currency

1975 1976 1977 1978 1979 1980 1981 1982 1983 1984 1985 1986 1987 1988 1989 1990 1991 1992 1993 1994 1995

Source: Standard & Poor's Sovereign Reports of June 2, 1996

Historical perspective

Having examined the types of country risk and the situations in which they can arise, the next step is to try and quantify the size of the problem. How often do sovereign defaults occur, how long do they last and what are the consequences in terms of likely losses?

Standard and Poor's in their annual *Sovereign Default Study*[1] provide statistics that give a useful insight into these questions, and which show a number of interesting historical trends. Firstly, both the number of issues in default and the value of sovereign debt in default are declining. Figure 3 shows the number of sovereign debt issuers in default. These rose sharply in the early 1980s as a result of the Latin American debt crisis and jumped again in 1985 mainly as a result of sub-Saharan African and eastern European issuers.

The second interesting feature is the sharp distinction between rated and unrated countries. Since 1975 no sovereign issuer has defaulted on any local or foreign currency debt rated by Standard & Poor's. Defaults by unrated issuers over the same period have been numerous. This trend, however, may not continue as a significant proportion of new sovereign ratings are now being assigned to lower rated countries.

A clear distinction also currently exists between the default rates of loans and bonds. In the period since 1975, whilst a total of 68 sovereigns have defaulted on bank debt, only six have defaulted on their bonds, suggesting that sovereigns effectively treat bond issues as senior obligations. In large part, this is because historically governments have relied upon bank loans for the majority of their overseas financing. Issuance of

international bonds is a relatively new phenomena, really only having started in the 1990s with the issuance of Brady bonds by several Latin American countries. As the market for emerging country debt has grown, so the level of bond issuance has increased dramatically (with a total of $51.4 billion of Latin American international debt issuance in 1996, for example). In the future, therefore, sovereigns may not be able to keep servicing their bond issues at the expense of bank lenders.

Figure 3 also shows a marked difference between the frequency of default on foreign currency debt compared with local currency debt, with the ratio since 1975 running at an average of 8:1. This is hardly surprising, given a government's ability to manage its domestic financial system.

The S&P report also offers some interesting findings on the duration of default (Table 2). Once again, we can see marked differences between loans and bonds, and between foreign and local currency debt. Whilst the average default duration for local currency debt is only one year, by contrast it is eight years for bank loans. A glance at the table, however, reveals the wide range of amounts of time taken to resolve problems from less than one year for the likes of Angola and Egypt to more than 10 years for several other countries.

The nature and consequences of a default can also vary widely from a simple rescheduling of interest and/or principal payments, to exchanges of one obligation for another or buy-backs for cash at a discount. During the Latin American crisis of the 1980s, exchanges became the norm as a result of the growth of the Brady bond market. More recently, however, buy-backs have been more frequent. As with duration of default, the loss suffered can vary widely from country to country and also with the type of debt held. According to S&P the lowest losses were suffered on foreign currency bond issues, with bondholders losing on average less than 15% and substantially less in some cases. In general, the longer the period of default, the greater loss suffered. The average losses on bank debt, at 30%, were double and showed greater variation. Local currency debt, however, whilst less likely to default, showed the greatest losses (averaging 40%) and also the greatest variation (with some lenders losing 100%).

It should be stressed before leaving this review of historic events that the market is changing all the time. As already noted, with a

Table 2. Duration of sovereign defaults: unrated issuers, years in default since 1975

Issuer	Local currency	Foreign currency	Foreign currency bank	Issuer	Local currency	Foreign currency	Foreign currency bank
Albania			1991–95	Liberia			1981–95
Algeria			1992–95	Macedonia			1992–95
Angola			1992	Madagascar			1981–84, 1986–95
Bolivia			1980–81, 1984–93	Malawi			1982, 1988
Bosnia & Herzegovina			1992–95	Morocco			1983, 1986–90
Bulgaria			1990–94	Mozambique			1984–91
Cameroon			1989–95	Myanmar (Burma)	1984		
Congo			1986–95	Nicaragua			1979–82, 1986–95
Costa Rica		1984–85	1981, 1983–90	Niger			1983, 1986–91
Côte d'Ivoire			1983, 1986–95	Nigeria		1986–88, 1992	1982–92
Croatia			1992–95	Panama		1987–94	1983–95
Cuba			1982–95	Peru			1976, 1978, 1980, 1984–95
Dominican Republic			1982–83, 1989–94	Sao Tome & Principe			1987–94
Ecuador			1983–95	Senegal			1981, 1990, 1992–95
Egypt			1984	Serbia			1992–95
Ethiopia			1991–95	Sierra Leone			1983, 1986–95
Gabon			1986–94	Sudan			1979–81, 1983–95
Gambia			1986–90	Tanzania			1984–95
Ghana	1979		1987	Togo			1979–80, 1988, 1990–95
Guatemala		1989	1986	Uganda			1980–93
Guinea			1986–88, 1991–95	USSR/Russia	1993		1991–95
Guyana			1979, 1982, 1984, 1986–92	Vietnam	1975		1985–95
Haiti			1982–95	Yemen			1990–95
Honduras			1981, 1986–95	Yugoslavia		1992–95	1983–91
Iran			1978, 1992–95	Zaire			1979–80, 1985–95
Iraq			1990–95	Zambia			1982, 1986–94
Jamaica			1978, 1981, 1987–93	Zimbabwe		1975–80*	
North Korea			1986–95				

* Bonds initially defaulted in 1985 *Source:* Standard & Poor's Sovereign Reports of June 2, 1996

higher degree of reliance by sovereigns on international bond financing, and the associated spread of ratings to less creditworthy sovereign issues, the trends of the past may well not be a good guide to the future.

Using credit derivatives to hedge country risk

Credit derivatives can be used to hedge both sovereign default risk and currency constraint risks. There are a variety of products available to do this including default swaps, total return swaps, credit-linked notes and hybrids such as spread options and downgrade protection. The examples below demonstrate how each can be appropriately applied in different circumstances.

DEFAULT SWAPS

Default swaps are the simplest form of credit derivative and are the building blocks for several of the more complex variants. Default protection on sovereigns is one of the most actively traded, and hence liquid, sectors of the credit derivative market, and prices are readily available for a range of countries and maturities. Figure 4 shows a typical broker's page for default swaps for Latin American countries. The page gives details of the

4. Example of sovereign default swap quotations

```
Enter 99 <GO> for list of story options.              Equity ICRD
                                                      Page 1 of 2
ICD    INTERCAPITAL LATIN AMERICAN CREDIT DERIVATIVES 1-800-382-4265
       Mar 3 1998 16:15
CREDIT    TERM   BID  OFFER AMOUNT STRUCTURE REFERENCE
ARGENTINA 6MOS   120  180*  10X10  DEF PUT   TBD
ARGENTINA 1      150  200*  10X10  DEF PUT   TBD
ARGENTINA 2      240  310   10X10  DEF PUT   TBD
ARGENTINA 3      300  360   10X10  DEF PUT   TBD
ARGENTINA 4      330  385*  10X10  DEF PUT   TBD
ARGENTINA 5      350  410   10X10  DEF PUT   TBD
ARGENTINA 7           500          DEF PUT   GLOB 06
BRAZIL    3      300         10     CONV
BRAZIL    3MTH   200*        10     DEF PUT   TBD
BRAZIL    6MTH   220  260*  10X10  DEF PUT   TBD
BRAZIL    1      250  325   10X10  DEF PUT   EI
BRAZIL    2      280  365*  10X10  DEF PUT   GLOBAL
BRAZIL    3      330  390   10X10  DEF PUT   GLOBAL
BRAZIL    4      360  430   10X10  DEF PUT   TBD
BRAZIL    5      390  470   10X10  DEF PUT   TBD
COLUMBIA  1      100         10     DEF PUT   TBD
COLUMBIA  5      185  235    10     DEF PUT   TBD
ECUADOR   2           550    10     DEF PUT   TBD
MEXICO    1      75   150*  10X10  DEF PUT   TBD
MEXICO    2      140  200   10X10  DEF PUT   TBD
Bloomberg-all rights reserved.  Frankfurt:69-920410  Hong Kong:2-521-3000  London:171-330-7500  New York:212-318-2000
Princeton:609-279-3000   Singapore:226-3000   Sydney:2-9777-8600   Tokyo:3-3201-8900   Sao Paulo:11-3048-4500
                                                      I422-132-1 04-Mar-98 17:25:54
```

Source: Bloomberg
The screen shown here presents prices for default swaps for Latin American countries provided by Intercapital Brokers. The TERM is the maturity of the default swap in months or years. BID and OFFER represent the price in basis points per annum at which protection is bought and sold respectively. AMOUNT is the size in millions of US dollars for which the prices are applicable on each side of the market (ie bid and offer). STRUCTURE shows the type of protection in question, which in most cases is default risk, though for three-year Brazil the currency convertibility structure is also quoted.
REFERENCE refers to the reference asset for determining whether a credit event has taken place

country to which the default swap relates, the maturity of the default swap, the price in basis points per annum where protection is bought and sold and the amount in millions of US dollars for which the prices apply. The structure in most cases is a default put ("DEF PUT") ie a default by the country concerned gives the buyer of protection the right to "put" or sell the reference asset to the protection seller either by physical delivery or through cash settlement. In the case of three-year Brazil, however, the protection that is bid for is currency convertibility ("CONV") and not default.

It is interesting to note that this broker's page shows bid and offer prices for most maturities up to five years in sizes of at least $10m, which shows that reasonable liquidity does exist in the default swap market, at least for country risk.

Deals cannot be struck, however, simply on the basis of screen prices. Firstly the prices shown are only indicative, and the bid/offer spreads are quite wide, with most deals actually being struck somewhere in between these levels. Secondly, and perhaps more importantly, many crucial details are not contained on the screen. These include:
❑ The credit events that will act as a trigger for credit event payments. In addition to a failure to pay, these may include cross-default, bankruptcy, reorganisation, repudiation or credit rating downgrade.
❑ The reference asset or assets that will be used to determine whether a credit event has occurred.
❑ The level of materiality required for a credit event.
❑ The method for determining the amount of the credit event payment (see discussion below).
❑ Whether physical delivery is acceptable, and a definition of the deliverable obligations.
❑ Type of documentation ie ISDA or other.

There is currently no market standard for the above (with the possible exception of documentation) and therefore all these details are open to negotiation. The exact terms agreed upon will affect the level of protection bought or sold and may also affect the price; currently, therefore, most deals are not considered to be finalised until the documents are agreed. This is in con-trast to the more mature interest rate derivatives market, where the details of transactions are often based on market standards – hence, most deals are struck over the phone with documentation following on after.

Let us consider the example of a bank that has loans outstanding to a particular sovereign and wishes to reduce its exposure to that country. The bank could buy protection through the default swap shown in Figure 5.

In this deal, the bank pays an amount to the protection seller (usually in the form of a periodic payment in basis points of the swap notional amount) in return for receiving a Credit Event Payment (CEP) if and when a predefined credit event occurs. The credit events are agreed in advance and can include any of failure to pay, bankruptcy, cross default/cross acceleration, repudiation or restructuring. The method for calculating the CEP is also agreed in advance. It can be made in three ways:
❑ *Physical delivery* In this case the protection buyer (buyer) delivers the defaulted "reference asset" to the protection seller (seller) in return for receiving the nominal amount of the assets. The advantage of this method for the buyer is that it is a perfect hedge provided he owns the reference assets – if he does not it can cause problems. The advantage for the seller is that, in the case of default, he becomes the owner of the asset and so can try to maximise the returns from the asset during the workout process. The main disadvantage is that if the reference assets are loans there may be restrictions on their transferability. Also, if the buyer does not own the reference assets he may have problems obtaining them in order to deliver. This problem could arise even where the deal is entered into as a hedge, if a reference asset is similar but not identical to the owned assets.
❑ *Dealer poll* This method involves establishing a market price for the reference assets by obtaining bids for them from an agreed panel of dealers a specified number of days after the credit event has occurred. The seller then pays the buyer the difference between the market price and par. Probably the most common method in use, this pricing methodology avoids the problems of physical delivery but has certain drawbacks. In the event of a default by a major sovereign borrower there are likely to be severe market disruptions, in which case it simply may not be possible to obtain any bids from the market and, where it is possible, the bids are likely to be very low in the days following such an event. This

5. Default swap example

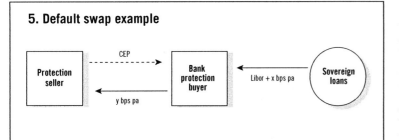

may ultimately be more disadvantageous for the seller, particularly bearing in mind that the actual average loss on defaulted sovereign bonds is historically only 15%. For this reason, some dealers will quote a higher price for writing protection with cash settlement based on a dealer poll than for writing protection based on physical delivery. Some people also take the view that, given that sovereign bond trading is dominated by a relatively small number of houses, which tend also to be the major players in the default swaps, there is the possibility of market distortion in such an event.

❏ *Fixed payment* It is possible, although unusual, to agree the size of a Credit Event Payment in advance. This is not really satisfactory for either party, given the large variance in losses resulting from a sovereign default, but it has the advantage of simplicity and can be used as a last resort if no satisfactory reference asset can be found.

Some participants in the market try to retain the right to choose between two or more of the above methods. Since presumably they will choose the most advantageous terms for themselves, this may result in an inferior hedge and is not to be recommended.

TOTAL RETURN SWAPS
Whilst the default swap allows a counterparty to transfer the default risk of an asset without transferring the asset itself, the total return swap allows the whole economic risk of the asset to be transferred without selling the asset, and can be used for hedging both debt and equity holdings. The example illustrated in Figure 6 shows how a total return swap can be used by an investor to hedge the risk of fixed rate sovereign bonds.

During the life of the TRS the protection buyer passes on all and any coupons received in return for receiving Libor plus margin. At the maturity of the TRS the market value of the reference assets is calculated and any increase or decrease from the initial value is paid or received by the buyer. The two important differences between the TRS and the default swap are that the buyer of the TRS has hedged the interest rate risk and has hedged any fall in the value of the reference assets for *any* reason ie not only reductions caused by default. The considerations in calculating the market value are similar to those that apply to default swaps. The seller would commonly be a member of the dealer valuation panel, giving him the option to make the best bid

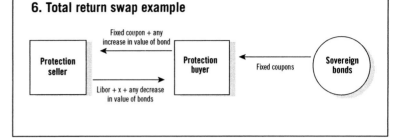

6. Total return swap example

and thereby effectively take physical delivery of the reference assets.

The maturities of default swaps or total return swaps need not be as long as the maturities of the reference assets. This means that an investor in sovereign bonds or loans who wishes to reduce his risk, but only for a limited period of time, can do so without actually having to sell the assets. This tactic was used extensively by investors during the recent debt crisis in South Korea, as discussed in Panel 1. At the start of the crisis the value of bonds plummeted and most investors were reluctant to sell at these low levels – especially if they felt that, provided the country could weather the initial storm and agree terms with the IMF, the worst would be over. They therefore bought protection for a period of six months to one year, thus hedging themselves during the perceived riskiest period but retaining ownership of the assets so that they could benefit from any "upside" later on.

Chapter 7 of this volume discusses TRS in more detail.

CREDIT-LINKED NOTES
Credit-linked notes are simply a securitised form of credit derivative ie a security, typically a debt instrument, with an embedded credit derivative. Most often the note issuer is the buyer of protection while the investor is the seller of protection. They may be used as an alternative to the naked derivative if, for example, the issuer wishes to raise cash concurrently with hedging a country exposure. They also allow investors who, for regulatory reasons, may not be able to enter into derivative agreements to write default protection. The investor has the risk of both the issuer of the credit-linked note and the embedded country risk. The return should therefore theoretically equal the default-free return plus the sum of the risk premiums for the issuer and the country, less an adjustment for the correlation between the two. This may be overridden by supply and demand factors, especially if the maturity of the CLN is one for which the sovereign issuer has little outstanding debt in the inter-

national markets. Several leading banks have developed so-called "limited recourse debt issuance medium term note" (MTN) programmes specifically for the issuance of sovereign-linked notes.

Suppose that a bank has a branch or subsidiary in Brazil that wishes to make a US dollar denominated loan to a local company, but that the bank's overall line of credit to that country is full. The bank could issue a Brazil-linked note in order to both fund the loan and at the same time buy country risk protection (Figure 7).

In this example, the bank has no direct credit exposure to the country, only to the company, but will only be repaid by the local company if it is able to access US dollars ie no currency constraints are imposed in Brazil. For this to be an effective hedge, therefore, the credit events contained within the note terms and conditions will relate to the imposition of currency constraints rather than sovereign debt default. The type of wording for this is covered in the next section on documentation.

If a credit event occurs, this can be dealt with in one of two ways:
❑ payments of principal and interest continue to be made, but in local currency at the then prevailing exchange rate; or
❑ no further payments are made until such time as the currency constraints are lifted, when the note will repay accrued interest and principal in US dollars.

Ideally, from the bank's point of view the terms should reflect those of the loan to the local company, although investors may have a preference for one over the other.

Chapter 8 of this volume discusses the structuring and valuing of credit-linked notes in more detail.

HYBRID DERIVATIVES
Other more specific types of credit derivatives are also available which may be useful for hedging in certain situations. Credit spread options give the buyer the right but not the obligation to

sell a reference asset to the option seller at a specified spread over either Libor, in the case of floating rate assets, or government bond yields in the case of fixed rate assets. These options come in two variants. Firstly, American-style options where the investor can "put" the bonds at any time and even in the event of default – this is not really a spread option at all but effectively a default put. Secondly, there are European or Bermudan options where the option can only be exercised on a limited number of dates and provided that no event of default has occurred. The option buyer can protect his downside risk whilst still benefiting from the upside if the credit improves.

A similar and related type of option is one that gives the option buyer the right to sell the reference assets to the option writer if the rating falls below a certain level. This is again useful for investors in sovereign debt who have to observe a minimum rating on all investments. Currently these hybrid derivatives are less liquid than the vanilla default or total return swaps, as they are harder to hedge precisely. However, they are easier to price theoretically since there is far more data available on credit spread movements and ratings migrations for sovereign debt than there is for sovereign defaults. These products are therefore likely to gain more prominence as banks become more comfortable with running credit derivative position risk.

Documentation considerations
The legal aspects of credit derivatives require particular attention in relation to country risk. They include the choice of reference asset, definition of default events and currency constraints, the settlement method and calculation of the settlement amount. The market generally uses the ISDA Credit Swap Transaction Confirmation, which has been recently updated, and the terms used here are largely consistent with that.

In choosing the reference asset, the objective should be to obtain the best hedge for the country exposure and ideally to find an asset with reasonable liquidity. These two objectives may not lead to the same conclusion, so a compromise may be necessary. If the asset is a loan, the protection seller may not accept this as a reference asset due to its lack of liquidity and there may also be problems with confidentiality, especially for bilateral agreements, and with transferability in the case of default. Protection sellers will generally prefer the most liquid bond issues which, if cross-default language is included, should theo-

7. Credit-linked note example

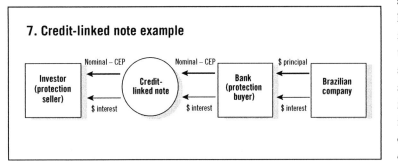

PANEL 1

HEDGING BONDS DURING THE ASIAN CRISIS

When the extent of the debt crisis in South Korea became fully apparent in October 1997, the value of all the bonds issued by Korean entities fell sharply, and the credit spread curve became steeply inverse. This reflected the fact that the market believed there was a significant likelihood of default and hence the debt of all maturities traded at very similar prices, making the yield on the short-dated debt much greater than the longer dated debt. Thus the negative spread curve.

At this time, there were intense negotiations taking place between the South Korean government and the IMF. Many investors felt that, provided the government could agree terms for the IMF funding package to be extended and that necessary reforms were implemented, the inherent strengths of the country would pull it through. On the other hand, if agreement could not be reached the country would almost certainly have to default on its debt obligations within months since it clearly had insufficient liquidity to cover forthcoming repayments.

At the time there was very little trading volume in bonds since few people wanted to invest more in South Korea, and few holders wanted to realise substantial losses by selling at the prevailing low prices. As a consequence, the bid/offer spreads quoted on bonds were very wide.

Faced with this scenario, the investor in Korea seemed to have two choices: selling into the very low bids, and hence realising his losses and missing any upside if an agreement was reached with the IMF; or holding on but facing the very real chance of a default and hence suffering even greater losses. In fact, many investors adopted a new tactic: they bought default protection for six months, thereby covering the risk of default over the perceived riskiest period yet retaining ownership of the asset to benefit from any later upside. The economics worked as follows for a five-year KDB bond:

Price of bonds before IMF agreement 65% bid/75% offer

Cost of six-month default protection 18% per annum

Price of bonds after IMF agreement 90% bid/92% offer

Assuming an investor owned the bonds at par, if he bought protection his situation after six months would be as follows:

Loss on bonds (to mid-market)   91% − 100% = (9%)

Cost of protection   8% for 6 months = (9%)
Net   (18%)

Compare this with the investor who sold immediately:

Loss on bonds   65% − 100% = (35%)

and the investor who took no action:

Loss on bonds (to mid-market)   91% − 100% = (9%)

Clearly, as things turned out the investor who took no action fared best, but this would not have been the case had default occurred. Assuming South Korea had defaulted, and that the value of the bond was 40% after this credit event, the economics would have been as follows:

For the investor who bought protection:

Loss on bonds   40% − 100% = (60%)

Cost of protection   (9%)

Credit event payment   (60%)

Net   (9%)

For the investor who sold immediately, as before:

Loss on bonds   (35%)

For the investor who took no action:

Loss on bonds   40% − 100% = (60%)

In summary the outcomes are as follows:

	Actual outcome	Outcome had default occurred	Average
Buyer of protection	−18%	−9%	−13.5%
Immediate seller	−35%	−35%	−35%
No action	−9%	−60%	−34.5%

Now, if it is assumed that there was an equal likelihood of the IMF agreeing or not agreeing to extend the funding package, then the expected outcome is merely the average of the two possible outcomes. In this case the buyer of default protection has by far the lowest expected loss.

Of course, weighting the outcomes in this way is purely subjective and for each investor to determine for themselves. It should also be noted that this analysis is for illustrative purposes only; although it is intended to be realistic the values used are not necessarily the values available in the market at the time. It is also possible that after six months, even if Korea had not defaulted, the debt could still have been trading at 65% − in which case the outcomes would be different.

PANEL 2

BUILDING COUNTRY CREDIT CURVES

The sovereign debt of countries with the highest credit ratings is generally considered to be as close to "risk free" as one can get. The US Government Treasury Bonds are the accepted benchmark for the risk-free US dollar yield curve. When investing in corporate debt or lower-rated countries the investor expects a higher return, the risk premium being designed to compensate the investor for the default risk inherent in these "risky" securities.

The difference between the risk-free rate and the risky rate is the *credit spread*, and this will vary with maturity as the risk of default varies. By plotting this for different maturities a *credit spread curve* can be built for risky countries.

Theoretically, it is also possible to calculate the risk premium or credit spread by calculating the probability of default. However, given the relatively small number of countries (compared with corporations), the very small number of historic defaults and the political factors involved this is not practical. It is therefore necessary to infer the credit spread from the bond market and adjust it as necessary to derive a default swap price.

Since the maturity of the default swap to be priced will not necessarily coincide with the maturity of an outstanding issue, a credit spread curve needs to be built from which the spread for any maturity can be read. In theory this is a simple matter of plotting the credit spread against the maturity of all outstanding issues and drawing a line through the data points. In practice, however, it is not so simple. In the case of a country with many issues outstanding, the data points tend to form a scattergram rather than a curve as in the example for Sweden issues (Figure A). This is due to market imperfections, such as the fact that

high coupon bonds, low coupon bonds and floating rate bonds will all tend to trade differently due to investor preferences. Also liquidity, a function of the size and age of an issue (among other things), will have a significant impact on the credit spread. It is possible to try and adjust for this subjectively or, if sufficient points exist, to estimate a function through them using regression analysis or some similar technique.

In the case of countries with few outstanding issues the problem will be insufficient data points from which to build a meaningful curve, as is the case for US dollar issues for Greece (Figure B). In this case one can simply join the points that do exist using linear or log linear interpolation, but this is not very satisfactory. An alternative approach is to use a "proxy" security to fill in the missing data points. The idea is to find an issue by another country that is as similar as possible in terms of rating, geographic area and key risk characteristics to the country in question. Although this approach can work quite well for building corporate credit curves where there is a large pool of issuers, it is less satisfactory for country credit curves due to the relatively small number of countries from which to select a proxy.

It must be borne in mind when building credit spread curves that market data is not always reliable, particularly for illiquid issues, and that it is important to ensure that the securities used to obtain data points are all of the same seniority.

Once a basic term structure of credit spreads has been built, it is possible to derive forward spreads in much the same way as for interest rates. These forward spreads are necessary for pricing spread options.

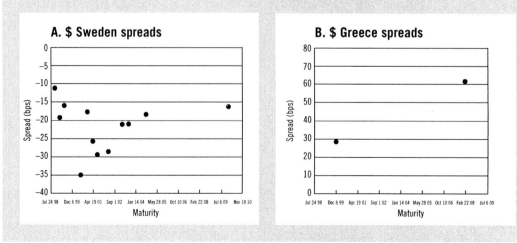

A. $ Sweden spreads

B. $ Greece spreads

retically be a good hedge for other direct *pari passu* obligations of the issuer. Historically, however, sovereign bonds have a significantly higher recovery rate than loans, following an event of default.

The ISDA confirmation lists seven credit events that may be included: bankruptcy, credit event upon merger, cross default/acceleration, downgrade, failure to pay, repudiation and restructuring. For sovereign risk protection failure to pay, cross-default/acceleration, repudiation and restructuring are normally included. This is becoming standard, although still often a point of debate, and the omission of any one of these events will weaken the quality of the hedge. The meaning of each of these is defined in the ISDA document and so need not be repeated here. It is, however, worthwhile examining the definition of "Restructuring":

A waiver, deferral, restructuring, rescheduling, standstill, moratorium, obligation exchange or other adjustment occurs with respect to any Obligation of the Reference Entity and the effect of such is that the terms of such Obligation are, overall, materially less favourable from an economic, credit or risk perspective to the holder of such obligation.

Since this covers a large percentage of the sovereign credit events that have taken place in the last 20 years, it should be regarded as essential. ISDA does not define currency constraint events, but the following paraphrased example of wording is taken from the Rabobank Nederland Limited Recourse Debt Issuance Programme:

(i) any action by the banking or monetary authorities of the Relevant Jurisdiction, with respect to foreign exchange market transactions (A) which results in the withholding of approval or permission for the exchange of Local Currency for the Relevant Currency by the Issuer or (B) that has the effect of preventing such exchange or the transfer of any Relevant Currency out of the Relevant Jurisdiction by non-local banks.

(ii) any event that results in the unavailability of the Relevant Currency for purchase by non-local banks with Local Currency and settlement through the banking system of the Relevant Jurisdiction which includes foreign exchange market transactions of

non-local banks.

Other events affecting foreign exchange markets can also be specifically mentioned including (i) banking moratoria, (ii) expropriation, confiscation, requisition and nationalisation and (iii) war, revolution, insurrection or hostile act.

The commercial factors concerning the choice of settlement method between cash settlement or physical delivery were covered earlier. For cash settlement, ISDA defines standard methods for calculating the settlement amount, while for physical delivery it is possible to specify more than one deliverable obligation. This should be acceptable, provided they are of the same seniority and may be a wise precaution for country risk transactions. It is believed that in the recent South Korean debt crisis default swaps with physical delivery of certain reference bonds were written with nominal amounts far exceeding the nominal amount of the relevant issue. This means that should these events ever be triggered, it will be impossible for all the protection buyers to fulfil their obligations to deliver. ISDA is currently considering the implications of this, but for this reason alone it is worth ensuring that the Dispute Resolution wording of any deals is satisfactory regarding this point.

Finally a point on Valuation Dates. The market standard seems to be to have these very soon after any Credit Event, but it may be advantageous for the hedger to make this period relatively long since the market turmoil immediately following a sovereign default may be greater than in the case of a corporate default.

Advantages and disadvantages compared with other products

Country risk managers have traditionally had a fairly limited number of products to choose from when hedging exposures, and those products that have been available have tended to focus on trade rather than investment. Export guarantees have been available for many years from both government agencies wishing to promote trade, such as ECGD in the UK, Hermes, Coface, and MITI in Japan and some private companies. Traditional trade finance products such as export letters of credit have also played a major role for exporters. Drawbacks of these methods include the fact that they require a specific transaction or project and that they tend to be quite short-term in nature. Also, letters of credit are sometimes issued by local banks: the country risk element of the credit risk of these institutions will be highly correlated to that of local companies.

PANEL 3

VOLATILITY OF CREDIT SPREADS

Panel 2 described how to derive the credit spread for a given sovereign issuer for a specific maturity. A glance at Figure 1 in the main text, however, shows that in the case of a KDB five-year bond the credit spread increased by 700 basis points in around three months. Clearly then, as well as knowing the credit spread itself, having some knowledge of how the spread behaves over time or its volatility is desirable. In fact, for pricing spread options it is essential.

The measure generally used for volatility in option pricing is the standard deviation of the spread given by:

Standard Deviation or

$$\sigma = \frac{1}{T-1} \sqrt{\sum_{t=1}^{t=T} \left(S_t - S_{avg} \right)^2}$$

where
S_t is the spread at time t
S_{avg} is the average spread
T is time to Maturity

In order to make this calculation, however, historic data is required for the yields on bonds over a reasonably significant period of time. Whilst several information providers do give historic bond yields, the data is not always reliable (particularly for less actively traded issues), and yield data may not be continuous over the period required. There is also sometimes rogue data, which can distort the end result. Assuming these problems can be overcome, however, it is a relatively simple matter to

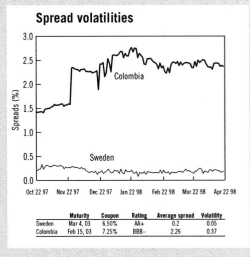

Spread volatilities

	Maturity	Coupon	Rating	Average spread	Volatility
Sweden	Mar 4, 03	6.50%	AA+	0.2	0.05
Colombia	Feb 15, 03	7.25%	BBB–	2.26	0.37

calculate the volatility figures.

The graph and table above give the average credit spread and the volatilities, in basis points, for two sovereign issues, Sweden and Colombia, for October 1997–April 1998.

Once a satisfactory source of historic credit spread data has been established, another interesting exercise is to derive the correlation in the spread behaviour between different countries. This is of use to the credit derivative practitioner but may also help the hedger to hedge his entire country exposures on a portfolio basis. It should be remembered, however, that correlations for general spread movements may not be the same as default correlations.

See also discussion in Chapter 9 of the present volume.

Credit insurance can overcome some of these problems, but the market remains fairly limited at present. None of these products, however, is particularly useful for hedging general exposures to a country, exposures which recur regularly or which continue for long periods of time, or exposures arising from major investments in emerging countries. Export guarantees, for example, are of limited use to the bank lender or emerging country fund manager wishing to reduce his exposure to a particular country. Credit derivatives on sovereigns on the other hand are available in large size and for maturities of up to 10 years. They therefore offer a very deep and flexible means of hedging financial exposures for reasonably long periods of time.

For example, a company exporting to a partic-

ular country on a regular basis and concerned more with the recipient's ability to pay in hard currency than its actual creditworthiness, could consider buying term currency convertibility protection rather than entering into a series of export finance arrangements. Or a company involved in a long-term infrastructure project backed by a particular government, could consider buying default protection on the sovereign. Credit derivatives in these cases offer a more general hedging method, and whilst not as perfect a hedge as export guarantees (as they are not tied to specific transactions), they provide reasonable protection over a long period and may prove to be more cost effective. Of course, traditional methods will undoubtedly continue to have a role to play, particularly in the more "exotic" emerging markets.

The biggest users, however, are likely to be the financial institutions to whom they offer a highly cost effective and flexible means of hedging investments in countries.

The liquidity of the credit derivatives market is still questioned from time to time. This is less of a problem for sovereign credits, which according to the latests BBA survey make up a significant fraction of the entire market (see Panel 1, Chapter 2).

Liquidity is improving all the time as the market grows, and pricing will become more competitive as new players enter the market.

The documentation of credit derivatives is no more complex than traditional export finance agreements and is rapidly becoming standardised under the auspices of ISDA. Also, the settlement procedures for credit derivatives are no more complex than for interest rate derivatives, and transactions can be recorded under existing ISDA master agreements. For potential users who are unable to use derivatives for regulatory or operational reasons, credit-linked notes will enable them to participate in the market.

For new users of credit derivatives there may be some drawbacks. The documentation and many of the terms may be unfamiliar, although existing users of interest rate derivatives should be familiar with ISDA documentation so this will be less of a problem.

There will also be legal considerations for new users to ensure that credit derivatives are intra vires and that they do not fall foul of any local insurance regulations. Finally there will be operational considerations. Credit derivatives, like interest rate derivatives, include periodic payments, event monitoring, counterparty exposure and marking-to-market. All of these require a reasonable level of sophistication by users, suggesting that, initially at least, they will be confined to the larger corporations and financial institutions.

Credit derivatives as part of an integrated risk management approach

Traditionally banks have set country limits on a country by country basis, based on either their own or external subjective research. These limits are then handed out to various parts of the organisations. The advent of country risk credit derivatives will potentially have a major impact on the way this is done. Firstly, since a country risk manager can now effectively "sell" his country limits in the market by writing default protection, he can now put a specific value on each country

limit. He is therefore able to on-sell the limits to the users within the organisation and to quantify the cost of doing business in these countries. This in turn may cause institutions to re-assess and re-price business in emerging markets. A corollary of this is that the company will also be able to buy limit extensions as their internal limits become full.

Secondly, many of the advanced pricing techniques developed in the interest rate derivatives market are now being applied to credit derivatives. This means that over time the pricing of country risk may become less subjective and based more upon default and recovery rates and price and rating volatility.

Since the country risk manager is now able to buy and sell country risk using credit derivatives, he is in a position to manage actively the company's country exposures as a whole. There is already sufficient liquidity in the market for it to be feasible to sell credit lines that are not being used in order to generate revenue, to cover excesses by buying protection and to charge internal users. As discussed further in Chapter 6, it is therefore possible for the country risk manager to run a revenue centre, acting like a portfolio manager as well as a risk manager. This does not mean that credit research can be dispensed with (unless all risks are covered) but it does mean that returns can be maximised for the overall level of country risk that an institution is prepared to take.

Since the country risk manager will potentially be able to buy exposure to countries where the company has no natural risk it will be possible for him to truly manage country risk on a portfolio basis, taking advantage of systematic risk reductions through diversification, and using the correlation between countries in the same region.

Pricing

Theoretical approaches to modelling and pricing credit risk are covered in detail in Chapters 10 and 11 of this volume, and so will not be described here. A common problem with theoretical pricing, however, is getting sufficient and reliable data to give meaningful results. This is particularly true for pricing country risk due to the relatively small number of countries that exist, in comparison with the number of companies, and the very small number of defaults. In addition, country risk is complicated by political factors, such as intervention from external sources – as when the IMF stepped in recently to provide liquidity to South Korea. (See Panel 1 of this chapter, and also Panel 3 of Chapter 9.)

Due to these problems with data and political factors, an alternative arbitrage-free approach to pricing default protection is to observe market yields on defaultable bonds and then adjust these for liquidity, funding and counterparty risk considerations.

1 *Standard & Poor's Sovereign Reports of June 2, 1996.*

The drawback of this method is that it requires a bond of the same maturity as the derivative from which to price the default swap. If this is not available then a credit curve will have to be created in order to give the margin for the appropriate maturity – a key challenge discussed in Panel 2.

4

Aggregating Market-driven Credit Exposures

A Parameterised Monte Carlo Approach and Implications for the Use of Credit Derivatives

David M. Rowe and Robert D. Reoch

Bank of America

Considerable financial and intellectual resources are now being devoted to the development of highly analytical approaches to evaluating, measuring and controlling credit risk. A brief look at the history of the credit derivatives market reveals just how quickly this situation has evolved. As recently as 1995, the marketing of credit derivatives involved a significant amount of education as to what the products actually were as well as how to use them. The applications neatly fell into two categories:

❑ synthetic assets; and
❑ credit risk management.

The first was embraced enthusiastically by the investment community as an alternative way of doing what they had always done: investing in credit-sensitive instruments. The synthetic approach added a degree of flexibility not available in the cash markets.

The second category involved a significant shift in the way that credit risk management could be conducted and hence faced more of an up-hill struggle. This was for a number of reasons. Credit risk management decisions are typically taken by credit departments that, in the past, have viewed derivatives with considerable scepticism. Often credit department staff were less than enthusiastic when derivatives professionals suggested that they could assist in the process of credit risk management – a view reinforced by some big derivative-related upsets and losses in 1994. All in all, the mid-1990s were not the best time to launch credit derivatives as a new risk management product; the very name was interpreted as containing both the best and the worst of the financial markets. Reminders

that the greatest loss suffered by a financial institution at that time was due to old-fashioned bad lending decisions by a certain French bank tended to fall on deaf ears.

Furthermore, in 1994 and 1995 the credit markets were incredibly competitive, with an abundance of loanable funds chasing too few assets. New issues were priced very aggressively and a large section of investment-grade borrowers saw their credit issuing cost converge towards Libor. For banks seeking a home for their mounting pool of deposits, it was hard to find assets that generated a positive carry over their own funding costs, let alone an adequate return on regulatory or economic capital. Most fund managers struggled to meet the aggressive return targets set in an increasingly competitive market. In this environment, it was very difficult to persuade banks that they should pay away valuable spread income to mitigate a risk that, at the time, seemed very remote. The credit derivative marketing pitch made for a great conversation, but few banks rushed out to pay for risk mitigation. For most, the possible benefits of credit derivatives took the form of being paid to take *more* risk.

But the most far-reaching reason for the slow acceptance of credit derivatives related to most users' limited ability to identify exactly which risks needed to be managed. A common reaction to a credit derivative sales-pitch was that "this is a great product but it solves problems that I haven't identified yet." For many banks, the ability to generate a consolidated report of credit risk did not exist. Different units kept track of their exposures but there was no efficient way of pulling this information together. For the few who could identify the exposures, quantifying

CREDIT DERIVATIVES: SUFFICIENT FOR PORTFOLIO MANAGEMENT?

While the development of the credit derivative market may have led the development of credit risk management analytics during the 1990s, the market will have to evolve rapidly to keep up with the increasingly sophisticated needs of the portfolio manager. Whereas most deals to date have involved the hedging of single risks with single dedicated transactions, the deals of tomorrow will involve hedges using indexes and proxy credits to provide different levels of protection. This might be driven by the need to reduce the overall cost of hedging, the need to hedge less liquid credits, or the need to hedge different types of credit risk.

the risk analytically was seen as a very complex and daunting task. It was partly in response to the frustration of credit derivative marketers that JP Morgan started work on its CreditMetrics product.

Credit risk modelling is now a hot topic in financial institutions, and many are devoting considerable resources to developing such a capability. Simultaneous with this burgeoning interest in credit risk modelling, credit derivatives have evolved from a marginal curiosity to a serious market with the kind of broad and widely-recognised applications described in Chapter 2 of this volume. The concurrence of these two developments is certainly not coincidental. In the past, more quantitative and disciplined insights into credit risk were of limited value to financial institutions since there were few tools available for active management of these risks. Often the only way to adjust portfolio concentrations was to alter basic business strategy, cutting back on originations in some areas and building business volume in others. Loan sales have provided a more flexible alternative, but they can have undesirable consequences for customer relationships. Credit derivatives are a much more flexible and confidential tool for active credit risk management. As such, they give a practical value to more rigorous quantitative insights into the credit risks of an institution's portfolio. This has, in turn, justified the effort in developing such insights.

All these developments make this is an exciting time for the credit derivatives market. Issues remain, however, that will obstruct a seamless transition from credit risk modelling to credit risk management. In the following sections we present a technical approach to one of these obstacles – hedging market-driven credit exposures of uncertain magnitude. In Panels 2-4 we discuss some key issues in the market as it exists today and offer some possible solutions.

Credit exposure and credit risk

Unfortunately, the close association of credit derivatives with a more analytical approach to evaluating credit risk has lead to a frequent confusion of two distinct issues:

❏ the risk of counterparty default; and,

❏ the uncertainty about the exposure in the face of default.

For most traditional sources of credit exposure, the issue of uncertainty as to amount does not arise. Virtually all credit derivative transactions to date relate to the hedging of credit exposures that are easily quantifiable: loan and bond exposures where the principal amount subject to impairment is known and fixed. Following a credit event, the buyer of protection merely wants the loss to be made whole. On the other hand, there are many capital markets contracts, such as swaps and other traditional financial derivatives, where the exposure is highly uncertain and dependent on future market conditions.[1] Hedging of this more "dynamic" form of exposure has not been highly successful in the credit derivative market. Solutions employed so far have included either hedging the peak exposure or dynamically hedging with a series of short-term contracts.

HEDGING THE PEAK EXPOSURE

At the time of a swap's inception, the amount of any credit exposure is highly variable at various times in its life. Given certain assumptions, it is possible to calculate the probability distribution of potential credit exposure at each point in the future. It is then possible to calculate the average or expected exposure at every point,[2] the average exposure over the full life of the swap, or the peak potential exposure based on a given confidence level. Some institutions use average exposure, sometimes referred to as "loan equivalent exposure", as their proxy for the credit risk in a swap that needs to be hedged. A more conservative approach is to hedge the peak exposure using a confidence interval of 95% or greater. Not

PANEL 2

THE COST OF HEDGING

One of the main forces behind the need for different hedging tools relates to the cost of using plain vanilla hedges for plain vanilla risks. In a simple single-name transaction, where a loan to a corporate name is fully hedged with a default swap, the cost of the hedge is equal to most of the economic benefit of owning the underlying loan. So this only represents a viable hedging strategy for a small percentage of the portfolio as the portfolio's performance is measured primarily by its income, and such a strategy would eventually result in no risk but virtually no income.

In order to justify a credit hedging strategy, the portfolio manager looks for hedges that do not pay away the full economic benefit. There are simple and complex ways of achieving this, but whatever structure is adopted in theory, the portfolio will generally be left with some residual risk. The theory is based on the simple relationship of risk and reward and assumes that the credit markets are efficient. The cases where this is not true in practice are due to credit markets being far from perfect, which allows the portfolio manager to exploit an anomaly in pricing or credit perception.

Shorter hedge
An example of a simple strategy which leaves some residual risk is where an asset is hedged with a shorter-dated credit derivative; a five-year loan hedged with a one-year default swap, for instance. In most cases the existence of a positive credit curve would ensure that the earnings on the long five-year position would more than cover the cost of the one-year short position. The risk in such a strategy is, of course, the un-hedged forward position. At the end of Year One the then four-year position can be re-hedged with a new one-year default swap at the one-year cost then prevailing. Depending on the credit condition of the issuer at the end of Year One, there may or may not continue to be a positive carry. The risk of an increase in the future hedging costs can be partly mitigated by reserving the positive carry in the early years. Such a strategy ensures that default risk is always hedged, but the reward of generating significant savings to hedge costs in the early years is offset by the risk of future price deterioration.

Basket hedging
A strategy that also results in partial protection involves the use of basket default swaps – structures whereby a number of credits are hedged using a contract that pays out only on the first to default. The basket of credits, typically less than five, is chosen for its low correlation to ensure that the likelihood of multiple defaults is low. Such

unexpectedly, however, hedging the peak exposure is an uneconomic way of running a swap business. A ten-year cross currency swap with a single counterparty is likely to have a peak exposure greater than 50% of the principal of the swap. The credit derivative market might require a payment of 20 basis points per year to hedge single-A credit risk for 10 years. This would translate into a cost of 10bp per year on the principal amount of the contract, which is likely to be greater than the profit on the swap. This could only be justified by relationship or other economic advantages.

DYNAMIC SHORT-TERM HEDGING
An alternative approach is to use short-dated contracts to hedge the credit risk of a swap for the next couple of months, and adjust the notional of the hedge at each roll-over date for any increases or decreases in the average exposure over the next period. The credit derivative market now caters to contracts as short as a few weeks, and this (almost) enables a credit risk manager to replicate a perfect hedge whereby the mark-to-market of a swap is guaranteed at any time. What such a strategy does not achieve, however, is an effective hedge against the credit deterioration of the swap counterparty that stops short of default during the term of any one contract. Naturally, the cost of these short-term credit hedges will rise as the swap counterparty's credit quality worsens. It is a bit like buying life insurance by the month and watching the premiums rise as your health deteriorates. Hedging swap credit exposure with short-dated contracts does little to hedge the risk of that exposure over the full life of the transaction. At the point where the protection is most needed, it becomes too expensive or even unavailable.

Since the risk of counterparty deterioration and exposure volatility are assumed by every institution that enters into a swap, how is it that multiple defaults represent the residual risk in such a transaction. This structure, despite being simple in appearance, is very complex in practice. After a brief period of popularity in 1993 and 1994, it has been seen less frequently. The buyer of protection struggled to quantify and report the benefits of the hedge; the seller was never clear about how to allocate the risk against each of the individual names. Often the seller ended up either allocating line usage to the riskiest name (which showed no risk against the other names in the basket) or allocating line usage to all the names (which massively overstated the risk and used up credit lines).

As a small number of sophisticated investors have emerged who are interested in taking second or subsequent losses, some progress has been made in providing the buyer of protection with a better or even a full hedge. Such investors might, for example, agree to take the second to default of a three-name basket, thus reducing the buyer's residual risk to a situation in which all three names defaulted. The pricing of such transactions might provide the buyer with some positive carry, which could, of course, be reserved against the residual risk. It is likely that such transactions will evolve since the risk profiles are similar to those taken in collateralised bond obligation (CBO) structures. The basket default swap tried, and arguably failed, to re-invent CBO pricing from the bottom up. Currently the rating, and hence the

pricing, of such CBO structures is based on diversification scores provided by the rating agencies (see also Chapter 8). As CBO pricing becomes more complex, and tools develop for pricing basket default swaps, the two methodologies are likely to converge.

Fixed loss and capped loss

Certain types of credit derivatives have evolved to provide fixed pay-outs following a credit event, in situations where there were no credit instruments to satisfy cash or physical settlement requirements. This does not represent a significant part of the market as such needs are few and far between. However, the mechanism appeals to protection buyers who wish to reduce the cost of hedging by either specifying a fixed payment following a credit event, or by capping the pay-out on a cash-settled structure. While the theory might appeal to both buyers and sellers, uncertainties over pricing and risk management mean these trades really require more sophisticated credit models. In turn, these models will depend on better data about recovery rates. The trades executed to date have only worked where the two participants had a substantially different view on recovery rates. If the buyer of protection feels that a 90% recovery is likely, then capping the loss at 10% is acceptable. If the seller feels that a 50% loss is likely, then capping the loss at 10% also looks attractive.

such institutions have become comfortable with a risk that would seem very difficult to hedge? One approach is to include language in the swap agreement that addresses the credit deterioration of either party. This typically involves posting collateral, early termination or the right of assignment if the credit rating of the counterparty falls below a threshold. These measures are very effective when they can be negotiated successfully. Clearly, however, there will continue to be market pressures for professional swap dealers to assume unsecured credit exposure on swap transactions. (Presumably this would be reflected in wider bid-offer spreads on such deals to compensate for the additional risk.) In addition, if relative bargaining strength requires that credit risk mitigating provisions be two-way in nature there is an incentive for both parties to avoid them.[3] As a result, there will continue to be a need for tools to manage and hedge unsecured credit exposure where the amount of exposure is driven by

uncertain market conditions. Since hedging potential exposures over the life of a deal is too expensive to be economically attractive and rolling short-term hedges are not very effective, an alternative approach is required.

Portfolio concentrations and credit derivatives

It is a long-established tradition in credit risk management that excessive portfolio concentrations in specific regions or industries should be avoided. Indeed, the ability of credit derivatives to reshape existing portfolio exposure distributions in favourable ways is one of their primary attractions. The problem with market-driven credit exposures, however, has been that simplistic estimation methods distort portfolio measures even more than they distort individual counterparty estimates. This is primarily because a robust treatment of netting is essential for reliable portfolio results. Netting treatment can introduce distortions at the individual counterparty level as well, but these can be minimised by an appropriate choice of where to set limits and what constitutes the operational definition of a counterparty. For portfolio exposures to multiple counterparties, however, it is clearly necessary to combine pools of transactions that may be nettable within each pool but which are not nettable across pools. In these cases the most straightforward way to assure proper treatment is to simulate exposures at the deal level using a Monte Carlo process. It then is simple to combine the exposures in a way that is consistent with any definition of what constitutes nettable pools of transactions within the total portfolio. The result is a statistically robust estimate of the exposure distribution for whatever collection of counterparties is specified.

Another advantage of a robust method for estimating portfolio exposures is that these are often more stable than individual counterparty exposures. The more diversification that exists across the trading patterns of different counterparties, the smaller is the dispersion of their combined exposure at any point in the future. This can reduce the frequency with which the amount of credit coverage needs to be adjusted because of changing market conditions. The most obvious tool with which to hedge an aggregate credit exposure profile is a total return swap (TRS) where the total return is based on a customised portfolio of corporate bonds. Ideally, the size and mix of the underlying bond portfolio could change over the life of the TRS to reflect projected changes in the characteristics of the aggregate exposure profile.

Of course, hedging portfolio concentrations is less precise than hedging exposure to individual names. The correlation of the payoff on the hedge and the loss on the original position is considerably lower than it would be if a series of name-specific hedges had been used. On the other hand, name-specific hedges only provide protection relative to the specific names involved. If the "wrong" counterparties deteriorate, a series of name-specific hedges may be useless. In any case, a portfolio concentration hedge is sure to be less expensive than a series of name-specific hedges.

In effect, it is our view that credit derivatives can best be used to hedge market-driven credit exposures if they are viewed as a tool to reduce excessive portfolio concentrations. Attempting to hedge individual counterparty exposures on a systematic basis is like trying to purchase guarantees for individual loans; it simply is not an economically-viable approach to the problem.

The remainder of this chapter presents a parameterised Monte Carlo approach to the aggregation of market-driven credit exposures. It builds on, and is a logical extension to, the system capabilities required for simpler single market or directionally consistent multi-market portfolios.[4]

The evolution of market-driven credit exposure measurement

For much of the past decade, most institutions approached the measurement of market-driven credit exposures on a transaction-by-transaction basis. This involved estimating one potential value amount for each contract. This figure was intended to be "the most" the institution is likely to be owed at any time during the remaining life of the contract. Naturally, "the most" means a statistical confidence estimate of the amount that only would be exceeded with some small probability. The level of probability used differs among institutions. It is usually between 1% and 5%, with 2.5% being the most common convention. We will refer to such an estimate as a "probabilistic maximum". Exposure for a counterparty was simply the sum of all these probabilistic maxima across all contracts with the counterparty.

Two extremely useful extensions to this framework have become common at major institutions:

❑ To make estimates of the probabilistic maximum exposure at a series of points over the remaining life of the contracts, rather than confining the analysis to a single maximum value over the remaining life. It then is possible to add up these maximum values at consistent simulation dates rather than summing non-contemporaneous peaks.

❑ To model all contracts with a counterparty as a portfolio, thereby recognising the risk-reducing effect of offsets from two-way trading and diversification across multiple markets and risk sources.

When trading is confined to a single market, such as the dollar swaps market (and assuming transaction values are monotonically related to market rates) constructing such an exposure profile is relatively simple. It is possible to construct confidence bands for future market rates at various times and to price the transactions at their outer limits. The exposures can be added up across transactions for common simulation dates and common market scenarios.

The problem becomes more complicated when trading is conducted in multiple markets

TYPES OF CREDITS BEING HEDGED: SOME OBSTACLES

During the early years of the credit derivatives market, transactions were linked to credits that were well known, publicly rated and liquid. This catered to the concerns of early investors, who felt that the structure provided enough to focus on without the need for making a demanding credit decision. It so happened that much of the credit risk hedged in 1993 and 1994 was associated with interest rates swaps. Huge activity in the swap market by well-known A- and AA-rated borrowers had used up credit lines. As a result, the large investment banks were keen to free up these lines for more profitable swap business. The very names that they needed to sell conveniently matched the names whose risk investors were prepared to assume by way of credit derivatives.

Those days are long past, and the credit derivative market of today focuses on a broad spectrum of credit risk. New transactions continue to push out the envelope of credits that can be "derivatised" and we are moving rapidly towards a situation in which a derivative can be used to transfer the credit risk of most cash instruments. A number of obstacles remain and to overcome them the market will either have to provide a more sophisticated product, or existing instruments will have to be used in a more sophisticated way. Typical obstacles are related to liquidity, assignability and identification.

Liquidity

Most structures assume the existence of an underlying that does, or could, trade in the secondary market. For those credits that do not meet this criteria, there are concerns that settlement of a default swap or total return swap might fail. As we will see below and in Panel 4, physical delivery is not a fail-safe mechanism. A situation may arise in which there is no way to settle a transaction other than the standard fall-back of employing the services of some independent third party to determine fair value.

Assignability

As soon as a credit derivative moves away from the relative simplicity of the bond market, the practicalities of dealing with an underlying that is not freely transferable have a significant impact. Bank loans are often not transferable or require the consent of the borrower which, the language typically states, would not be "unreasonably withheld". This last test is too vague and provides little comfort to the buyer of protection looking for a watertight hedge.

This obstacle is being addressed in two different ways. First, banks are working with clients to explain the prudence of a credit portfolio management system and the need for improved assignability in a default situation. The success of this initiative is both a function of how well the credit derivative strategy is explained to the client, and of how happy the client is to risk a change of bank group during a loan work-out – arguably the one time when it would be nice to know who is going to be sitting around the table! The second approach is at the lender level, where there has been discussion about standardising assignment language in new facilities to, among other things, assist the credit derivative process. It is likely that these two initiatives will result in improved assignability.

Identification

This term relates to small- to medium-size credits where the true nature of the credit risk is hard to identify. In most cases, the current market will not accommodate the hedging of smaller credits; it is focused on better-known names that can be traded using derivative contracts in a minimum size of $5 million. The only hedge that the market can offer is a proxy hedge that could address the credit risk of a number of smaller credits which happen to be correlated by industry, region or some economic factor, such as the price of oil. In these limited and currently rather specialised situations, the use of the proxy hedge is compelling. It is likely to form a more significant part of the market over the next few years.

with the same counterparty. In this case, it is necessary to aggregate exposure across markets that exhibit varying degrees of correlation. Often there is some broad directional consistency across all these markets. The two most common examples include portfolios of interest rate swaps in multiple currencies and forex portfolios where trading is almost exclusively against the institution's home currency. In the former, the level of global interest rates is the source of directional consistency. In the latter, it is the value of the home currency. In such cases, an *ad hoc* shortcut involving correlated aggregation of the differences in the values of transactions at implied forward rates and at extreme upper and lower bounds of market variables offers a simple and acceptably accurate approach for most purposes.[5]

Unfortunately, the *ad hoc* aggregation approach breaks down badly when there is no source of such directional consistency across markets. A very common example is a portfolio of foreign exchange contracts involving not only forward positions versus the home currency but positions in multiple cross-currency combinations as well. At this point, it becomes necessary to introduce an explicit Monte Carlo process into the analysis. The problem is to do so in a way that allows rapid intraday recalculation of exposure and acceptable trading desk response times to what-if analysis of proposed deals. Without such a level of performance, the official measure of risk is relegated to an overnight batch process while, on the desk, trading credit decisions are controlled by a parallel and usually far more simplistic system of calculations.

Simulating at the outer boundaries of market conditions

Since the transformation from market conditions to a transaction's price is non-linear, especially for transactions with option features, the probability density function of the price is not tractable theoretically. Since this holds for a single transaction, it is obviously true for a portfolio of transactions. The "primary risk source" approach addresses this problem by simulating transaction prices at the centre and at the outer boundaries of the distribution of the relevant market variable. Specifically, the data produced by this approach are the hypothetical values of each transaction in three different scenarios at a series of future simulation dates. These are:

❑ the "upper bound" values (such as the 97.5th percentiles) of the primary risk source on the various simulation dates;

❑ the implied forward values of the primary risk source on the simulation dates; and

❑ the "lower bound" values (such as the 2.5th percentiles) of the primary risk source on the various simulation dates.

We will define $U_{i,s,t}$ as the simulated value of transaction i at the "upper bound" of risk source s on simulation date t. $M_{i,s,t}$ and $L_{i,s,t}$ are similarly defined as the transaction's simulated values at the implied forward and "lower bound" values of the primary risk source. We then make the simplifying assumption that the value of the transaction at other points in the distribution of the

primary risk source can be approximated by linear interpolation (or extrapolation) based on these three values.[6] Specifically, if primary risk source s is $\tilde{n}_{s,t}$ standard deviations *above* its implied forward value on simulation date t, then the value of transaction i is assumed to be:

$$V_{i,s,t} = M_{i,s,t} + (\tilde{n}_{s,t}/2)(U_{i,s,t} - M_{i,s,t})$$

If primary risk source s is $\tilde{n}_{s,t}$ standard deviations *below* its implied forward value on simulation date t, then the value of transaction i is assumed to be:

$$V_{i,s,t} = M_{i,s,t} + (\tilde{n}_{s,t}/2)(L_{i,s,t} - M_{i,s,t})$$

If the primary risk source in its most common expression is not normally distributed, it may be possible to transform it in such a way that it becomes normal. Thus, if an interest rate is the primary risk source and it is assumed to be log normally distributed, then the natural log of the interest rate becomes the form of the primary risk source used in the above formulation and $\tilde{n}_{s,t}$ refers to a number of standard deviations of $\ln(r)$ from its implied forward value.

Aggregation and netting

Assume we have a sample of 2000 values corresponding to draws from a standard normal distribution. We will refer to these as $\tilde{n}_d$ for d = 1 to 2000, where d refers to the number of the draw. By sequentially substituting these 2000 values for $\tilde{n}_d$ into the above equations, we derive a 2000-element distribution of the value of transaction i (which is subject to primary risk source s) at simulation date t. We will designate any one of these simulated market values as $V_{i,s,t,d}$ where d refers to the number of the Monte Carlo draw. We then can find the 97.5th percentile of these 2000 values by inspection. For monotonic exposure to a single risk source, this procedure gains nothing. The 97.5 percentile of these 2000 transaction values will (subject to some small sampling error) be equal to the $Max(U_{i,s,t}, L_{i,s,t})$.[7]

Consider a more complicated portfolio, however, with two nettable deals involving exposure to two different risk sources. Assume that the corresponding market variables have a correlation coefficient equal to ρ. Further assume that we have two sets of 2000 draws from a random normal distribution, and that they have an empirical correlation equal to ρ. We will refer to the dth draw from the sample corresponding to risk source 1 as $\tilde{n}_{1,d}$ and the corresponding draw from the sample corresponding to risk source 2 as $\tilde{n}_{2,d}$. We now construct 2000 simulated market values at simulation date t for transaction 1 driven by risk source 1, and refer to them as $V_{1,1,t,d}$ where d

PANEL 4

PORTFOLIO IMPLEMENTATION: A CASE STUDY

Consider a situation in which a bank has a relationship with XYZ Corporation, resulting in a number of different transactions. Loans and letters of credit generate fees and coupons and create exposures. Cash management and financial advisory services bring in fees with no additional exposure. The bank regards the relationship as generating an overall return for taking an overall risk.

XYZ approaches the bank to request an additional letter of credit. The exposure requested would exceed the relationship cap on exposure, and initially the bank's credit department denies the application.

Analysis reveals that the letter of credit is priced very favourably: it could be hedged in the credit derivative market and still generate an attractive fee. Failure to provide this facility might spur the customer to go to the competition and thus jeopardise existing facilities as well as the new business under discussion. The solution suggested by the credit derivative group involves using a default swap to hedge the exposure.

Issues and solutions
Issue XYZ has not issued any liquid credit instruments. Hence, there is some concern that a cash settlement mechanism would be unreliable. Physical delivery would work in theory but, in practice, the facility cannot be assigned even in default.
Solution Use physical delivery with a silent participation to avoid the assignment obstacle. Following a credit event, the seller of protection would receive a participation that would transfer all the economic risk.

Issue The seller of protection would require that the participation transfer voting rights, enabling the seller to direct the bank's action in the "workout" following a credit event. The bank is unwilling to risk a situation in which it has no control over how it votes and may be forced to take a conflicting position from the rest of the bank group (resulting in reputation risk).
Solution The bank approaches XYZ to request modification of some credit agreements to enable transfer following a credit event.

Issue XYZ takes deep offence at the idea that the bank might need to reduce its credit exposure and not only refuses to modify any credit agreements but also further stipulates that credit derivatives should not be used in any situation in which an unexpected institution may end up sitting at the negotiating table during a workout.
Solution Reconsider cash settlement.

The scenario above summarises a range of issues facing banks as they embark on implementing a credit risk management strategy. It is likely that the majority of the portfolio consists of credits that, one way or another, fit into the mould of XYZ company. In many cases, these issues are resolved by dialogue and a good relationship, but where they are not the banks will be forced to take the risks that the case study above tried to mitigate: relying on cash settlement for illiquid names; relying on the consent of the borrower for assigning a facility in default; or risking the reputation risk of being directed by the protection seller at a workout.

---

varies from 1 to 2000 and corresponds to the index of the draw from the standard normal distribution for risk source 1. We define $V_{2,2,t,d}$ analogously for transaction 2 subject to risk source 2. Now we can define a sample of 2000 values of the combined portfolio at simulation date t as the sum of the values of deals 1 and 2 for each draw d. Thus $V_{\Sigma,\Sigma,t,d}$ is the total portfolio value on simulation date t for random draw d and is defined as:

$$V_{\Sigma,\Sigma,t,d} = \sum_{S} \sum_{i|s=S} V_{i,s,t,d}$$

In other words, for each risk source s we sum across all relevant deals i and then sum across all risk sources.

The essential point is that the correlation ρ between the two samples of 2000 standard normal variables $\tilde{n}_{1,d}$ and $\tilde{n}_{2,d}$ will flow through into the total portfolio value distribution in the appropriate way. For example, if the risk sources are highly correlated and the positions are in opposite directions (one is a "pay fixed" swap and the other is a "receive fixed" swap in highly correlated interest rates, for example) the corresponding values of $V_{1,1,t,d}$ and $V_{2,2,t,d}$ for any value of d will tend to be of opposite sign and the total portfolio value distribution (assuming netting applies) will have a correspondingly low dispersion. If the correlation is low, there will be no consistent pattern to the signs of the sample val-

RAROC AND CREDIT PORTFOLIO MANAGEMENT

A review of a bank's relationship with XYZ Corporation reveals that the overall relationship RAROC (risk-adjusted return on capital) is low compared to the portfolio average.

Analysis reveals that the RAROC is mainly affected by a large facility that generates little return for the amount of risk that it contributes. Hedging this risk with credit derivatives would have a greater impact on reducing the risk than the cost of doing so would have on the return. In fact, the analysis may show that the entire facility fee and more can be paid away and still improve the relationship RAROC. The solution suggested by the credit derivative group involves a default swap. The Bank pays a fee to a third party and receives protection in the event of a default by XYZ. The Bank's credit group agrees that this effectively reduces the bank's exposure to XYZ.

Issues and solutions
The analysis sounds good in theory but there are a number of obstacles to surmount.
Issue The in-house systems will need to capture the benefit of the hedge so that the exposure to XYZ is reduced accordingly. The relationship manager does not want to pay away valuable spread only to see the exposure still on the books.
Issue The relationship Raroc will need to be adjusted to capture the benefit of the hedge. This is the main driver of the transaction.
Issue The impact on earnings needs to be factored in and this can be very subjective. Improving the Raroc is a desirable goal, but not at the expense of a noticeable drop in earnings. There is a "size consideration" that needs to be thought about at an early stage and senior management needs to be involved.
Solution Implement far-reaching changes to the management information systems to ensure that all the benefits of a credit derivative transaction are captured.

This scenario summarises some of the many issues associated with implementing a credit derivative business. At a general level, there are questions such as where to locate the credit derivative group and how to integrate its products into the existing infrastructure. There also are many quantitative issues that have to be faced. However, the issues touched on above are particularly relevant in the context of "portfolio" credit risk management and relate to the reporting of the organisational and customer benefits of each transaction.

Ideally, organisational benefits should align individual and group objectives and actions. As more portfolio management activity, especially distribution activity, is centralised within a dedicated group, a dual ownership of the loan portfolio emerges, and with that comes the issue of which unit should be rewarded for credit derivative deals. Even if a transaction is initiated by a centralised group, the business unit will certainly get involved because it has expert knowledge of the underlying borrower. This input is necessary and needs to be rewarded with partial credit for the economic profit captured.

Customer allocation is a matter of defining "customer". How this term is defined helps guide the profitability allocation. If a customer is defined as a *relationship*, it is easy to argue that profitability should not be allocated. However, if a customer is defined as a *manageable risk source*, the risk component of RAROC calculations should be allocated. For purchased protection, the fact that the exposure to the underlying borrower has decreased should be stored, and if the counterparty and the borrower are highly correlated, the second-order joint probability risk should also be allocated. This process is vital in ensuring that all the benefits of credit derivatives are reflected in the reporting of the overall customer risks and returns.

Until the impact of credit derivatives is fully integrated into relationship reporting, there will be difficulties in managing the portfolio. A strong desire to reduce exposure at a central level often gets a lukewarm reception at the customer level: managers of the relationship see the benefits of individual facilities taken away with no "compensation" at a local level.
See also discussion in Chapter 6.

ues of the individual deals, and it will make little difference whether the deals are in the same or opposite directions (both pay fixed, both receive fixed or one of each, for example).

The above formulation assumes that all the deals under discussion are legally nettable. It is an easy extension to generalise this to a portfolio containing pools of deals that are nettable against each other, but not against deals in other pools in the portfolio. First add another subscript p to the above expression to identify the pool to which a deal belongs. Thus, $V_{p,i,s,t,d}$ will refer to the value of deal i in pool p subject to risk source s on simulation date t in Monte Carlo draw d. $V_{p,\Sigma,\Sigma,t,d}$ refers to the simulated *net* value of all deals in pool p on simulation date t in Monte Carlo draw d. The aggregate simulated credit exposure for the portfolio on simulation date t in Monte Carlo draw d is defined as:

$$V_{\Sigma,\Sigma,\Sigma,t,d} = \sum_{p} Max(V_{p,\Sigma,\Sigma,t,d},0)$$

In other words, in going from one pool to another we have crossed the "perimeter of nettability". Thus, the summation must set the impact of any pool with negative simulated market value to zero and not allow this negative mark-to-market to offset positive simulated values in other pools.

The implications for estimating portfolio concentrations should be obvious. Even in a perfectly nettable world, the "perimeter of nettability" is crossed in going from one counterparty to another. Applying the above approach to estimating the exposure distribution for multiple counterparties gives results that:

❑ capture diversification within each counterparty's portfolio;

❑ capture diversification in the trading patterns across distinct counterparties; and

❑ recognise netting to the exact extent that it is deemed to be legally enforceable.

If trading patterns vary across the counterparties in the calculation, then the variability of the exposure will be reduced by this diversification. As a result, a total return swap used as a portfolio concentration hedge, and structured to reflect the resulting pattern of exposure through time, is likely to require less frequent adjustment than would be required for similar hedges of individual counterparty exposures.

Conclusion

Banks are spending an increasing amount of time discussing the need for implementing a prudent credit risk management system, and senior management is generally well aware of the various parts of the jigsaw puzzle that need to be correctly assembled for the goal to be achieved. Credit derivative specialists have provided extensive education about the pros and cons of various credit risk management tools, and sophisticated credit risk models are producing three-dimensional graphs that illustrate previously unobserved risks and opportunities within the credit portfolio. Meanwhile, the market provides painful reminders of the realities of credit risk (as was seen during the months either side of the close of 1997), and regulators emphasise the need for better management of these risks. For some institutions, the puzzle is almost complete and the remaining piece, too often overlooked, is the difficult process of implementation. As many are finding, this one word represents the most significant obstacle to meeting senior management demands for improved credit risk management systems.

Appendix

IMPOSING CORRELATION ON A RANDOM SAMPLE – THE CHOLESKY TRANSFORM

The main mathematical insight needed to implement this approach is how to impose historically-observed correlations between various risk sources onto the unit normal distributions driving the Monte Carlo simulations. Fortunately there is a standard method for doing this, generally known as the Cholesky Transformation. As documented in most theoretical numerical analysis sources, the procedure is as follows.

The theory

The construction of random variables with predetermined correlations depends on the ability to decompose the correlation matrix R into the product of an upper-triangular matrix A and its lower-triangular transpose A′ such that A′A = R. The process starts with a series of m realisations for n independent random normal variables contained in an m by n matrix X. Given the decomposition of R into A and A′, a matrix Y of m realisations for n multivariate normal variables with the correlation matrix of R can be constructed by defining Y = XA.

The derivation of A can be illustrated with a simple 3×3 example, but the process generalises to the N × N case.

Define:

$$R \equiv \begin{bmatrix} \rho_{1,1} & \rho_{1,2} & \rho_{1,3} \\ \rho_{2,1} & \rho_{2,2} & \rho_{2,3} \\ \rho_{3,1} & \rho_{3,2} & \rho_{3,3} \end{bmatrix} \quad A \equiv \begin{bmatrix} a_{1,1} & a_{1,2} & a_{1,3} \\ 0 & a_{2,2} & a_{2,3} \\ 0 & 0 & a_{3,3} \end{bmatrix} \quad A' \equiv \begin{bmatrix} a_{1,1} & 0 & 0 \\ a_{1,2} & a_{2,2} & 0 \\ a_{1,3} & a_{2,3} & a_{3,3} \end{bmatrix}$$

Then we wish to solve for the elements of A such that A′A = R, or

$$\begin{bmatrix} a_{1,1} & 0 & 0 \\ a_{1,2} & a_{2,2} & 0 \\ a_{1,3} & a_{2,3} & a_{3,3} \end{bmatrix} \begin{bmatrix} a_{1,1} & a_{1,2} & a_{1,3} \\ 0 & a_{2,2} & a_{2,3} \\ 0 & 0 & a_{3,3} \end{bmatrix} = \begin{bmatrix} \rho_{1,1} & \rho_{1,2} & \rho_{1,3} \\ \rho_{2,1} & \rho_{2,2} & \rho_{2,3} \\ \rho_{3,1} & \rho_{3,2} & \rho_{3,3} \end{bmatrix}$$

Multiplying out the matrix product on the left, this becomes:

$$\begin{bmatrix} a_{1,1}^2 & a_{1,1}a_{1,2} & a_{1,1}a_{1,3} \\ a_{1,2}a_{1,1} & a_{1,2}^2 + a_{2,2}^2 & a_{1,2}a_{1,3} + a_{2,2}a_{2,3} \\ a_{1,3}a_{1,1} & a_{1,3}a_{1,2} + a_{2,3}a_{2,2} & a_{1,3}^2 + a_{2,3}^2 + a_{3,3}^2 \end{bmatrix} = \begin{bmatrix} \rho_{1,1} & \rho_{1,2} & \rho_{1,3} \\ \rho_{2,1} & \rho_{2,2} & \rho_{2,3} \\ \rho_{3,1} & \rho_{3,2} & \rho_{3,3} \end{bmatrix}$$

Now it is possible to solve for the elements of A recursively as follows:

$$a_{1,1}^2 = \rho_{1,1} \text{ so } a_{1,1} = \sqrt{\rho_{1,1}}$$

$$a_{1,1}a_{1,2} = \rho_{1,2} = \rho_{2,1} \text{ so } a_{1,2} = \frac{\rho_{1,2}}{a_{1,1}}$$

$$a_{1,1}a_{1,3} = \rho_{1,3} = \rho_{3,1} \text{ so } a_{1,3} = \frac{\rho_{1,3}}{a_{1,1}}$$

$$a_{1,2}^2 a_{2,2}^2 = \rho_{2,2} \text{ so } a_{2,2} = \sqrt{\rho_{2,2} - a_{1,2}^2}$$

$$a_{1,2}a_{1,3} + a_{2,2}a_{2,3} = \rho_{2,3} \text{ so } a_{2,3} = \frac{\rho_{2,3} - a_{1,2}a_{1,3}}{a_{2,2}}$$

$$a_{1,3}^2 + a_{2,3}^2 + a_{3,3}^2 = \rho_{3,3} \text{ so } a_{3,3} = \sqrt{\rho_{3,3} - a_{1,3}^2 - a_{2,3}^2}$$

The more general result in the $N \times N$ case is that:

$$a_{i,j} = \frac{\left[\rho_{i,j} - \sum_{k=1}^{i-1} a_{k,i}a_{k,j} \right]}{a_{i,i}} \text{ where } i \neq j$$

$$a_{i,i} = \sqrt{\rho_{i,i} - \sum_{k=1}^{i-1} a_{k,i}^2}$$

Now constructing Y such that $Y \equiv XA$ results in columns of Y that exhibit the desired correlation R. The simplest way to see this is to normalise the original data (the columns of X) so that each series has mean zero and standard deviation one. We do this by subtracting the column mean from each element in each column of X and then dividing the resulting values by their column standard deviations. Having thus normalised the data, the sample estimate for R, the correlation matrix for the columns of these normalised variables X, reduces to $X'X/(m-1)$.

If the columns of X are statistically independent, the off-diagonal elements of R will equal zero and R equals the identity matrix I. That is:

$$\frac{1}{(m-1)}X'X = I$$

Having defined Y as $Y = XA$, we can show that the mean and standard deviation of the columns of Y also will have means equal to zero and standard deviations equal to one. That the means equal zero follows directly from the observation that columns of Y are weighted sums of one or more columns of X. Since the means of the columns of X have been constructed to equal zero, any weighted sum of them will also have a mean of zero.

That the standard deviations of the columns of Y also are all equal to one is less obvious. Consider, however, the following observations. For any random variable x with variance var(x), a new random variable y defined as a scalar multiple kx will have variance $k^2 var(x)$. More generally, assume that for a series of *statistically-independent* random variables x_j with variances var(x_j), a new random variable y is defined as

$$y = \sum_{j=1}^{n} w_j x_j$$

where w_j are fixed weights. Then the variance of the random variable y will be

$$var(y) = \sum_{j=1}^{n} w_j^2 var(x_j)$$

Further note that any column of Y is a weighted sum of the columns of X where the weights are the elements in the corresponding column of A. Examining the derivation of the columns of A, however, makes it clear that:

$$\sum_{k=1}^{i} a_{k,i}^2 = \sum_{k=1}^{i-1} a_{k,j}^2 + a_{i,i}^2 = \sum_{k=1}^{i-1} a_{k,i}^2 + \rho_{i,i} - \sum_{k=1}^{i-1} a_{k,i}^2 = \rho_{i,i} = 1$$

Since the variances of all the columns of X have been forced to equal one in all cases, the variance of column i of Y is

$$var(Y_i) = \sum_{k=1}^{i} a_{k,i}^2 var(X_k) = \sum_{k=1}^{i} a_{k,i}^2 = 1$$

One practical problem remains. In constructing the original matrix X for a modest value of m, say 2000 rows, there will always be spurious non-zero correlation in the off-diagonal elements of the actual correlation matrix. For all the above properties to hold for Y, the original columns of X must be strictly uncorrelated in the actual matrix that is being used. (In mathematical terms, the dot product of any two distinct columns of X must equal zero or, stated differently, the columns must all be orthogonal to each other.) Fortunately, it is possible to apply the Cholesky methodology to X to achieve this result. Recall that we modified the original matrix X by forcing the column means to zero and the column standard deviations to one. The next step is to calculate the empirical correlation matrix for X. Call this correlation matrix (which is approximately but not exactly equal to the identity matrix) R. Now define a Cholesky matrix B that would transform a perfectly uncorrelated set of variables into series with the correlation matrix R. If we now transform X by the *inverse* of B, the columns of the resulting matrix Z will be *exactly* orthogonal and will exhibit exactly zero correlation for any two distinct columns. In specific mathematical terms, if

$$Z = XB^{-1}$$

then the empirically calculated correlation matrix for Z will be exactly equal to the identity matrix.[8] Thus if we now use the columns of Z as the initial set of uncorrelated variables, all the above results will hold empirically as well as theoretically. The Cholesky transform will create resulting variables Y = ZA that exactly exhibit the desired correlations and the zero means and unit standard deviations will be preserved empirically for the reasons outlined previously.

Finally, since the zero mean and unit standard deviations are preserved in Y, the correlation matrix for the columns of Y can be written as

$$R_Y = \frac{1}{(m-1)} Y'Y = \frac{1}{(m-1)} (A'Z')(ZA)$$
$$= \frac{1}{(m-1)} A'(Z'Z)A = A'IA = A'A = R$$

since A is constructed explicitly such that A'A = R.

---

1 *Many will make the point that even loan exposure is not as simple as we have implied here. In fact, rising or falling interest rates affect the true economic value of a loan just as they affect the value of a bond that is marked to market. Just because, by GAAP convention, we carry loans at historical cost does not alter the fact that the true economic value has changed. Even if we did mark loans to market, however, the impact of market conditions on a contract such as a swap is more dramatic than for a loan. For a fixed-rate term loan, general market conditions might create a 5% to 10% discount or premium relative to face value. In any case, however, the exposure will be a large fraction of the face value. (This assumes, of course, that the loan is denominated in the base currency of the lender. If this is not the case, then changes in the foreign exchange rate between the currency of the loan and the base currency of the lender can have a much larger impact on the amount of credit exposure as viewed by the lender.) For a swap, there is a significant likelihood that the exposure is zero (the lender will owe money to the defaulting counterparty) accompanied by possible positive exposures up to a substantial fraction of the notional amount, depending on the exact nature of the contract.*

2 *Even if the expected market value is zero, the expected credit exposure is positive. This is because negative market values correspond to zero credit exposure. Hence, expected credit exposure is the sum of the probability of each outcome times the maximum of the mark-to-market value for that outcome or zero. Obviously this will lead to positive expected credit exposure whenever any outcome has a positive market value. Only when all outcomes can never have a positive market value, such as a series of sold options with the premiums paid in advance, will the portfolio have zero credit risk.*

3 *For example, if collateralisation tied to a credit rating downgrade is two-way, the swap provider may find it neces-*

sary to post considerable collateral at just the time when liquidity for its obligations is shrinking, making it difficult to raise the necessary funds.

4 *See, for example, D. Rowe, 1995, "Aggregating Credit Exposures: The Primary Risk Source Approach", Derivative Credit Risk: Advances in Measurement and Management, London: Risk Publications, pp. 13-22; D. Lawrence, "Aggregating Credit Exposures: The Simulation Approach", Derivative Credit Risk, op. cit., pp.23-31.*

5 *See Rowe, op. cit.*

6 *The number of scenarios can, of course, be increased to construct a more detailed price grid as a function of the value of the relevant market variable. It must be remembered, however, that these "pre-aggregation" values are computationally expensive, since they require full repricing of the transaction or its constituent parts. For most standard derivative contracts, the increase in accuracy is modest relative to the added computational burden. An alternative means of attaining greater accuracy is to preserve the fully-repriced values of each leg of a deal and to utilise quadratic interpolation to mimic the non-linearity of the price response to changes in market conditions.*

7 *This is not true, of course, for a position such as a straddle where the market value of the trade is not monotonic with respect to changes in the relevant risk source. Such a trade is best handled by breaking it down into two components, a purchased put and a purchased call, each of which does have a value that is monotonic with respect to the underlying market variable.*

8 *Richard Libby of the Bank of America Risk Management Information Analytics group was the first to point out to the authors this handy procedure for forcing exactly zero correlations on the original variables.*

5

Actively Managing Corporate Credit Risk

New Methodologies and Instruments for Non-financial Firms

Richard Buy, Vincent Kaminski, Krishnarao Pinnamaneni and Vasant Shanbhogue
Enron Corp

During the last few years, many financial institutions have applied the tools of financial engineering to the problems of credit management. New and powerful techniques have been developed to estimate the credit exposures of individual financial transactions and of entire portfolios, to incorporate credit risk into the pricing of different instruments, and to manage credit risk efficiently by separating it from other risks and selectively transferring it to other institutions.[1]

Historically, the management of credit risk has been limited to exercising judgement in selecting credit counterparties, to monitoring developments once the decision has been made to enter into a transaction, and to working with a counterparty to resolve unfolding problems. The main tool used in this process was diversification – a policy designed to avoid excessive concentration of credit exposures and implemented through credit line limits. The new techniques of financial analysis and new financial instruments have changed credit management in sophisticated financial institutions. In this chapter, we evaluate these new tools from the point of view of a non-financial company, and offer a viewpoint on credit derivatives that other non-financial firms may find useful.

The chapter is based on the experience acquired by the authors in the process of managing various aspects of credit risk in Enron Capital & Trade Resources (ECT) – a unit of Enron Corp. ECT has four principal businesses:

❏ cash trading of the full spectrum of energy commodities: natural gas, gas liquids, crude oil, refined products, coal, and electricity;

❏ origination of energy-related risk management products, both for other units of Enron and external customers;

❏ provision of equity and debt capital to other companies, primarily in the energy business; and

❏ acquisition and operation of long-term physical merchant assets related to energy production and transportation.

Two features of our business have a profound impact on the credit process. First, our transactions combine, often in one deal, financial and physical aspects. Many ECT contracts for delivery and purchase of physical energy commodities have options embedded in them. These options are aggregated in predefined portfolios (or "books" in our internal jargon) and are managed in a systematic and disciplined way. Credit risk management, like price risk management, must be performed at the level of groups of these portfolios so as to capture the exposure to counterparties across all markets and transaction types. Second, ECT often acts as a lender or as an equity investor, either directly, or by embedding the loan component in a physical or financial commodity transaction.

These aspects of our activities require a strong and multidimensional credit culture. One special feature of our approach is a heavy reliance on quantitative methods, as discussed below.

Financial vs commercial credit

The main difference between financial and commercial credit is that the latter cannot be separated from transactions involving sales and purchases of goods and services. In commercial transactions, delivery of goods and services may take place well in advance of receipt of payment, and the time lag may extend from a few hours to many years; the amount at risk may range from an insignificant sum to a very substantial exposure. Credit exposure arises from, in effect, the embedding of a loan in the sale of goods and services. Commercial credit is borne by practically every business in a developed market economy – perhaps 90–95% of all commercial transactions in the United States between firms involve the use of credit. Commercial credit is not only bigger in volume than financial credit but also an important engine of economic development. Even a relatively small reduction in the volume of commercial credit would profoundly affect the prosperity of a developed market economy.

The fact that commercial credit is effectively a process of embedding a loan in a business transaction makes credit risk management similar to the management of a lending relationship in a commercial bank. The main difference is that for a commercial firm, the act of extending credit is typically a precondition of making a sale. A non-financial firm is thus much less able to diversify its credit exposure, and will typically experience relatively higher concentrations of credit risk with respect to a single customer and/or certain sectors of the economy by region or industry. Most industrial and trading firms have, like

banks, the ability to select out customers who do not meet pre-established credit standards, but in doing so they may face a difficult internal conflict. Curtailing business may be a good decision in the long run, but it may not be recognised as such by the management and the sales force in the short run.[2]

Credit process in ECT: the importance of being quantitative

Traditionally, the credit process in non-financial firms (Figure 1) has been limited to a review of the quality of counterparties and of the decision to extend credit, through a direct loan or a commodity transaction. The credit department of ECT plays a much more active role, which goes beyond an uncoordinated analysis of stand-alone credit exposures to different counterparties.

The first step is to see how a new transaction fits into the entire portfolio of deals with a given counterparty and the entire portfolio of commodity transactions. Key issues include:
- ❑ netting of transactions;
- ❑ the distinctions between physical and financial transactions;
- ❑ exposures to major risk factors; and
- ❑ concentration of credit risk.

The credit department may even assume an active role in structuring the transaction to mitigate credit risk. These modifications may be limited to a straightforward change of the duration of the contract, its size and/or payment terms. More active measures involve the inclusion of contractual provisions such as collateral requirements, MAC clauses (material adverse change in the counterparty's financial position), or the use of credit derivatives to transfer credit risk. This new type of process is described in Figure 2.

One of the major recent changes in credit risk management in ECT is the application of quantitative tools, derived from financial economics and financial engineering. There are a number of reasons for this trend. One is the increased use of derivative instruments by companies in the energy industry. Derivatives allow a company to restructure the balance sheet in a relatively short period of time, and especially to increase leverage inherent in the balance sheet. The importance of understanding the potential impact of derivative transactions on the creditworthiness of a company is illustrated by the case of Metalgesellschaft Marketing and Refining, a company brought down by excessive and poorly hedged long-term commodity swaps. The use of derivatives increases the opacity of a company's

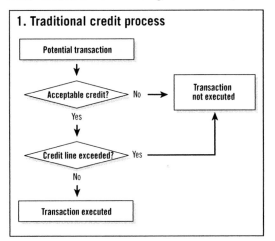

1. Traditional credit process

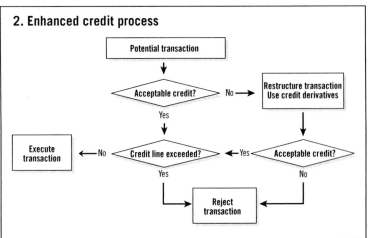

2. Enhanced credit process

finances, and requires more frequent and comprehensive credit reviews. A full understanding of the risks of derivative positions often requires sophisticated quantitative analysis.

Even more important to credit risk analysis is the way in which derivatives, by their nature, make the size of the credit risk uncertain. As we explain in more detail below, derivatives can generate widely varying exposures throughout the life of the deal. For example, at inception a commodity swap generally represents an exchange of equal cashflows; the credit exposure at inception is therefore equal to zero. Over its life, a commodity swap may become an asset or a liability, and its credit exposure may continue to be zero, or may become positive. If the swap is an asset from the marketer's point of view, the value of the swap may be lost if the counterparty is made bankrupt. However, if the swap is "under water" from the marketer's perspective (ie is an asset to the swap counterparty), the bankruptcy judge will insist that this transaction be continued and that all claims be resolved as part of the bankruptcy proceedings. This is known as "asymmetry in credit risk", and is a critical consideration in the estimation of credit exposures (see Figure 3).

As other chapters in this book make clear, another key development in the area of credit risk management in the last few years has been the invention and application of credit derivatives. These financial engineering tools allow users to isolate credit risk from underlying transactions. They facilitate the transfer of credit risk to, or the acquisition of credit risk from, another institution. Credit derivatives are fairly complicated to value and risk manage, and underline how heavily advanced credit risk management relies on quantitative analysis (Table 1).

DEFINITION OF CREDIT RISK
Credit risk is typically defined as a failure to meet contractual requirements related to the promise to repay a loan, or to pay for the delivery of goods and/or services within an agreed time. Recent financial literature evolves around measuring and managing credit risk embedded in financial instruments, primarily corporate debentures and interest rate and currency swaps. Most credit derivatives have been designed to mitigate and hedge the risk embedded in such instruments.

One major difficulty that we encounter in our work is that credit risk in commodity-related contracts is different from the credit risk of a bond. Most analytical tools developed in the literature

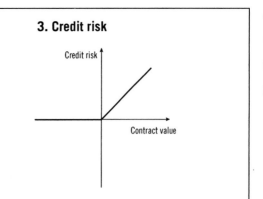

3. Credit risk

Credit risk

Contract value

Table 1. Areas of credit risk management reliant upon advanced quantitative analysis

1.	Definition and estimation of credit risk
2.	Quantitative measurement and representation of credit quality
3.	Estimation of probabilities of default
4.	Estimation of credit exposure and determination of credit reserve
5.	Pricing of credit risk
6.	Valuation and structuring of credit derivatives

revolve around bond defaults, and use the history of bond defaults or bond yield spreads to estimate the probability of default (as described below). One can argue that the probability of default on a corporate bond exceeds the probability of default on a commodity swap. This is supported by the historical performance of such contracts as well as by other considerations. Commodity swaps with a physical component play an important role in the production process of an end-user or a producer. It may be difficult to replicate the same physical transaction given the rigidities of related physical assets, such as transportation or storage or requirements regarding reliability and volume of deliveries. Therefore, even in bankruptcy, a counterparty that continues its economic activities will make an effort to perform on a commodity contract. There are, of course, cases when such factors are not important, and when a defaulting counterparty may renege on its obligations and go to the market to obtain the same supply/purchase contract on better terms.

Another important distinction between these two types of defaults is that a default on a commodity transaction has many shades of grey and may not involve a straightforward suspension of payments. Any counterparty acting in bad faith has a wide range of tools at its disposal when it wishes to engage in contract frustration, including complaints about quality or timeliness of deliveries, and even court action questioning the legal foundations of a contract. In any case, all this highlights the fact that most of the information available on historical or expected credit risks is based on a narrow definition of default, limited to a non-performance on corporate debentures. (Some general techniques that may be used to remedy the lack of historical default information are discussed below in the section on "Alternative estimation techniques".)

The standard approach to measuring credit exposure with respect to an individual counterparty distinguishes between current and potential exposure. Current exposure is defined as value that could be lost if a counterparty defaults today. Future exposure is defined as the exposure that might occur in the future as a result of fluctuation of market prices, interest rates, and exchange rates. For a loan, current and future exposures are typically very close, except for amortising loans with balances decreasing gradually over time. Technically speaking, potential exposure on a loan includes accrued interest and may diverge from the principal, but typically stays within narrow bands (100, 100 + accrued interest).

As we mentioned above, complications arise in the case of derivative contracts. A standard example is that of a commodity or interest rate swap. At inception, a swap generally represents an exchange of two equal (in terms of net present value) cashflows, and its market value at that point is equal to zero. The value of the fixed leg is easy to calculate: it is equal to the net present value of the future cashflows calculated by multiplying the agreed future volumes by the fixed prices for those volumes. The floating leg is evaluated by using the forward prices, which represent the best guesses of the future spot prices used for settlement.

Over the life of the swap, forward prices may evolve and turn the contract into an asset (or liability) from the point of view of a marketer. This variability in the potential prices increases the potential exposure, until at some point the shrinking future volumetric obligations begin to offset the combined effects of price variability and time. By the end of the swap's life the expected exposure is zero again, as no more cashflows remain to be exchanged. However, the market exposure during the lifetime of the contract is not known in advance and can only be estimated probabilistically.

Credit exposure may be calculated at the deal or counterparty level. Exposure at the counterparty level should take into account the effects of netting, ie the result of adding together the exposures generated by multiple transactions with a given counterparty. Here, complications arise for two main reasons:
❑ There are legal restrictions regarding the extent that financial and physical transactions may be netted. The current legal interpretation is that physical transactions may be netted only against other physical transactions; the same is true of financial transactions. Netting of physical transactions may sometimes be limited to one, or a small number of, commodities.
❑ There are legal issues related to the netting of transactions with different units of the same counterparty, operating in the same or different jurisdictions.

Any good portfolio management system for commodity transactions should be able to produce a report on credit exposure by single transaction, and in terms of a portfolio defined according to certain criteria. More sophisticated portfolio reporting systems can report both current and potential credit exposures by a number of different criteria, eg in terms of different credit ratings or counterparties. Other possible schemes for aggregating exposures include those based on vulnerability to various macroeconomic factors. For example, an energy marketer may be interested in balancing exposures to energy producers and consumers. This creates a natural hedge to rising or falling energy prices, as one group of customers is likely to benefit when the other group is negatively affected. Other classifications include aggregations by industries, geographical areas and countries.

QUANTITATIVE MEASUREMENT AND REPRESENTATION OF CREDIT QUALITY
The credit quality of a company is traditionally measured using the credit ratings developed by companies such as Standard & Poor's, Moody's and Fitch. The credit ratings developed by these institutions describe the credit quality of corporate debentures. The quality is represented by the well-known symbols shown in the table in Panel 1. Credit ratings offer obvious advantages: they are widely and easily available for most companies and are backed by large and sophisticated institutions, employing experienced analysts who combine industry knowledge with credit experience. The cost of obtaining information is relatively low and information is generally reliable. One complication for a non-financial company in the commodity business is that it deals with many small counterparties that may not be

MEASURING CREDIT QUALITY FROM FINANCIAL RATIOS

Financial ratios, such as debt-to-equity or return on assets, convey important information about companies to investors. These ratios can be easily computed for a public company from the data in the company's balance sheet and income statement. It is often useful to have a model that combines all the relevant financial information about a company into a single number representing its credit quality. For example, such a model can be used to rate private companies in which a potential equity investment is considered. Using the same quantitative model for evaluating different companies provides us with an objective comparison of these companies.

We gathered financial information on 90 public electric utilities for years 1994–96. For each of these companies, we obtained the Standard & Poor's (S&P) credit ratings given in the January of years 1995–97, associating each rating number with the financial data for the prior year. The S&P ratings were converted to a numerical credit code using the conversions given in the table. Since this represents cross-sectional and time-series data, we use the regression equation

$$Y_{it} = a + b_1X_{it,1} + b_2X_{it,2} + \cdots + b_KX_{it,K} + e_{it}$$

where the subscripts i and t refer, respectively, to company number and year, Y_{it} are the credit codes, $X_{it,k}$ are the financial ratios, and e_{it} are the errors. We use an error component model[1] assuming that the error term e_{it} is composed of three independent components – one associated with time, one associated with the companies, and a third varying with both. According to this model,

$$e_{it} = u_i + v_t + w_{it}$$

Conversion of S&P and Moody's ratings to numerical codes

S&P rating	Moody's rating	Code
AAA	Aaa	2
AA+	Aa1	4
AA	Aa2	5
AA–	Aa3	6
A+	A1	7
A	A2	8
A–	A3	9
BBB+	Baa1	10
BBB	Baa2	11
BBB–	Baa3	12
BB+	Ba1	13
BB	Ba2	14
BB–	Ba3	15
B+	B1	16
B	B2	17
B–	B3	18
CCC+	Caa	19
CCC	Ca	20
CCC–	C	21

where u_i, v_t, w_{it} are independent and are normally distributed with zero means.

The results of the regression analysis shows that three ratios are important determinants of the credit code of a company: total debt-to-assets ratio (DR), return on assets (ROA) and book value per share (BVPS). The model can be given by

Credit Code = 8.65 + 0.17 * DR – 1.08 * ROA – 0.06 * BVPS + Error

The model has an R^2 of 66.5% and an adjusted R^2 of 65.7%.

1 J. Kmenta, *Elements of Econometrics*, New York, 1971, pp. 625–29.

followed in detail by analysts, so obtaining a credit rating for these firms may be difficult.

There are other disadvantages with credit ratings from our point of view. One problem is that the credit ratings are subject to a periodic review, and a counterparty's financial position may undergo rapid change in the interim period. The misuse of derivatives can accelerate this process of credit quality decay. More serious problems result from the basis risk, mentioned above, between risk of default on a debenture and on a commodity transaction. This distinction led us to

develop an alternative credit rating system for measuring risk as it is defined and perceived by ECT.

Another reason why an alternative credit rating system is necessary is the proliferation of energy commodity marketers (especially in the area of natural gas and power), who are either independent, or are established as unregulated units of utilities or large energy companies. Some marketing companies are thinly capitalised and some lack the explicit credit guarantee of their parents. Recent cases indicate that parent companies may not always honour the obligations of their affiliates, as described in Lapson (1997). This means that the credit rating of a parent cannot be automatically extended to the affiliated company and, given that no alternative ratings are available, a special internal, company-supported system has to be designed to address this gap.

An additional problem arises from the fact that credit ratings (internal or developed by agencies) may be available only for a subset of potential clients. Sometimes, it is necessary to produce a rating for a new client on very short notice. One possible approach to the derivation of credit ratings is to use an approach based on cross-sectional regression, linking available credit ratings (converted into numerical scale) to a set of financial ratios characterising the performance of companies. Such ratios are derived from the financial statements of the companies and are used to characterise asset and liability structure, liquidity, profitability and other aspects of performance. Panel 1 shows an example of this procedure for a sample of electric utilities in the US.

Of course, the quantitative approach can be used only as the first step in the evaluation of creditworthiness of a counterparty and in assignment of internal credit ratings. The credit decision is based on a number of factors, which often do not lend themselves to numerical representation. Some of the most important considerations are the quality of management, and the position of a company relative to its peers.

From the point of view of senior management, it is critical to provide information both about the creditworthiness of a given counterparty and also about the quality of the entire portfolio of contracts. This can be accomplished by showing the distribution of the portfolio by different synthetic credit ratings, and also by showing quantitative measures of concentration with respect to a given counterparty and to homogeneous groups of customers. Tracking the position with a given counterparty is complicated by the dispersion of transactions with a counterparty between different units of the same company, which are sometimes located in many countries and on many continents. An additional problem arises from the fact that a given counterparty may transact under many different names in many jurisdictions. Keeping track of relationships between different counterparties is a difficult problem and requires a good customer database.

Measuring and reporting of exposures to a group of homogeneous counterparties may be as important as, or even more important than, measuring and reporting of exposures by individual counterparties. Heavy reliance on a group of customers vulnerable to the same market conditions, with concentration in one industry or geographical location, or dependent on the same technology, may amplify the impact of adverse market developments. It is important that a company develops sophisticated ways of measuring concentrations of credit risk.

ESTIMATION OF PROBABILITIES OF DEFAULT
Once credit ratings have been assigned to different counterparties, we must estimate the probability of default for each one. There are two methods for estimating probabilities of default: the bond spreads method, and the Markov chains method. For simplicity, it can be assumed that two companies with the same credit rating have the same probabilities of default regardless of their respective industries and financial conditions. In the discussion below, we also assume that default probabilities are derived from publicly-available external credit ratings.

Bond spreads method
The probability of default of a company in a given year can be estimated from the yield curves for bonds of the same credit quality as those of the company. For example, if we wish to estimate the probability of default of a company with a rating of BB, we would obtain the yield curve for a BB-rated bond. Financial data vendors, such as Bloomberg Financial Systems, offer information on different bond prices and their yields. The yield curves that may be used are aggregate yield curves (also called "fair market yield curves"), which apply on average to the group of all bonds with the same rating. The estimation of the probabilities of default is based on an assumption of risk-neutrality.

To understand how this method works, let r_f be the current one-year risk-free interest rate and r the one-year rate on a risky loan or bond. For a $1 principal, the repayment on the risk-free and risky borrowings are $(1 + r_f)$ and $(1 + r)$, respectively. Given that repayment under the risky borrowing is uncertain, the payoff of $(1 + r)$ occurs with a probability of $(1 - p)$, where p is the probability of default on the risky loan over the course of one year. Assuming that investors are risk-neutral, the expected repayment under the risky loan should equal the repayment from the risk-free loan. If we assume a fraction s of the loan is recovered in case of default, then

$$(1+r)(1-p) + sp = 1 + r_f$$

which gives us

$$p = \frac{r - r_f}{1 + r - s}$$

Here we derived the probability of default for a period of one year from now. We can derive the *marginal* probability of default for any given period in the future by a similar approach. To do this, let r_{fn}, r_n respectively be the current forward one-year rates on risk-free and risky bonds for year n respectively. The marginal probability of default for year n is given by

$$p_n = \frac{r_n - r_{fn}}{1 + r_n - s}$$

This analysis can be performed not only at the one-year level but also at the one-month, quarterly, or multi-year levels.

Markov chains method

This method uses rating migration probability matrices derived from historical data to estimate default probabilities. Such a matrix can be generated from historical data on transition of companies from one rating group to another over time. This data is available from credit rating agencies such as Standard & Poor's and Moody's. Table 2 shows an example of a one-year rating migration probability matrix. Different credit ratings are shown at the top and at the side of the table. The diagonal elements contain probabilities that a company's credit rating will remain unchanged in one year. For example, for a company rated AAA, the probability of remaining a AAA company during one year is 89.1%. The probability of a downgrade to AA is 9.63%. There is a zero probability of a downgrade to any level lower than BB during one year. It is, of course, possible for a AAA company to become a non-investment grade (BB or below) company, through a series of downgrades over several years.

The last column in the matrix corresponds to bankruptcy, which is defined as an "absorbing state". In the language of Markov chains theory, this means that the probability of moving from bankruptcy to any higher rating is zero, as indicated by the last row of the matrix. This corresponds to Moody's convention of treating a company emerging from bankruptcy as a new entity.

Two assumptions underlie the Markov chains

approach. The first is that the rating transition probabilities for a company in each succeeding year depend only on the company's rating in that year and not on its rating during previous years. The second is that the rating migration probability matrix giving the probabilities of transition of a company from one rating to another in one year does not change from year to year. This second property is called *stationarity*. With these two assumptions and a rating migration probability matrix given, we can compute the probability that a company moves from one rating to another in a given number of years. The CreditMetrics Technical Document[3] compares the matrices developed by Standard and Poor's and by Moody's, and also indicates how a stationary matrix may be constructed to match historical default data over multiple years.

To show how to compute the probabilities of default, let P be the annual rating migration probability matrix that gives the marginal probabilities of rating migration of companies from one rating to another rating in one year. We assume that P is stationary. The (i, j)th element of P gives the probability that a company with rating i moves to rating j in one year. The rating migration probability matrix for a period of n years is just the n-fold product of rating migration matrices for successive years. Assuming that the annual probability matrix is constant and equal to the historical rating migration matrix P, the n-year rating migration matrix is obtained by raising P to the nth power, or

$$P_1 P_2 \cdots P_n = P^n$$

where P_i is the rating migration probability matrix for year i. The last column of the n-year rating migration matrix P^n corresponds to the default or absorbing state and gives the cumulative probabilities of default in n years for initial ratings given by each row index. If we are interested in computing the probabilities of default only, and not other transitions, we can compute them more efficiently as follows. Let d be the

Table 2. One year rating transition probability matrix

	AAA	AA	A	BBB	BB	B	CCC	Default
AAA	0.8910	0.0963	0.0078	0.0019	0.0030	0.0000	0.0000	0.0000
AA	0.0086	0.9010	0.0747	0.0099	0.0029	0.0029	0.0000	0.0000
A	0.0009	0.0291	0.8894	0.0649	0.0101	0.0045	0.0000	0.0009
BBB	0.0006	0.0043	0.0656	0.8427	0.0644	0.0160	0.0018	0.0045
BB	0.0004	0.0022	0.0077	0.0920	0.7596	0.1020	0.0125	0.0236
B	0.0000	0.0019	0.0031	0.0066	0.0517	0.8246	0.0435	0.0685
CCC	0.0000	0.0000	0.0116	0.0116	0.0203	0.0754	0.6493	0.2319
Default	0.0000	0.0000	0.0000	0.0000	0.0000	0.0000	0.0000	1.0000

ESTIMATION OF DEFAULT PROBABILITIES FROM BOND PRICES

In the main text, we discuss how to derive probabilities of default from bond prices. Here we show the details of this computation with an example. We then discuss an alternative approach to computing probabilities of default through the risk-neutral bond pricing approach suggested by Fons (1994).[1]

For the sake of simplicity, we use corporate par bonds paying annual coupons to illustrate both methods. The assumption of a par bond means that the coupon of the bond is equal to its yield-to-maturity and that the market price of the bond is equal to par. The calculations for bonds with semi-annual coupons are similar though more cumbersome.

The equation for the price of an n-year bond with an annual coupon C is

$$\text{Bond price} = \sum_{t=1}^{n} \frac{C}{\left(1 + i(t)\right)^{t}} + \frac{1}{\left(1 + i(n)\right)^{n}}$$

where i(t) is the (zero) interest rate for t years. We use z(t) to represent the price of a zero-coupon bond price, which is the same as the discount factor corresponding to time t, that is

$$z(t) = \frac{1}{\left(1 + i(t)\right)^{t}}$$

We start with a hypothetical market yield curve y(t) (shown in column 2 of Table A) for BBB-rated par bonds and derive the zero-coupon bond prices z(t) for each year by bootstrapping. For the n-year par bond, we have bond price = 1 and coupon = y(n). Using this information, we can rewrite the bond price equation as

$$1 = \sum_{t=1}^{n} y(n)z(t) + z(n)$$

This identity is used to compute recursively the zero-coupon bond prices. One-year forward rates r(t) are derived from the zero-coupon bond prices and are used to compute the probabilities of default. The details of the computation are given in the algorithm below. Here, the yields, zero-coupon bond prices, and interest rates corresponding to the risk-free (Treasury) bonds are represented by yf(t), zf(t) and rf(t) respectively. Marginal probabilities of default and survival are given by d(t) and s(t) respectively. Also, the cumulative probabilities of default and survival are given by D(t) and S(t) respectively.

Algorithm 1. Calculation of probabilities of default
1. Initialise z(0) = zf(0) = 1, S(0) = 1, and t = 1.
2. Compute BBB zero coupon bond price for year t using

$$z(t) = \left(1 - y(t) * \sum_{i=1}^{t-1} z(i)\right) / \left(1 + y(t)\right)$$

This equation follows from the identity for the price of a par bond discussed above. Zero-coupon bond price for Treasuries zf(t) is computed similarly using the Treasury yields yf(t) (shown in Table B).
3. Compute the one-year BBB forward rate from

$$r(t) = \frac{z(t-1)}{z(t)} - 1$$

The forward rates for Treasury bonds rf(t) are calculated similarly using zf(t-1) and zf(t).
4. Compute the marginal probabilities of default and survival using

$$d(t) = \frac{r(t) - rf(t)}{1 - r(t) - a}$$

where a = recovery rate on the notional of the bond (assumed 40% for BBB-rated companies), and

$$s(t) = 1 - d(t)$$

5. Compute the cumulative probabilities of survival and default using

$$S(t) = S(t-1) * s(t)$$

and

$$D(t) = 1 - S(t)$$

The calculations for the next year are done by setting t = t + 1 and jumping to step 2.

Table A gives the results of applying this algorithm on a sample yield curve for a BBB bond. The Treasury yield curve used for this example is shown in Table B.

Alternative method of Fons

With the notation introduced above, we can write the certainty-equivalent version of the equation for the price of an n-year bond with annual coupon C as

$$\text{Bond price} = \sum_{t=1}^{n} U(t)zf(t) + S(n)zf(n)$$

where U(t) is the expected payoff to the bond-holder in year t and is given by

Table A. Calculation of probabilities of default by algorithm 1.

# years	BBB bond yields	BBB zero bond price	BBB 1-year forward rate	Marginal probability of default	Marginal probability of survival	Cumulative probability of survival	Cumulative probability of default
t	y(t)	z(t)	r(t)	p(t)	s(t)	S(t)	D(t)
1	6.10%	0.943	6.10%	0.010	0.990	0.99047	0.010
2	6.22%	0.886	6.35%	0.008	0.992	0.98259	0.017
3	6.27%	0.833	6.38%	0.010	0.990	0.97258	0.027
4	6.31%	0.783	6.45%	0.009	0.991	0.96363	0.036
5	6.37%	0.734	6.65%	0.014	0.986	0.94987	0.050

$$U(t) = S(t)C + S(t-1)d(t)a$$

Here, a is the recovery rate on the notional of the bond, as assumed before. Note that, in his paper,[1] Fons assumes that the recovery rate applies to the notional plus accrued coupon. One other difference in our discussion of Fons' method is that we feel it is more appropriate to discount each period's risk-adjusted cashflow by the risk-free zero rate for that period, rather than by the yield-to-maturity of the risk-free bond. The equation above follows from risk-neutrality and absence of arbitrage. Also, for a par bond, we have bond price = $1 and C = y(n). This equation can be used to compute the probabilities of default. The following algorithm gives the details of this method. Here we assume that the zero bond prices for treasuries zf(t) have already been calculated as shown in Algorithm 1. The formulae in steps 2 and 3 below follow from the above bond price equation.

Algorithm 2. Calculation of probabilities of default

1. Initialize S(0) = 1 and t = 1.

2. Compute V(t − 1) from

$$V(t-1) = \sum_{i=1}^{t-1}\left[S(i)y(t) + aS(i-1)d(i)\right]zf(i)$$

This is simply the expected present value of the cashflows in the first (t − 1) years of a t-year par bond. Note that y(t) is the coupon of the t-year bond, the principal is 1, and zf(i) for i = 1 to t−1 are the discount factors for the first (t − 1) years.

3. Compute the cumulative probabilities of survival S(t) and default D(t) from

Table B. Calculation of risk-free forward rates from Treasury bond yields

# years	Treasury yield	Treasury zero bond price	Treasury 1-year forward rate
t	yf(t)	zf(t)	rf(t)
1	5.47%	0.9481	5.47%
2	5.64%	0.8960	5.82%
3	5.66%	0.8476	5.70%
4	5.70%	0.8009	5.83%
5	5.70%	0.7577	5.70%

$$S(t) = \left(1 - V(t-1) - B(t)\right)/A(t)$$

and D(t) = 1 − S(t) where

$$A(t) = \left(1 + y(t) - a\right)zf(t)$$

and B(t) = aS(t − 1)zf(t).

4. Compute the marginal probabilities of survival and default from

$$s(t) = \frac{S(t)}{S(t-1)}$$

and d(t) = 1 − s(t).

To perform the calculations for another year, set t = t + 1 and go to step 2.

Table C below gives the results of applying this algorithm to the BBB and Treasury yield curves shown in the above tables. The probabilities of default obtained from the above two methods are similar, as Tables A and C show.

[1] J.S.Fons, 1994, "Using Default Rates to Model the Term Structure of Credit Risk," *Financial Analysts Journal*, Sep–Oct, pp. 25–32.

Table C. Calculation of probabilities of default by algorithm 2.

# years	BBB bond yields	Treasury zero bond price	Cumulative probability of survival	Cumulative probability of default	Marginal probability of survival	Marginal probability of default	
t	y(t)	zf(t)	S(t)	D(t)	s(t)	d(t)	V(t)
1	6.10%	0.948	0.990	0.010	0.990	0.010	0.061
2	6.22%	0.896	0.984	0.016	0.994	0.006	0.120
3	6.27%	0.848	0.973	0.027	0.989	0.011	0.176
4	6.31%	0.801	0.964	0.036	0.991	0.009	0.229
5	6.37%	0.758	0.952	0.048	0.987	0.013	0.281

vector of probabilities of default in one year, given by the last column in P. Then the cumulative probabilities of default for n years are given by

$$d_n = P^{n-1}d$$

or, equivalently

$$d_n = Pd_{n-1}$$

for n = 2, 3, etc. The last equation allows us to compute the cumulative probabilities of default $d_1, d_2, d_3, \ldots$ in successive years without computing the matrix powers.

To determine the expected loss of mark-to-market values resulting from counterparty defaults, we need to know the marginal probabilities of default. Using the Markov assumptions, it is easy to show that

$$d_{nj} = d_{n-1,j} + m_{nj}(1 - d_{n-1,j})$$

where m_{nj} is the marginal probability of default for year n for rating j, and d_{nj} is the cumulative probability of default for n years for rating j. This gives us the result

$$m_{nj} = \frac{d_{nj} - d_{n-1,j}}{1 - d_{n-1,j}}$$

Comparison and critique of the two methods
Both approaches to the computation of default probabilities described above have particular shortcomings. The certainty equivalent approach assumes that the investors are risk-neutral. This means, for example, that if the expected returns are identical an investor will be indifferent between the following:

❑ invest $1 million which gives a 50% chance of a $3 million profit, but a 50% chance of losing the entire investment; and
❑ invest $1 million with a guaranteed profit of $1 million.

In reality, people are risk-averse, preferring the second alternative to the first. Risk aversion implies that probabilities of default are overestimated by the bond spreads approach.

Another disadvantage of the bond spreads approach concerns the nature of the input data available for the model. Corporate bonds typically have options embedded in them and it is difficult, if not impossible, to extract prices of pure bonds from the data. Also, factors other than credit quality can affect bond prices in the short run. For example, the spread over the treasury rates for corporate bonds of a given rating can be affected by the available supply of bonds

in that rating relative to the treasury bonds. Also, the liquidity of the US Treasury market far exceeds that of any other bond market, and so corporate bonds require a premium to compensate for their liquidity risk.

The probabilities of default are sensitive to the recovery rates. Recovery rates depend upon many factors including bond seniority. In practice, recovery rates are difficult to measure due to the complexities involved in the bankruptcy process and its prolonged nature. Also, the recovery rates are usually not constant over time.

The main drawback of the Markov chains method is that it is based on historical data about the evolution of the credit quality of companies. Though we use the current rating of a company in establishing its default probabilities, there is no guarantee that future rating migration probabilities are the same as those computed from past data. The historical rating migration matrix is thus highly dependent on the time period used to collect default history.

Another disadvantage with the Markov chains approach is that it ignores the issue of autocorrelation in the time-series of credit quality changes. For example, Altman and Kao (1992) find that downgrades of S&P ratings of companies are likely to be followed by downgrades in the following periods, giving rise to positive autocorrelation.

A general problem in using probabilities of default is the possibility of a rapid deterioration of the credit quality of a financial company. This is a possible scenario for some companies given how easy it is to reorganise a portfolio of derivatives with minimal transaction costs and in a very short time. A company's financial health may deteriorate quickly as the company's leverage is increased, escaping the scrutiny of the market place. On the other hand, derivatives help to reduce financial friction: they cut the time required to reorganise a portfolio and minimise transaction costs, thus improving overall economic efficiency.

Alternative estimation techniques
The two techniques for the estimation of default probability described above are currently the most widely used mathematical tools in credit analysis. In addition to these, we believe that discriminant analysis and other mathematical tools are very useful for a company that has a large customer population and only limited information regarding each client.

Historically, the first application of quantitative tools in this area was to the analysis of financial ratios. Financial ratios are indicators derived from the set of financial statements of a company, designed to summarise information about its liquidity, profitability, leverage and other aspects of its operations.[4] The first step, going back at least one century, was to use different financial ratios derived from company financial statements, combined with rules-of-thumb regarding the critical values of such indicators.

The predictive power of financial ratios may be enhanced by using them as inputs to a more general index of the company's financial health. Such an index may be built using trial-and-error and intuition, or through more sophisticated statistical techniques. Such an effort was started by Altman (1968), who applied the statistical technique known as multivariate discriminant analysis. This technique requires that a population of objects (firms, households) be divided into two or more predefined groups. Such groups, in the case of credit analysis, may correspond to highly creditworthy customers with a sterling reputation, customers who are considered creditworthy but require additional review if the exposure exceeds a certain amount, and customers who should be rejected automatically without any additional process.

The next step is to select, from many different indicators of financial health, the set that discriminates the best between these groups, and to develop an overall single indicator, calculated as a weighted sum of the indicators included in this set. This single credit score may be used to classify the new observation when it arrives. This can be accomplished by calculating the value of the discriminant function (or Z-score, as Altman called it) and comparing this to a certain critical value that the discriminant method produces. Several software packages, for example, Dun and Bradstreet's Risk Assessment Manager, adopt this approach. In his 1968 paper, Altman identified the financial ratios that in combination have the highest predictive power for corporate bankruptcies:

❑ Working capital/total assets
❑ Retained earnings/total assets
❑ EBIT as a percentage of total assets
❑ Market value of equity/book value of debt
❑ Sales/total assets

One runs, of course, the risk of misclassification – of committing a Type I error (a good firm is rejected), or a Type II error (a bad firm is accepted). These terms come from statistics where hypotheses about a population are being tested using a sample from that population: a Type I error is rejection of a hypothesis, when it is in fact true; a Type II error is committed when a hypothesis is accepted when it is false.

Altman's technique has been applied and enhanced by a number of other authors.[5] The objections to his method mentioned in the literature mostly relate to its mechanical and static nature. The critics objected that a method that was developed for applications in biology to classify Indian skulls or newly discovered species would be unable to capture the texture and dynamics of business developments. However, the use of discriminant analysis can reduce the cost of pre-screening customers and direct the attention of credit officers to a subset of potential or current clients.

Another quantitative tool used to estimate probabilities of default is regression analysis. This approach requires compilation of historical information about the cases of default (1) and no-default (0) of different companies (or households, countries), together with information about the financial and economic conditions of these entities preceding (with some lead time) the observations of default (no-default) events. The obvious task is then to relate these two information sets using regression techniques.

One limitation of the straightforward linear regression method is that the nature of the dependent variable (0 or 1), in conjunction with the standard regression specification:

$$y = \alpha + \beta'x + \varepsilon$$

implies that for any given value of the vector of explanatory variables, x, the error term may assume only two values:[6]

$$-\alpha - \beta'x$$

or

$$1 - \alpha - \beta'x$$

This violates the standard assumption of normality of errors (and also, as one can prove, homoskedasticity) and invalidates classical tests of significance. In addition, the predicted values of the dependent variable may be outside the (0,1) interval, making it impossible to interpret the regression results as inputs to default probability estimation and to use the estimates of α and β for prediction.

An alternative regression formulation links a vector of financial and economic indicators to probability of default (y), using the so-called logit formulation:

$$y = \exp(\beta'x)/(1 + \exp(\beta'x))$$

The left-hand side variable is not observable, but one can define a variable, d, such that $d = 1$ if a default takes place, 0 otherwise (Feder and Just 1977). It implies:

$$P(d = 0|x = x_i) = 1/[1 + \exp(\beta'x)]$$

$$P(d = 1|x = x_i) = \exp(\beta'x)/[1 + \exp(\beta'x)]$$

where P stands for probability. The use of non-linear regression techniques allows the estimation of the coefficients of this equation.

ESTIMATION OF CREDIT EXPOSURE

Credit exposure results from an interaction between default probabilities, commodity price movements, interest rate movements and foreign exchange rate movements.

Since we do not know in advance when, if ever, a counterparty is going to default on its deal, we have to consider potential values of the deal throughout its life. There are two ways that this can be done:

❏ Single shift of commodity prices, interest rates and foreign exchange rates

❏ Multiple shifts via simulation of commodity prices, interest rates and foreign exchange rates

ECT uses both of these approaches to estimate credit exposure. This allows us to gain different viewpoints on credit exposure, and stops us getting tied down to the various assumptions that lie behind each of the approaches.

Single-shift calculation

As discussed above, we can obtain probabilities of default for each time interval in the future, conditional on the counterparty not defaulting before the start of the time interval. We may choose the time interval to be a day, a week, a month or a year. Typically, we believe that a month is an appropriate choice. We then calculate the probability of the counterparty defaulting in that time interval and not earlier. Assuming independence between the event of no default until the beginning of the time interval, and the event of default in the time interval conditional on no default earlier, the desired probability is simply the product of the probabilities associated with these two events.

In the case of a single-shift exposure calculation, the crucial decision is how to calculate the deal value in a forward month. The simplistic answer would be to value the remaining part of the deal (the part that has not settled before the default date) using the current forward commodity price curve, and the current interest rate curves. However, this calculation ignores the impact of volatility on commodity prices, which gives rise to a wider distribution of possible deal values in the future. One would expect that

wider deal value distributions would translate into greater credit exposure, and so higher volatility commodity deals would tend to have higher credit exposure than lower volatility commodities.

One way to try to factor the impact of volatility into the calculation is to consider a shifted commodity price curve instead of the regular price curve. For each forward month, we may then calculate the value of the remaining portion of the deal (the part of the deal that extends from that forward month to the end of the deal) using the shifted price curve. This value may be positive, zero or negative. We refer to the greater of zero and this value as the "exposure value". The series of exposure values by forward month gives credit exposure as a function of time.

The shift in the forward price curve may be accomplished in many different ways. One possibility is a parallel shift of the price curve. However, for commodity prices, the volatility curve tends to be downward sloping and not flat. In other words, the volatilities for the forward prices closer to today (the "front" of the volatility curve) are much higher than the volatilities for the forward prices far from today (the "back" of the volatility curve). As a result, a parallel shift of prices would either overstate the shift towards the back of the price curve, or understate the shift at the front of the price curve.

A better way to approach this problem is to recognise that:

❏ the value of the remaining portion of the deal at any future point in time is unknown;

❏ the probability distribution of this value may be derived using mathematics or by using certain conventions and shortcuts; and

❏ the exposure at that point in time may be selected from this distribution.

Each forward price is considered to have a certain probability distribution, with the means centered on the current forward price curve, dependent on the volatilities given by the forward volatility curve. Then we can use a shifted price curve that is defined as a function of the price distributions. The shift may be chosen to be some percentile of the commodity price distribution. To be conservative, a higher percentile should be chosen when deal value increases with increasing commodity prices, and a lower percentile should be chosen otherwise. One should note that the median or 50th percentile is not appropriate unless we believe that the commodity price distribution is symmetric.

Using the 95th percentiles or the 5th percentiles for the shifted price curve might be regarded as one way to calculate a "worst-case" credit exposure, while using a percentile closer to the 50th percentile might be seen as an attempt to calculate an "expected-case" credit exposure. However, the exact percentile to be used for the expected-case calculation would depend on the choice of probability distribution for commodity prices. Some probability distributions, such as the normal distribution, have an expected value equal to the 50th percentile, whereas other probability distributions, such as the lognormal distribution, have an expected value that is different from the 50th percentile.

A completely different way of incorporating volatility into the calculation is to borrow some ideas from options theory. The expected loss from a counterparty default in some forward month, say month i, may be viewed as the value of an option that the counterparty has with strike price of zero to "put" the deal to us whenever the deal value is negative for him (or positive for us). If the deal is a swap, then his option is simply a swaption. If the deal is an option expiring in some month later than month i, then the option to default becomes a compound option. The only problem with this methodology is that the valuation of these options can quickly become quite complicated, when the deal increases in complexity from a single swap or a single option to strips of options, compound options, swaptions, or even more intricate deal structures.

Simulation

In this methodology, we have to assume a price process for each forward price. This implies a pricing equation relating the price at the end of a time step with the price at the beginning of the time step. The relationship is not deterministic, and it includes the impact of one or more random variables on the price at the beginning of the time step. The exact relationship depends on the price process assumed for each price.

The simulation of prices involves sampling these random variables from their distributions to obtain a time series of prices. When the entire forward price curve is to be simulated, there are many different ways that the random variables may be generated – these relate to the assumptions about correlations between the different forward prices along the price curve. Typically, for commodities, we find a high degree of correlation between prices along the curve, with the correlation being higher the closer the prices are

to each other on the curve. At one extreme, one may generate a set of random variables for each forward price, and correlate them using a full correlation matrix of size N by N, where N is the number of forward prices in the price curve. This solution is very computer-intensive and is probably an overkill. At the other extreme, one may assume either completely uncorrelated shocks between forward prices or perfectly correlated shocks.

Neither assumption is realistic, but the assumption of perfect correlation does provide a link to the single-shift methodology. Under the single-shift methodology, as described earlier, one has to decide how to shift the forward price curve in order to incorporate the effect of volatility. The shift will be either up for every forward price or down for every forward price. This is exactly the definition of perfect correlation between the prices in the forward price curve.

A middle ground that makes a lot of sense is to use a multifactor model that describes the perturbation of each forward price as a linear combination of a small number of factors, modelled as random variables. The same factors apply to every price in the forward curve, but the linear combinations are different, so the shocks to each price are not exactly the same. The advantage of this methodology is that it is not necessary to simulate as many independent shocks as there are prices. One needs only to simulate a small number of factors, and thus describe the movement of the entire forward price curve. This technique of simulation also allows for different kinds of curve reshaping, ie not only may parallel shifts be simulated, but also steepenings and flattenings, and cases where one part of the curve behaves differently from the other parts of the curve. This methodology was first pioneered by Heath, Jarrow and Morton (1992) in the context of interest rate curve simulation, and has been extended to commodities by Cortazar and Schwartz (1994). Enron uses this methodology for its value-at-risk calculation, and other applications include the pricing of deals by simulation, and calculation of credit exposure.

Once we have determined how we are going to simulate prices, we can move on to simulate counterparty defaults. To do this, we will assume that we have available the cumulative probabilities of no default for each time period extending from today to a forward month. These are easily obtained from the calculation of probabilities of default discussed above. Then, for each simulation, we sample a uniform random variable over the interval 0 to 1, and look for the forward month for which the realised value of the uniform random variable exceeds the cumulative probability of no default for the time period from today to that forward month. If deals with that counterparty extend beyond that month, then the counterparty is assumed to default in that forward month, else the counterparty is assumed not to default for this simulation.

A certain (large) number of simulations is agreed upon and, for each simulation, times of default are simulated for each counterparty. If deals with a counterparty extend beyond the time of default for that counterparty, then prices are also simulated up to that time, and these deals (whole or part) extending beyond this time are valued. If this value is positive, it is recorded as loss for this simulation for this counterparty. Otherwise, zero is recorded as the loss.

One advantage that simulation has over single-shift calculation is that we may generate a distribution of losses due to counterparty default and not just a point estimate. This allows us to look not just at the expected loss, but also at any percentile of the loss distribution. Although it may seem that we can do this in the single-shift case also by choosing the appropriate percentiles of the price distributions as the single shift, this is not correct in general, especially for types of deal (eg options) where the deal value is a non-linear function of prices.

Another important advantage of simulation is that it is easier to handle multicommodity deals such as spread deals, in which a company simultaneously agrees to go long one commodity and short the other. An example of a transaction that is getting more and more popular is the spark spread – a spread between the value of generated electricity and the value of the natural gas fuel required to generate that electricity. Another example is a deal where ECT agrees to buy natural gas at one location and sell it at another. Although the physical commodity is the same at both places, the commodity may not be economically fungible across delivery locations. In other words, for simulation purposes, we treat natural gas at different locations as completely different commodities whose prices have some correlation between them.

A third important advantage of simulation is that it can handle the effect of diversification. Since most companies would not expect all counterparties to default together, the 95th percentile loss on a portfolio of deals with many different counterparties would be less than the sum

of the 95th percentile losses for each deal considered in isolation. Simulation can easily handle uncorrelated or correlated defaults across different counterparties, whereas for the single-shift case, it is hard to implement relationships between counterparty defaults.

PRICING CREDIT RISK

The energy industry has failed, so far, to develop effective ways of incorporating default risk into the prices of commodity-related swaps and options. This stands in a sharp contrast with the rationalisation of the pricing of credit risk that is currently taking place in the interest rate and currency markets. It can be explained in terms of the much smaller volume of energy-related derivatives, limited price transparency and lack of publicly available data.

In theory, one can identify several methods of pricing credit risk. One approach available for swaps is to use a higher discount rate for a riskier counterparty. Otherwise, we would overvalue the deal. However, in the case of a liquid market with many different participants, this may be very hard to do. In the case of bilateral deals, we can address this issue more easily. There are two main approaches:

❑ Determine one price that includes a consideration for credit risk; for example, by using a higher interest rate for discounting than the Treasury rate, with the interest rate being higher for worse credit ratings.

❑ Determine one price without any consideration for credit risk, and then determine an adjustment (subtraction from value) to account for credit risk; for example, by using a common interest rate to value all deals, but then adjusting the deal value by a credit reserve number.

Ultimately, the true value of a deal should be evident from the marketplace if a liquid market exists. Since the credit derivatives market is in a nascent stage, calculating the "correct" value of credit adjustments to deal value relies quite heavily on negotiations between the counterparties involved in the deal. An individual company may devise a consistent methodology for calculating credit reserves, but it is unlikely that this will match the counterparty's calculation as there is no standard way to calculate probabilities of default, and there is no universal approach concerning the use of single shifts of prices and simulation.

An alternative solution is to adjust swap prices explicitly for probabilities of default. Surprisingly, the adjustment is in most cases relatively low. This is explained by the fact that, just as ECT

CREDIT DERIVATIVES AND COMMODITY TRANSACTIONS: AN EXAMPLE

Suppose that ECT enters into a five-year commodity swap with Counterparty XYZ, whereby ECT agrees to exchange (receive) the floating price of natural gas for delivery at the Henry Hub facility on the first of each month for (pay) a fixed price of $2.20 per MMBtu. The volume to be considered for each month is 100,000 MMBtu. The cashflow (monthly volume times the difference between floating price and fixed price) is to be settled on the first of each month. The swap extends from March 1, 1998 up to and including March 2003.

ECT incurs credit risk to the extent that if floating prices go up, XYZ may default while the value of the deal is positive. To protect against this credit exposure, ECT enters into a deal with Counterparty ABC in which ECT pays ABC a monthly cash amount, in return for which ABC agrees to take over all of XYZ's obligations to ECT in case of a default by XYZ. This reduces the credit exposure to ECT because now ECT suffers a loss only if the deal value is positive and both XYZ and ABC default. The extent of the reduction in

credit exposure depends upon the correlation between defaults by XYZ and by ABC. It might be reasonable to assume a very low correlation if the two counterparties are in different industry sectors.

In the figure, the solid arrows are in effect as long as XYZ does not default. As soon as XYZ defaults, the dotted arrows come into effect and the solid arrows are no longer in effect.

Simulation may easily be used to estimate the distribution of credit losses due to price movements and correlated defaults. The variables to simulate include: the default times of XYZ and ABC, and forward prices for natural gas for delivery at Henry Hub.

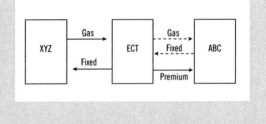

determines an exposure with respect to counterparty XYZ, the counterparty also determines an exposure to ECT. In the case of swaps, for transactions between counterparties with the same credit standing, there would be no adjustment to pricing at all. The adjustment necessitated by insignificant differences in credit ratings is likely to be small, and only big differences in credit ratings (for example, AA versus B) tend to affect prices to a large extent.

The fact that credit risk is not factored explicitly into deal prices does not mean that it has no effect on valuations. Instead, credit considerations are reflected in collateral provisions, contractual provisions enhancing claims of one party in the case of a default (for example, the choice of applicable laws for resolving disputes or the choice of jurisdiction), payment terms, bid–offer spreads, etc. This is a rather inefficient and expensive way of handling credit risk, but it does not mean that the industry is oblivious to it.

VALUATION OF CREDIT DERIVATIVES
Credit derivatives are contracts that separate credit risk from the underlying assets and allow it to be transferred to another party (see Panel 3).

Credit derivatives are an important tool in the arsenal of a risk manager, who is given the task of minimising company risk at lowest cost, using all available physical and financial instruments. The credit risk manager is primarily interested in managing the credit risk in the entire portfolio of deals that he oversees. This provides an interesting situation, as the value of a credit derivative to the risk manager may be different in the context of his portfolio from the value of the credit derivative in the context of an unprotected portfolio.

This means that when two counterparties strike a deal, it is quite possible for both to benefit. Suppose Counterparty A is willing to buy some credit risk for $2 million, and Counterparty B is willing to sell that credit risk for $1 million. If Counterparty A buys the credit risk for $1.5 million, then both A and B will benefit. This is a key reason for the success of the credit derivatives market, and suggests that incremental credit exposure is an extremely important concept in the valuation of credit derivatives.

In particular, a portfolio manager with highly concentrated credit risks and with few counterparties is likely to benefit by selling parts of that risk and buying the credit risk of other counter-

WHAT'S UP YOUR SLEEVE?

Recent turbulence in the US power markets demonstrates the importance of developing a strong credit culture, and the fact that credit risk and market risk can be two sides of the same coin.

Towards the end of June 1998, a combination of unusually hot weather in the Midwest and outages of several generation units and transmission lines created the conditions for price spikes in several regions, including ECAR and MAIN.[1] The power price for "next hour" delivery reportedly reached $5,000 per MWh on June 25 in ECAR, and levels of $1,000–4,000 in other regions such as SERC and SPP.[2] At these levels, prices clearly exceeded the cost of production at the units required to meet marginal demand. It turned out that the spike in price was amplified by credit problems.

Credit sleeve

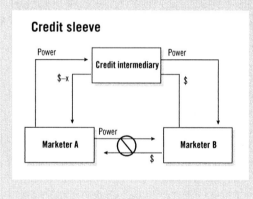

The development of the wholesale power market in the US over the last few years has been characterised by a rapid growth in the number of power marketers. Some of these are thinly capitalised companies, while others are affiliates of strong regulated utilities that do not extend a credit guarantee to their (unregulated) trading units. Undercapitalised marketers are often not considered to be acceptable counterparties by stronger or more credit savvy companies, or often even by other companies of the same credit standing. Transactions between weak and strong counterparties, or between weak counterparties, were thus in some cases made possible by a practice known as sleeving.

Under this arrangement, a third counterparty steps between the two weak or mutually unacceptable credits (see Figure). The intermediary enters into a trade with one counterparty and offsets the trade with a mirror transaction with the second company. The spread between the prices in the two deals compensates the intermediary for assuming the credit risk. In many cases, a transaction between a generator and a final buyer involves a sequence of transactions, referred to in industry jargon as a "daisy chain".

In June 1998, as electricity prices climbed, these arrangements began to break down. The

parties. The manager will also be interested in adding regular deals to his portfolio that diversify his group of counterparties. Ideally, the correlation of default among these counterparties should be low. However, the fortunes of companies in the same industry tend to be closely linked, and the correlation may not be the result of any causal link between one company and another; it may flow from common economic factors, such as commodity prices, that affect two companies in the same way. It is, therefore, important to identify counterparties with low correlations of default even within a single industry sector.

In reality, of course, a non-financial company is limited in its ability to choose industry sectors and counterparties. Also, selling a deal with one counterparty to another counterparty in order to try to sell credit risk may jeopardise existing business relationships. Credit derivatives provide a way to transfer credit risk synthetically.

Having identified correlation of default as an

important parameter, it should be noted that it is not easy to calculate this, primarily because default is rare and therefore historical data captures too few default events. There may also be evidence of serial correlation – higher or lower number of defaults (than historical average) in one month may indicate higher or lower number of defaults in the next month. This complicates the calculation of contemporaneous correlation, between defaults of different companies in the same month, since this calculation typically assumes that there is no serial correlation.

Also, one has to consider whether the correlations calculated from historical data will be stable over time. This leads to the standard econometric problem of choosing between (1) using only recent data and obtaining relatively current but statistically less precise numbers; and (2) using many years' of historical data and obtaining less current but statistically more meaningful numbers.

default of one counterparty caused a chain reaction of defaults down the line. Counterparties upstream from a defaulting company feared that they would not be paid, while counterparties downstream from a defaulting company suddenly had to find power in the market or pay liquidated damages to their customers. The supply portfolio of some marketers, whose suppliers had defaulted, began to fall apart and resulted in a scramble to cover short positions. Prices started to reflect the desire of marketers to avoid a default at any price, and the compulsion of potential suppliers to build a credit risk premium into their price. Prices reached historically unparalleled levels as the market groped to find equilibrium. The problem was exacerbated by the withdrawal of a number of generators from the power markets, as many utilities decided to preserve power to service their own native (committed) load.

After a few days, prices returned to more usual levels, as more information became available in the marketplace. However, the episode proved that:
❑ market fluctuations can increase credit risk by (1) increasing the exposure to the counterparty, and (2) eroding its financial strength and driving it into default;
❑ credit risk can then easily translate back into a market risk. When previously closed positions suddenly open up, they may have to be closed again at any price in extreme market conditions.

Participants in physical commodity markets are exposed to additional layers of risk, related to physical operations. In the case of the US power markets, the recent price spikes were exacerbated by the problems related to physical outages of power plants and transmission lines.

All this underlines the need for a strong credit review of all transactions, constant monitoring, and the active credit management of existing exposures. In terms of quantitative analysis, the episode illustrated the importance of measuring the potential, and not just the current, credit exposure and of maintaining appropriate credit reserves and/or credit insurance. This is why, as mentioned in the main text, Enron uses a stochastic approach to determine the required credit reserve. It is also critical that the probabilistic approach is based upon price processes that correctly describe the price dynamics in different markets. Power prices, for example, are susceptible to jumps, especially in the spot markets and in the front part of the forward price curve. It is true that they tend to revert to the mean in the long run.[3] In the long run, however, some market players may be dead.

1 The North American Electric Reliability Council (NERC) has defined a number of reliability regions, including ECAR (East Central Area Reliability Coordination Agreement), and MAIN (Mid-America Interconnected Network). Other regions include SERC (Southeastern Electric Reliability Council), and SPP (Southwest Power Pool).
2 "Massive Spike Continues; ECAR hourly hits $5,000", *MegawattDaily*, Friday, June 26, 1998, p. 1.
3 See V. Kaminski, "The Challenge of Pricing and Risk Managing Electricity Derivatives", *The US Power Market: Restructuring and Risk Management*, Risk Publications, 1997, pp. 149-74.

Finally, we must again emphasise that the energy industry needs to develop contracts that explicitly accommodate default provisions, where the definition of default includes various shades of non-performance and not simply bond default.

Conclusion

Credit risk has always been an important issue for non-financial companies that have to worry about the promptness of settlement of receivables. In this chapter, we have considered an expanded universe of deals whose pricing depends on fluctuating commodity prices, interest rates, credit ratings and other factors. Recent innovations in the structuring and pricing of credit derivatives allow credit risk to be managed as a portfolio. This underlines the benefits of diversification and of avoiding over-concentration with respect to specific factors.

Credit risk management is an evolving discipline. ECT is continually trying to improve its methodology for credit risk measurement, and strongly emphasises the implementation of new ideas. The challenge is to apply or extend techniques that were originally developed for the fixed income markets to the commodity markets, and also to work within the limitations of existing information technology systems.

1 *A very useful summary and review of this area is contained in* Derivative Credit Risk: Advances in Measurement and Management, *London: Risk Publications, 1995.*

2 *This does not necessarily mean that banks avoid incorrect decisions and do not engage in lending with reckless abandon in order to maintain market share. Some banks, like industrial and trading firms, have a relatively narrow clientele base and by necessity face the problem of credit risk concentration.*

3 CreditMetrics - Technical Document, *JP Morgan & Co., 1997.*

4 *We will not provide definitions of different financial ratios in this paper. Discussion of financial ratios may be found in any introductory text on finance or accounting.*

5 *A paper by E. Rosenberg and A. Gleit. "Quantitative Methods in Credit Management: A Survey",* Operations Research, *Vol. 42, No.4, August 1994, pp. 589-613 contains a good summary of other contributions.*

6 *See J. Kmenta,* Elements of Econometrics, *New York, 1971, p.426.*

BIBLIOGRAPHY

Altman, E.I., 1968, "Financial Ratios, Discriminant Analysis, and the Prediction of Corporate Bankruptcy", *Journal of Finance* 23, pp. 589-609.

Altman, E.I., and D.L. Kao, 1992, "The Implications of Corporate Bond Ratings Drift", *Financial Analysts Journal* May/June, pp. 64-75.

Cortazar, G. and E.S. Schwartz, 1994, "The Valuation of Commodity-Contingent Claims", *The Journal of Derivatives*, Summer, pp. 27-39.

Feder, G., and R.E. Just, 1977, "A Study of Debt Servicing Capacity Applying Logit Analysis", *Journal of Development Economics* 4, pp. 25-38.

Heath, D.R., R. Jarrow and A. Morton, 1992, "Bond Pricing and the Term Structure of Interest Rates: A New Methodology", *Econometrica* 60(1), pp. 77-105.

Lapson, E., 1997, "Managing Credit Risk in the Electricity Market", *The US Power Market: Restructuring and Risk Management*, London: Risk Publications, pp. 287-93.

INVESTMENT MARKETS, CREDIT-LINKED SECURITIES AND CREDIT DERIVATIVES

6

Credit Derivatives

Linking Loan Portfolio Management and Bank Loan Investment Programmes

Elliot Asarnow

ING Capital Advisers

This chapter looks at how credit derivatives can be applied to manage loan portfolios, from the perspective of both commercial banks and investment funds that specialise in managing portfolios of corporate loans. The differing perspectives of these two types of organisation lead to different approaches to employing credit derivatives. Given the relatively recent emergence of credit derivatives, we describe not only current practices but also some potential applications.[1] We also take a look at some of the organisational implications of active credit portfolio management.

Commercial bank perspective

BARRIERS TO LOAN PORTFOLIO
MANAGEMENT
The prevailing corporate banking strategy of the vast majority of commercial banks is to maximise the profitability of corporate client relationships through the ongoing sale of multiple products and services by the banks' relationship management sales forces. The range and sophistication of product offerings varies widely across banks, of course. In addition to extensions of credit in the form of loans and letters of credit, cash management services are high on the list. Among more sophisticated banks, product offerings can be comprehensive, including foreign exchange, interest rate derivatives, M&A advice and securities underwritings (whether securitisations or general corporate financings). In most cases, relationship profitability is measured in terms of absolute revenue, perhaps supplemented by an assessment of the return on regulatory capital. There is generally not a great deal of focus on economic risk versus return at the relationship level, although this situation has begun to improve.

Given their focus on managing relationships, it should not be surprising that few banks are strongly focused on maximising the risk/return profile of the corporate loan portfolio. Banks may make compromises on loan pricing and covenants, as well as on the size and liquidity of portfolio "hold" positions, in the interests of relationship management – an issue that non-bank loan portfolio managers do not have to consider seriously. Even when banks adhere to their credit policies, those policies tend to be binary – ie an accept/reject decision based on conformity with stated criteria – and rarely encourage true relative value investing.

While major banks are moving in the direction of managing the loan portfolio on a more sophisticated risk/return basis, this movement is in its early stages. Implementation will take some years, and will be characterised by fits and starts – a function of the shifting internal political landscape. Though portfolio management is gaining recognition as a legitimate and distinct activity, the portfolio management function is rarely fully empowered. It tends most often to be either an information management function that is responsible for describing the portfolio or, at best, a risk management function that is responsible for establishing and enforcing portfolio policies such as concentration limits and possibly exercising some authority over individual loan approvals. It is rare for a portfolio management group to have direct revenue responsibility. Rather, the line bankers retain control of the revenue line in the income statement whereas the portfolio management group shares responsibility for the cost of the credit line.

Except during the worst of times, those who control the revenue line in a financial services institution tend to have the upper hand over those responsible for containing risk – especially in the corporate lending business. Since the performance measurement criteria for relationship managers tend to be driven by absolute revenue, there is a powerful constituency with an incentive to retain large positions in individual loan assets.

An additional concern is that the business origination effort of most banks is naturally concentrated in their geographic home markets. This natural concentration is exaggerated by:

❏ the fact that corporate borrowers frequently expect, and sometimes require, their banks to hold large, illiquid loan positions;

❏ the general reluctance by many banks to buy loans originated by others outside their home markets; and

❏ the internal bias towards holding large positions in self-originated loans.

Apart from internal constraints, a number of factors limit the liquidity of the underlying loans. We have already cited the desire of many borrowers that their relationship banks retain sizable levels of loans. The result is that banks hold many loans that they do not have the legal right to sell (ie they are not assignable). This is most common in the investment-grade sector, primarily because these companies are in a stronger bargaining position due to their ready access to the capital markets. Among the reasons that borrowers seek to restrict the assignment of their loans is that the loans provided by banks in this sector tend to be unfunded in normal circumstances. Borrowers are concerned, therefore, that strongly capitalised lenders stand ready to offer funding if the borrower does indeed need to draw on these loans. In addition, the dynamic nature of loan agreements, which may involve frequent amendments to accommodate changes in borrower requirements, means that borrowers try to ensure that the bank group is composed of "friendly faces".

Illiquid credit risk also arises for banks as a by-product of their trading activities in interest rate, foreign exchange and commodities contracts. To the extent that a bank is in-the-money (or potentially in-the-money) for a particular contract, and the counterparty has not provided 100% margin, the bank has "pre-settlement risk" exposure to the counterparty. For major corporate clients of major trading banks, pre-settlement risk exposures can be very substantial, even with netting agreements in place. This form of credit risk is inherently illiquid since it is not even represented by an explicit underlying, tradable contract but rather arises in generic form as a by-product of other activities.

THE CENTRAL ROLE OF CREDIT DERIVATIVES

We have described a number of barriers to implementing effective loan portfolio management by banks, both internal and external in nature. Credit derivatives can play a central role in eliminating these barriers.

Once a bank's senior management has made the conceptual shift in favour of portfolio management, the work has just begun. A number of years of development of systems and analytics probably lie ahead, along with a major requirement for consistent and repeated communication, education and encouragement – as well as significant organisational realignments. Here, let us assume that a bank has developed the basic technical infrastructure and has reached the point where it is looking at its ability to execute its portfolio management strategy from a market as well as an organisational perspective.

There are a number of possible strategies for striking a balance between:

❏ benefiting from relationship management and expertise in one's local markets, which tends to be associated with risk concentrations; and

❏ having a loan portfolio that is well-diversified and efficient from a risk-adjusted return perspective.

It is not necessary to be perfectly diversified. That is, not every portfolio has to be identical, as is the case with similarly defined index funds. Perhaps the most natural approach is to permit a core concentration in selected self-originated credits (while avoiding "break the bank" size exposures) in order to take maximum advantage of the bank's specific credit expertise and value-added loan origination activities, while moving forcefully to diversify the bulk of the portfolio.

Given a specific view about rebalancing the portfolio, the key requirement is liquidity. In light of the illiquid nature of much bank credit risk as described above, credit derivatives represent an elegant solution. With credit derivatives, it is possible to sell the economic risk of an underlying credit exposure in a manner that is unthreatening to the borrower, since ownership of the underlying asset is not transferred. Also, since credit derivatives do not involve exchanges of principal, they offer greater operational simplicity than loan sales that require principal to be exchanged. This is especially true for revolving credits, which can involve quite frequent borrowings and repayments. Finally, credit derivatives offer a means of liquefying credit risk that arises as a by-product of non-lending activities, such as pre-settlement risk arising from trading activities.

While credit derivatives provide a market-

PANEL 1

THE FULLY DEVELOPED LOAN PRODUCT FUNCTION

The figure below describes schematically how a fully developed loan product function might be deployed within a bank:

❑ Relationship manager (origination) identifies opportunity with prospective borrower.

❑ Loan product group responsible for loan structuring.

❑ Loans structured to clear the market per criteria of loan syndications.

❑ Loan is syndicated.

❑ Loan portfolio management is a potential buyer based on:

● Loan portfolio management's own interest.

● Loan portfolio management accommodating relationship management.

❑ If loan portfolio management accommodates relationship management on an illiquid deal, the transfer pricing group becomes involved.

❑ Portfolio management has exclusive responsibility for the portfolio on an ongoing basis; including full authority to purchase and sell non-originated assets.

Schematic view of fully developed loan product function

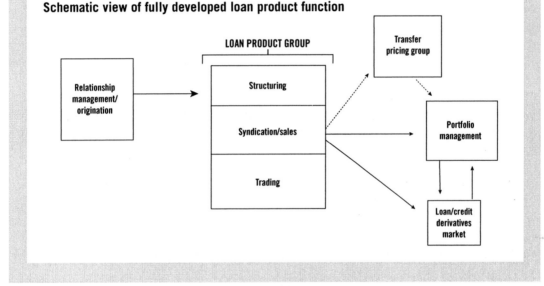

based solution to liquefying credit risk for banks, they can be employed effectively only if the appropriate organisational changes are made. At a minimum, focusing primarily on risk containment, lending officers can be held to some system of concentration limits for their individual borrowers. Ideally, limit sizes are directly related to both the riskiness of the borrowers and specific features of the credit facilities. If seriously enforced, this approach should naturally lead lenders to maximise the (risk-adjusted) return on their permitted balance sheet exposure for each client. Since the lenders' ability to do new business with their clients may be curtailed until they free-up balance sheet capacity, they have a strong incentive to sell credit exposure whether by selling loans outright or by employing credit derivatives. These asset sales increase the velocity of the bank's balance sheet. Assuming that the bank is able to retain some form of income in return for the credit risk that it sells, as compensation for its efforts (eg for trading or loan origination)

the higher balance-sheet turnover should result in a higher return per unit of retained exposure.

While the above approach can provide substantial benefits, it does not provide a framework for maximising the overall risk/return performance of the credit balance sheet. This latter objective requires a broader perspective than that which results from the sum of decentralised decisions by individual lending officers. In its fully developed form (Panel 1), a centralised portfolio management function is established with ultimate profit and loss responsibility for, and control of, the credit balance sheet. Loans are structured for sale by origination/product groups while the portfolio management group determines initial underwriting and hold positions, as well as subsequent portfolio sales. The portfolio management group buys loans from the origination group at relevant market-based transfer prices – including credit derivative market prices. (A separate transfer pricing group can be established to facilitate the process.)

Portfolio management not only has authority to approve/reject and sell credits that have been sourced by the origination group (with some means of accommodation for key borrower relationships), but also has authority to buy additional credits in the market, both in cash and derivative form, independent of relationship considerations. The credit purchasing authority of the portfolio management group is a function of the bank's overall goals with respect to revenue, capital, return, etc. An ideal arrangement is one in which the portfolio management group has authority not only to replace the exposures that it sells, but also to grow the credit portfolio incrementally.

The performance of the portfolio management group is measured as other true portfolio managers are measured, eg relative to market benchmarks and/or in terms of risk/return ratios and absolute return targets, within the constraint of allocated capital. This system has the potential to establish an equal balance of power between the portfolio management and relationship management functions. As with any balance of power, there will naturally be tensions, but if properly managed these tensions can be healthy.

This fully fledged credit portfolio management approach is not likely to be the first step taken by most banks as they move to implement a portfolio management approach. Given the current power imbalance in favour of origination over portfolio management (if such a function exists at all), it may well be more effective to employ a "back door" approach as an interim step on the path towards portfolio management rather than attempt a frontal assault on the entrenched control of origination. Such an interim step is described below.

In this interim approach, the portfolio arising from the activities of the origination group is referred to as the "core" portfolio. Portfolio management has authority to sell credits from the core portfolio in cash or credit derivative form. Origination retains a "shadow" long position in loans thus sold while portfolio management retains a "shadow" short position (Panel 2). While the shadow long and short positions are artificial MIS conveniences, the net position of the institution is properly captured. Since origination's measured income is not affected by portfolio management's sales of core exposure, origination should be at worst neutral to portfolio management's activities and may well be very supportive, since portfolio management's sales out of the core portfolio create capacity for origi-

nation to execute more business with its clients without sacrificing income attributed to origination.

It is critically important that portfolio management not only be responsible for managing risk but also be structured as a profit centre. Being responsible solely for activities that reduce absolute income is politically difficult. Portfolio management therefore must have authority to reinvest the proceeds of asset sales, whether in cash or derivative form. Given the tracking of the shadow long and short positions, portfolio management can readily be measured on its incremental contribution to (risk-adjusted) income and return.

Investment fund perspective

Credit derivatives tend to play a very different role for investment funds that specialise in corporate loan investing than they do for most commercial banks. This is a function of the differing business objectives of banks and loan funds. A generic statement of the business strategy of loan investment funds might be that they seek to maximise assets under management and investment advisory fee income by:
❑ designing investment programmes that meet investor needs; and
❑ maximising the long-term return/risk of portfolios within their investment guidelines.

INVESTMENT APPLICATIONS
With respect to asset purchases, credit derivatives offer many potential advantages. It may be possible to purchase credit exposure to a particular issuer in derivative form on better economic terms than in the cash market. This could arise, for example, when a bank seeks to reduce its pre-settlement risk exposure to a major investment grade trading counterparty. The bank's only tool for reducing this exposure is probably the credit derivatives market. Given the relative immaturity/thinness of the market, it may well be that the buyer can achieve better execution than by buying a bond of the same issuer. Stated more generally, in combination with the cash market the credit derivatives market creates arbitrage opportunities for trading in the credit risk of a specific issuer.

Credit derivatives can also help to expand the range of a fund's investment universe. For example, if a particular fund's investment objectives effectively set a minimum Libor spread standard for individual loan purchases then lower spread assets are not likely to be of interest. However, a

PANEL 2

INTERIM APPROACH TO PORTFOLIO MANAGEMENT: AN EXAMPLE

In the figure below we present an example transaction to help clarify how an interim approach to portfolio management might work:

❑ Origination holds a $50 million loan in the core portfolio generating a 2% spread above funding cost ($1 million per year in net revenue).

❑ Portfolio Management executes a sale of the loan into the market (eg at the carrying cost of the loan).

❑ Origination is credited with retention of the loan.

❑ Portfolio Management pays Origination funding cost plus the $1 million per year net revenue ("shadow income").

❑ Portfolio Management records a short position in the asset and receives a credit for eliminating the funding cost.

❑ Portfolio Management reinvests the proceeds of the loan sale in a new $50 million loan of comparable risk that earns 2.25% above funding cost and receives credit for the earnings ($1.125 million per year).

❑ Portfolio Management has created $125,000 per year in value on a risk-adjusted basis without increasing the bank's balance sheet.

❑ Relationship Management maintains its revenue, preserves its customer relationship and increases its capacity to do new business.

Schematic view of sale and purchase MIS

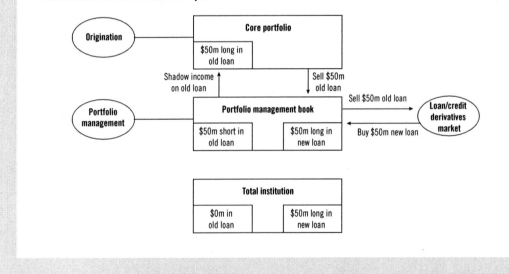

credit derivative such as a first-loss position in the individual asset can be used to leverage a position in a lower-spread asset, thus bringing its leveraged spread up to the fund's target range (Table 1).

Assume that a term loan exists in the market that provides a spread of 125 basis points over Libor, and which is rated BB+. This spread may be too low for an investor with perhaps a "Libor plus 250bp" target, while the rating may be too low for another investor who is limited to investment grade assets. By reapportioning the risk and return, both investors obtain an attractive asset that would otherwise be unavailable. In our example in Table 1, the more aggressive investor agrees to take the full risk of the first 40% loss on the asset in the event of a default. This position

Table 1. Analysis of spread split between first and second loss position

Assumptions

Underlying coupon (in excess of Libor)	125bps
Upfront fees for market purchase	25bps
Average life	2.0 years
First loss position	40%
First loss coupon and fee multiple	2.00

Results

	Total	1st loss	2nd loss
Loan principal	$50,000,000	$20,000,000	$30,000,000
Coupon income	$625,000	$500,000	$125,000
Upfront fee:			
per annum amortisation	$62,500	$25,000	$37,500
Total income	$687,500	$525,000	$162,500
All-in spread	1.38%	2.63%	0.54%
Coupon income	1.25%	2.50%	0.42%

might be rated BB– or B+. The more risk-averse investor holds a position that might be rated perhaps BBB. The first loss provider receives a multiple of the underlying spread on his position while the second loss provider receives a spread that is lower than that of the underlying loan.

If the underlying loan has sufficient spread on a risk-adjusted basis, the result should be that both parties end up with attractively priced assets relative to comparably rated loans available in the cash market. In addition, if the underlying asset is a term loan then the second loss provider ends up with a fully funded BBB synthetic loan, which is a rarity in the cash market for loans. The risk analysis hinges on the probability of default as well as potential loss in the event of default. The latter is best analysed not only in terms of an expected value but also with some thought as to the potential range of values.

Alternatively, leverage can also be created by combining individual lower-spread assets in a first-default loss basket, again amplifying the spread available relative to that of any individual underlying asset. A first-default loss basket trade can be helpful not only as a way of packaging loans viewed as particularly desirable, but also as a means of efficiently packaging loans that might be viewed as a "by-product" of other purchases. For example, most loan fund managers prefer buying term loans rather than partially unfunded revolving credits. Yet often it is necessary to purchase revolving credits and term loans on a pro-rata basis. One solution is to find a balance-sheet provider willing to combine in a basket a number of revolving credits selected by the fund man-

ager, and then sell the first-default risk to the fund. This simplifies the fund's cash management activities (the fund is not subject to potential daily cash funding requirements) and provides leverage, which creates a potentially attractive absolute return.

The resultant return can be quite attractive, as seen in Table 2a. The table illustrates an instance in which the revolvers are at least partially utilised (this is normally the case for revolving credits extended to non-investment grade companies). If the revolvers are totally unused, the returns can be thin even with a basket trade, as demonstrated in Table 2b. The return modelling is similar in many ways to that performed when bifurcating a single asset into first and second loss positions. However, the risk analysis, which is not addressed here, is more complex since it includes consideration of the potential default correlations between the assets in the first-default loss basket.

The discussion above regarding the creation of additional leverage by means of credit derivatives applies equally in reverse. In situations where an asset is riskier than the fund's normal criteria, a derivative structure can be used to bring into the transaction an investor with a higher risk tolerance who is interested in taking a first loss position while the fund takes a second loss position.

Bank regulatory capital rules do create some problems when non-banks wish to purchase credit exposure from banks in the form of total return swaps and first default positions. Since there is no initial exchange of principal, banks

---

Table 2a. Example of revolver fee and spread split between first and second loss position: partially funded loans

Assumptions

Number of revolvers in basket (equal sized)	3
Weighted average commitment fee	50bps
Weighted average drawn spread	250bps
Weighted average upfront fee	50bps
Weighted average usage rate	40%
Average life	2.0 years
First loss position	33%
First loss coupon and fee multiple	2.50

Results

	Total	1st loss	2nd loss
Aggregate commitment			
amount in basket	$50,000,000	$16,666,667	$33,333,333
Commitment fee income	$150,000	$125,000	$25,000
Spread income	$500,500	$416,667	$83,333
Upfront fee:			
per annum amortisation	$125,000	$41,667	$83,333
Total income	$775,000	$583,333	$191,667
All-in return	1.55%	3.50%	0.58%

Table 2b. Example of revolver fee and spread split between first and second loss position: unfunded loans

Assumptions

Number of revolvers in basket (equal sized)	3
Weighted average commitment fee	50bps
Weighted average drawn spread	250bps
Weighted average upfront fee	50bps
Weighted average usage rate	0%
Average life	2.0 years
First loss position	33%
First loss coupon and fee multiple	2.50

Results

	Total	1st loss	2nd loss
Aggregate commitment			
amount in basket	$50,000,000	$16,666,667	$33,333,333
Commitment fee income	$250,000	$208,333	$41,667
Spread income	–	–	–
Upfront fee:			
per annum amortisation	$125,000	$41,667	$83,333
Total income	$375,000	$250,000	$125,000
All-in return	0.75%	1.50%	0.38%

incur counterparty risk when selling credit risk in derivative form. If the credit buyer is a non-bank, bank regulatory capital rules do not provide the selling bank with any capital relief. One remedy to this problem is for the credit purchaser to provide cash margin dollar-for-dollar against the nominal contract size, which eliminates the potential for certain forms of leverage (such potential is not eliminated in some instances, eg a first-loss structure). Alternatively, the transaction can be structured as a loan participation, which is similar to a total return swap although principal does change hands.

Funding applications

Senior secured corporate bank loans continue to gain wider recognition as an attractive asset class, offering low volatility floating-rate returns of Libor plus 250 basis points or more while preserving principal. There are classes of investors who find these fundamentals appealing, but in general seek higher absolute returns. It is possible to meet these investors' objectives by incorporating financial leverage in a senior secured corporate bank loan investment programme. This leverage can be provided in a number of ways: collateralised loan obligations, which are loan securitisation vehicles, are financed by issuing various tranches of securities and can offer investors in the bottom tranche leverage in the order of 10:1; similarly, it is possible to leverage a loan portfolio by means of a bank credit line.

In the investment application section, we discussed the use of credit derivatives to create leverage in order to increase the absolute return of a lower yielding but fundamentally attractive asset up to a threshold minimum level. The potential for creating leverage by purchasing credit risk in derivative form can be used systematically as the basis for financing an entire investment programme. This can be achieved one asset at a time. Conversely, rather than negotiate the implicit financing terms of each swap with the credit seller, the fund manager can arrange for a balance-sheet provider to finance each purchase as part of a committed (or uncommitted) credit line.

Though credit derivatives have interesting applications for financing bank loan investment programmes for investors seeking high returns, there is also the separate question of the legal form of the investment held by the end investor. Thus, regardless of how an investment programme achieves leverage for its asset purchases, if it does so at all, an end investor may wish to hold its investment in some form other than that offered directly. In effect, the character and/or leverage of the investment programme can be transformed on a customised basis for an individual investor by means of further structuring outside of the investment programme itself.

For example, a loan investment programme may be offered to investors in the form of an equity investment in a special purpose vehicle. A particular investor, perhaps to comply with regulatory, legal, tax or its own prospectus requirements, may prefer to receive the economics of its fund investment in the form of a credit-linked note or total return swap. This offers the investor the further opportunity to adjust the overall leverage of its position. For example, if an investor owns a position in a fund with 5:1 leverage but prefers 10:1 leverage, the additional leverage can be achieved by adding a separate layer of leverage outside the loan investment programme (eg by means of a total return swap with 50% margin). This situation is illustrated in Tables 3a–b.

Table 3a. Use of swap as supplemental financing source for loan fund investment ($000)

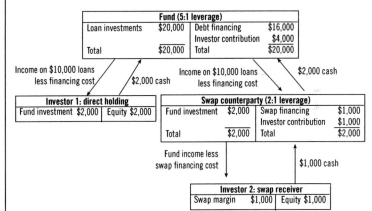

Table 3b. Use of swap as supplemental financing source for loan fund investment ($000)

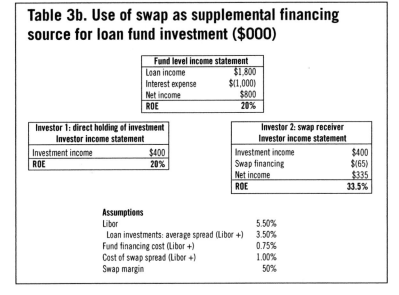

Risks

Credit derivatives pose some additional risks beyond those inherent in the underlying assets. The most obvious risk pertains to the increased leverage and resultant volatility made possible by investing in credit derivative contracts. The leverage can be simple in form, as with a straight total return or credit default swap executed with a stated cash margin. More complex is a first-loss position in a single asset where, as discussed above, in addition to understanding the probability of default, it is necessary to understand the distribution of potential recovery values in the event of a default in order to fully understand the economic risk that is being assumed. Also more complex is a credit swap that involves taking the loss on the first-to-default of a basket of loans; here, understanding default correlations is crucial.

The risk of increased leverage is related to other issues. For example, it highlights the need to ensure that any credit derivatives that are purchased are consistent in letter and spirit with the credit policies of a bank or the investment guidelines of a fund. Credit derivatives have many use-ful and legitimate applications, but they also create the potential for abuse through the taking on of inappropriate amounts of leverage in disguised form.

In addition, the leverage and potential complexity of credit derivatives elevate the need to perform a careful economic analysis of the required return. Fortunately, this follows naturally from properly understanding the risk inherent in the structure.

Finally, given the early stage of market development for credit derivatives, secondary liquidity is limited. To the extent that secondary liquidity does develop, it would seem likely to develop more slowly for more complex instruments such as basket trades, where a potential secondary buyer must be comfortable with the inclusion of each name in the basket. This contrasts, for example, with a total return swap on a single underlying issue. Apart from secondary market liquidity, however, it is possible to structure the credit derivative transaction itself so that the buyer and/or seller have early termination rights.

---

1 *Throughout this chapter, references to credit derivatives are intended to include total return trades (either as swaps or embedded in notes) as well as purely default-based structures.*

Total Return Swaps

Jessica James and Phyllis Thomas
First Chicago NBD

Total return swaps are proving to be one of the most important types of credit derivative, and a key link between the investment and risk management sectors of the market. Although exact volumes are difficult to estimate, it is clear that the nascent credit derivatives market is dominated by two types of transaction: default swaps and total return swaps.

In this chapter, we first define a total return swap and explain how the combination of market and credit risk in these instruments sets them apart from other financial contracts (Panel 1). We introduce readers to the theory that lies behind sophisticated attempts to price total return swaps, and make plain the practical steps that most investors need to take to ascertain "fair value", when this is possible. Risk managing new types of instrument is always problematic, and we conclude with an extended illustrative example that points up some of the credit and operational risk pitfalls that await the unwary investor.

What is a total return swap?

It is possible to divide modern credit derivatives into two classes: insurance instruments such as default swaps, and exchange instruments that enable investors to obtain tailored exposures. Total return swaps fall into the second category, being more similar to traditional swaps than other credit derivatives. (It is also possible to construct hybrid instruments that have characteristics of both insurance and exchange instruments.)

A total return swap enables an institution to acquire the cashflows that would originate from selling or buying a bond or other financial instrument, without having to sell or buy the instrument physically. Bank A might hold a definite opinion that Bond X is seriously overvalued in the market because, in the opinion of Bank A, the company that issued the bond is more likely to default than the market appears to allow in its pricing of the bond. However, Bank A cannot monetise this opinion, because Bond X is not liquid enough to be easily shorted in the market.

There are many other reasons why Bank A might not be able to short Bond X, including tax constraints and "political" concerns. Perhaps the bond is the debt of an important client who would be offended that Bank A wishes to sell.

Given this situation, a total return swap appears to hold the answer. Let us say that Bank B sells a total return swap to Bank A (Figure 1). Bank B is known as the receiver in the swap, and Bank A is the payer. Bond X is known as the reference asset. Bank A agrees to pay the total positive return on a notional amount of the reference asset to Bank B. The total return in this case means all interest, dividend and fee payments, plus any increase in market value. In return, Bank B will pay Bank A an interest rate on the notional amount, usually equal to Libor, plus a spread, plus any fall in value of the notional amount of the bond (ie, if the value of the bond falls by 10 basis points, Bank B will pay Bank A 10bp). The interest rate is known as the reference rate.

What is the overall result? Bank A, which wanted to sell the bond, is now in exactly the situation it wanted. The cashflows that it receives and pays net out to exactly those that would have been generated by selling the bond and investing the proceeds at Libor. Bank B, on the other hand, now has cashflows consistent with owning the notional amount of Bond X; it may hedge or warehouse these cashflows. Possibly it wished to gain exposure to Bond X because it does not

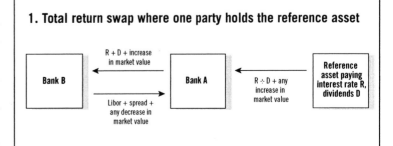

1. Total return swap where one party holds the reference asset

TOTAL RETURN SWAPS VERSUS DEFAULT SWAPS: A COMPARISON

Although default swaps are not the major subject of this chapter, it is worth discussing them, as they probably share the honours with the total return swap as the most frequently used credit derivatives. Default swaps are also confusingly known as credit swaps, default options or default puts. A default swap is, in its simplest form, simply an insurance agreement. For example, suppose that we held a large quantity of Italian government bonds (BTPs) and that we were concerned that the Italian government might default on its debt. We can purchase a default swap which, in the event of default, will pay us a predefined sum, in a previously specified currency. The sum will have been decided on the basis of the likelihood of recovery of any part of the debt, and the premium that we pay for the protection will be determined by the perceived likelihood of default by the Italian government. This type of simple default swap is illustrated in the figure below.

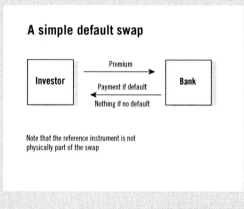

A simple default swap

Note that the reference instrument is not physically part of the swap

It has been possible to insure against default for some time, which makes the growth of the default swap market something of a surprise. However, making an insurance claim is a lengthy business, and the insurance company may decide that in the event the claim will not be upheld. A default swap is far more efficient; if a predefined default event occurs, then an agreed amount is paid, with no fuss. Thus they are preferred in many cases.

One problem with this type of deal is how to agree upon what constitutes default. If the Italian government defaulted upon one type of debt, but not all of its debts, should the payment be triggered? Careful definition of the default event is needed. This becomes even more important when it is a "credit event" such as a re-rating, rather than an actual default, that is the trigger for the payment.

Default swaps and total return swaps are very different animals. The value of a default swap is determined largely or completely by the probability of default (or a credit event). This default may or may not happen by a specified time, and thus the payoff of the instrument is determined by a single event. In contrast, a total return swap offers total economic exposure to an instrument, including the market risk: its value is dependent upon a continuously changing variable. Default swaps are usually entered into for insurance reasons, while total return swaps have a wider range of applicability.

share Bank A's belief that the bond is overvalued.

Of course, total return swaps are useful for many reasons other than reducing exposure to assets that are perceived as overvalued. It might well be that an investor wishes to gain exposure to a risky but high-yielding asset, for example a Czech Republic bond. However, the investor may be forbidden from purchasing the bond itself, or the bond may be unavailable in the market. As the receiver (rather than the payer) in a total return swap, the investor can gain this exposure in any desired amount.

There are several variants on this simple theme. The reference asset need not be a bond, but might instead be a loan basket, a collection of debt or equity securities or, in theory, any

other financial instrument; the precise terms of the swap can vary as well.

Why have total return swaps evolved?

Like all financial innovations, credit derivatives were the answer to a market need. The need originated in the increasingly sophisticated techniques used to manage portfolios. The total risk of loss on any portfolio has two components: market and default risk. Both market and default risk have probability distributions, and combine to produce a total risk of loss distribution. The characteristics of the distributions are shown in Figure 2. The uncertainty about future values is derived from the width of the loss distributions.

Any such portfolio of risky assets needs to be

assigned capital to support possible losses due to default; if the width of the total loss distribution is large, then the capital required is also relatively large. To make efficient use of capital, the width of the loss distribution needs to be made as small as possible.

Careful hedging can reduce the width of the market risk distribution, but until recently little could be done to reduce the contribution to the risk of loss distribution that came from the default distribution, apart from diversifying the portfolio by adding new credits. With the advent of credit derivatives, however, for the first time credit risk could be hedged rather than diversified, enabling the default risk distribution to be manipulated as well as that of market risk. This is an incredibly powerful new tool for portfolio management.

Total return swaps, as opposed to credit derivatives in general, evolved to allow investors to take long or short positions on the total risk (market + default risk) of a huge range of instruments, without actually dealing in the instruments themselves. There are many reasons why an investor might wish to do this:

❑ The market in the reference asset may be illiquid.

❑ There may be accounting, tax or legal reasons why the investor should or should not hold the asset, even though there is a financial advantage that makes a short or long position desirable.

❑ The investor may desire a customised exposure which can be constructed by referencing available assets.

❑ The investor may want to engineer a high degree of leverage.

Pricing total return swaps

PRICING THEORY
Pricing a total return swap is beset with all the same problems and complexities as the pricing of credit derivatives in general. The first question that arises is, "Can we use risk-neutral pricing?" The essence of risk-neutral pricing is that investors are indifferent to how much risk they accept as long as the probable return on the deal is appropriate. Thus an investor is equally happy to enter into a low risk investment with a low return or a high risk investment with a suitably higher return. In fact, an additional factor due to the "price of risk" also needs to be included, but risk-neutral pricing provides the foundation.

However, while it may be reasonable to apply risk-neutral pricing in well-established markets,

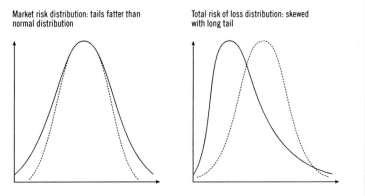

2. Characteristics of market and total risk of loss distribution

Market risk distribution: tails fatter than normal distribution

Total risk of loss distribution: skewed with long tail

where all instruments are regularly purchased and sold, it is not at all certain that risk-neutral pricing will apply in the world of credit derivatives (particularly while the market is young). After all, the main reason that most early credit derivatives were executed was because portfolio managers were averse to the credit risk that they held in their portfolios. A significant bar to the development of the market has been the fact that people are far keener on buying protection than selling it!

However, as the market slowly grows, it becomes apparent that the other side of the coin, which may provide overall risk neutrality, is the fact that investors desire exposure to high-yield assets. While it is not yet certain, it seems possible that risk-neutral pricing methods may be correct for credit derivatives once the market has matured.

The next problem is default probabilities. If we agree that risk neutral pricing is the way to go, then we need to discover the distributions of both market and default risk to price a total return swap correctly. The distribution of market risk is similar to a normal distribution, but with fatter tails. There is plenty of data available that can be used to determine market risk distributions, although it is always necessary to make a judgement about how relevant this data is. The default distribution of a single counterparty is very skewed, as there is a high probability of no default and a low probability of some degree of default. If defaults were uncorrelated, this skew would not matter, because as long as there were plenty of different credits in the portfolio then the central limit theorem would apply and the overall distribution for the risk of loss would be similar to a normal distribution. However, there is a small but significant correlation between defaults, and this means that the risk of loss distribution inherits a lot of the skewness that origi-

PANEL 2

WHO ENTERS INTO TOTAL RETURN SWAPS – AND WHY?

We can divide those institutions that wish to enter into total return swap into two classes: those that are total return receivers (asset sellers) and those that are total return payers (asset receivers).

The asset seller acquires a synthetic, off-balance sheet instrument that does not require funding. The swap replicates the performance of the asset, and moreover the asset seller may choose the degree of leverage. While a collateralised loan duplicates some of these features, a total return swap is frequently simpler, more flexible and has smaller transaction costs. Also, the asset seller gains access to assets and financing in markets that might otherwise be unavailable. There may be additional tax and accounting benefits.

Thus asset sellers (Total return receivers, Libor + spread payers) are desirous of financing an asset. They might include:

❏ Large corporations
❏ Insurance companies
❏ Mutual funds/pension funds
❏ Banks (regional and international)
❏ Securities companies
❏ Leveraged investment funds
❏ High net worth individuals
❏ Government agencies

The asset buyer, or total return payer, will enjoy far more favourable BIS capital treatment for a total return swap than they would for a loan. Also, the spreads above Libor that they will receive are better than those available for traditional asset swaps, FRNs etc. A total return swap can provide a hedge for an exposure in a particular asset or basket of assets, or the buyer can obtain identical exposures to those from shorting an asset (which may itself be impossible). Again, almost any degree of leverage may be chosen.

Thus asset buyers are using their balance sheet to achieve above-Libor returns. They include:

❏ International banks
❏ Institutional money managers
❏ Insurance companies
❏ Large corporations

---

nated with the default distribution of a single counterparty.

This skewed distribution is not of itself a problem, if we had sufficient default data to construct it. However, default data is difficult to obtain and very sparse when it is found, due to the small number of defaults that have occurred historically. Due to this small quantity of data, it becomes necessary to model defaults. There are two popular methods of doing this:

❏ Assuming that the credit spreads seen in the marketplace provide a good indication of default likelihood and modelling them.

❏ Assuming that credit ratings live up to their claims, and are closely related to default probabilities and modelling them.

The first of these alternatives, modelling credit spreads, is popular because credit spreads are observable market parameters that change in response to events that might be supposed to affect the probability of default. A credit spread for a company bond is the difference between the value of the bond and the value of a default-free bond of the same maturity in the same currency – usually taken to be a government bond. The credit spread method is the one preferred by academics, and a considerable amount of research has been devoted to extracting the probability of default from credit spreads so as to allow the pricing of credit derivatives (see technical discussion in Chapter 10).

However, all of this theory relies upon the assumption that the credit spread is only affected by the probability of default of the company. In practice, a number of other variables - such as supply and demand, and tax issues - also affect credit spreads. What happens when we apply the theory to estimate the cost of default risk? The credit spread between corporate bonds and government debt in the interest rate swaps markets seems to be about 2 or 3 basis points, which is consistent with market prices. But for cross currency swaps, the same theory suggests that spreads should be in the order of 20bp, which is very much larger than the spreads observed from market prices. If these calculated spread values were correct then the seller of the swap would have to pass them on to the buyer to cover the default risk, so the only conclusions that it is possible to come to are that:

❏ Currency swaps are being bought and sold with far too small a bid-offer spread; or

❏ The spread values given by the theory are not

KEY ISSUES WHEN CALCULATING THE EXPECTED LOSS COMPONENT OF CREDIT DERIVATIVE PRICING

The exposure that an institution may have to a derivative depends upon the probability of default by the counterparty, and the possible loss in the event of default. It is obvious that these two quantities are not unconnected – very large positions can lead directly to credit events. An example is the fall of Barings, where huge unhedged positions on the Nikkei led directly to the bank's demise. The following equation describes a situation in which these quantities may be correlated:

Expected loss = $E[D \times V] = E[D]E[V] + \text{cov}(D,V)$ (1)

Here D is 1 if default occurs, and 0 if not. V is the present value of the exposure at time T, after any recovery of losses.

However, most useful theories disregard this connection and assume that the default probability and the loss in the event of default are uncorrelated. If this assumption is made, then (1) simplifies to

$$E[D \times V] = p(T)E[V(T)]$$

Here p(T) is the probability of default at time T. If we assume that the expected loss will be equal to the difference in value between a credit-risky bond and a similar risk-free bond, then we can say

$$p(T) = (V_1 - V_2)/(V_2{}^*f)$$

where V_1 is the value of the risk-free bond, V_2 is the value of the credit-risky bond, and f is the percentage of the value of the bond that would be recovered after default. This equation is only true for the simple case of a single period T, but may easily be extended

One last point of interest is the relationship of credit risk exposure to a derivative and the value of that derivative. This is one of the ways in which the differences between loans and derivatives become sharply apparent. If we lend a sum of money to a client, our exposure is the whole of the loan, less any recovered amount. However, if we sell a derivative to a client, the value of the derivative may be positive, negative or zero. Only if the client owes us money at the time of default will we have any exposure. If we owe him money and he defaults, then we experience no loss. This exposure profile looks very like the payoff from an option, as illustrated below.

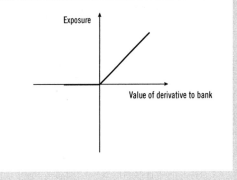

correct, probably because credit spreads are affected by factors other than the probability of default.

The other way of modelling default is to model credit ratings. The useful feature of ratings is that there is a reasonable amount of upgrade and downgrade data available, compared with very little data on actual default. It is possible to model rating lifetimes, rating momentum and many other ratings features. Default is possible at any stage, but an investment grade company is far more likely to downgrade prior to default than to default while it is still classed as investment grade.

While this is quite a rich area in which to build models, it is only reasonable to do so if ratings are indeed directly related to default probabilities. Rating agencies devote many man-years of research to ensuring that this is the case, and yet it may not be quite true. There is a "lag" effect, whereby ratings only change some time after it seems appropriate for them to do so. A recent example is the Korean crisis, where institutions were sharply downgraded only after the crisis struck. In some cases, there were defaults before a downgrade took place. However, credit ratings may be used as estimates of default probability, and are certainly better than nothing.

Some other interesting issues in calculating the expected loss component of credit derivatives are outlined in Panel 3. It is worth mentioning that most of the problems encountered in the pricing of total return swaps are due to the "credit" or default part of the instruments. The market risk of the underlying asset in a total return swap is a more familiar, and better understood, problem.

IS PRICING THEORY USED IN PRACTICE?
At the time of writing, a few brave institutions

are using theories such as those outlined above to price and warehouse total return swaps and other credit derivatives. However, the majority of institutions that deal in credit derivatives operate on the time-honoured principle of "we do it where we can hedge it". Let us illustrate this robust, if somewhat limiting, approach with an example of a total return swap.

Imagine that a bank has a potential counterparty that wishes to gain exposure to a particular reference asset without actually buying it; the bank suggests a total return swap according to which it pays the counterparty the total returns (interest, dividends and any increases in value), and the counterparty pays to the bank any reduction in value. The bank can put in place a perfect hedge for this contract by simply holding the reference asset. If this is feasible, then it is ideal. A variation would be to purchase an option to buy the asset, and include the cost of the option in the price of the credit derivative. A bank that sticks to this kind of policy when dealing in credit derivatives will always be fully hedged, but will be limited in the number and type of derivatives it can enter into.

FAIR VALUING TOTAL RETURN SWAPS

Theoretical discussions do not, unfortunately, give an investor much idea of whether the price that he is being quoted is correct. Although this is an inevitable problem in a new market, there are a few steps that a cautious investor can take to reduce the chance of buying a total return swap at a poor price. These are:

❑ Estimate the expected price of a collateralised loan. It will almost certainly give a different result, but may in some circumstances provide a "ballpark" estimate (see also discussion below).

❑ Do some calculations based on your own estimates of default probabilities, possibly making use of Moody's and Standard & Poor's default probability matrices.

❑ Most important – call around! If an investor is uncertain about whether he has a fair price, the best and most efficient way to check is to ask other banks for similar quotes.

These steps may not always be possible, particularly when a tailored transaction is being constructed. However, in these circumstances it is expected that some charge will be made by the bank for the amount of work involved.

Real live total return swaps

MARKET EXAMPLE OF A TOTAL RETURN SWAP

The example that follows outlines the definition and structure of a total return swap that might indeed be sold by a bank to a customer. We illustrate the cashflows that would occur in this type of transaction in Figures 3–5. These show the three stages of the structure: the initial asset purchase, the swap and the asset sale.

Different institutions may have slightly different methodologies, but the details we give here are an accurate representation of how such a transaction might be structured in practice. We assume that the bank prefers to hold the reference asset as a hedge, thus bypassing any problems with pricing theory.

We refer to the seller of the total return swap as "the Bank" and to the purchaser as "the Customer". Also, two subsidiaries, the Bank Funding Corporation and Bank Hedging Services, are involved in the transaction.

❑ The basic total return swap is a transaction which transfers the risk and return of holding an investment asset from one party's balance sheet to another:

■ In the standard transaction, the bank buys the reference asset or pool of assets from the customer or market, and Bank Hedging Services holds the asset(s) as a hedge on its balance sheet (Figure 3). Alternatively, the bank may enter into an offsetting swap with another customer to move the asset off balance sheet.

■ The customer pays Libor plus a spread to the bank.

■ The customer receives the total return on the reference asset, ie price change plus interest or dividends, depending upon the nature of the asset.

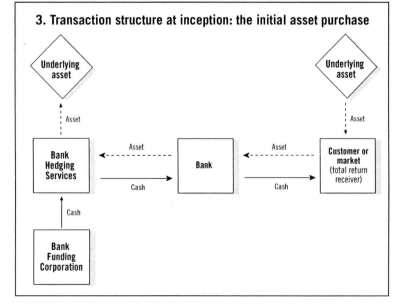

3. Transaction structure at inception: the initial asset purchase

■ At each reset date (which may be weekly, quarterly or monthly) the customer and the bank exchange net payments (Figure 4). The net payment is the difference between [total return on assets] and [Libor + spread]. The bank pays the total return if it is positive and receives it if it is negative.

■ At the end of the total return swap transaction, the bank sells the reference asset at current market rates, but the counterparty has "last look" – ie the right to purchase the asset at its highest market bid price. The total return swap terminal net payment is based on the final sale/purchase price (Figure 5). The asset is removed from the bank balance sheets, and any collateral is released.

❑ The total return swap transaction described above is likely to be documented as up to three separate trades: two asset purchase or sale transactions, and one swap transaction.

■ Initial asset purchase for cash (Figure 3).

■ Swap to exchange total return of reference asset for Libor plus a spread (Figure 4).

■ Final reference asset sale for cash (Figure 5).

■ The asset purchase and final asset sale are executed and confirmed as standard buy and sell transactions.

■ The exchange of total return on the asset for Libor plus a spread is executed as a swap transaction under ISDA.

❑ Total return swaps are most often used for off-balance-sheet financing of securities by the party that owns and initially sells the asset:

■ The Bank finances the asset for the total return receiver in return for a spread above Libor.

■ Alternatively, the total return swap can be used by an investor to create a synthetic asset position in the underlying reference asset.

Total return swaps versus collateralised loans

A total return swap is often compared to a loan collateralised with the underlying asset. They are economically very similar, as a total return swap provides full exposure to the reference asset. However, the various differences between a total return swap and a collateralised loan mean that total return swaps are preferred in a number of situations, both by those who sell them and

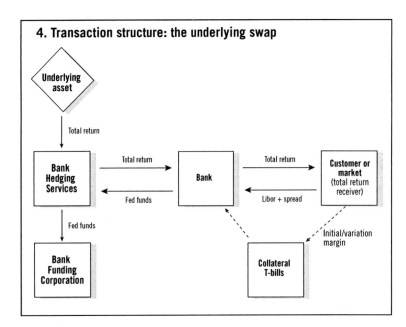

4. Transaction structure: the underlying swap

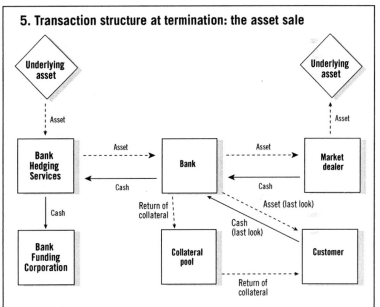

5. Transaction structure at termination: the asset sale

those who purchase them. We list the important differences below:

❑ *Claim of one counterparty upon the other* In the case of a loan, a claim would be made upon the full principal amount of the loan, plus any accrued interest. For a total return swap, the amount involved in any claim would only be the net difference between the total return and Libor plus a spread, in any single period. The amount resets to zero at each reset date (weekly, monthly or quarterly).

❑ *Loan-equivalent credit risk* In the case of a loan, the whole principal amount is subject to credit risk, whereas in a total return swap, the credit risk is only on the exposure of the notional amount. This exposure has a large range but is usually from 1% to 50% of the notional. Only in very rare deal structures such as long-term zero-coupon deals will the exposure approach 100% of the notional amount. This is one of the important differences between loan credit risk and derivative credit risk.

❑ *Capital allocation* Because of the difference in credit risk, the capital allocation is very different. Capital must be allocated to cover the risk of default on 100% of the loan, but only on the exposure amount of the total return swap.

❑ *Return on equity* Because much less capital needs to be allocated to a total return swap than to a loan, and yet spreads are similar, ROE is much higher for a total return swap.

❑ *Costs* The costs of a loan will be due to administrative factors, product cost factors and a factor proportional to the size of the principal amount of the loan. For a total return swap, while the first two costs may be comparable, the third will only be proportional to the exposure of the loan.

❑ *Balance-sheet treatment* In the case of a loan, the whole of the loan asset will be maintained on the lender's balance sheet. For a total return swap, the hedging asset will be held on the balance sheet of a holding company, or may be matched by a reverse total return swap.

❑ *BIS risk-adjusted capital of asset* For a secured loan, this will be 8% of the principal amount. For a total return swap, it is less than 1% of the notional amount (post 1997).

❑ *Legal documentation* A collateralised loan requires a loan agreement, with a collateral pledge on the underlying assets. A total return swap is likely to be based on an ISDA agreement with a credit support annex describing initial and variation margin of liquid collateral.

❑ *Recourse to underlying assets in the event of bankruptcy* In the case of a loan, in the event of bankruptcy, assets are subject to an automatic stay, or period of time when no-one may take possession of them until various legal procedures have been gone through. Counterparties of the bankrupt party need to apply to the bankruptcy court for permission to take possession of the collateral, but they risk delay and may even be denied access to the collateral if the court decides that another party has a superior claim. In the case of a total return swap, the hedged counterparty can simply sell the reference asset that it held as a hedge against the swap, and the swap itself can be closed out without delay. There is also immediate access to variation and margin collateral.

❑ *Initial margin* This is a cash amount which is calculated as a safety margin. In the event of default, closing out a deal may take a few working days, in which time the value of the assets may well have changed. The initial margin is designed to cover this risk. For a loan, the initial margin is usually a pledge of more than 100% of the underlying asset, and this is subject to all the problems mentioned in the previous point. For a total return swap, the initial margin is posted, usually in the form of US treasury bills, and there is no automatic stay.

❑ *Variation margin* In the case of a total return swap, the mark-to-market value of the swap will vary, and will only be refixed to zero at the reset dates. In the interim, an amount equal to the mark-to-market of the swap may be posted daily in the form of Treasury bills. In the case of a loan, there is no provision for variation margin.

❑ *Leverage* In the case of a loan there is only one way of increasing exposure: lending more money. Consider a bank which lends money at a high rate of interest to a company that does not seem financially secure. The bank has a view that the company will do well and would like to lend it more money (and thus receive more interest at the high rate). Naturally, however, the company only requires loans up to a certain amount. By contrast, in the case of a total return swap, the degree of leverage can be anything within reason. For example, if the bank wished to acquire the cashflows that would result from shorting a particular illiquid bond, it could use a total return swap to short a lot more of the bond than ever was available in the market.

Types of reference asset

So far in this chapter, despite continuous use of the term "reference assets", exactly what kind of assets can be used in total return swaps has been left to the reader's imagination. To end the suspense, we here list the types of reference asset that are commonly used in the market. This is by no means comprehensive – the variety of assets which in theory may be used is huge – but it does provide a representative sample.

❑ Sovereign government bonds
❑ Corporate debt
❑ Investment grade corporates
❑ Sub-investment grade corporates
❑ Eurobonds
❑ Trade finance paper
❑ Convertibles
❑ Asset-backed securities
❑ Syndicated bank loans
❑ Equities and warrants (both single stocks and baskets)
❑ Company equities

- ❏ Closed-end funds
- ❏ Warrants
- ❏ Restricted stocks
- ❏ Brady bonds
- ❏ Mortgages/CMOs

Advantages and risks

HOW TOTAL RETURN SWAPS CAN INCREASE
EFFICIENCY

Most of the useful features of total return swap have by now been mentioned, as summarised in Table 1, but it is worth noting that total return swaps and other credit derivatives provide links between three previously separate markets: the bank loan market, the corporate bond market and the equity market. Without the link, the price placed upon credit risk in each of these markets will not necessarily be the same. Now that credit derivatives have "completed" the market in this way, it seems likely that there will be a standardisation of the value of credit risk, much like the standardisation of option pricing that was introduced by risk-neutral pricing and the Black–Scholes equation.

Market, credit and operational risks of total return swaps

In this section, we first briefly describe some of the special risks that arise when institutions begin to use credit derivatives, and then present a more detailed example of how things can go wrong. Key classes of risk include:

❏ *Market risk* Only the total return receiver has any market risk with a total return swap. The danger here is that the asset may under-perform so that the total return will not on average be equal to the "Libor plus a spread" payments. It is possible to hedge this risk away with an offsetting position, however. Also, the total return receiver takes issuer risk on the dividends, principal and coupons of the reference asset. Thus if the reference asset is a company bond and the company defaults, the total return receiver will lose out.

The total return payer, on the other hand, has no issuer risk and no market risk, as long as the counterparty does not default. This default risk is reduced by the frequent resets.

A useful feature of total return swap is that the market risk is always dependent upon the price volatility of the reference asset – and this is an exposure calculation that most institutions are already able to perform.

❏ *Credit risk* The ever-present risk that the

Table 1. Advantages of total return swaps

- ❏ High yield potential
- ❏ Efficient access to loan market
- ❏ Off-balance-sheet investments
- ❏ Minimal back-office administration: a total return swap can give the cashflows of deals that would otherwise require back and middle office capabilities which the company may not have
- ❏ Low capital requirements
- ❏ As much leverage as you like
- ❏ Legal advantages: a total return swap will probably be viewed as a swap agreement under the bankruptcy code, which would be a significant advantage. Clarification of this issue is expected from ISDA in the near future
- ❏ No exchange of principal
- ❏ Access to previously unreachable markets

---

counterparty may default may be mitigated by collateralisation, using initial and variation margin techniques. A significant advantage which total return swaps have over loans is that they count as derivatives and are governed by ISDA rules. In the event of bankruptcy, transactions and collateral under ISDA are specifically excluded from the automatic stays that apply to a loan, allowing for quick liquidation.

❏ *Regulation/netting risk* Total return swaps may, in principle, be used to manage the credit risk of a portfolio – for example, a risky asset could be synthetically "sold" via a total return swap. This eliminates the asset risk from the portfolio, providing the returns from the asset and the swap may be netted. However, it is not certain that total return swaps may be used to net out credit risk in a portfolio under all circumstances. In theory they provide a powerful tool for the reduction of credit risk and therefore the reduction of capital needed to support the portfolio. Regulatory bodies are currently in the process of issuing guidelines as to the netting allowed, and it is worthwhile investigating these before transactions are entered into for netting purposes.

❏ *Concealed exposure risk* Total return swaps do not only reduce risk; if used incorrectly they can hide it. Consider a company whose treasurer has considerable freedom to use credit derivatives, and considerable pressure to enhance the return of his portfolio. He may use total return swaps to gain leveraged exposure to a number of high-yield, high-risk assets. However, the swaps themselves will be executed with reputable market counterparties, and the nature of the assets may thus be concealed from all but the most curious eyes. In a less extreme situation, underlying assets may be rather more correlated than is immediately obvious from looking at the names of swap counterparties.

❏ *Operational risk* Precisely because credit derivatives are new, there are risks associated with the setting up of new procedures and documentation. Middle- and back-office staff may make errors because they are unfamiliar with the instruments, and there may be a few loopholes left in ISDA agreements which have yet to be discovered. However, these risks will steadily reduce as credit derivatives become more widely used.

❑ *Risk management risk* Currently there are not so many credit derivatives around that you will find them in every derivatives portfolio. However, they are increasing in number, and risk managing a portfolio of this nature will require a whole new set of mathematics and software. Outside a few large and innovative institutions, development of these tools will lag behind the development of the credit derivatives market, and it may be that some companies will discover unexpected risk concentrations in their portfolios the hard way. In particular, valuing credit derivatives is difficult. If credit derivatives are added to a portfolio to manage credit risk, then they need to be valued for a market risk calculation, which may not be trivial.

❑ *Price discovery risk* As discussed earlier, the "true" price of a credit derivative is a matter of some debate. Valuing a portfolio containing credit derivatives will entail a few heroic assumptions. This risk is largely removed by hedging with the reference asset or with an opposing position.

❑ *Liquidity risk* As with all new products, it may be difficult to buy or sell credit derivatives in the market. In particular, some highly tailored deals may be very difficult to unload. However, this risk will reduce as the market develops.

HOW MIGHT IT GO WRONG?
In order to appreciate how total return swaps could increase risk, we give an outline of a worst-case scenario, where a deal that should not have been done in the first place leads to a high exposure to a risky asset and then to a loss.

Company A has a subsidiary, Sub1. Company A is US-based, but Sub1 is based in Europe. Sub1 has only recently been set up, and is under pressure to produce good results. The treasury of Sub1 is fairly independent, with freedom to hedge and to take positions in the market. However, Company A has imposed some restrictions upon the contracts that Sub1 may enter into. These are that Sub1 may not purchase equity or company debt of companies with credit ratings below A, it may not enter into options on those instruments, and it is also pre-

vented from dealing in certain structured derivatives. Swaps, however, are allowed. In addition, it is not allowed to deal with any company in any way whose credit rating is below BB.

In the first half of the year, the returns to Sub1 are disappointing. However, the treasury is one department that has done well, purchasing some equities which have outperformed. The treasurer KnowItAll wishes that he were able to purchase a selection of rather more risky instruments, whose returns are higher. In particular, he believes that company bond X, issued by Company HighRisk, will do very well in coming months. However, this company does not have a good enough credit rating for him to purchase it.

However, some little while later, he gets a marketing call from Bank SellAnything. The marketer, Gung Ho, asks careful questions, and discovers that Sub1 is keen to gain exposure to bond X. He suggests a total return swap.

In the course of several meetings, KnowItAll becomes convinced that he is allowed to enter into such a transaction, because it is a swap and his counterparty is Bank SellAnything, whose credit rating is more than good enough to meet his dealing criteria. Gung Ho suggests that as KnowItAll holds such a strong view on the performance of bond X, he might consider a leveraged transaction. KnowItAll agrees. Gung Ho is keen to sell the deal, and does not do sensitivity analyses.

Gung Ho is required to obtain the approval of a Credit Officer prior to implementation of high-risk transactions, and has to submit warnings in varying degrees of detail to the client according to Table 2. He judges optimistically that Sub1 is a sophisticated client, and is obliged to assume that the transaction is high risk due to its leverage. Thus he has to submit a warning to Sub1 about possible risks, and is obliged to ensure that this warning is passed on to a higher level officer within Sub1 than KnowItAll. However, this warning does not have to include great detail or sensitivity analysis. Had he more realistically assumed that the client was unsophisticated, then Bank SellAnything would have had to ensure that a very detailed warning about the possible risks of the transaction was understood by a superior of KnowItAll within Sub1 or Company A.

The warning is read by a superior of KnowItAll at Sub1, who is not concerned at the possible risks as he is reassured by KnowItAll. He does not pass on the warning to the parent company.

The transaction is entered into, and the deal is put onto the books of Sub1. It shows up as a

Table 2. Keeping clients informed

Level of client sophistication	Level of product risk		
	1	2	3
Sophisticated	No warning necessary	No warning necessary	Warning and approval
Unsophisticated	No warning necessary	Warning	Detailed warning and approval
Individuals/first-time users	No warning necessary	Warning	Prohibited

swap with allowed counterparty Bank SellAnything, and the name of Company HighRisk does not appear on summary reports which go from Sub1 to Company A. It does appear on more detailed reports, but these are not routinely seen by the credit officers at Company A who might be expected to pick up on the name.

Now, the inevitable happens. Company HighRisk does very poorly and the value of bond X plummets. The losses suffered by Sub1 are exacerbated by the leverage factor. Initially KnowItAll holds on, hoping that the situation will improve and that the losses will be recouped. The situation worsens, and he tries to get out of the deal but has great difficulty in doing so due to its illiquidity. Company A is eventually called upon to make good the losses and thus discovers the true nature of the deal for the first time.

This scenario could have been interrupted at many points. Tighter procedures and more detailed reporting requirements on the parts of both Sub1 and Bank SellAnything could have prevented the disaster. For example:

❑ The restrictions upon the deal types which Sub1 was allowed to enter into should have been far more detailed and should have included leveraged transactions and those which resulted in exposure to undesirable credits. If they had, KnowItAll of Sub1 would not have been able to enter into the transaction, however much he wanted to.

❑ Gung Ho should have performed extensive sensitivity analyses for KnowItAll, showing him what his losses would be in the event of a fall in value of bond X. This might have persuaded KnowItAll that it was a bad idea to proceed with the deal.

❑ Gung Ho should have checked with the Credit

Officer that the client actually did fall into the category of "sophisticated". The Credit Officer would have ensured that a very detailed warning was passed on to the superior of KnowItAll, which might well have prevented the deal from going through.

❑ The Credit Officer himself should have checked that the client was sophisticated, and upon realising that he was not, should have ensured that the parent company was aware of the deal and that a detailed warning had been submitted.

❑ The reporting requirements for Sub1 should have been more detailed, and the detailed reports (as opposed to the summary reports) should have been viewed by credit personnel with the experience to spot the deal.

❑ Sub1 should have notified Company A as soon as the deal started to go wrong. Instead it waited and the situation worsened. Immediate stop-out might have mitigated the losses. The subsidiary should not have been in a position where it was able to conceal significant losses for any length of time.

Conclusion

There is no doubt that the credit derivatives market is growing, although estimates as to its size vary widely. It has been given a boost in recent times by sympathetic regulation, and many institutions have now set up whole teams to market and distribute the products. Growth of the market seems inevitable, given the potential uses of credit derivatives to improve portfolio management. However, not all of the risks associated with this product are widely understood as yet, and credit derivatives have the dangerous potential to conceal risks and exposures.

BIBLIOGRAPHY

Hull, J.C., and A. White, 1995, "The Price of Default ", *Derivative Credit Risk*, London: Risk Publications, pp. 79–83.

ISDA, "Developing a Supervisory Approach to Credit Derivatives" and "Credit Derivatives: Issues for Discussion on Interim Prudential Treatment", February 1, 1997. See also Chapter 12 of the present volume.

Jarrow, R.A., and S.M. Turnbull, 1993, "Pricing Options on Financial Securities Subject to Credit Risk", Working paper, Cornell University.

Jarrow, R.A., and S. M. Turnbull, 1995, "The Forex Analogy", *Derivative Credit Risk*, London: Risk Publications, pp. 72–8.

Jarrow, R.A, D. Lando and S.M. Turnbull, 1994, "A Markov Model for the Term Structure of Credit Risk Spreads", Working paper, Cornell University.

8

Buying and Selling Credit Risk

A Perspective on Credit-linked Obligations

Arturo Cifuentes, Isaac Efrat, Jeremy Gluck and Eileen Murphy
Moody's Investors Service

The markets for credit derivatives, credit-linked notes (CLNs) and collateralised debt obligations (CDOs) are, to a considerable extent, complementary. While there are instances when different instruments can be used to achieve the same economic goal, this does not mean that credit derivatives will ultimately displace structured instruments offering similar risk/return profiles. Indeed, the relationship between credit derivatives and, say, credit-linked notes, closely parallels the one between interest-rate derivatives and synthetic debt instruments; rather than replacing debt instruments, interest-rate derivatives have made it possible for debt offerings to be made more appealing to investors.

Throughout this chapter, we will discuss the markets for CLNs and CDOs, giving examples of the instruments and our rating methodology, as well as the particular risks associated with these investments. Panel 1 highlights a general feature of Moody's analysis of structured instruments: the analysis of credit risk revolves around an assessment of expected loss.

Credit derivatives versus physical instruments

The credit derivatives market gives sophisticated players the scope to achieve very specific credit risk profiles. Banks, non-bank dealers and portfolio managers can hedge existing risks, diversify across a range of credit risks, and seek new opportunities for yield that might otherwise be difficult to exploit.

But for many investors trying to achieve a credit risk profile, the OTC derivatives market is a less suitable arena than the market for "physical" instruments. There are several factors behind the desire to invest in CLNs, CDOs and conventional (non-structured) debt rather than

the credit derivatives market, including:
❑ the opportunity for the buy-and-hold investor to capture a liquidity premium;
❑ a preference for avoiding the derivatives market; and
❑ a preference for rated instruments.

A number of studies have suggested that a diversified portfolio of high-yield bonds offers better returns than less risky bonds over a long horizon.[1] High-yield instruments offer a liquidity/default premium that has more than compensated for the default risk.

Investments in high-yield bonds via OTC derivatives instruments typically require the surrender of this premium. An investment in a single bond or portfolio of bonds via a total return swap, for example, normally requires the investor to compensate the dealer somehow for the cost of hedging. Hedging costs are high in comparison to, say, interest-rate derivatives because there is no set of suitable exchange-traded contracts for hedging credit risk, and credit risk is also inherently difficult to hedge. So the premium that a buy-and-hold investor would achieve in the high-yield bond market would be likely to be absorbed in a credit-derivative transaction aiming to offer the same risk profile.

Of course, many investors, either by choice or by statute, simply do not have access to the credit derivatives market. In some cases, corporate charters or fund indentures do not allow the use of OTC derivatives. More frequently, company boards or investment fund managers will limit the use of derivatives to "plain-vanilla" interest-rate products, such as swaps and caps. The market for credit derivatives is still young, and many senior managers are not yet comfortable with it. This discomfort may extend to credit-linked notes, which were tainted by problems in the structured note market in the mid-1990s.

THE EXPECTED LOSS CONCEPT

Moody's ratings of CLNs, CDOs and other structured instruments reflect our assessment of the expected loss (EL) posed to the investor. Although other criteria could be used to assign a credit rating, we believe that EL is the single most useful measure. It is easily understood as the product of the likelihood of default in each possible loss scenario, multiplied by the actual loss to the investor in such an event. Thus,

$$EL = \sum_s P_s L_s \qquad (1)$$

where L_s is the loss experienced by the investor under scenario s and P_s is the probability that the scenario will occur.

For the institutional investors that typically buy structured instruments, EL is more meaningful than a mere probability of default criterion. Any rational investor should be interested in both the likelihood and consequences of default, just as a rational market participant would not price an option by focusing solely on the likelihood of exercise. For institutional investors, it is true that a single default within a diversified portfolio is not traumatic. Holders of large fixed-income portfolios recognise that defaults will occasionally occur; indeed, they are compensated for this risk. What matters is the frequency of default and the losses

that will ensue – the expected loss.[1]

The concept of "loss" itself is subject to a number of possible interpretations. For the purpose of assigning a credit rating, we view a loss as any shortfall in the present value of payments received in a given scenario, relative to the present value of the cashflows embodied in the promise to investors. The promise is usually well defined: the pledge to pay a fixed coupon of 8% plus the return of principal upon maturity, say; or a coupon of Libor plus a spread and the return of principal. In some cases the promise may only include the return of principal, or the return of principal plus a below-market coupon (with the expectation on the investor's part that unrated "excess" cashflows will also be received). In some circumstances, the pledge may be simply to "pay you what we have got." Because such implicit promises contain little useful information for the investor, we treat the standard against which losses are measured as the present value of a riskless note.

1 One might imagine still other measures of risk, such as those that include some measure of the dispersion of returns, or even their skewness. But it remains true that within a diversified portfolio, such measures would be of limited use. Some "beta-like" indicator could be more relevant, but since there is no clear "market portfolio" within the fixed-income world, it is unlikely that investors would find a single measure any more useful than EL.

Pure credit derivative transactions are generally not rated by Moody's, nor by competing rating agencies.[2] Many investors prefer, or are restricted to, investments in rated instruments. There is comfort in having an independent entity evaluate both the contracts surrounding an investment, as well as the pure "economic" component of credit risk (which, for Moody's, entails an analysis of the expected loss posed to investors, described more fully in Panel 1.) For some institutions – US insurance firms for instance – the purchase of unrated instruments may be permitted, but an onerous regulatory capital charge is usually entailed. For investors restricting themselves to rated instruments, the choices are limited to conventional notes, or bonds and CLNs.

Credit-linked notes

DEFINITION AND EXAMPLES
A credit-linked note (CLN) is a note which, under normal circumstances, pays out a conventional

stream of cashflows such as periodic coupons and principal at redemption. However, these cashflows are altered upon the occurrence of a credit event experienced by some pre-specified reference credit(s). The event is most often a credit default by the reference, but other occurrences such as credit rating migration or changes in the legal or regulatory status of the reference credit may also apply.

In order to effect such a structure, a special purpose vehicle (SPV) is typically established, which places the proceeds of the sale of the CLN into some plain-vanilla, investment-grade instruments. Simultaneously, the SPV enters into a credit derivative agreement with a highly-rated counterparty, where the derivative's underlying is the credit of the CLN's reference (see Figure 1). Common examples of credit derivatives include default options or credit swaps, where, in exchange for a periodic premium, one party undertakes to compensate the other party for losses that might be incurred as the result of a future default; or total return swaps, where one party pays to (receives from) the other party the rise (fall) in the value of a debt issuance by a credit-sensitive name.

A CLN can be as simple as a structured note that passes through the cashflows from a low-rated bond. More substantial constructs include CLNs that protect the full redemption of principal via the purchase of a default put on the reference that is struck at par; and a CLN that enhances the investor's yield through the sale of a default call, thus taking on a synthetic long position in the underlying name's credit.

The more elaborate example of the Russian roulette note in the box to the right incorporates these and other typical CLN traits. Here, the investor has in effect sold his counterparty insurance against the first event of default in a small portfolio, for which the counterparty pays him a periodic premium. We will use this example and its possible variants to illustrate the main advantages of participation in the CLN market.

REASONS FOR TRANSACTING IN CLNS

A major reason for issuing a CLN is the desire to lay off some existing credit risk. As is clear in the Russian roulette example, the swap counterparty has succeeded in hedging away its risk of one out of five defaults (while retaining the risk of two or more). More generally, it has reconfigured its credit risk exposure, perhaps because it wants to mitigate requirements imposed by regulators, auditors or internal risk-management practices, or to release capital for other, potentially more attractive, investments.

This is accomplished without the physical need to unload the instruments that gave rise to exposure to the reference credits. The corresponding lack of unnecessary disclosure assists the portfolio manager in maintaining client relationships that might otherwise be adversely affected by shorting or selling the reference credits. And tax liabilities arising from the physical sale of an asset may be delayed or eliminated.

We now turn from the seller of credit to the buyer. A major reason for investing in CLNs is the potential they offer for enhanced returns, via an entry into a long position in the references' credit when this is perceived to be undervalued. In the Russian roulette transaction, an additional annual spread of 100 basis points (two semi-annual payments of 50) is collected for as long as the reference portfolio remains intact. It has been repeatedly documented that credit spreads quoted in the market significantly exceed those implied by the observed historical probabilities

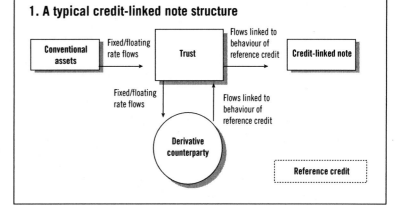

1. A typical credit-linked note structure

Conventional assets → Fixed/floating rate flows → Trust → Flows linked to behaviour of reference credit → Credit-linked note

Trust → Fixed/floating rate flows → Derivative counterparty → Flows linked to behaviour of reference credit

Reference credit

EXAMPLE: THE RUSSIAN ROULETTE NOTE

After investing the proceeds of the note in a 3-year, A1-rated, vanilla floating rate note that pays 6-month Libor plus a small spread, the SPV enters into a credit swap with a Aa1-rated counterparty, stipulating a semi-annual payment of 50 basis points. However, should *any* of five predetermined reference names – all rated Baa1 but otherwise uncorrelated – default, the trust terminates and fully compensates the counterparty for the severity of the default.

of default and recovery rates.[3] A well-designed portfolio of credit positions can be an effective, yet prudent, investment vehicle.

And as well as potentially increasing returns, CLNs allow investors to participate in an asset class that is distinct from a portfolio's more traditional equity or fixed income components. The added diversification can lower portfolio volatility and, ultimately, better approximate the efficient frontier.[4]

The synthetic nature of the CLN enables the buyer to leverage his exposure to the underlying name. In the example of the Russian roulette note, the investor has leveraged his Baa1 exposure by a factor of five-to-one, thereby earning a spread that is associated with a higher, Ba1 risk.[5] This synthetic character also enables the issuer to customise the CLN according to the prospective buyer's needs. So an investor who wishes to avoid potential ambiguities in the extent and timing of default losses, for example, can negotiate an a priori severity rate that would change hands immediately upon the determination of a default event occurring.

THE APPROACH TO RATING CLNS

As we have already seen, Moody's assignment of a rating centres around the calculation and benchmarking of an appropriate notion of

PANEL 2

EL: AN EXAMPLE

Suppose that an SPV purchases a Ba2-rated one-year note that carries an 8% coupon. It then pays a 2% premium to a Aaa-rated dealer in order to purchase a put on the Ba2-rated note with a strike at par. The SPV issues a note offering a 6% coupon. Thus, the investor in the note has paid a 2% premium to assure the return of principal with Aaa confidence.

Assuming that the promise on the note is to be the standard return of principal and payment of the full 6% coupon, the EL is calculated as follows. Using a one-year (idealised) Ba2 default rate of 1.56% and a one-year Treasury yield of 5.5%, and noting that the Aaa default rate is immaterial in comparison to the Ba2 default rate, we have:

$$EL = 1.56\% * (106/1.055 - 100/1.055)/100$$
$$=0.08872\%$$

In words, the expected loss is the probability of default on the Ba2 note, multiplied by the loss should the default occur, and expressed as a percentage. The loss is the present value of the promised payments, minus the present value of the payout on the put (par). This computed EL is most closely aligned with the 0.098% EL of a Baa2 benchmark bullet (assuming a recovery rate of 45%).

expected loss (EL).[6] This EL is defined in relation to a promise that is being made to the holders of the note, and its identification constitutes the initial step in the rating process. Once the promise is identified, we take the following additional steps:

Enumeration of credit scenarios

The credit returns on a CLN typically depend on whether or not its underlying reference credits default, as well as on the time (in years) in which these defaults occur. This means that there are many possible credit scenarios, and these can often be explicitly specified. Among them is the most likely scenario of no defaults, while all other scenarios may impose actual credit losses on the investor.

In cases where an analytic description of all eventualities is impractical, a Monte Carlo simulation can be performed, which generates credit scenarios according to Moody's idealised default probability tables.[7] Here again, the loss scenarios are those where the cashflow realised by the investor falls short of that which has been promised.

Determination of the EL

EL is the average of the losses (the latter are often zero) over all possible credit scenarios, expressed as a percentage of the initial CLN proceeds. When an analytic description of the outcomes has been used, the average is weighted by their various likelihoods. Should a simulation be required, all scenarios are of course taken to be equally likely.

Benchmarking to plain-vanilla bonds

To transform the EL percentage into a letter rating, we compare the CLN's EL to those of conventional bullet corporate bonds of like duration where, as before, the latter are computed based on our default probability table. The assigned alphanumeric is the rating of the bullet that most closely matches the EL of the CLN. So two investments with similar reward-to-risk profiles, as expressed by their ELs, end up being associated with the same rating.

PITFALLS OF THE CLN MARKET

Despite the attractions of CLNs, certain pitfalls await the prospective investor. These are primarily because of the market's relative immaturity, and can be categorised in the following way:

Legal and documentation risk

Legal and accounting firms, as well as regulatory bodies and trade organisations, have recently initiated an effort to define, standardise, and document credit derivatives.[8] Even so, the current situation cannot yet be compared to the better-established derivative markets, where instruments such as fixed-to-floating swaps and forex options are thoroughly understood and their terms agreed upon by all participants.

Because of differing investor needs and counterparty goals, practices may vary over such crucial terms as physical or cash delivery upon the occurrence of a credit event, materiality standards for the occurrence of credit events, the requirement for publicly-available or privately-ascertained information regarding events and, perhaps most importantly, the identification of specific or generalised reference credits. As a result, credit investors need to be particularly wary of any special nuances that might affect the risks entailed in a particular transaction.

Modelling risk

While there has been some recent work on the valuation of risky bonds,[9] the subject of event risk and credit default modelling in the context of the capital markets is still very much open. The stochastic processes that govern the dynamics of credit migration, or the catastrophic nature of certain credit events, for instance, have not been thoroughly analysed.[10] In particular, analogues to the Black–Scholes formalism or other arbitrage-free pricing methodologies have not been developed (as discussed further in Chapter 10 of the present volume). The investor may therefore face a wide range of dealer quotes, a difficulty that is exacerbated by an inability to validate them against an accepted benchmark.

Liquidity risk

As a result of the absence of price transparency, as well as the lack of uniformity of terms, CLN investors cannot expect to unwind their positions should the need arise. Additional illiquidity may be caused by circumstances similar to those experienced in other derivative arenas. So investors who are short an upgraded credit on a leveraged basis may have trouble offsetting their position by taking a long position in the reference debt, for example.

Correlation risk

Correlations between events of default are notoriously difficult to estimate, due to the lack of relevant data, the absence of a unified theory of event risk, and the cyclical nature of economic conditions. As a result, the investor who is long credit risk may find that he has sold more credit insurance than originally intended. In other instances, a hedge of credit exposure may later prove to be less comprehensive than at the time of purchase. For example, if the credits that underlie the Russian roulette transaction described above turn out to be significantly positively correlated, one event of default may be accompanied by additional events. The issuer may then find that he has paid a premium otherwise associated with that of a higher Ba1 risk, in return for laying off a less risky exposure that is closer to the Baa1 of the individual components in the pool.

Collateralised debt obligations

As we observed earlier, credit risk is particularly difficult to hedge. One alternative to hedging is diversification, the attempt to eliminate "idiosyncratic" risk through the pooling of many assets.[11] Though one cannot remove all credit (or market) risk from a portfolio of debt instruments via diversification, bond returns, particularly within a global portfolio, have sufficiently imperfect correlations to permit a substantial risk reduction through diversification. Such pooling can also be achieved at relatively low cost.

For years, mutual funds have been the primary vehicles for the assembly of a diverse pool of fixed-income instruments. More recently, institutional investors have come to view collateralised debt obligations (CDOs) as an attractive mechanism for gaining fixed-income exposures. Through the slicing of a CDO's liabilities into two or more tranches, the issuer of debt can appeal to investors with markedly different risk preferences, such as:

❑ those that seek highly-rated, low-risk instruments that offer yields slightly more favourable than those of more "traditional" asset-backed securities; and

❑ investors that prefer low-rated or unrated, high-risk instruments that promise equity-like returns.

Hence, CDOs, like other products of securitisation (mortgage-backed securities, credit-card backed securities, and so on) represent a mechanism for altering the risk characteristics of a pool of financial instruments.

A typical CDO structure, which may incorporate bonds (collateralised bond obligations, or CBOs) or loans (collateralised loan obligations, or CLOs) is depicted in Figure 2. In this example, the SPV issues three tranches of debt to finance the purchase of a portfolio of high-yield bonds.

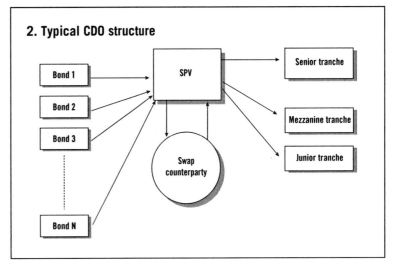

2. Typical CDO structure

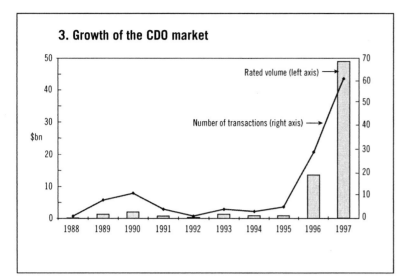

3. Growth of the CDO market

The senior and "mezzanine" tranches might carry ratings of, say, Aa2 and Baa3, respectively, while the most junior, or equity tranche, would normally be unrated. A swap is used to offset any mismatch in the interest rate basis between the assets and liabilities.

MARKET EVOLUTION

Nearly any sort of commercial obligation can be included in a CDO collateral pool. In the early days of the market during the late 1980s, US high-yield bonds were most prominent, though bank loans were also found among the assets. The market contracted sharply in the early 1990s (see Figure 3) in sympathy with the disruption of the high-yield market that was, in turn, the product of a surge in defaults and the failure of market-maker Drexel Burnham Lambert .

The CDO market awakened from its slumber in 1996 as investors shed some of their concerns about speculative grade instruments against the backdrop of a strong US economy. At the same time, yields on CDOs began to look attractive as the spreads over Libor for other asset-backed securities tightened. Collateral managers ultimately moved beyond more pedestrian instruments such as high-yield bonds and leveraged

loans to incorporate emerging market sovereign and corporate obligations, trade-related instruments, project loans and even tranches of structured finance transactions into their asset pools.

Most of the volume can be attributed to bank loans, primarily in connection with large "balance sheet" transactions in which banks securitise portions of their balance sheets. The surging volume of balance sheet CLOs reflects the banks' realisation that commercial credit can be securitised in the same way as mortgages and credit-card receivables; indeed, it is attractive to do so in the face of the high capital costs associated with holding these assets on bank balance sheets. So banks can retain origination and servicing fees, while freeing up capital and improving reported returns on equity. Not surprisingly, Japanese banks, which tend to face tight capital constraints and relatively high borrowing costs on unsecured debt, have been particularly active as CLO issuers.

Table 1 lists some of the more interesting CDOs among the 160-plus that Moody's has rated since 1988.

SYNTHETIC COLLATERAL

One of the more interesting developments on the asset side of CDO structures is the inclusion of synthetic instruments – credit-linked notes or credit swaps – in the pools. This is partly because of cost: participants in the US high-yield bond market have observed that the prices of some bonds (which have come to be known as "CBO bonds") have been bid up because of their suitability for inclusion in CBOs. Rather than sacrifice yield by buying these scarce instruments, portfolio managers have synthesised suitable assets by, for example, creating CLNs that bear the characteristics of the underlying securities, but with a shorter maturity. The ability to shorten maturity is particularly useful because it eliminates the market risk that would otherwise be present if assets with lives longer than those

Table 1. Selected CDOs

Transaction	Rating date	Collateral manager	Underwriter	Comment
Long Run Bond Corp.	Nov 1, 1988	Imperial S&L	Drexel Burnham	First Moody's-rated CBO
IFC Latin America & Asia Loan Trust	July 6, 1995	International Finance Corp.	CS First Boston	First primarily emerging market CDO
PPM America Special Investments Fund	June 21, 1996	PPM America	Rothschild	Market-value deal with primarily distressed collateral
ROSE Funding No. 1	Nov 29, 1996	Natwest Markets	Natwest Markets	First balance-sheet CLO; $5 billion volume
Oakmont	July 31, 1997	Chancellor LGT	Chase	First exclusively CLN collateral pool
NationsBank Commercial Loan Master Trust	Sep 24, 1997	NationsBank	NationsBank	First balance-sheet deal to use master trust structure
Project Loan Funding Corp. I	Mar 5, 1998	CS First Boston	CS First Boston	First project-loan CDO

of the liabilities had to be sold when the liabilities mature.

A second reason for including synthetics arises within the bank balance sheet transactions. Rather than place actual loans into a portfolio, some banks[12] have used CLNs to hedge exposures to select counterparties. Banks can apply the CLN approach to hedging exposures that arise through OTC derivatives activity. Though this may leave the bank with imperfect hedges, because the fixed size of the CLNs will not precisely mirror the variable exposures to counterparties, a portfolio of fixed-principal CLNs will appeal to many investors. The synthetic approach also permits banks fully or partially to offset credit risk without having to assign loans, a procedure that might require notification to the affected borrowers.

One key drawback to the use of CLNs in these structures is the additional risk attributable to the issuer of the CLNs (or, in the case of credit swaps, the counterparty to the trades). When the rating of the issuer/counterparty is roughly equivalent to, or below, that of the senior CLO tranche, the incremental contribution to expected loss is substantial. In effect, the rating of the sponsor acts as a ceiling on the ratings of the CLO liabilities.

THE APPROACH TO RATING CDOs
As in the case of CLNs, Moody's ratings of CDOs are intended to reflect the expected loss faced by an investor in any of the rated tranches, where the loss represents the percentage shortfall in the present value of cashflows vis-à-vis the promised value.

Since interest-rate risk is normally hedged out of these structures, and because assets and liabilities are normally denominated in a single currency, the primary determinant of loss is the number of defaults within the collateral pool. In theory, default losses could be modelled through a Monte Carlo simulation in which defaults are generated for each period, based on the marginal default rates associated with each credit, as well as correlations in default rates.

In practice, it is convenient to rely instead on the Binomial Expansion Technique (BET). The BET must be considered an approximation to the simulation result; its value lies in the similarity of the outcome to a full-fledged simulation and the computational savings. Simulations become impractical when a large number of transactions must be evaluated and a number of possible portfolios, liability structures and structural tests

must be considered for each transaction.

The BET represents the application of basic probability theory to a simplified version of the true portfolio. The simplified portfolio consists of a set of assets, which each have the same face value, coupon and rating, and a likelihood of default independent of those of the other assets. The number of assets in this idealised pool is known as the diversity score (see Panel 3 overleaf) of the portfolio. After the characteristics of the homogeneous, idealised pool have been identified, the losses under each possible default scenario can be calculated. The probability-weighted average of these losses is the EL for the CDO tranche under consideration.

CALCULATING EXPECTED LOSS
The diversity score (D), in combination with the average characteristics of the collateral pool – the Weighted Average Rating Factor (WARF), the Weighted Average Coupon (WAC), and the Weighted Average Recovery Rate) – permits the calculation of expected loss without having to resort to a simulation. The rating factor is merely the 10-year cumulative (idealised) default rate, multiplied by 10,000. The WARF thus represents the "average rating" of the portfolio.[13] The WARF and the amortisation profile of the portfolio jointly determine the average probability of default of the pool, by permitting comparison of the anticipated life of the assets to the idealised default rate table described earlier.

Having determined the diversity score and the average characteristics of the pool, one can, in this simplified environment, describe the default behaviour of the assets by considering $D + 1$ possible scenarios: 0 defaults, 1 default, 2 defaults, ..., D defaults. (In a properly structured cashflow transaction, there cannot be any losses in the absence of defaults.) The probability P_j that any particular scenario j (j defaults) will occur can be computed using the so-called binomial formula

$$P_j = \frac{D!}{j!(D-j)!}(\lambda p)^j (1-\lambda p)^{D-j} \qquad (2)$$

where D is the diversity score, p is the cumulative probability of default for any one of the identical assets and λ is the appropriate stress factor.

The stress factor is necessary to account for the fact that the relationship between the probability of default and the rating is far less stable for low-rated instruments (the assets) than for highly rated instruments (the liabilities). The factor is thus an adjustment for the risk that a given pool will not necessarily perform in accordance with

CALCULATION OF THE "DIVERSITY SCORE"

The diversity score is intended to represent the number of independent, identical assets that poses the same loss distribution as the actual collateral portfolio. In a transaction with credit enhancement, such as that provided by the tranching of a CDO, we are primarily interested in the left tail of the return distribution (where losses to the rated tranches may occur). We want to approximate this tail closely.

One way of calculating an approximate diversity score is to match the first two moments (mean and standard deviation) of the return distribution associated with the actual collateral pool.

Assume the actual collateral pool consists of n bonds, each with face value F_i and a default probability p_i that is implied by the rating and maturity of the bond. Let X_i be the non-default indicator for the bond ; $X_i = 0$, when bond i defaults and $X_i = 1$ otherwise. Thus $X_i = 0$ with probability p_i and $X_i = 1$ with probability $q_i = 1 - p_i$. Assume also that the correlation coefficient of default between bond i and j is ρ_{ij}. After allowing for defaults, the remaining notional amount of the collateral pool is

$$P = \sum_{i=1}^{n} X_i F_i \qquad (1)$$

Assume there exists a homogenous pool with D identical, uncorrelated bonds and that each identical bond has the same face value F, the same rating and the same maturity (which is the average life of the actual collateral pool). Let the default probability implied by the average rating and maturity be p and the indicator of bond i non-default be Y_i; hence, $Y_i = 0$, with probability p and $Y_i = 1$ with probability $q = 1 - p$. If P^* is the total notional of the homogenous pool, then

$$P^* = \sum_{i=1}^{D} Y_i F \qquad (2)$$

We intend to use this homogenous pool of identical assets to approximate the default profile of the original collateral pool. Of course, the initial notional amount of two pools has to be the same so that

$$\sum_{i=1}^{n} F_i = DF \qquad (3)$$

In addition to (3), we match the first two moments of P and P^*. That is, the expected value of the notional amount of the two pools are equal

$$E(P) = E(P^*) \qquad (4)$$

and the variance of the notional amount of the two pools are equal:

$$Var(P) = Var(P^*) \qquad (5)$$

In order to match the first two moments, we observe that:

$X_i \sim$ Binomial $(1, q_i)$, corr $(X_i, X_j) = \rho_{ij}$, i = 1...n and
$Y_i \sim$ Binomial $(1, q)$, corr $(Y_i, Y_j) = 0$, i = 1...D.

Thus, $E(X_i) = q_i$, $Var(X_i) = p_i q_i$, and
$E(Y_i) = q$, $Var(Y_i) = pq$.

The first two moments of P are given by

$$E(P) = E\left(\sum_{i=1}^{n} X_i F_i\right) = \sum_{i=1}^{n} E(X_i) F_i = \sum_{i=1}^{n} q_i F_i \qquad (6)$$

and

$$Var(P) = Var\left(\sum_{i=1}^{n} X_i F_i\right)$$
$$= \sum_{i=1}^{n} \sum_{j=1}^{n} \rho_{ij} \sqrt{Var(X_i) Var(X_j)} F_i F_j$$
$$= \sum_{i=1}^{n} \sum_{j=1}^{n} \rho_{ij} \sqrt{p_i q_i p_j q_j} F_i F_j \qquad (7)$$

The first two moments of P^* are:

$$E(P^*) = F \sum_{i=1}^{D} E(Y_i) = FDq \qquad (8)$$

$$Var(P^*) = F^2 \sum_{i=1}^{D} Var(Y_i) = F^2 Dpq \qquad (9)$$

We can substitute (6)–(9) into (3)–(5) to obtain

$$\text{Average face value: } F = \left(\sum_{i=1}^{n} F_i\right) / D \qquad (10)$$

$$\text{Average default probability: } p = \frac{\sum_{i=1}^{n} p_i F_i}{\sum_{i=1}^{n} F_i} \qquad (11)$$

$$\text{Diversity score: } D = \frac{\left(\sum_{i=1}^{n} p_i F_i\right)\left(\sum_{i=1}^{n} q_i F_i\right)}{\sum \sum \rho_{ij} \sqrt{p_i q_i p_j q_j} F_i F_j} \qquad (12)$$

Though we have not explicitly addressed the skewness of the return distribution, experimentation with a variety of portfolios suggests that the homogeneous portfolio consisting of D assets closely approximates the tail of the return distribution.

average default behaviour – it might, for example, deviate from the mean during an economic downturn, but the elevated default rate would typically remain within two standard deviations from its mean.[14] The stressing factor depends on the rating anticipated for the tranche under examination: the greater the discrepancy between the rating of the tranche and the average rating of the collateral, the higher the stressing factor. No stress would be applied if the two ratings were the same. Alternatively, within a simulation, one could treat the default rates themselves as being random.

Finally, the EL for the tranche under consideration is

$$EL = \sum_{j=1}^{D} P_j L_j \qquad (3)$$

where L_j represents the loss under scenario j.

Losses for each tranche are calculated by defaulting a proportion of collateral in the homogeneous portfolio that is consistent with the number of defaults associated with the scenario. Losses are allocated over time by considering several different possible default patterns, but with an emphasis on early defaults, which are particularly likely for the non-investment-grade assets that populate most CDOs.

Consistent with our treatment of CLNs, the loss in a particular scenario is the percentage shortfall in the present value of the cashflows received by the investor relative to the par value of the note (or the present value of the promised flows in cases where the promise is unconventional). The rating is then determined by looking at the idealised expected losses of conventional corporate bullet bonds of the appropriate maturity.

TAKING ACCOUNT OF CASHFLOWS

When collateral default losses are considered in the homogeneous portfolio, cashflows are correspondingly reduced. Interest flows to the various tranches and, potentially, principal flows may be lost or postponed. The computation of L_j must accurately reflect the priority of payments (which could be sequential, pro rata, or a combination of these two arrangements) and the payment of all the fees involved in the transaction. Depending on the nature of the assets, recoveries for defaulted instruments may be assumed to be immediate or delayed. In cases where the pool includes a small basket of zeroes or step-up bonds, the model must take account of the fact that the WAC will vary with time.

Even in the absence of defaults, the cashflows from the asset pool will not precisely match the flows to the liabilities. Typically, the most senior tranche offers a floating-rate coupon, while more junior tranches tend to pay a fixed-rate coupon. The collateral may be either fixed rate, as in the case of most high-yield bonds, or floating rate, which is typical of bank loans. In nearly all cases, there is something of a mismatch between the interest-rate basis of the assets and that of the liabilities.

It is common for swaps or caps to be used to reduce the interest-rate risk and timing mismatches that would otherwise be present in CDOs. To the extent that swaps/caps are not sufficient to offset interest-rate risk fully, the residual is addressed by considering several potential interest rate scenarios; for example, a current forward curve and stressed high- and low-rate environments. Of course, the presence of the swap counterparty may be a source of additional credit risk. The incremental expected loss associated with a lower-rated counterparty must be incorporated into the rating. Typically though, a very highly-rated entity is chosen to avoid such complications, or collateral may need to be posted should the counterparty be downgraded below some threshold.

Despite the various simplifying assumptions that are made to accommodate the BET procedure, the results closely match those of more elaborate and time-consuming Monte Carlo simulations. In view of the extreme computational burden of considering portfolio behaviour when the portfolio changes, as it often does during the proposal phase, the BET approach is quite effective.

STRUCTURAL PROTECTIONS

Cashflow CDOs generally incorporate a number of protections beyond the subordination of junior tranches. Most notably, principal- and interest-coverage tests are normally introduced. For example, the senior-class tests might require that the face value of the assets exceed the face value of the liabilities by a ratio of 1.30:1, and that the interest-flows available for the next CDO coupon payment exceed the interest due by a ratio of 1.05:1. Should the principal coverage test be failed, principal payments would have to be redirected toward the senior class. Should the interest-coverage test not be met, interest flows would be diverted to the senior class. The modelling of cashflows must incorporate these features to reflect expected loss accurately.

Other protections relate to the potential for price risk that has not been addressed in the cashflow modelling. For example, it is typical that only a very small fraction of the collateral may mature beyond the life of the liabilities in order to limit price and liquidity risk from the sale of the assets. During any "ramp-up" period, there are usually intermediate targets for diversity, WAC, WARF, and so on, that must be achieved in order to continue acquiring assets; the risk here is that the assets will appreciate after the debt is issued, making it impossible to achieve the anticipated portfolio.

MARKET VALUE TRANSACTIONS

Most CDO transactions have been of the "cashflow" variety, meaning that rather than marking the assets to market, the focus is on the sufficiency of the inflows generated by the assets to meet the outflows to the noteholders. When collateral defaults begin to threaten the health of the senior classes, cashflows are normally redistributed in favour of the senior noteholders. Assets need not be liquidated to meet any shortfall.

A minority of deals have instead been structured to ensure that with a high degree of confidence, the market value of the assets will exceed the (face) value of the obligations. In the event of a shortfall in the value of assets, some or all of the collateral must be liquidated in order to restore the balance between the values of assets and liabilities. The price volatility and liquidity of each asset class, as well as the transaction's structural protections, are normally reflected in a set of "advance rates" or "haircuts" – the "haircut" value of the assets must exceed the liabilities.

It is not surprising that most CDOs are of the cashflow, rather than market-value variety. We have observed that these high-yield assets carry a significant liquidity premium and are thus attractive to buy-and-hold investors. The liquidity premium is sacrificed when the collateral must be sold. Still, the market-value approach is attractive where assets do not generate a well-defined stream of cashflows, as in the case of distressed instruments. Even for more traditional fixed-income collateral, mutual or hedge funds (or those that invest through them) may be more comfortable in a mark-to-market environment.

Moody's relies on a historical simulation approach to determine the expected loss facing an investor in a market-value CDO. Our preference for historical simulation reflects a concern that a "parametric" approach is unlikely to account for the price volatility of the portfolio accurately. The usual value-at-risk issues are relevant here: the return distributions have fat tails, are skewed, and are characterised by parameters that vary over time. Of particular importance is the fact that when a market crashes – precisely the circumstance that is of greatest interest – both volatilities and correlations tend to rise sharply.

As with cashflow CDOs, the loss calculation must reflect the transaction's structure. Hence, the historical simulation must incorporate the standards imposed for concentration by asset size, industry or asset class. The calculation must also take account of any tranching in the liabilities; it is common to have senior debt, mezzanine debt and equity in market-value CDOs.

LEGAL ISSUES FOR CDO TRANSACTIONS

CDO issuers and investors should be aware of the unique legal risks found in these structures. Although the main concerns are shared by structured finance transactions in general – bankruptcy remoteness of the issuer, true sale of assets to the issuer, substantive consolidation and effectiveness of subordination – special attention must be given to the legal issues arising from the nature of the collateral in CDOs. These include potential problems involving custody, ownership and transfer of assets, loan origination and participation risks (especially in CLO transactions), taxes, emerging market legal uncertainty, and regulatory issues.

When a bank loan is purchased by a CDO, it is possible that, under certain circumstances, the CDO could be deemed to be engaged in loan origination, an activity with possible adverse consequences for its US tax status. Additionally, a CDO's status as lender under a revolving loan agreement could conceivably lead to its liability for the consequences of a failure to fund a borrower's draw. Moody's asks that transactions be structured effectively to minimise or eliminate such risks.

Other risks arise from the nature of the CDO's interest in the assets. If the CDO holds a loan participation, possible risks include the interruption of cashflows to an issuer because of the insolvency of the entity that sold the participation to the SPV. These risks can be minimised by purchasing participations only from highly-rated sellers and limiting exposure to any one counterparty. Regulatory treatment of participations sold by financial institutions which might become insolvent, especially where "delinkage" (the achievement of a rating for a tranche that exceeds the rating of the CLO's sponsor) is desired, should be explored. Even if a CDO holds commercial credit assets, custodial, security interest and transfer issues can still affect the strength of its interest in such assets. Many structures now include a basket for credit-linked notes, which allow managers to tailor securities with a custom fit for the portfolio. Since the payment on CLNs is dependent on the continued solvency of the issuer of, or counterparty under, the CLN, the same type of counterparty risks found in participations are applicable here.

Some legal risks arise from the uncertainty of treatment of an asset where laws are undeveloped or unfriendly to securitisation. For instance, the creation, perfection and enforceability of security interests and the insolvency treatment in foreign jurisdictions can create considerable uncertainty in emerging market structures. In addition, custodial arrangements in emerging market jurisdictions, especially with small unrated or low-rated custodians, support using significantly lower recovery assumptions in these transactions. Finally, obligors in emerging market transactions must be able to make payments to the SPV that will not be subject to withholding tax (unless the obligor makes "gross-up" payments or some other accommodation).

As the range of assets underlying CDOs continues to broaden, new issues will arise. In some jurisdictions, the potential inclusion of catastrophe-linked notes within the collateral pool could raise issues as to whether the purchaser might become subject to regulation as an insurer. Or the inclusion of project loans into structures will require a sophisticated sovereign or political risk analysis that takes into account possible legal changes affecting a project and enforcement of agreements underlying the project financing.

RISKS INVOLVED IN THE PURCHASE OF CDO TRANCHES

We believe that the credit risk entailed in CDO investments is accurately captured by our ratings. However, potential investors should be aware that:
❑ only credit risk relative to the stated promise is captured; and
❑ the ratings do not address the risk that market loss may result should a note issued from a CDO be sold prior to maturity.

To date, the ratings of CDOs have been quite stable, but bear in mind that most of these structures have been issued within a fairly benign environment – US corporate default rates over the past five years have tended to fall below the mean. The relative health of the US high-yield market has eased the burden on collateral managers to stay within the boundaries set by the CDOs' trust indentures. As long as the managers stay within these boundaries, the ratings tend to be stable. To date, six transactions have been downgraded, while two have been upgraded.[15]

The economic environment outside the US has been less kind to CDOs. The recent instability in Asia has had some impact on emerging markets. Because the investment-grade tranches within a CBO are cushioned from a deterioration in the credit quality of the collateral pool, CDO ratings have only been marginally affected by the dramatic downgrades of fundamental credits. As of January 1998, 16 transactions had at least 5% of their collateral invested in the countries at the centre of the crisis – Indonesia, Thailand and South Korea. Of these, Moody's placed two of the ratings on review for potential downgrade. The initial ratings of these two transactions were confirmed after the portfolios were improved through selective trading. However, a third CDO was ultimately downgraded in connection with the emerging markets turmoil.

As a rule, the ratings of the more junior tranches are not only more risky to begin with, but are more subject to possible downgrades. Because these are relatively small "residual" pieces, the expected losses associated with the junior tranches may vary widely as the credit quality of the pool changes.

Since Moody's ratings address only credit risk vis-à-vis a promise, the investor must be very careful to understand what has been rated. In some cases, the rating may only address the return of principal by the stated maturity date. In others, the rating may address the return of principal plus a below-market coupon; the investor may also anticipate "excess" coupons, but this anticipated payout is not associated with a Moody's rating. Indeed, if this excess coupon were rated, it would certainly receive a lower rating than has been assigned to the promise to return principal plus the low coupon.

Finally, market risk may arise from the sale of a CDO piece prior to its maturity. Moody's credit ratings are not intended to address the likelihood of losses arising from such sales. Moreover, the ratings are not meant to express a view toward the manager's ability to achieve returns in excess of some market benchmark. Though any such expertise would, of course, be of great interest to the equity investors in a CDO, it does not have an immediate impact on credit risk. Rather, Moody's is concerned with the manager's commitment to operate within the guidelines set forth by the documents, as well as setting up the controls and systems in place to run a portfolio effectively.

1 *See, for example, Bencivenga, Joseph C., "The High-Yield Corporate Bond Market" in* The Handbook of Fixed Income Securities, *Frank J. Fabozzi, ed., Chapter 15.*

2 *This, however, is beginning to change. We are now being asked to evaluate credit risk in cases where there is no conventional debt offering.*

3 *Please refer to Footnote 1.*

4 *We refer, of course, to the curve that depicts the highest return possible for a given portfolio standard deviation. See, for example, Sharpe, W.A., 1970,* Portfolio Theory and Capital Markets, *McGraw Hill, New York.*

5 *The independence of these five default events implies that the probability of at least one default during the three year life of the note is approximately five times the Baa1 three year probability, which is close to that of a Ba1. A more precise determination of the rating of the Russian roulette is a result of the EL process described below. Note however that, somewhat contrary to intuition, the higher the diversity in this underlying pool, the riskier the CLN. If, for example, this pool of five bonds behaved instead like an uncorrelated pool of, say, three bonds, then the resulting rating would be Baa3.*

6 *This section is taken, in somewhat abbreviated form, from "Moody's Refines its Approach to Rating Structured Notes", Special Report, July 1997.*

7 *Moody's idealised default rates represent a smoothed version of the historical default figures.*

8 *For example, see Chapters 12 and 13 of the present volume. Panel 3 in Chapter 2 discusses the particular issue of physical default under credit default transactions.*

9 *Consult J. Hull and A. White, 1995, "Pricing Credit Risk", in* Derivative Credit Risk, *Risk Publications, London, pp. 67-71, and references therein.*

10 *See Chapter 11 of the present volume, as well as "Moody's Rating Migration and Credit Quality Correlation, 1920-1996",* Moody's Special Comment, *July 1997.*

11 *Here we consider the vast majority of structures in which diversification is beneficial. The Russian roulette case discussed above is one of the few exceptions.*

12 *The sponsors of these transactions include Swiss Bank Corporation and Credit Suisse.*

13 *This is not to suggest that 10-year default rates are necessarily applied to the collateral pool; rather, the 10-year default rates are used as a metric so that the non-linearity in the rating/default rate relationship is recognised in calculating the average rating of the pool. The actual default probability applied to the assets must be consistent with the weighted average life of the asset pool.*

14 *Alternatively, within a simulation, one could treat the default rates themselves as being random.*

15 *Most of the downgrades have been the result of Japanese banks that have sponsored CLOs. In these cases, the SPVs did not have a perfected security interest in the collateral. Even in a favourable environment, Moody's does not typically upgrade the ratings of CDO tranches because it is generally possible for collateral managers to trade down to the standards established in the governing documents. Only in cases where gains - which might be reflected in better-than-assumed asset quality, higher coupons or cash reserves - are effectively trapped in the portfolio do we regard an upgrade as appropriate.*

9

Emerging Market Credit Derivatives and Default Estimation

Volatility, Business Cycle Correlation and Portfolio Diversification

David K.A. Mordecai and Samantha Kappagoda
Fitch IBCA, Inc; Caxton Corporation

In a few short years, the market for over-the-counter credit derivatives has grown to exceed $200 billion. A large segment of that market is comprised of emerging market credit derivatives, in particular sovereign emerging market credit derivatives. These derivative transactions reference the forward credit spread curve of a sovereign debt obligation as a benchmark security, or the rating of a sovereign entity.

This chapter surveys the literature on, and proposes original research into, correlation between countries in an effort to suggest an analytic framework for assessing credit exposures at a portfolio level – and hence an approach for estimating default expectations and setting concentration limits to manage the exposure profile of credit portfolios using credit derivatives. More specifically, it offers a rationale for the risk management and portfolio optimisation activities of those contemplating investments in high-yield emerging market credit derivatives as an asset class.

The chapter begins with a discussion of portfolio credit risk and the relationship between correlation and diversification. We review one approach to evaluating credit-risk and default correlations: analysis of the correlation between equity prices. (Most of the relevant finance research on industry and country risk involves the use of equity indexes, because equity data is more easily available than bond or loan default data.) We also try to answer the key questions set out in Table 1.

To discover how to set justifiable concentration limits for global industries, countries and regions, we explore risk exposure in terms of international volatility and duration measures, as well as common risk factors for sovereign and corporate credits. To put these findings in context, we review some key ideas in the asset pricing, credit risk modelling, and investment literature. We draw upon observations from a preliminary country correlation study, independently conducted by the authors, in which GDP served as the proxy for business conditions (economic growth cycles). In Panel 3 we look at how all this relates to the real-world credit crunch in Asia during 1997/8.

We finish by suggesting that the systematic credit risk of a portfolio is a function of the covariance of credit exposures in the portfolio, which is itself a function of the sensitivity of those exposures to common economic factors. This provides market participants with a framework that will help them manage credit exposure(s) in a portfolio, either by setting concentration limits according to the level of reserves, or by setting premiums to compensate for the assumed credit risk.

The relationship between portfolio credit risk and correlation

Asset diversification is fundamental to active portfolio management, both from the perspective of portfolio optimisation and portfolio risk

---

Table 1. Key questions in emerging market credit portfolio analysis

❑ What are the risk characteristics of sovereign and non-US corporate debt?
❑ What is the relationship between market risk, credit risk and default risk?
❑ What is the relationship between risk (ie, asset volatility) and correlation between (a) industries, and (b) countries?
❑ When does industry correlation matter for non-US corporate bonds?
❑ When do regional concentrations matter?

Table 2. Summary statistics

	Stocks			Bonds		
Countries	Monthly (dollars)	Monthly (local currency)	Weekly (local currency)	Monthly (dollars)	Monthly (local currency)	Weekly (local currency)
Correlation						
Germany/US	0.346	0.359	0.298	0.241	0.288	0.257
France/US	0.371	0.386	0.327	0.172	0.184	0.359
UK/US	0.446	0.482	0.417	0.223	0.239	0.328
Switzerland/US	0.467	0.539	0.369	0.120	0.186	0.075
Japan/US	0.235	0.278	0.297	0.161	0.197	0.230
EAFE($)/US	0.473	0.473	0.435	na	na	na
France/Germany	0.517	0.459	0.444	0.518	0.213	0.615
Volatility						
Germany	0.194	0.170	0.166	0.117	0.058	0.035
France	0.213	0.195	0.167	0.102	0.049	0.049
UK	0.214	0.192	0.156	0.139	0.083	0.063
Switzerland	0.191	0.168	0.140	0.102	0.027	0.044
Japan	0.205	0.173	0.172	0.109	0.050	0.040
EAFE($)	0.150	0.150	0.120	na	na	na
US	0.142	0.142	0.134	0.060	0.060	0.044

Source: Solnik et al. (1996)

management. The objective of active credit risk management is to reduce the portfolio credit risk by diversifying the individual credit exposures in the portfolio across national, industrial and regional markets that have a low correlation of asset volatility.

In keeping with modern portfolio theory (Markowitz), two loans or bonds held to maturity will have a much lower default correlation than the stock price correlation of their respective firms, given the low likelihood that two extremely low-probability events will occur simultaneously. Hence, the consequence of low default correlation is that the systematic risk in a portfolio of credit instruments is small relative to the risk contributed by each individual credit. Assuming a low (or zero) correlation with the rest of the portfolio, the lower the relative weight of an individual credit within a portfolio, the smaller its contribution to the risk of that portfolio. Higher correlation results in higher volatility (ie risk) of the portfolio.

Much of the recent literature presents evidence that correlation is time-varying. Solnik, Boucrelle and Le Fur (1996) examine 37 years of monthly stock data (1958–95) and 36 years of monthly bond data (1959–95), as well as 13 years of weekly stock and bond data (1982–95). They find that the international correlation of bond markets increased in the early 1980s, but had no discernible trend in the past ten years (Table 2). Their results suggest that national factors still strongly affect local asset factors. However, they limit the sample in their study to correlation between major industrial foreign markets with the US markets.

From a credit-risk perspective, the more crucial element in their study and in similar studies is the existence of a volatility "contagion" across markets. Another important empirical question is whether industrialised markets (80% of world market capitalisation) are more or less correlated than emerging markets. Later on, we provide evidence about this, as well as results on the correlation of industrial markets with emerging markets.

Numerous studies find evidence for the transmission of volatility across markets. Although long-term trends in US and foreign (industrial) market bonds remain low (<0.3 in US dollar terms), market covariances tend to increase faster than market variances when markets become more volatile. Solnik et al. find evidence not only for wide fluctuations in international correlation of both stocks and bonds, but also that international correlation increases in periods of high market volatility (Table 3).

This suggests two things. The first is that it may be justifiable to set lower concentration limits during credit expansion (compressed credit-spread) periods. The second is that the unconditional variance (ie a constant variance or correlation estimate over long periods) is a less informationally-efficient measure of risk than another approach, such as a downside risk measure, eg semi-variance (the average over all n-observations of the squared deviations below the mean value). The use of semi-variance to measure portfolio volatility in a portfolio of credit instruments is consistent with the left-skewed, fat-tailed distribution of returns exhibited by credit portfolios. (It is this distribution that makes portfolio credit risk estimation a much thornier problem than the estimation of portfolio market risk for the purposes of risk management and portfolio optimisation.)

Market volatility, duration and the term structure of credit risk

The assumed distribution of returns to emerging market credit instruments is fundamental to the performance of credit derivatives. For example, the performance of a total return swap is directly derived from the credit-spread performance of the pre-specified benchmark security.

Emerging market sovereign (and corporate) debt (EMD) behaves more like high-yield domestic debt than industrialised country sovereign or investment-grade corporate debt. The credit and interest-rate sensitivity of a sovereign domicile compounds the local business conditions that

119

EMERGING

MARKET

CREDIT

DERIVATIVES

AND DEFAULT

ESTIMATION

Table 3. Link between correlation and market volatility
(t-statistics in parentheses)

	Monthly (1958-95)				Weekly (1982-95)			
Correlation	Constant (%)	Volatility (Non-US)	Volatility (US)	Adjusted R-squared	Constant (%)	Volatility (Non-US)	Volatility (US)	Adjusted R-squared
STOCKS								
Germany/US	0.078	1.610	2.100	0.147	0.081	1.080	2.750	0.191
	(0.350)	(4.070)	(5.030)		(0.770)	(4.030)	(9.920)	
France/US	-0.130	1.280	2.770	0.254	0.075	0.770	3.010	0.169
	(-0.070)	(4.510)	(8.130)		(0.650)	(2.670)	(9.970)	
UK/US	0.118	0.770	2.070	0.193	0.079	1.130	3.330	0.385
	(0.630)	(4.710)	(5.820)		(0.860)	(6.800)	(12.000)	
Switzerland/US	0.075	2.460	1.260	0.311	0.068	1.800	2.810	0.341
	(0.450)	(8.680)	(3.690)		(0.700)	(8.360)	(10.100)	
Japan/US	0.130	1.740	1.150	0.086	0.021	1.000	3.470	0.268
	(0.600)	(4.910)	(3.050)		(0.200)	(4.890)	(12.900)	
EAFE($)/US	-0.001	1.510	2.520	0.211	0.029	1.950	3.520	0.424
	(-0.000)	(4.320)	(7.070)		(0.310)	(8.340)	(12.800)	
		Volatility France	Volatility Germany			Volatility France	Volatility Germany	
France/Germany	0.104	1.640	1.420	0.203	0.041	0.670	2.050	0.160
	(0.620)	(6.140)	(4.660)		(0.460)	(3.000)	(9.030)	
BONDS								
Germany/US	0.129	-0.80	-5.65	0.221	-0.013	0.41	10.10	0.300
	(0.59)	(-1.10)	(9.32)		(-0.10)	(0.34)	(12.6)	
France/US	0.025	-0.62	6.03	0.164	0.103	4.38	7.51	.361
	(0.09)	(-0.91)	(7.73)		(0.81)	(4.46)	(7.48)	
UK/US	0.002	0.76	4.27	0.125	0.039	3.56	7.33	0.258
	(0.01)	(1.30)	(6.24)		(0.30)	(4.74)	(9.23)	
Switzerland/US	0.037	3.86	4.74	0.117	-0.035	1.53	-2.18	0.036
	(0.13)	(1.61)	(5.68)		(-0.25)	(1.60)	(-2.89)	
Japan/US	-0.006	3.02	3.88	0.136	-0.121	2.37	4.36	0.077
	(-0.03)	(3.45)	(5.85)		(-0.84)	(2.28)	(5.29)	
		Volatility France	Volatility Germany			Volatility France	Volatility Germany	
France/Germany	0.282	5.66	-0.38	0.180	0.175	8.49	3.31	0.435
	(0.99)	(8.16)	(-0.40)		(1.80)	(13.9)	(3.58)	

Source: Solnik et al. (1996)

influence the credit of emerging market corporate debt. As a risk factor, the default risk of developing country debt is essentially absent in bonds of industrialised countries. Dym (1996) addresses this unique feature of emerging market sovereign debt by developing a risk measure that adjusts for duration and credit risk.

For emerging market bonds (sovereigns and corporates), duration-adjusted credit risk is distinct from both interest-rate sensitivity (yield volatility of the risk-free rate) and credit sensitivity. Hence, the duration-adjusted credit-risk (as opposed to the credit sensitivity) of an emerging market sovereign bond can be measured by the following:

$$\text{Credit risk} = \frac{\text{Duration}}{1-d}\text{Stdev}(\Delta d)$$

where d = the market's assessment of the bond's default probability.

The risk of a sovereign (or a corporate) emerging market reference credit's risk is the product of its credit duration and the volatility of its expected default rate (the implied volatility of the risky option). Therefore, the bond's total risk reflects its likely price movements in response to changes in interest rates, changes in expected default rates, and their interactions. It follows that the credit risk of EMD is captured by the volatility of the expected default rate (and its covariance with the risk-free rate, ie credit-spread variability). Table 4 overleaf provides a sample of the relationship between credit risk and total risk for sovereign EMD.

Much like domestic high yield bonds, emerging market corporate debt returns are better explained by equity factors than by term structure factors. Depending on the domicile of a corporation's operating assets and its revenue base (the domicile and credit quality of its customers), a corporation is more or less subject to the sovereign rating ceiling of its parent's domicile. As we discuss later, sovereign debt returns have corresponding indicators related to economic country

Table 4. Developing country risk measures

Government or agency bonds

	Argentina	Brazil	Brazil (Exit)	Mexico	Venezuela
Yield volatility ($\times$ 100)	0.3011	0.3296	0.2047	0.2935	0.3389
Default rate volatility ($\times$ 100)	5.6849	1.5929	2.0030	0.5912	1.0854
Yield-default rate covariance ($\times 100^2$)	0.0560	−0.2286	0.0290	−0.1116	−0.0689
Interest rate risk	0.0014	0.0057	0.0165	0.0109	0.0084
Credit risk	0.0201	0.0205	0.1166	0.0134	0.0175
Total risk	0.0202	0.0187	0.1189	0.0105	0.0179
Interest rate risk share	0.0049	0.0932	0.0192	1.0745	0.2205
Credit risk share	0.9905	1.1978	0.9617	1.6267	0.9951
Covariance share	0.0046	−0.2910	0.0192	−1.7012	−0.1716

Collateralised Brady bonds

	Costa Rica	Mexico	Venezuela
Yield volatility ($\times$ 100)	0.2205	0.2040	0.2041
Default rate volatility ($\times$ 100)	1.1205	0.3904	0.7702
Yield-default rate covariance ($\times$ 100^2)	−0.1351	−0.0393	−0.0461
Interest rate risk	0.0239	0.0239	0.0238
Credit risk	0.0298	0.0250	0.0454
Total risk	0.0261	0.0247	0.0447
Interest rate risk share	0.8408	0.9385	0.2829
Credit risk share	1.3045	1.0325	1.0342
Covariance share	−1.1453	−0.9710	−0.3171

Source: Dym (1996)

factors that compete with term structure as predictors of default and credit risk.

The relevance of equity values and correlations

For the purposes of fundamental or "bottom-up" analysis of portfolios of sovereign credits, there are a number of key economic indicators that can be monitored. Among them are GDP growth, current account, real exchange rates, inflation, debt (short- and long-term) and foreign exchange reserves. These economic indicators for countries can be viewed as corresponding to the following fundamental corporate accounting measures of idiosyncratic business conditions (company operating risk and leverage): operating income, total liabilities, current liabilities and current assets.

Both domestic high yield corporate debt and EMD (corporate and sovereign) exhibit equity factors in their returns. In fact, for high yield debt, business conditions subsume term structure factors in explaining returns. More generally, credit quality correlations for corporate debt can be inferred from equity prices. However, this requires a model that links the asset value of the firm to changes in firm credit quality. If we assume that firm value is randomly distributed according to some distribution, and that liabilities are constant, then the face value of the liabilities act as the threshold level that triggers default.

If we treat credit risk as a default option, then both defaults and recoveries are a function of the variability of equity prices (ie asset volatility or the variability of expected future cashflow). Since equity prices are more easily observed (and indexes of equity values are more easily constructed) than indexes of debt values, we should consider employing equity values to infer asset volatility and hence to infer the value of the default option implicit in risky corporate debt. This embedded default option can be viewed as a credit derivative embedded in a debt instrument.

Asset volatility: implications for credit and default risk

Since a default option (an implicit credit derivative) is priced within every debt instrument, if we model default risk as a knockout or barrier option, then the volatility of asset values directly predict the probability of default. The relationship between market risk and credit risk is based on the valuation of the option of default. The Black–Scholes–Merton models provide an option-theoretic approach for using equity prices to value a risky debt claim on corporate assets.

According to Merton, the option value of debt is a function of the face amount (K) and maturity of the debt (T), the risk-free rate of interest (r), and the volatility of the equity price (σ^2). In the Merton model, the volatility of equity serves as an informative signal on cashflow variability in relation to business risk, and financial/operating leverage.

$$\text{Bond} = VN(-z) + Kr^{-T} * N\left(z - \sigma\sqrt{T}\right),$$

where

$$z = \frac{\log\left(V / Kr^{-T}\right)}{\sigma\sqrt{T}} + \tfrac{1}{2}\left(\sigma\sqrt{T}\right).$$

For a portfolio, much of the covariance dominates the variance of any single credit. Covariance is the product of the variances of the assets and the correlation between those assets. The magnitude of the correlation determines the extent to which individual credit variances offset one another. As stated previously, the objective of diversification, asset allocation, portfolio optimisation and active credit portfolio management is to use correlation as a tool to minimise portfolio variance subject to a target level of expected returns. In the context of a global credit (derivative) portfolio, the objective is to manage the geographic exposure as a proxy for other less observable credit-sensitive economic factors that may influence the default risk of the portfolio, as a function of business and political conditions.

121

EMERGING

MARKET

CREDIT

DERIVATIVES

AND DEFAULT

ESTIMATION

DEFINING CREDIT RISK

Credit risk can be described as the sensitivity of the market value of an asset or a portfolio to expected losses on future payments. Default risk can be defined as the realisation of those losses on future payments. The credit risk premium prices the risk of migration to a state of default for a loan or bond (and the related deterioration in market value).

A risky bond can be analysed as the combination of a risk-free bond (eg US treasury bond) and a long call (a short put) option on some asset (ie the underlying assets of a firm in the case of a corporate bond). In pricing the call (put) option embedded in the bond, one can derive the probability of default for that bond. The value of the call (put) option and the implied credit-risk premium is a function of the volatility of the underlying asset values. Assuming constant interest rates, these underlying asset values vary with changes in future cashflows expected to accrue to those assets.

The downside risk to a buyer of a credit swap is a function of the unexpected occurrence of default, the use of leverage, and the realised recovery rate. One proxy for potential losses are published historical default and recovery rates

compiled by the rating agencies and other sources.

Rating agencies, and buyers of corporate, mortgage-backed and asset-backed securities typically model and measure default risk in terms of the probability of default (inferred from the historical sample frequency of default), and expected loss. The probability of loss measure can be interpreted as the marginal probability of losing a non-zero amount. This measure of risk represents the risk aversion profile for an investor who is sensitive to losing any amount. Alternatively, it can be viewed as a risk measure that treats any default as a total loss. (In the simplest cases, the frequency of default approximates the probability of default.) Expected loss is conditioned upon a given level of defaults:

Expected (Net) Loss =
Gross Defaults * (1 – Expected Recoveries)

Or alternatively, expected losses can be described as the net difference between expected defaults minus expected recoveries. Both the probability (frequency) of default and expected loss are estimates of random variables, and hence have variances associated with them.

Business conditions and common factors in credit risk

All credit derivatives – default swaps and options, credit spread options, and total return swaps – reference the default risk premiums of benchmark securities in order to determine their respective payoffs. The finance literature has attempted to quantify the default-risk premiums of corporate bonds, in other words, the sensitivity of bonds to changing business conditions. In addition, evidence for a common factor in the returns of both stocks and bonds related to economic conditions has been documented both by the Roll–Ross Arbitrage Pricing Theory (1976, 1986), and by the Fama–French three-factor model (1992). This relationship between business cycles and risk premiums for stocks and bonds further defines using GDP as a measure of consumption to proxy for economic growth (Chan, Chen & Hsieh, 1983; Chen, Roll & Ross, 1986). Global research further confirms and generalises the relationship between cashflow volatility, asset prices and risk premiums (Hoshi,

Kashyap & Scharfstein, 1993).

In decomposing the risk premiums of debt instruments, the difference between systemic market risk and idiosyncratic (ie asset-specific) price risk can be illustrated in a simpler context using metaphors from cross-sectional regression analysis of risk factors and event studies of pricing residuals. In event studies based on the market model, abnormal idiosyncratic returns in pricing residuals signal changes in market expectations regarding future cashflows to an asset as a function of new information:

$$r_i = \alpha + \beta_i(R_m) + \varepsilon_i$$

where

r_i = return on asset i

α = abnormal return

β_i = the coefficient of variation

R_m = the return on the market

ε_i = error term ($E[\varepsilon_i] = 0$).

In the Capital Asset Pricing Model (CAPM) and other equilibrium asset-pricing models (variants of the CAPM), excess returns (returns in excess of the risk-free rate) represent idiosyn-

122

EMERGING
MARKET
CREDIT
DERIVATIVES
AND DEFAULT
ESTIMATION

CREDIT RISK MEASURES AND CREDIT PRICING

Derivatives dealers and Derivative Product Companies (DPCs), portfolio managers of credit risky securities, buyers of the residual tranches of these securities, and risk managers currently use different variants of the value-at-risk methodology to measure the risk of their portfolios.

Value-at-risk (VAR) approaches employ methods such as Monte Carlo simulation in order to forecast and summarise with a single statistic the expected maximum loss, over a target horizon and within a given confidence interval. A correctly implemented Monte Carlo approach to VAR can capture both market risk and credit risk of a portfolio, and can compute both probability of default and expected loss as by-products. In addition, VAR directly calculates portfolio value losses from

an asset's migration in credit quality to default by inferring a transition matrix from historical data.

As with other derivative instruments, constructing and valuing these structures involves the use of default estimation applications, such as the Stein estimator, and volatility estimation and simulation methodologies, such as Markov Chain Monte Carlo algorithms and stratified sampling techniques.

As a rating agency, Fitch IBCA has conducted research to incorporate elements of JP Morgan's CreditMetrics and CSFP's CreditRisk+ models into its rating analytics. CreditMetrics employs a value-at-risk approach to default and recovery estimation. In contrast, CreditRisk+ is a sensitivity analysis tool that employs an actuarial approach to correlation and volatility that is similar to the methodology employed for insurance portfolios. McKinsey & Co. subsequently introduced its CreditPortfolio View model. This approach employs cross-section and time-series regressions to empirically estimate the incidence of default for various credit instruments relative to changing economic variables (eg GDP, interest rates, etc.) on a regional and an industry basis. The CreditPortfolio View model is not a factor model in the sense that it does not analytically incorporate term structure into its parameter specification as do the Asset Value Models or the Spread Models.[1]

Models for contingent claims analysis

1st generation - asset value models	
Merton (1974)	
Black–Cox (1976)	
2nd generation – asset value models	
Hull–White (1995)	
Longstaff–Schwartz (1995)	
3rd generation – term structure models	
Jarrow–Turnbull (1995)	
Jarrow–Lando–Turnbull (1995)	
Das–Tufano (1996)	
Risk management models based on contingent claims approaches	
KMV, CreditMetrics	
Creditrisk+	
Creditview	

1 The authors refer the reader to the technical documents of CreditMetrics, CreditRisk+, and CreditPortfolio View for further descriptions of these credit risk models.

---

cratic returns not priced by the market:

$$r_j - r_f = \alpha_0 + \beta_j(R_m - r_f) + \varepsilon_j$$

where

r_j = return on asset j

r_f = risk-free rate of interest

α_0 = where α_0 = 0, o.w. excess returns

β_i = the coefficient of variation

ε_j = error term ($E[\varepsilon_j] = 0$).

The Arbitrage Pricing Theory (APT) and other multi-factor asset models (also variants of the CAPM, eg Consumption CAPM, Intertemporal CAPM) add to the market return factor other macroeconomic and term structure factors. The APT decomposes the risk in asset returns into (at least) two components: a common (systemic) macro factor and a firm-specific (idiosyncratic) micro factor. In the APT, the common factor F

represents new macro-economic information and thus has a zero expected value. In the APT model ε_k represents idiosyncratic risk and also has a zero expected value. This latter risk can be diversified away.

$$r_k = E(r_k) + \beta_k F + \varepsilon_k$$

where

r_k = return on asset k

$E(r_k)$ = expected return on asset k

β_k = the sensitivity of k to F

F = innovations in the common factor

ε_k = firm-specific risk ($E[\varepsilon_k] = 0$).

The discount factor for the idiosyncratic price risk of any asset including any debt instrument (as a present value of expected future cashflows) includes the market expectation of credit risk. Credit risk is the product of probability of default

123

EMERGING
MARKET
CREDIT
DERIVATIVES
AND DEFAULT
ESTIMATION

times the market's sensitivity to losses from defaults. Defaults are not directly observable and there is missing data for both debt trading prices and for defaults. Also, debt prices are incomplete due to discontinuous trading, illiquidity and the bid-ask spread. Although noisier, equity prices tend to provide smoother, more observable measures of asset volatility. To determine when a default will be "costly" (ie, when expected net losses are expected to be significant), credit swaps traders employ tests of the materiality of default using prices, or the market value of debt. The market value of debt can be derived from the option value of default, based on asset volatility inferred from equity prices.[1]

Both market value and credit quality correlations for corporate debt can be inferred from equity prices. However, this requires a model that links the asset value of the firm to changes in firm credit quality. If we assume that firm value is randomly distributed according to a probability distribution, and that liabilities are constant, then the face value of the firm's liabilities act as the critical threshold level for triggering default when firm value approaches this level, much like the exercise price of an option. In this way, the option of default can be modelled as a barrier option. If we treat default risk as a barrier option, then both defaults and recoveries are a function of the variability of equity prices (ie asset volatility or the variability of expected future cashflow).

Comparing equity correlation forecasts between countries

Countries vary in their degree of global integration (or conversely, market segmentation). In a study on the excess equity returns of 24 countries conducted by BARRA, Inc., the United States was the most globally integrated or "open" economy, followed by the Netherlands, Canada and Japan (Table 5). Mexico, Malaysia and Hong Kong were the most segmented markets, ie exhibited the most "closed" economies. In this study, excess returns are a proxy for barriers to global integration.

Erb, Harvey & Viskanta (1994) present evidence that changes in correlation through time are linked to economic activity. They show that equity correlation is higher for two countries in economic recession, than for two countries with business cycles that are out-of-phase. They find correlation between US equities and other G-7 countries to be much higher in recession. The evidence is consistent with the observation that

correlation increases with downside variance. This affirms the rationale for our analysis of GDP correlation as a state variable for the default and volatility estimation of sovereign credit risk. In this approach, GDP correlation is a state-variable related to economic conditions (country or regional). As a state variable, GDP influences both correlation and volatility on an industry, country and regional basis, and hence captures the effects of volatility contagion that can magnify credit risk between markets.

The relative roles of industry and country factors in corporate credit risk

As further motivation for analysing GDP correlations, country correlation usually subsumes industry correlation. Also risk levels (as measured by the standard deviation of returns) vary more widely among countries than among industries. With respect to secular trends in country correlation, Beckers, Connor and Curds (1996) find significant evidence that the trend toward increasing integration is restricted to western Europe. Certain industries are more influential than countries. In fact, the most influential industries dominate the effect of the least influential countries. From the perspective of portfolio risk, the industries that matter most are global

Table 5. Global market correlations and standard deviations of country factor returns

Country	Factor/local market correlation	Rank	Annual standard deviation
Australia	0.83	13	20.5
Austria	0.80	10	20.0
Belgium	0.82	12	19.5
Canada	0.72	2	15.7
Denmark	0.79	8	20.8
Finland	0.85	17	26.2
France	0.83	14	21.5
Germany	0.79	9	20.1
Hong Kong	0.92	23	32.9
Ireland	0.85	18	22.2
Italy	0.84	16	25.1
Japan	0.72	4	17.0
Malaysia	0.91	21	28.1
Mexico	0.97	24	57.0
Netherlands	0.72	3	18.7
New Zealand	0.85	19	28.7
Norway	0.83	15	24.5
Singapore	0.91	22	27.0
South Africa	0.74	6	18.9
Spain	0.86	20	23.0
Sweden	0.80	11	20.5
Switzerland	0.73	5	16.3
United Kingdom	0.75	7	14.5
United States	0.70	1	13.7

Source: BARRA, Inc

124

EMERGING
MARKET
CREDIT
DERIVATIVES
AND DEFAULT
ESTIMATION

Table 6. Global model: standard deviation of industry factor returns

Name	Annual standard deviation
Banks	16.0
Financial institutions	17.8
Life insurance	14.4
Property insurance	15.2
Real estate	14.8
Holding companies	14.5
International oil	17.1
Non-oil energy	18.2
Utilities	10.5
Transportation	13.8
Automobiles	17.2
Household durables	21.5
Textiles	16.1
Beverage	13.7
Health	15.5
Food	13.0
Entertainment	14.0
Media	15.0
Business service	16.0
Retail	14.5
Wholesale	16.0
Consumer goods	15.0
Aerospace	15.5
Computers	14.7
Electrical	14.4
Electronics	18.4
Machinery	15.1
Heavy engineering	16.0
Automobile components	14.9
Manufacturing	15.1
Construction	14.2
Chemicals	15.2
Mining	17.5
Precious metals	21.4
Forestry	15.1
Container products	15.5

Source: Becker et al. (1996)

businesses that fall into the following categories: banking, oil, precious metals and mining, forest products (Table 6).

Business conditions and default risk

As with derivative pricing, credit analysis should focus on volatility or variance estimation. Many proponents of implied volatility and arbitrage pricing of credit risk compare the use of historical default rates, recovery rates and yield spreads for risk management to "driving by looking in the rear-view mirror".

Historically, both the probability of loss (loss frequency), and expected loss (loss severity) exhibit considerable variability over time. Often, both historical and stochastic model estimates rely on the highly questionable assumption of uncorrelated default likelihood between assets, sectors, regions or industries. Default probabilities in rating transition matrices estimated from historical data are highly dependent on how

many states are assumed to exist between AAA and D (eg 9 vs 18 rating categories or "states").

Loss severity or recovery values also exhibit significant variance that increases progressively from the higher to the lower ratings in the credit spectrum. Over the last ten years, the average annual default frequency for B-rated US corporate bonds has varied from 7% to 21%. Iterative shrinkage techniques such as Stein estimation can employ cross-sectional variation to derive a more predictive long-run average from a sample of events than the historical arithmetic average. Prediction intervals are non-linear and confidence intervals for non-normal distributions are not meaningful (credit distributions are skewed, fat-tailed distributions).

In contrast to the historical approach, and consistent with the time-varying patterns between business cycle correlation and market volatility of the countries documented above, country/industry concentration limits for credit derivative portfolios can be weighted according to distribution functions (rather than estimates) in the corresponding variance-covariance matrix. This simulation approach uses probability distributions to model parameters as random variables rather than as constants. The authors propose modelling the state-dependencies of credit and default risk for a portfolio of EMD credits using a Bayesian hierarchical model approach. In this model, GDP correlation serves as the country factor state-variable (proxy for business cycle correlation). Industry equity correlations can capture the influence of those industry factors (oil, mining, banking, etc.) that subsume country factors. Country risk factors and correlations as a function of short-term interest rate sensitivity (term structure volatility) can be proxied by country equity index standard deviations and correlations.

$$\text{Credit risk}_p = f(\Sigma \gamma_i, \sigma_i, \delta_i | \phi_j, \phi_j, \theta_j, \rho_j)$$

where

γ = weight of i in p

σ = credit spread of credit i in portfolio p

δ = duration of i in p

ϕ = business cycle correlation (GDP correlation) for country (domicile of i) j

ϕ = global industry correlation for country j

θ = weight of ϕ in country j

λ = country j equity index volatility

ρ = country j equity index correlation with p

v = term structure volatility of j.

Probability distributions and correlations can be fitted to each of these distributions and simulated values can be generated. Given sufficient

EMERGING
MARKET
CREDIT
DERIVATIVES
AND DEFAULT
ESTIMATION

data, nonparametric estimation techniques will prove particularly well-suited to fitting probability distributions. In the probabilistic version of this hierarchical model simulation, correlation is modelled as a jump-diffusion process. A more deterministic sensitivity analysis can also be run for specified levels of portfolio volatility and correlation. A reduced-form approach might employ three-stage regression estimates of ϕ, φ, λ, and ρ to compute the multi-variate probability of default in high-correlation, high-volatility country regimes. In applying regression analysis to estimate parameters, assuming that many of these variables are endogenous, instrumental variable approaches and simultaneous equation estimation techniques will prove useful (eg two-stage or three-stage least squares).

In addition to the non-parametric approaches for estimating volatility, Arch/Garch (Auto-Regressive and Generalised Auto-Regressive Conditional Heteroskedasticity) and GMM (Generalised Method of Moments) techniques have proved helpful. Some researchers have begun to apply a time-series approach similar to Arch for volatility estimation, in order to estimate correlation (the Auto-Regressive Conditional Correlation technique). In modelling both volatility and correlation as a function of the state-variable, the Bayesian models proven by Zellner (1997) in predicting regime-switching in inflation factors should prove useful.

We propose conducting further time-series and cross-sectional analysis in order to estimate distribution functions and correlations for industry and country factors. We leave the reader to explore the hierarchy, specification and subset of parameters specific to their purposes.

The impact of political risk: regional influences on EMD

Political risk is the principal driver of regional "concentrations" of credit exposure, in which an economic or political event in one country affects other countries in the same region. Political risk is intimately linked to other key regional economic influences, such as trade flows (embargoes, cartel activity), tariffs and transfer payments. The ten-year impact of political risk on correlation and volatility of expected default can be significant.

Erb, Harvey & Viskanta (1996) analysed the links between various political risk measures and fundamentals such as price-to-book ratios within each economy. The results of their analysis suggest that country risk measures are correlated with future equity returns and with equity valuation measures.

Diamonte, Liew and Stevens (1996) found a statistically significant difference between the impact of political risk on emerging markets (11% per quarter) vs developed markets (2.5% per quarter). They also found that during the past ten years political risk has decreased in emerging markets and increased in developed markets. They conclude that if this trend continues, the differential impact of political risk on asset prices may narrow over time.

Panel 3 overleaf illustrates the limitations of a fundamental analysis approach that does not incorporate the effects of investor sentiment and regional contagion into global credit risk analysis.

Default estimates and the indexing of credit risk

With the growing interest in credit risk management and credit derivatives, there is an increasing demand for credit risk and default indexes. As indexes might conceivably form a tool for managing some of the exposures we discussed above, in this section we look at some considerations in constructing and interpreting them.

A credit event index can be an index of loss amounts, an aggregate number of events (defaults, failure rates), changes in implied credit spreads, or credit (rating) migrations. In themselves, indexes are not new. For many years, they have been constructed for commercial and residential mortgage debt to describe defaults and prepayments, and have also been used in the consumer loan and credit card markets. Indexes of business failures or personal bankruptcies are published by private organisations such as Dun & Bradstreet, and by various government agencies such as the US Commerce Department or the Census Bureau. Rating upgrades and downgrades have been tracked for several years by the Nationally Recognized Securities Rating Organisations (NRSROs) and, recently, transition matrices and default studies by these organisations have proliferated.

However, the indexes now being promoted in the corporate markets take a greater variety of forms, such as the total return index or model portfolio of credit spread performance. They are devised primarily by investment banks as a credit derivative trading tool.

Traditional indexes of corporate credit events were unsuitable for trading purposes because of their lack of transparency, measurement error

EMERGING

MARKET

CREDIT

DERIVATIVES

AND DEFAULT

ESTIMATION

PANEL 3

EAST ASIA CRISIS CASE STUDY:
The Impact of Asset Bubbles, Contagion and Informational Cascades on Regional Credit Risk Portfolios

The East Asian Crisis was unanticipated by many market participants and analysts. Macroeconomic fundamentals in East Asia were stable in the early 1990s, and some of the warning signs usually associated with problems were not apparent. Government budgetary positions within each country were maintained at reasonable levels and were sometimes even in surplus prior to 1996. Inflation remained below 10% and domestic savings rates and investment rates were high throughout the region. Current account deficits were large and, between 1990 and 1996, averaged 4% of GDP for all five countries (Indonesia, Korea, Malaysia, the Philippines and Thailand), however due to increased capital inflows, there was a net increase in foreign exchange reserves in all countries except Malaysia. (In all countries, reserves exceeded four months of imports, and in South Korea, they were equivalent to 2.8 months.) Furthermore, global market conditions were favourable; interest rates remained low and commodity prices were relatively stable.

During 1996 and 1997, there were increasing signs of financial weakness, dismissed at the time as temporary imbalances that could be rectified. Current account deficits continued to increase; in 1996, Malaysia's deficit increased by 8% of GDP, Thailand's by almost 5% and Philippines by about 3% of GDP. With hindsight, it is clear that real exchange rates had become overvalued, particularly after 1994, with the appreciation of the US dollar. Following the local currency appreciation, export growth slowed, dropping from an average of 25% for all five countries in 1995, to 7.2% in 1996.

Financial sector weakness increased, as banks struggled to keep up with growing income, demand for increasingly sophisticated financial services and large capital inflows. Private sector credit had expanded rapidly, following partial financial liberalisation in the late 1980s and early 1990s. This was primarily financed by offshore borrowing by the banking sector. A large part of the credit was directed at speculative investments such as real estate, rather than to increase productive capacity (as had been the case in earlier years).

Foreign liabilities of commercial banks increased at rapid rates, thus exposing the banking system to significant exchange rate risk, since they had local currency revenue streams and dollar liabilities. Even if domestic loans were denominated in dollars, borrowers earning local currency faced problems in the event of depreciation. The proportion of short-term to total debt outstanding increased. The ratio of short term debt to foreign exchange reserves, which compares a country's short term foreign liabilities to its liquid foreign assets available to service those liabilities, grew. (This had also been the case in mid 1994 in Mexico and Argentina.) In mid-1997, this indicator exceeded 1.0 for Indonesia, Thailand and Korea. Although this by itself does not create a

and significant basis risk. These are also the hurdles that the current generations of credit indexes must overcome. There is also the expense of setting up and maintaining an index, and the problem of building consistent definitions for credit events.

Although indexes can be employed for both exchange-traded instruments and over-the-counter transactions, indexes constructed and widely employed by exchanges can more easily be referenced for OTC trades than vice-versa. Different models of credit risk will deploy different indexes, depending on the objective of the model and its structure and specification.

There are three or four general classes of mod-els: forecasting (estimation/prediction) models and, closely related, valuation models, portfolio optimisation (asset allocation) models, pricing (arbitrage) models, and hedging models (typically a by-product of a pricing model). Different indexes can be constructed for valuing, hedging, pricing, and trading credit risk, depending on whether the objective is to estimate:

❑ the number of defaults in an industry, a sector of a market, an economy, or an asset-class (ie, the frequency or rate of default);

❑ the economic losses associated with defaults (ie, the severity of default);

❑ the asset volatilities (implied probability or distance to default) associated with a credit; or

127

EMERGING
MARKET
CREDIT
DERIVATIVES
AND DEFAULT
ESTIMATION

crisis, it increases the vulnerability of a country to any period of instability. These financial risks were generally ignored.

In late June of 1997, the Thai government removed support from a major finance company, Finance One, announcing that creditors would incur losses – contrary to their previous position and market expectations. This shock accelerated the withdrawal of foreign funds and the depreciation of the Thai baht on July 2, which developed into a financial panic.

Once the crisis was in progress, contagion spread for a variety of reasons. One reason was that many creditors treated the region as one entity, rather than distinguishing between the individual countries. This was exacerbated by a loss of government credibility throughout the region. Furthermore, there was additional political uncertainty due to potential changes in government in Korea, Thailand, the Philippines and Indonesia.

The depreciation resulting from the withdrawal of funds was followed by new withdrawals of foreign exchange as domestic borrowers with unhedged currency positions rushed to buy dollars. These withdrawals set into motion a liquidity squeeze and a sharp rise in interest rates. Firms that were profitable prior to the crisis could no longer obtain working capital. The absence of clear laws on bankruptcy and workout mechanisms accentuated the withdrawal of credit as foreign lenders feared little recourse.

The banking sector came under pressure, the balance of non-performing loans rose rapidly, and depositors withdrew funds, either due to concerns for the banking system or to meet their foreign exchange obligations. The short-term liquidity squeeze triggered bank runs which resulted in a longer term liquidity crisis. Thailand and Korea attempted to defend their exchange rate pegs, using a large proportion of their reserves to no avail. Malaysia and Thailand introduced controls on foreign exchange transactions. Inflammatory statements by government officials and market participants served to underline the problems. Undercapitalised Japanese banks with heavy South East Asian exposure began to call in their loans, as did Korean banks. The regional crisis spread when the Hong Kong dollar came under pressure in November and the banking sector reacted by calling in loans from the rest of the region.

Although IMF intervention can often strengthen investor confidence, the first round of IMF programs included recommendations for immediate suspensions or closures of financial institutions, and served to incite panic. The first programmes in Thailand, Korea and Indonesia failed after the first few weeks and the second programme did nothing to restore confidence as stock markets kept falling and local currencies continued to depreciate. Bank closures in Indonesia and Thailand added fuel to the fire, and credit ratings for these countries collapsed after the agreements were in place.

This account illustrates the limits of fundamental analyses that do not take account of regional interdependencies, market perception and investor sentiment. In advocating regime models for regional credit risk, the authors direct readers to the academic literature on asset bubbles, contagion, and informational cascades, as well as the Diamond-Dybvig and Grossman-Stiglitz models of asset markets with imperfect information (see main text bibliography).

❑ credit spreads for pricing or inferring default probabilities, total return, etc.

The first step in constructing an index of credit spreads is identifying reference assets (ie benchmark instruments) or, in some cases, reference parties (credit names or counterparties). A second step is to specify for each type of credit instrument the mapping of heterogeneous covenants and default/recovery behaviour into consistent and uniform performance within the index. The potential for basis risk and moral hazard are key considerations in constructing an index, and index values are likely always to be subject to broad interpretation.

For example, the construction and mainte-nance of a total return index, which is most like an equity or commodity index, is still subject to far more sample bias, survivor bias and heteroskedasticity than an equity or commodity index, because of the informational inefficiency in debt prices. Most debt indexes employ dealer quotes and interpolated values (matrix pricing) to fill in gaps in traded prices. These information deficiencies further complicate the criteria and procedures involved in tracking benchmarks with minimal tracking error, and in portfolio rebalancing.

Particularly problematic is the definition of credit events for default or loss indexes. Only costly defaults should be included. Often, credit

EMERGING
MARKET
CREDIT
DERIVATIVES
AND DEFAULT
ESTIMATION

swap triggers employ materiality tests of credit events and credit migration. However, these tests are often not feasible to apply to an index of events. Similarly, recovery values are difficult if not impossible to observe. In addition, the values associated with credits that have defaulted or that have been downgraded are often non-synchronous, and can either lead or lag the event occurrence.

Conclusion

We have attempted in this chapter to present an analytical framework and methodological rationale for assessing regional, country and industry exposure in an actively managed credit (derivative) portfolio. In doing so, we addressed the relationship between asset volatility, duration and the

term structure of credit risk, and the role of correlation and the covariance of the portfolio.

In assessing the impact of credit risk on the portfolio our analysis has drawn on principles from portfolio and option theory, asset pricing and interest-rate modelling. Our suggestions for estimating defaults have addressed the idiosyncrasy, discontinuity and opaqueness of credit risk, and have proposed Bayesian approaches for computing robust estimates of correlation and volatility regimes. We believe that the above tools are aids to decision-making. As such, they are meant to be complements, not substitutes, for experienced and rational judgements based on thoughtful, carefully formulated and clearly articulated assumptions.

1 *The credit risk modelling firm KMV is particularly active in applying contingent claims analysis to imply default*

probabilities from firm equity prices and correlations.

BIBLIOGRAPHY

MODELS AND MODEL RISK

Credit Suisse Financial Products, 1997, Creditrisk+ Technical & Marketing Documents.

Derman, E., 1996, "Model Risk", *Risk* 9/5, May, pp. 34-7..

Jorion, P., 1997, *Value-at-Risk: The New Benchmark for Controlling Derivative Risk*, New York: Irwin.

JP Morgan, 1997, CreditMetrics Technical & Marketing Documents.

McKinsey & Company, Creditview Technical & Marketing Documents, 1997.

Zellner, A., 1997, *Bayesian Analysis in Econometrics and Statistics: The Zellner View and Papers*, Chicago: University of Chicago Press.

INTERMEDIATION, OPTION PRICING AND PORTFOLIO THEORY

Markowitz, H., 1990, *Portfolio Selection*, Oxford: Blackwell.

Markowitz, H., 1994, *Mean-Variance Analysis with Portfolio Choice and Capital Markets*, Oxford: Blackwell.

Merton, R., 1990, *Continuous-Time Finance*, Oxford: Blackwell.

IMPERFECT INFORMATION AND CASCADES IN ASSET MARKETS

Bikchandjani, S., D. Hirschleifer and I. Welch, "A Theory of Fads and Fashions, Customs and Cultural Changes as Informational Cascades", *Journal of Political Economy* 100 (5), pp. 992-1026.

Diamond, D.W and Dybvig, P.H., 1983, "Bank Runs, Deposit Insurance and Liquidity", *Journal of Political Economy* 91 (June), pp. 401-19.

Grossman, S.J. and J.E. Stiglitz, 1976, "Information and Competitive Price Systems", *American Economic Review*, no. 66, May, pp. 246-53.

Grossman, S.J. and J.E. Stiglitz, 1980, "On the Impossibility of Informationally Efficient Markets", *American Economic Review*, no. 70, pp. 393-408.

BUBBLES AND CONTAGION IN EMERGING MARKET ECONOMIES

Annual Report, 1988, Bank for International Settlements.

Dornbusch, R., 1988, *Asian Crisis Themes* (mimeo).

Global Development Finance, 1998, World Bank, Washington DC.

Krugman, P., 1998, *What Happened to Asia?* (mimeo).

Radelet, S. and J. Sachs, 1998, *The Onset of the East Asian Financial Crisis* (mimeo).

RESEARCH ON GLOBAL MARKET VOLATILITY AND CORRELATION

Beckers, S., G. Connor, and R. Curds, 1996, "National versus Global Influences on Equity Returns", *Financial Analysts Journal* 52/2, March/April.

Chen, Nai-Fu, R. Roll, and S. Ross, 1986, "Economic Forces and the Stock Market", *Journal of Business* July.

Diamonte R. L., J. M. Liew, and R. L. Stevens, 1996, "Political Risk in Emerging and Developed Markets",

129

EMERGING

MARKET

CREDIT

DERIVATIVES

AND DEFAULT

ESTIMATION

Financial Analysts Journal 52/3, May/June, pp.71-8.

Dym, S., 1994, "Identifying and Measuring the Risks of Developing Country Bonds", *Journal of Portfolio Management* 20/2, Winter, pp. 61-72.

Erb, Claude, C. R. Harvey, and T. E. Viskanta, 1994, "Forecasting International Equity Correlations", *Financial Analysts Journal* 50/6, Nov/Dec, pp. 32-45.

Erb, Claude, C. R. Harvey, and T. E. Viskanta, 1996, "Political Risk, Economic Risk and Financial Risk", *Financial Analysts Journal* 52/6, Nov/Dec, pp. 29-74.

Fama, E.F., 1988, "Permanent and Temporary Components of Stock Prices", *Quarterly Journal of Economics* 96/2, February.

Fama, E.F., and K.R. French, 1989, "Business Conditions and Expected Returns on Stocks and Bonds", *Journal of Financial Economics* 25/1, February, pp. 23-49

Fama, E.F., and K.R. French, 1993, "Common Risk Factors in the Returns on Stocks and Bonds", *Journal of Financial Economics* 33/1, February, pp. 3-56

Grinold, Richard, A. Rudd, D. Stefek, 1989, "Global Factors: Fact or Fiction?", *Journal of Portfolio Management* 16/1, Fall, pp. 79-89.

Kashyap, A., T. Hoshi and D. Scharfstein, 1991, "Corporate Structure, Liquidity and Investment: Evidence from Japanese Industrial Groups", *Quarterly Journal of Economics* 106/1, pp. 33-60.

Ross, S., 1976a, "Arbitrage Theory of Capital Asset Pricing", *Journal of Economic Theory*, December.

Ross, S., 1976b, "Risk Arbitrage", *Risk and Return in Finance*.

Ross, S., 1986, "Testing the APT and Alternative Asset Pricing Theories", *Journal of Business*.

Rudd, A., 1996, *Industry versus Country Correlations*, BARRA, Inc.

Solnik, B., C. Boucrelle and Yann LeFur, 1996, "International Market Correlation and Volatility", *Financial Analysts Journal* 52/5, Sept/Oct, 1996, pp. 17-68.

CREDIT MODELLING, TRANSITION ANALYSIS AND CREDIT DERIVATIVES

10

Rational Modelling of Credit Risk and Credit Derivatives[1]

Richard K. Skora

Skora & Company Inc.

For the last couple of decades, and especially the last several years, the derivatives market has worked feverishly to develop new and better interest rate models. All this knowledge and understanding is quickly being adapted and extended to credit models. Nevertheless, credit risk modelling is still in its infancy.

This chapter offers an introduction to this developing science and explains how the various approaches relate to the pricing of credit risk and credit derivatives. We start by explaining the ways in which credit risk is different from interest rate risk and other market risks. As a result many of the assumptions underlying interest rate models, and therefore the models themselves, are not applicable to credit risk. We then look at capital-based pricing of credit risk and explore how this relates to credit risk modelling. The next section discusses whether risk-neutral pricing theory can be applied to credit risk and credit derivatives.

Finally, we look at the four broad divisions of credit risk models, particularly as they relate to credit derivatives. As this chapter is intended to provide a framework for those coming into the field, our discussion is substantially more general than the discussions of credit risk modelling in, for example, Cooper and Martin (1996), Cossin (1997), Madan (1998), and Das (1998), and makes liberal use of a bibliography of key texts presented at the end of this chapter. Newcomers to the credit derivatives field may find it particularly useful to read Hull and White (1995) and Cooper and Mello (1991), who make several important observations about credit risk and how it affects the price of over-the-counter derivatives. Sorensen and Bollier (1994) give a particularly clever, practical explanation of pricing the credit risk in an over-the-counter swap, while Wall and Fung (1987), Iben and Brotherton-Ratcliffe (1994) and Duffee (1996) discuss credit risk as it applies to portfolio risk management.

To illustrate the implications of the main text, we present examples in Panels 1 and 2. The first panel describes a credit default swap in detail and explains how it is priced. The pricing exercise highlights the advantages and disadvantages of risk-neutral pricing. The second panel demonstrates how a slight variation in the structure of the swap demands that a completely different approach to pricing be used.

Credit risk is unique

Credit risk is the risk of loss on a financial or non-financial contract due to the counterparty's failure to perform on that contract. Credit risk's two components are default risk and recovery risk. Default risk is the possibility that a counterparty will fail to meet its obligation, and recovery risk is the possibility that the recovery value of the defaulted contract may be less than its promised value.

Methods and models for evaluating and pricing credit risk have been around for as long as individuals and institutions have extended credit. Banks, insurance companies, and credit rating institutions employ thousands of experts at evaluating individual institutions. For example, a credit officer of a bank analyses fundamental data about a firm, industry, or country such as financial statements and economic data to determine the creditworthiness of a client. The findings of their efforts translate almost directly into the price of a loan or bond, or a decision on whether or not to buy a bond or make a loan.

These methods and models are not sufficient for pricing credit derivatives. In order to price a credit derivative one needs a model that describes the dynamics of credit risk. These dynamic models start with the creditworthiness of the firm, industry, or country or some other known measure of credit risk. The model then describes the possible ways that the creditworthiness may evolve over time.

Credit risk has both similarities and differences to other risks such as interest rate risk or equity risk. These latter risks are usually referred to as market risks. Credit risk can be traded just as interest rate risk may be traded. A corporate bond or emerging market bond is an excellent mechanism for taking credit exposure to a particular issuer. The price of the bond is affected by changes in the credit risk or perceived credit risk of the issuer. Of course a bond is not a perfect instrument for trading credit risk: its price is also affected by changes in the general level of interest rates.

On the other hand credit risk has many properties that make it different from market risk – especially for modelling purposes. A US Treasury bond is the quintessential example of a security that has interest rate risk, but no credit risk. The US Treasury market represents the entire debt of the US government. The Treasury bond markets are liquid, so the Treasury rate is set through the trading activities of thousands market-makers and end-users. As a result one may take both long and short positions in the Treasury bond market of almost any tenor while incurring relatively small transactions costs.

In contrast, the market for credit risky debt is illiquid. The illiquidity is partly because the market is segmented – each corporation issues its own debt which trades at prices representing the investors' perceptions for that particular corporation. As a result, instruments that would allow one to assume the credit risk of a particular corporation at a particular tenor may simply not exist; sometimes those that do exist either do not trade or trade for large transaction costs.

A second difference between market risk and credit risk is that changes in credit risk often cause the price of the associated debt instrument to "jump". And that jump can be very large, particularly when it is caused by default. In default the recovery value can be a small fraction of the face value of the debt instrument; furthermore, the recovery value is highly uncertain and may only be determined after a (possibly lengthy) negotiation process.

While we will not argue further whether credit risk is or is not a kind of market risk, it is important to remember these key differences when modelling credit risk. Most of the models described later in this chapter use techniques that are particular to credit risk modelling. The success of these models may be judged with respect to how well they capture the idiosyncrasies of credit risk.

Capital-based pricing

Since banks are market makers in credit derivatives, it is natural to review one of the traditional ways in which banks price risk.

It is complicated to define bank capital. A technical definition is that bank capital is the bank's net worth. More immediately, capital is also the bank's cushion against possible losses due to various risks such as market, credit, and operational risk. This cushion capital is held mostly in the form of liquid, secure assets. (There are various tiers of capital.) When losses exceed the total amount of capital, the bank defaults and the excess loss is passed along to the creditors. Therefore it is important that a bank holds enough capital so as to have a small likelihood of default.

The amount of capital is the sum of its expected loss and unexpected loss as described by the equation

Capital = Expected Loss + Unexpected Loss

The unexpected loss is a measure of the uncertainty of loss. As actual losses may be either smaller or larger than the expected loss, the potential for loss can only be described using a probability distribution. The expected loss plus the unexpected loss is thus an expression of the losses that a bank might suffer at some appropriate confidence level. A bank that uses a larger confidence level should be more secure.

We ought to mention that in practice bankers speak of at least two kinds of capital: regulatory capital and economic capital. Regulatory capital is determined by rules set by the regulators. The calculation of regulatory capital has to apply to all banks, so it is simple and conservative.

Economic capital is determined by each bank's own internal policies. So it is customised to its own products and its own view of risk. The calculation of economic capital has generally been more scientific and has evolved to keep up with the new banking activities. It is sometimes calculated using an actuarial methodology. This means that the calculation of risk is statistical in nature and is based on historical experience.

Purportedly, both regulatory and economic capital are a measure of the bank's risks. When banks were simply lending money, the two kinds of capital were nearly equal. At present, the two

135

RATIONAL
MODELLING OF
CREDIT RISK
AND CREDIT
DERIVATIVES

kinds of capital are diverging. Indeed, banks are lobbying hard to convince regulators to adopt new rules to bring regulatory capital more in line with banks' economic capital. (This is the theme of Chapter 12 in the present volume.)

Regardless of whether the two kinds of capital are the same, it is true that the capital concept is one kind of measure of risk and therefore is relevant to determining a fair price for that risk. For the following pricing exercise, we will assume that one has a formula for calculating capital and that it accurately measures risk.

The *cost of capital* is the total return that the bank expects to generate from its capital. It is usually calculated as 100% of the expected loss plus the bank's predetermined rate of return times the unexpected loss. This is expressed by the formula:

Cost of Capital = (100%) * Expected Loss
+ (Rate of Return) * (Unexpected Loss)

One way of pricing credit derivatives or any risky bank asset is to base the methodology on the cost of capital. The revenues from the asset should compensate the bank for its cost of capital. The price of an asset may be measured by the change in the cost of capital when the asset is added to (or taken away from) the bank's portfolio.

Using this pricing model, one would price each new asset by considering the marginal effect that it has on the bank's capital. Actually, the marginal effect alone may not be exactly accurate. One should look at more than just the local affect of the asset. For example an asset by itself may significantly increase the capital, while an asset considered as one of the next one hundred new assets may account for only a small fraction of the total capital for those one hundred new assets. (This brings to mind the Capital Asset Pricing Model, under which one cannot determine the price of an asset by itself, but only as part of a larger market portfolio.)

Here are two observations about capital-based pricing. First, to determine the expected and unexpected losses, the bank either implicitly or explicitly assigns probabilities to future events that are likely to affect its cashflows.

Second, banks naturally try to hedge their risks, that is, to minimise their unexpected losses. If they cannot directly offset their risks, then they will try to minimise their risks in relation to their total assets by diversifying.

For example, the two primary risks of a bank that makes markets in over-the-counter interest rate swaps are market risk and credit risk. The market risk is usually perfectly hedged, so the unexpected losses due to market risk are zero. This leaves non-zero expected and unexpected losses due to credit risk.

If the bank were able to diversify its credit risk so that unexpected losses due to credit risk were negligible in comparison to the expected losses, then the cost of capital would approximate to the bank's expected losses. It would follow that the price for the trade would be equal to the expected losses. (Compare this with risk-neutral pricing below.)

In practice, a bank's risks, especially credit risks, cannot be diversified away – and unexpected losses are not zero. Moreover, in reality credit markets are not perfectly liquid. Not every bank has the same opportunities. Banks and other institutions execute deals as opportunities come along. Sometimes a new deal fits nicely into a portfolio and increases the overall risk/return ratio, and sometimes it does not. So capital-based pricing theory suggests that different banks should offer different prices for the same credit risk. This is exactly what can be observed in the credit markets today.

The next section discusses an alternative pricing theory called "risk-neutral pricing". It will be seen that risk-neutral pricing theory has some similarities to capital-based pricing theory. If the markets were complete, there were no transaction costs, and all risks could be hedged, then the two theories would give identical prices.

It is not the purpose of this paper to select the correct pricing theory – both have advantages. In particular, as the prudent banker should always consider the cost of capital, the capital-based method is a check of whether a trade "makes sense".

Risk-neutral pricing and credit risk

RISK-NEUTRAL PRICING

Black, Scholes (1974) and Merton (1974) famously developed a pricing theory for valuing equity call options called risk-neutral pricing theory. The two key steps in their theory are to:
❑ model equity prices; and
❑ hedge the equity risk.

In the first step, they model equity prices as a lognormal Brownian process. This is the simplest process that succeeds in describing much of the randomness of equity prices. The Brownian process is also easy to work with and leads to a simple formula for the price of the option. It is easy to replace the Brownian process and model the equity prices by other processes. (Of course these models give different prices, and this has led to a serious debate among practitioners over the selection of models.)

Black, Scholes and Merton's second step contains the important, new idea. Hedging the equity risk means that one can synthetically replicate the equity call option using a dynamic, self-financing portfolio of the underlying equity and a money market account. In particular, at the time of the option's expiry the portfolio and the equity call option have exactly the same value. If there is no arbitrage, then they must always have the same value. The price of the option is the price of the portfolio.

The construction of the portfolio leads to a partial differential equation for the price of the equity call option. The solution is well known. One readily deduces that the price of the option is the expected value of the present value of future cashflows. The expectation is taken with respect to what is called the risk-neutral probability measure. This means that the expected return on the equity (and equity call option) is the riskless rate and the present value is calculated by discounting by the riskless rate. See Derman (1997) for a practical discussion of modelling and risk-neutral pricing.

The key assumptions in risk-neutral pricing theory are that the market is complete and arbitrage free. To be complete, a market must allow a participant efficiently to take a long or short position in the underlying cash instrument. In particular, the market must be liquid.

Looked at from the probability-theoretic viewpoint, risk-neutral pricing simply selects a probability distribution of future events that affect the cashflows of the product under consideration. The distribution is then calibrated to known market prices. That means that the model correctly prices the known market products. So in some sense risk-neutral pricing is simply interpolating prices of simpler products to obtain prices of more complicated products. See Harrison and

Kreps (1979) and Harrison and Pliska (1981) for a general probability-theoretic description of risk-neutral pricing theory.

RISK-NEUTRAL PRICING APPLIED TO CREDIT RISK

The key ingredient in the Black–Scholes and Merton theory is the ability to hedge the equity call option. If one could hedge credit risk, then risk-neutral pricing would apply perfectly to credit derivatives. But what if one cannot hedge credit risk? We have already pointed out that the credit markets are not complete – for example, one may not efficiently "short" a corporate bond. So the assumptions in risk-neutral pricing theory are not satisfied.

On the other hand, risk-neutral pricing remains a useful tool. For credit derivatives it can be used to give a good approximation of the correct price. In practice, the estimated price may be adjusted to account for known shortcomings or vagaries in the model. In any case, so far the market seems to have decided to apply the risk-neutral model: most of the pricing models for credit derivatives are based on risk-neutral pricing theory.

To apply risk-neutral pricing theory, a model must start by modelling the risks that affect the price. This amounts to selecting a process that describes the evolution of future events which affect the cashflows of credit-risky instruments. These future events may simply be future prices of credit risky instruments, or they may be future defaults and recoveries. Credit risk and market risk are the two risks that most obviously affect the price of a credit derivative (Figure 1). Usually the market risk is simply interest rate risk eg the price of a corporate bond depends on the general level of interest rates.

Thus, all credit risk models should be integrated with interest rate risk models to various degrees. However, the simplest approach is to ignore the interest rate risk and to assume that interest rates are static. In particular, this approach assumes that credit risk and interest rate risks are probabilistically independent. This assumption may or may not be appropriate depending on the credit derivative that is to be priced. So in the discussion below, we point out the models that allow for the non-independence of credit and market risk.

Strictly speaking, the second step in applying risk-neutral pricing is to replicate synthetically the credit derivative by means of a dynamic, self-financing portfolio of the underlying credit

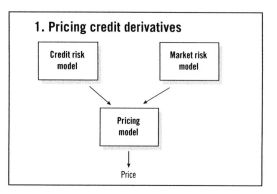

1. Pricing credit derivatives

Credit risk model → Market risk model → Pricing model → Price

137

RATIONAL
MODELLING OF
CREDIT RISK
AND CREDIT
DERIVATIVES

instruments and money market accounts. (Panel 1 overleaf describes how a credit default swap can be priced using risk-neutral pricing by explicitly constructing a hedge.) This step is implicit in the calibration process, whereby the model is adjusted so that it correctly prices known credit instruments. In the case of credit derivatives the underlying credit instruments are bonds or loans. As above, the bonds and/or loans and the credit derivative are assumed to have an expected return equal to the riskless rate.

In the end the price of the credit derivative is the expected value of the present value of the future cashflows. Future cashflows are discounted back at the riskless rate. (Panel 2 prices a credit default swap using risk-neutral pricing by calculating implied default rates from bonds.)

It is important to note the differences between risk-neutral pricing and other pricing methods. For example, note that the model is calibrated to bonds and loans that have known market prices. Thus the price of credit risk is implied by the price of these instruments. This is in contrast to pricing methodologies that infer the price from historical interest rates or historical default rates.

Approaches to modelling credit risk

CLASSIFICATION
The large number of competing credit risk models can be overwhelming. Classification offers one useful tool for comparing and understanding these models.

For classifications to be useful, one needs to identify characteristics that define a model and that distinguish it from other models. There are many superficial characteristics we might use: the numerical implementation, the pricing formula, the applicable credit risk products and so on. But the most important characteristic of a credit risk pricing model is its ability to accurately explain or describe the market dynamics of credit risk. Even if even one rejected risk-neutral pricing for credit derivatives, this characteristic would survive to be applied in some other pricing theory.

The following classification groups credit risk models according to how they explicitly or implicitly describe the default and recovery process. Figure 2 shows the four divisions of credit risk modelling. It shows one model on top of the other because, as will be explained below, the model on top provides "finer" information about the default and recovery process. This is

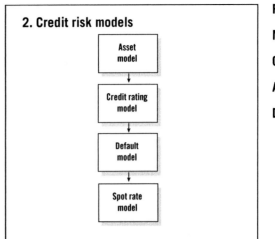

2. Credit risk models

Asset model → Credit rating model → Default model → Spot rate model

not to say that it is easy, in practice, to translate a model in one division to a model in the next highest division.

Each model has its own advantages and disadvantages. Since the models on top offer finer information, they are naturally more appropriate for pricing the more complicated credit derivatives. This flexibility does not come for free. The models on top are generally harder to implement and require more information to calibrate.

One will see that most of the models discussed below focus mainly on default and rather less on recovery. They usually model recovery as a constant, known number (see Tables 1 and 2). [2]

Table 1. First generation credit risk models

Model	Static default rate	Dynamic default rate
Asset		Black–Scholes (1974); Merton (1974); Bhattacharya, Mason (1981); Black, Cox (1976); Das (1995); Kim, Ramaswamy, Sundaresan (1989); Merton (1974); Nielson, Saa-Requejo, Santa Clara (1993); Shimko, Tejima, van Deventer (1993)
Credit rating		Carty (1997); Brand, Rabbia and Bahar (1997); Altman, Kao (1991); Jarrow, Lando, Turnbull (1997)
Default	Johnson (1967); Bierman, Hass (1975); Yawitz (1977); Jonkhart (1979); Rodriguez (1988)	Jarrow, Turnbull (1995)
Spot rate		Ramaswamy, Sundaresan (1986); Litterman, Iben (1991); Longstaff, Schwartz (1995b); Das (1998)
Forward rate		Madan, Unal (1994)

Table 2. Second generation credit risk models

Model	Dynamic recovery	Dynamic riskless interest rates	Multiple firms
Asset	Longstaff, Schwartz (1995a); Zhou (1997a); Madan, Unal (1998)	Longstaff, Schwartz (1995a); Hubner (1997); Madan, Unal (1998)	Zhou (1987b)
Credit rating	Das, Tuffano (1996)	Lando (1994)	CreditMetrics (1997)
Default	Duffie, Singleton (1996)		CreditRisk+ (1997)

138

RATIONAL
MODELLING OF
CREDIT RISK
AND CREDIT
DERIVATIVES

THE CREDIT DEFAULT SWAP

This panel shows how risk-neutral pricing theory can be applied to price a credit default swap. The price is obtained by explicitly constructing a hedge from the underlying cash market instruments.

A credit default swap is the most straightforward type of a credit derivative. It is an agreement between two counterparties that allows one counterparty to be "long" a third-party credit risk, and the other counterparty to be "short" the credit risk. Explained another way, one counterparty is selling insurance and the other counterparty is buying insurance against the default of the third party.

For example, suppose that two counterparties, a market maker and an investor, enter into a two-year credit default swap. They specify what is called the *reference asset*, which is a particular credit-risky bond issued by a third-party corporation or sovereign. For simplicity, let us suppose that the bond has exactly two years' remaining maturity and is currently trading at par value.

The market maker agrees to make regular fixed payments to the investor for two years, with the same frequency as the reference bond. In exchange the market maker has the following right. (For simplicity assume default can occur only at discrete times, namely, at the times just before the coupon payment is due.) If the third party defaults at any time within that two years, the market-maker makes his last regular fixed payment to the investor and puts the bond to the investor in exchange for the bond's par value plus interest. The credit default swap is thus a contingent put - the third party must default before the put is activated (Figure A).

In this simple example there is little difference in terms of risk between the credit default swap and the reference bond. Because the swap and the bond have the same maturity, the market maker is effectively short the bond and the investor is long the bond. (In the real world, it is often the case that the bond tenor is longer than the swap tenor. In this case the swap counterparties have exposure to credit risk, but do not have exposure to the full market risk of the bond.)

The simplicity of our example helps clarify how the instrument is priced. Pricing the credit default swap involves determining the fixed payments from the market-maker to the investor. In this case it is sufficient to extract the price from the bond market. One does not need to model default or any other complicated credit risk process. To apply risk-neutral pricing theory one needs to construct a hedge for the credit default swap. In this simple example, it is sufficient to construct a static hedge. This means the cash instruments are purchased once, and once only, for the life of the credit default swap; they will not have to be sold until the termination of the credit default swap.

The hedge is different for the market-maker and investor. If the market-maker were to hedge the credit default swap, then it would need to go long the bond. As illustrated in Figure B, the market-maker borrows money in the funding markets at Libor and uses those funds to purchase the corporate bond, which pays Libor + X basis points. The hedge is paying the market-maker a net cash-flow of X basis points.

If the reference asset does not default, then at the termination of the swap the market-maker simply unwinds the hedge at no net cost. If the reference asset defaults, then the market-maker

A. Credit default swap

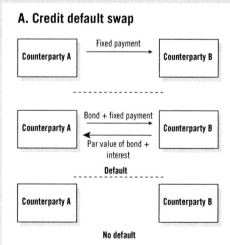

B. Market maker's hedge

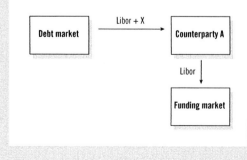

139

RATIONAL
MODELLING OF
CREDIT RISK
AND CREDIT
DERIVATIVES

immediately unwinds the hedge. It delivers the bond to the investor in exchange for the par amount, and repays its borrowed funding with the principal. This perfectly hedges the market-maker's risk in the credit default swap.

Now apply the same reasoning to the investor. If the investor were to hedge the credit default swap, then he would need to short the bond. As Figure C illustrates, the investor borrows the bond in the repo markets. In order for the investor to borrow the bond, he must lend the face value of the bond to the repo market at what will certainly be a sub-Libor rate. Suppose the investor lends the par value of the bond at Libor – Y basis points in exchange for borrowing the bond. The bond lender keeps the bond's coupon payments.

The value Y can be quite large, for two reasons. First the investor is making a collateralised loan. The bond is collateral against the loan, so the borrower expects a low borrowing rate. And secondly, the market for shorting the credit risky bond is inefficient. The value of Y might be anywhere from 20 to 150 basis points.

The investor then sells the bond in the debt markets and must pay Libor + X basis points to the bond buyer. The hedge is costing the investor a net cashflow of X + Y basis points. This perfectly hedges the investor's risk in the credit default swap.[1]

Notice that the hedges are not symmetric. The market maker is receiving X basis points from his hedge while the investor is paying X + Y basis points from his hedge. So the hedges determine the price of the credit default swap up to a range. The market is left with a spread of approximately Y basis points which cannot be arbitraged away. (For some real-world examples of bid/ask spreads, see Figure 4 of Chapter 3 in this volume.)

Exactly where the price of the credit swap falls in the range of X to X + Y depends on the counterparties and their motivations. Counterparties to credit default swaps are entering into a customised, off-balance sheet transaction that has certain intangible advantages over the cash markets. Market-makers or commercial bank lenders looking for credit protection on a certain name might be willing to pay as much as X + Y or more. On the other hand an investor looking for some extra premium may be willing to accept as little as X or less. Market makers with sub-Libor funding rates, and investors with above-Libor funding rates, would find the credit default swap even more favourable.

C. Investor's hedge

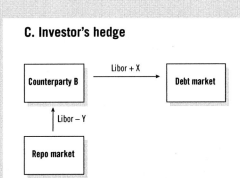

In general, pricing credit default swaps is not this simple. We mentioned above that the bond tenor may well be longer than the swap tenor, but it is also often the case that the bond is not trading at par, or that coupon payments are fixed instead of floating. The price also depends on the particular terms of the swap agreement and the reference security.

Despite the simplicity, the exercise demonstrates a couple of points. Firstly, risk-neutral pricing theory both works and does not work in the credit markets. It gives a good bound for the price of the credit default swap, but it does not give a single price because the assumptions of risk-neutral pricing (market completeness, liquidity and lack of transaction costs) do not apply. Note that the market uses risk-neutral pricing (with care) to price credit default swaps and other credit derivatives. In particular, pricing models are calibrated to the bond market, as opposed to calibrating to the historical price of credit. Sometimes looking at historical default rates and recovery rates serves as a good check of the final price.

Secondly, the credit default swap is somewhere in-between a cash instrument and a derivative product. The more complicated credit default swaps may not be perfectly replicated in the cash markets, but the cash markets give some guidance to the correct price of default swaps.

The credit default swap market will follow the interest rate swap market. While the credit default swap market will never be as deep nor as liquid as the interest rate swap market, the bid/ask spreads will decrease and the credit default swap will function like its own primary market Thus the default swap curve should serve as the starting point for pricing all other credit derivative models, just as the interest rate swap curve is the input into pricing all other interest rate derivatives.

1 Actually this is not a perfect hedge. The investor has taken on a very small amount of additional credit risk to the repo markets.

140

RATIONAL
MODELLING OF
CREDIT RISK
AND CREDIT
DERIVATIVES

PRICING CREDIT DERIVATIVES

In Panel 1 we looked at how to price a credit default swap by explicitly constructing a hedge to the swap. Here we look at a variant of the credit default swap where the hedge for the swap structure is not obvious. In this case the price is obtained by first calculating implied default rates from bond prices and then by using these default rates in a lattice to obtain the price.

In Panel 1, the market-maker agreed to make regular fixed payments, with the same frequency as the reference bond, to the investor for the duration of the swap. This was convenient for pricing the swap because, like the coupons of the reference bond, the regular fixed payments would cease upon default.

Here the market-maker agrees to make one fixed payment to the investor at the beginning of the swap. The exact time of default is important in order to present-value the future cashflows properly.

A. Non-default and default probabilities

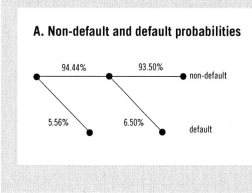

For simplicity, we will assume that the swap has a tenor of two years and that the coupon payments are annual. Also, we will assume that default can occur only at discrete times at the end of one year or of two years. In order to calculate the implied default rates we will need to calculate the full two-year term structure of both the riskless and credit-risky rates.

The market data is as follows. The riskless term structure is flat at 5% for each of one and two years. The credit risky issuer of the reference bond has a term structure at one and two years at 8% and 8.25%, respectively. In particular, the two-year credit spread is 3.25%.

Assume a loss rate given default of 50% , so the recovery rate given default is 50%. Then the one- and two-year forward default rates are 5.56% and 6.50%, respectively. The first default rate is easily calculated using the formula given in the main text in the section on Default Models. The second default rate depends on the first default rate and so must be solved for using a slightly more complicated formula. In any case, one can check that these default rates and loss rates price the one and two years bonds of 8% and 8.25%, respectively at par (Figure A).

Also, for the sake of simplicity, let us assume that default is independent of the general level of interest rates. So future scenarios are simple to analyse: either the reference asset does not

Spot rate models

This first division of models is already a bit of an exception to our scheme in that they do not directly model default or recovery. These models immediately attach a price to credit risk. The dynamics of default are in some sense implied by the dynamics of the price of credit risk. The price of credit risk is reflected in either the credit-risky spot rate, forward rate, or discount factor. These models focus on one of these three rates.

The credit-risky *spot rate* is today's rate for lending today for a specified tenor to a certain credit-risky counterparty. Actually there is a different credit-risky spot rate for each counterparty and each tenor.

The credit-risky *forward rate* is today's rate for lending at a certain time in the future for a specified tenor to a certain credit-risky counter-

party *conditional* on the fact that the counterparty has not defaulted before that time in the future. The fact that it is conditional is crucial. If lending were not conditional on not defaulting, then the forward rate would have to be higher to compensate for the higher risk, that is, the risk that one could be lending to a counterparty already defaulted.

The credit-risky *discount factor* is the present value of receiving one unit of money from a certain credit-risky counterparty at a specified time in the future. Let R be the spot rate at time 0 for lending for one year, that is, over the time interval from 0 to 1. Let F(t) be the forward rate at time 0 for lending over the time interval from t to t + 1 and D(0,t) be the discount factor for the time interval from 0 to t. If today is time 0, then the spot rate R(0) is equal to the forward rate F(0).

141

RATIONAL
MODELLING OF
CREDIT RISK
AND CREDIT
DERIVATIVES

default, or it does default and it defaults at some time before the maturity of the trade.

There are several ways of implementing credit models eg analytic formulas, Monte Carlo simulations, and lattices. The method selected depends on the credit model and the product that is being priced. For this example a collapsed lattice is sufficient. Since default is independent of the general level of riskless or risky interest rates, one may assume constant interest rates.

The previous panel suggested that the market-maker would expect the fair price for the credit default swap to be 3.25% per annum. We need to calculate the equivalent price when the market-maker pays it in full to the investor at the beginning of the transaction (Figure B).

The calculation of the price is illustrated in Figure C. Recall that the price is the expected value of the present value of future cashflows. The expectation is taken with respect to the risk-neutral default probabilities, which were calculated above. The present value is calculated with respect to the riskless rate of 5%, which corresponds to a one-period discount factor of 0.9524. The simple arithmetic gives a price of 5.88%. This means the market-maker makes an upfront payment to the investor at the beginning of the swap which is 5.88% of the par value of the reference asset.

Notice that in the above example the lattice is calibrated to the term structure of bond yields. This means that it correctly prices a long bond position. (The product is also naturally long the

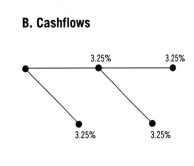

B. Cashflows

credit risk.) If one were to hedge the product, one would have to short the bond – and shorting is more expensive. Thus if one actually intended to hedge the position by shorting bonds, then the pricing model should be calibrated to the short bond prices and this would naturally give a higher price for the product.

Finally, the loss rate assumption influences the price. A different loss assumption would change the default rates and, therefore, change the non-default rates. This in turn would change the present value of the two coupons of 3.25%.

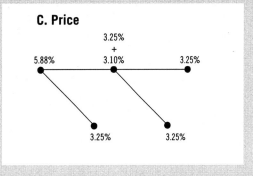

C. Price

It is not obvious whether the usual arithmetic relations between the spot rate, forward rate and discount factor are applicable. Consider the discount factor. In theory one is trying to use a single discount factor to explain two contingent cashflows: the cashflow in non-default and the cashflow in default.

Here is a specific, though subtle, example. Suppose one has calculated the discount factor for the principal repayment at maturity of a one-year bond. The discount factor implicitly contains assumptions about recovery rates – in particular, recovery rates with respect to a matured one-year bond. This discount factor is not necessarily appropriate for discounting the one-year coupon of a two-year bond. The reason is that the recovery rate on the matured one-year bond may not be the same as that of an un-matured, possibly off-market two-year bond.

Despite this, market partcipants seem to have chosen to employ the usual arithmetic relations between the spot rate, forward rate and discount factor. These are used generously in the corporate bond markets and emerging markets. Using such arithmetic, one may calculate the relationship between the forward rate and the discount rate as:

$$D(t + 1) = D(t)/(1 + F(t))$$

Notice that spot rate models model credit risk implicitly: its two components, default risk and recovery risk, are tied together into a single price. It follows that these models are inappropriate for credit derivative contracts that specify only default risk or only recovery risk. (The relationship between price, default and recovery is discussed below.)

Litterman and Iben (1991) model the credit-risky spot rate using a stochastic process.

Specifically, the spot rate follows a lognormal Brownian process as in the Black–Derman–Toy model. Ramaswamy and Sundaresan (1986), Longstaff and Schwartz (1995b), and Das (1998) also all model the spot rate using various stochastic processes. Madan and Unal (1994) model the forward rate using a stochastic process.

Besides the problem with the bond arithmetic mentioned above, these models all share another problem. For pricing anything with optionality, one needs a stochastic model of the credit-risky spot rate or forward rate. While a lognormal Brownian process may be sufficient for riskless rates, it is poor at capturing the "fat tails" of the probability distribution of credit-risky rates. (The "fat tails" are caused by the fact that the credit markets are much more likely to exhibit an abnormal event – say, a five standard deviation event – than is a normal distribution.)

Default models

The models discussed in this section of the chapter directly model the risk of default, and are closely related to the models in the previous section. Bierman and Hass (1975), Johnson (1967), Jonkhart (1979), Rodriguez (1988), and Yawitz (1977) derive formulas for the relationship between the default rate, the recovery rate and the credit spread. Here is a review of the arithmetic.

If r is the riskless rate, then it is convenient to represent the credit risky rate by r + s, where s is called the *credit spread*. Let p be the probability of default of the same term as the rates r and r + s apply. Let L be the loss rate given default, so 1 – L is the recovery rate given default.

To derive a formula for the relationship one needs to make certain assumptions. Though the spread is called the "credit spread", it is not really the credit spread. The spread accounts for several costs and risks including credit risk. For example the spread includes tax costs and liquidity risk and supply and demand.

Let us ignore these other costs and risks, and assume that the credit risky spread is simply the cost of credit risk. Further assume that risk-neutral pricing theory applies, so the price of the bond is the expected value of the present value of future cashflows. Then the expected returns on a riskless investment and a credit risky investment are the same, and one obtains the equation:

$$1 + r = (1 - p)(1 + r + s) + p(1 - L)(1 + r + s)$$

Here is a way to gain insight into the meaning of the credit spread s. One desires an equation that naturally describes the excess return above the

riskless return r. By moving the 1 + r term to the other side one obtains the new equation:

$$0 = (1 - p)s - p(1 + r - (1 - L)(1 + r + s))$$

As one would expect from the risk-neutral pricing assumption, the two events, non-default and default, have equal but opposite expected values. Specifically, in the event of non-default one receives the excess spread s. In the event of default one loses the difference between the value of a riskless bond and the recovery value of the risky bond.

One may also solve for the credit-risky rate giving the formula:

$$r + s = \frac{r + pL}{1 - pL}$$

Notice that the spread s is determined by both the default probability p and loss rate L. So, knowing only the spread, it is impossible to solve for both the default probability and loss rate (or recovery rate) simultaneously. Solving for the product pL gives the formula

$$pL = \frac{s}{1 + r + s}$$

It is important to keep track of assumptions. The first equation relating the interest rates and default and loss rates implicitly assumes recovery applies to both principal and interest. If one adjusts the first equation to reflect the assumption that in the event of default the recovery is on the principal only, then one obtains the equations

$$1 + r = (1 - p)(1 + r + s) + p(1 - L)(1)$$
and

$$r + s = \frac{r + pL}{1 - p}$$

Just as there is a relationship between the spot rate, forward rate, and discount factor, there is a parallel relationship between the marginal default rate, the conditional default rate, and the cumulative default rate.

The *cumulative probability of default* over the time interval t(0) to t(n) is the probability today of defaulting over the given time interval. Let d(n) be the cumulative probability of default over the time interval t(0) to t(n). It satisfies the inequalities $0 \leq d \leq 1$.

The *marginal default rate* over the time interval t(n – 1) to t(n) is the probability today of defaulting between times t(n – 1) and t(n). The marginal default rate is:

$$m(n) = d(n - 1) - d(n)$$

The *conditional default rate* (or *forward*

default rate) over the time interval t(n − 1) to t(n) is the probability today of defaulting between times t(n − 1) and t(n) conditional on not having defaulted before or at time t(n − 1). The conditional default rate is:

$$c(n) = m(n)/(1 − d(n − 1))$$

Default models directly model default and recovery. Default risk and recovery risk may be considered jointly or separately.

Jarrow and Turnbull (1995) models the forward default rate by a stochastic process. Duffie and Singleton (1996) model each of the forward default rate and recovery rate by a stochastic process.

CreditRisk+ (1997) models the marginal default rate by a stochastic process as well. The model also allows for multiple credit-risky counterparties. One novel feature of this model is that the counterparty defaults are non-independent because the marginal default rates are non-independent. The paper proposes one-factor and multi-factor models of the marginal default rates.

Credit rating models

Credit rating models generalise default models. In a default model there are two states: not defaulted and defaulted. In a credit rating model there is a state for each credit rating.

The credit rating system is a linear ordering of creditworthiness. The rating could be assigned by a credit rating agency, implied by market prices of the firm's debt, or calculated or assigned through some other means (eg Chapter 5, Panel 1). Usually the lowest state represents default. The important feature of these models is that the credit quality is modelled by a state variable that can take on only a finite number of values.

The state process may be modelled in either discrete or continuous time. The first and most natural way to model the credit rating is as a Markov process. In a discrete-time Markov process the probability of moving from one given state to another over the discrete time interval is independent of the specific firm, its rating history, or time.

A nice feature of the discrete-time Markov model is that it may be encoded in a finite n-by-n matrix, where n is the number of states. This matrix is called a *transition matrix*. The entry in the ith row and jth column is the conditional probability that if a firm is in the ith state at the beginning of the period, then it will be in the jth state at the end of the period. There is an analogous mathematical theory for continuous-time Markov processes, for example, see Lando (1994).

The credit rating agencies have reported the historical transition matrices for several years. Two recent studies are Brand, Rabbia, Bahar, (1997) and Carty (1997). It is clear that the matrix varies from year to year and is probably non-independent from macro-economic variables.

Altman and Kao (1991) propose two other models of the credit rating. They analyse a non-stationary Markov model and a Mover–Stayer model. In a non-stationary Markov process the probability of moving from one given state to another given state is again independent of the specific firm or its rating history, but may depend upon time.

In a Mover–Stayer process the firms are split into two groups: movers and stayers. Each group follows its own Markov process. The union of the two processes is usually not a Markov process, but has some potential for better fitting historical credit rating migration data.

Jarrow, Lando and Turnbull (1997) propose a one-factor non-stationary Markov process for the credit rating and try to fit it to transitions implied by market prices of debt. This is extended by Das and Tuffano (1996) who model recovery as a stochastic process.

One more credit rating approach is proposed in CreditMetrics (1997). This method extends the Markov model to incorporate more than one firm. The goal is to capture the apparent non-stationarity of the credit rating process, which is believed to be due to the non-independence of defaults. CreditMetrics uses a stationary Markov model for pairs of credit rating: the probability of two firms moving from a given pair of states to another given pair of states is independent of the specific firms or the time.

Lando (1994) proposes a new credit rating model. He allows both the credit rating and risk-less interest rate to be stochastic and non-independent. Also he works in the setting of continuous time Markov models, which he shows have certain theoretical and practical advantages (see Chapter 11 of the present volume).

Asset models

The models described in this last section generalise the credit rating models. As we have already observed, the credit rating models use a finite number of credit ratings. The asset approach is simply a continuous state limit of the credit rating approach. Although we are describing them last of all, models of this type were actually devised before default and credit rating models.

Black–Scholes (1974) and Merton (1974) proposed the first asset model of credit risk. They made the observation that the value of the corporation's assets is the sum of the corporation's equity and debt. The firm goes into default when the value of the assets drops below the face value of the debt. Viewed this way, both the equity and debt are contingent claims on the total assets of the firm and their prices may be modelled using the Black–Scholes and Merton option theory.

The value of the firm, V, is the sum of its equity, S, and debt, F, given by the formula:

$$V = S + F$$

Merton (1974) follows through on the analysis. He supposes the firm issues one zero-coupon bond which promises to pay B dollars to bondholders in T years. Assume the firm can only default at time T. At that time it defaults if the value of the assets is less than its promised payment to the bondholders. At time T the firms pays the bondholders:

$$\min(B, V) = V - \max(0, V - B)$$

One can see that the bondholder is short a put on the value of the firm. The bond is more valuable for larger values of V.

Merton models the value of the firm as a lognormal diffusion process:

$$dV/V = \alpha dt + \sigma dz$$

where α is the instantaneous return on the assets, σ is the instantaneous standard deviation of the return, and dz is the standard Brownian process. The above stochastic equation is identical to the equation in the Black–Scholes and Merton model. The equity option pricing formula applies and the present value of the debt is:

$$F = V - \left(VN(d_+) - Be^{-rT}N(d_-) \right),$$

$$d_\pm = \frac{\ln\left(Ve^{rT} / B\right) \pm \sigma^2 T / 2}{\sigma\sqrt{T}}$$

where N is the standard normal cumulative distribution function.

The constant drift and constant volatility of value of the firm does not capture the variability of the credit spread. This model is thus appropriate for only the simplest of credit derivative products. Nevertheless, it is an excellent theoretical springboard for other credit risk models.

The most obvious shortcoming of this approach is that it only allows for default at one time, namely T. This shortcoming has been eliminated by numerous authors including Bhattacharya and Mason (1981), Black and Cox

(1976), Das (1995), Kim, Ramaswamy and Sundaresan (1989), Nielson, Saa-Requejo and Santa Clara (1993), and Shimko, Tejima and van Deventer (1993).

Another interesting extension is offered by Longstaff and Schwartz (1995a). They extend the Merton model in two ways. They allow for non-independence between the credit risk and the interest rate risk, and they model recovery as a stochastic process. Hubner (1997) also models the value of the firm and interest rates as stochastic processes.

It has been observed that seemingly sound firms, even investment-grade firms, can default without warning. This means there is a non-trivial probability of default in the short term, and this is reflected in market prices. So another drawback of all the above models is that the output does not match either historical or implied default rates in the short term. In the above models the short-term probability of default is nearly zero. The reason is that the value of the firm follows a continuous diffusion process and thus the probability of the process hitting the default barrier in the short term is nearly zero.

One remedy for this problem is explained in Crosbie (1997). He describes the KMV model which unites the Merton framework with historical data. The model produces expected default probabilities by first modelling the current observable financial data of a firm and then adjusting the model's output so that it is calibrated to historically observed defaults.

Another remedy to the short-term default problem is given by Zhou (1997a) who models the value of the firm by a process that is the sum of a diffusion process and a Poisson process. The Poisson process is a discontinuous, jump process and, therefore, allows for the possibility of sudden defaults. This jump process model also implies that recovery is stochastic. A large jump into default would imply a smaller recovery rate. Madan and Unal (1998) also model the value of the firm as a stochastic jump process and model the riskless interest rate as a stochastic process.

In Zhou (1997b) the author extends the Merton model in another direction by simultaneously modelling the value of more than one firm. The value of each firm is modelled by a continuous diffusion process and these processes may be non-independent.

Conclusion

The market is a long way from settling on the "right" credit risk model. Firstly, credit risk models are at least as complicated as interest rate risk models, and eventually they will have to be integrated with market risk models to account for the non-independence of credit risk and market prices. The theory and implementation may make certain models cumbersome.

Secondly, most of the models are not flexible enough to fit either historical default data or implied bond and loan default data. Among those that are flexible enough to fit data, more work needs to be done to test whether the selected default and recovery processes do indeed match market experience. Where they do not, it may be because models are often chosen for their mathematical elegance or practical convenience rather than for their verisimilitude.

1 *The author thanks Don Chance, Jessica James, David Lando, Diana Woodward, and Chunsheng Zhou for their comments.*

2 *This discussion has tried to include all of the many examples of credit risk models. If a model was missed, apologies go out to its authors.*

BIBLIOGRAPHY

Altman, E.I. and D.L. Kao, 1991, "Examining and Modeling Corporate Bond Rating Drift", Working paper, New York University Salomon Center, New York.

Bhattacharya, S., and S.P. Mason, 1981, "Risky Debt, Jump Processes and Safety Covenants", *Journal of Financial Economics* 9/3, pp. 281-307.

Bierman, H., and J. Hass, 1975, "An Analytical Model of Bond Risk Differentials", *Journal of Financial and Quantitative Analysis* 10, pp. 757-73.

Black, F., and J.C. Cox, 1976, "Valuing Corporate Securities: Some Effects of Bond Indenture Provisions", *Journal of Finance* 31/2, pp. 361-7.

Black, F., and M. Scholes, 1973, "The Pricing of Options and Corporate Liabilities", *Journal of Political Economics* 81, pp. 637-59.

Brand, L., J. Rabbia, and R. Bahar, 1997, "Rating Performance 1996: Stability and Transition", Standard & Poor's.

Carty, L.V., 1997, "Moody's Rating Migration and Credit Quality Correlation, 1920-1996", Moody's.

Chance, D., 1990, "Default Risk and the Duration of Zero Coupon Bonds", *Journal of Finance* 45/1, pp. 265-74.

Cooper, I. A., and A. S. Mello, 1991, "The Default Risk of Swaps", *Journal of Finance* 46/2, pp. 597-620.

Cooper, I., and M. Martin, 1996, "Default Risk and Derivative Products", *Applied Mathematical Finance* 3/1, pp. 53-74.

Cossin, D., 1997, "Credit Risk Pricing: A Literature Survey", University of Lausanne.

CreditMetrics, 1997, JP Morgan.

CreditRisk+, 1997, Credit Suisse Financial Products.

Crosbie, P., 1997, "Modeling Default Risk", KMV Corporation.

Das, S.R., 1995, "Credit Risk Derivatives", *Journal of Derivatives* 2/3, pp. 7-23.

Das, S.R., 1998, "Pricing Credit Derivatives", Harvard Business School.

Das, S.R., and P. Tuffano, 1996, "Pricing Credit Sensitive Debt when Interest Rates, Credit Ratings and Credit Spreads are Stochastic", *Journal of Financial Engineering* 5, pp. 161-98.

Derman, E., 1997, "The Future of Modelling", *Risk* 10/12, pp. 164-7.

Duffee, G.R., 1996, "On Measuring Credit Risks of Derivative Instruments", *Journal of Banking and Finance* 20, pp. 805-33.

Duffie, D., and K.J. Singleton, 1996, "Modeling Term Structures of Defaultable Bonds", Graduate School of Business, Stanford University.

Harrison, J. M. and D.M. Kreps, 1979, "Martingales and Arbitrage in multiperiod securities markets", *Journal of Economic Theory* 20, pp. 381-408.

Harrison, J.M., and S. Pliska, 1981, "Martingales and stochastic integrals in the theory of continuous trading", *Stochastic Processes and their Applications* 11, pp. 215-60.

Hubner, G., 1997, "A Two-Factor Gaussian Model of Default Risk", INSEAD.

Hull, J., and A. White, 1995, "The Impact of Default Risk on the Prices of Option and Other Derivative Securities", *Journal of Banking and Finance* 19, pp. 299-322.

Iben, B., and R. Brotheron-Ratcliffe, 1994, "Credit Loss Distributions and Required Capital for Derivatives Portfolios", *Journal of Fixed Income* 3, pp. 6-14.

Jarrow, R., and S. M. Turnbull, 1995, "Pricing Derivatives on Financial Securities Subject to Credit Risk", *Journal of Finance* 50/1, pp. 53-86.

Jarrow, R., D. Lando and S.M. Turnbull, 1997, "A Markov

Model for the Term Structure of Credit Risk Spreads", *Review of Financial Studies* 10/2, pp. 481-523.

Johnson, R.E., 1967, "The Term Structure of Corporate Bond Yield as a Function of Risk of Default", *Journal of Finance* 22, pp. 313-45.

Jonkhart, M.J.L., 1979, "On the Term Structure of Interest Rates and the Risk of Default: an Analytical Approach", *Journal of Banking and Finance* 3, pp. 253-62.

Kim, I.J., K. Ramaswamy and S. Sundaresan, 1989, "The Valuation of Corporate Fixed Income Securities", Working Paper Rodney L. White Center for Financial Research, Wharton School, University of Pennsylvania.

Lando, D., 1994, "Three Essays on Contingent Claims Pricing", PhD thesis, Cornell University, Ithaca, NY.

Litterman, R., and T. Iben, 1991, "Corporate Bond Valuation and the Term Structure of Credit Spreads", *Financial Analysts Journal*, pp. 52-64.

Longstaff, F.A., and E.S. Schwartz, 1995a, "A Simple Approach to Valuing Fixed and Floating Rate Debt", *Journal of Finance* 50, pp. 789-819.

Longstaff, F.A., and E.S. Schwartz, 1995b, "Valuing Credit Derivatives", *Journal of Fixed Income* 5-1, pp. 6-12.

Lucas, D.J., and J. Lonski, 1992, "Changes in Corporate Credit Quality 1970-1990", *Journal of Fixed Income*, pp. 7-14.

Madan, D.B., and H. Unal, 1994, "Pricing the Risks of Default", Working paper, Wharton School, University of Pennsylvania.

Madan, D., 1998, "Default Risk", in David Hand and Saul D. Jacka, *Statistics in Finance*, John Wiley & Sons, Inc., London.

Madan, D.B., and H. Unal, 1998, "A Two-Factor Hazard-

Rate Model for Pricing Risky Debt in a Complex Capital Structure", Working paper, University of Maryland.

Merton, R.C., 1974, "On the Pricing of Corporate Debt: The Risk Structure of Interest Rates", *Journal of Finance* 29, pp. 449-70.

Nielson, L.T., J. Saa-Requejo, and P. Santa Clara, 1993, "Default Risk and Interest Rate Risk: the Term Structure of Default Spreads", Working paper, INSEAD Fontainebleau, France.

Ramaswamy, K. and S.M. Sundaresan, 1986, "The Valuation of Floating Rate Instruments: Theory and Evidence", *Journal of Financial Economics*, pp. 261-72.

Rodriguez, R.J., 1988, "Default Risk, Yield Spreads, and Time to Maturity", *Journal of Financial and Quantitative Analysis* 23, pp. 111-17.

Shimko, D., N. Tejima, and D. van Deventer, 1993, "The Pricing of Risky Debt when Interest Rates are Stochastic", *Journal of Fixed Income* 3, pp. 58-65.

Sorensen, E. H. and T. F. Bollier, 1994, "Pricing Swap Default Risk", *Financial Analysts Journal*, May-June.

Wall, L.D. and K-W Fung, 1987, "Evaluating the Credit Exposure Of Interest Rate Swap Portfolios", Working paper 87-8, Federal Reserve Board of Atlanta.

Yawitz, J.B., 1977, "An Analytical Model of Interest Rate Differentials and Different Default Recoveries", *Journal of Financial and Quantitative Analysis* 12, pp. 481-90.

Zhou, C., 1997a, "A Jump-Diffusion Approach to Modeling Credit Risk and Valuing Defaultable Securities," Finance and Economics Discussion Series, Board of Governors Federal Reserve Bank.

Zhou, C., 1997b, "Default Correlation: An Analytical Result", Finance and Economics Discussion Series, Board of Governors Federal Reserve Bank.

11

On Rating Transition Analysis and Correlation

David Lando

University of Copenhagen

Comparing the straightforward nature of binomial models for derivative pricing with the intricate continuous-time formulations, one might think that continuous-time models are meant to intimidate rather than to facilitate. While the "intimidation factor" cannot be banished entirely from work on continuous-time finance, it is worth emphasising that well-chosen continuous-time formulations provide us with tools that make calculations easier – and often increase the realism of the models as well.

One goal of this chapter is to demonstrate that continuous-time analysis does indeed facilitate transition modelling in credit risk analysis, most notably by allowing the model to account for time horizons that are arbitrary and which are not necessarily multiples of some chosen unit, such as one year. The tools we need here are not fetched from the heavy machinery of stochastic calculus and martingale theory, but are in fact only a little matrix algebra and some ordinary calculus.

After a short introduction to continuous-time Markov chain modelling, which focuses on the role of the "generator", we will see how to recover transition probabilities from the generator, how to read the behaviour of a chain from it, and how to recover a generator if all one has is a one-year transition probability matrix. This will be illustrated using the generator found in Jarrow, Lando and Turnbull (1997), which at the same time delivers a nice example of transition behaviour exhibiting monotone default probabilities (but not monotone barrier probabilities).

Another goal is to see how one can capture correlation in the continuous-time framework. We show how this can be done using the machinery developed in the chapter, and the first method presented seems mostly suited for "strong" correlations arising from firms whose fates are intimately linked to one another. The second method we present here models correlation between defaults and ratings changes of financial firms in a way that might hold the key to integrating credit risk and market risk. The moral of this approach is that a very smooth handling of correlation can be achieved when the primary focus is a "weak" correlation between entities – the kind that arises because entities respond to the same "exogenous" changes in market factors. Here, we present both a discrete-time version and a continuous-time version which, admittedly, does slip into some traditional continuous-time stochastic analysis.

Continuous-time Markov chains without tears

In all of the following we will be looking at rating processes that take values in some finite state space $\{1,\ldots,K\}$. Think of state 1 as the top rating category, state $K-1$ as the lowest non-default rating and K as the default state. Our presentation will assume familiarity with the notion of a transition matrix of a discrete-time Markov chain

$$P = \begin{pmatrix} p_{11} & \cdots & p_{1K} \\ \vdots & \ddots & \vdots \\ p_{K1} & \cdots & p_{KK} \end{pmatrix}$$

in which all of the entries are numbers between 0 and 1, the rows sum to 1 and the entry p_{ij} is the probability that a chain will be in state j in the next period given that it is in state i in the current period. When thinking of ratings we will often let the state K denote an absorbing state, which the chain may jump to but never leave. This is captured by letting $p_{KK} = 1$ and all other elements of that row equal to 0.

Matrix powers of P will give us transition probabilities over longer time horizons

$$P(X_n = j | X_0 = i) = (P^n)_{ij}.$$

where the right-hand side is the ijth element of the matrix P^n. Hence what one requires to describe the evolution of the Markov chain is a starting point (or perhaps a distribution over the starting points) and the transition matrix. Usually, the shortest period of time for which there are published transition data is one year.

A main application of transition matrices for risk management purposes is to compute probabilities of a certain entity defaulting or being downgraded before a given date in the future. In large portfolios of credit-risky securities it is important to be able to calculate transition probabilities corresponding to dates of the cashflows of the portfolios, and these will be spread out over different calendar dates. Clearly, if a transition matrix for a period of three months is available we could obtain the relevant probabilities for all multiples of three months by using the powers of the matrix. But what about cashflows occurring in a week, say, or in 17 days?

The continuous-time setup allows us to describe transition probabilities for all future dates at once and, more importantly, the behaviour can be summarised in one matrix, the so-called generator.

Before explaining the generator, let us note that what we want to describe in the following is a whole family of transition matrices:

$$P(t) = \begin{pmatrix} p_{11}(t) & \cdots & p_{1K}(t) \\ \vdots & \ddots & \vdots \\ p_{K1}(t) & \cdots & p_{KK}(t) \end{pmatrix}$$

Here, $p_{ij}(t)$ is the probability of reaching state j at time t when starting in state i at time 0. Note that other states may of course be realised in between. A chain is said to be time-homoge-

neous if what matters in describing transition probabilities is only the time between two dates and not the calendar time of the dates. If the calendar date matters, we have to keep track of matrices of the form $P(s,t)$ for all pairs of dates s and t, and for each such pair the matrix then contains information on probabilities of moving from a certain rating at time s to a possibly different rating at time t.

We will not discuss non-homogeneous chains in this chapter – the primary application of non-homogeneity is in the calibration of pricing models to observed term-structures of credit spreads for several different rating categories and this also will not be discussed here. But it is fair to issue a warning that the translation from generators to transition matrices in the non-homogeneous case is somewhat more complicated than for homogeneous chains.

Note that even for the homogeneous chain there is a lot to keep track of: one transition matrix for each time value. The generator can summarise everything that we need. The generator corresponding to a certain matrix of transition probabilities is a matrix for which

$$P(t) = \exp(\Lambda t) \quad \text{all } t \geq 0$$

where the matrix exponential function is defined through the series expansion

$$\exp(\Lambda t) = \sum_{n=0}^{\infty} \frac{\Lambda^n t^n}{n!}$$

Hence, if we know the generator, and if we know how to compute exponentials of matrices (and many software programs will do that for us), the whole family of transition probabilities for any time horizon can be computed. Table 1 shows the generator matrix used in Jarrow, Lando and Turnbull (1997); a note in that paper explains how to estimate the generator matrix from observations of rating transitions.

In that paper, an approximation procedure is given, while Panel 1 opposite presents a different procedure that can recover a generator from a one-year transition matrix. Note that in a generator the rows sum to 0, since the diagonal element is minus the sum of the other elements in the row. We sometimes refer to the sum of the off-diagonal elements in row i as λ_i and then denote the diagonal element $-\lambda_i$ instead of the usual λ_{ii}. If a whole row is 0 it means that the corresponding state is absorbing – hence a chain which reaches that state stays there forever. One may recall this by noting that the diagonal element contains information about the mean hold-

Table 1. Generator matrix: example from Jarrow, Lando and Turnbull (1997)

	AAA	AA	A	BBB	BB	B	CCC	D
AAA	−0,1153	0,1019	0,0083	0,0020	0,0031	0,0000	0,0000	0,0000
AA	0,0091	−0,1043	0,0787	0,0105	0,0030	0,0030	0,0000	0,0000
A	0,0010	0,0309	−0,1172	0,0688	0,0107	0,0048	0,0000	0,0010
BBB	0,0007	0,0047	0,0713	−0,1711	0,0701	0,0174	0,0020	0,0049
BB	0,0005	0,0025	0,0089	0,0813	−0,2530	0,1181	0,0144	0,0273
B	0,0000	0,0021	0,0034	0,0073	0,0568	−0,1928	0,0479	0,0753
CCC	0,0000	0,0000	0,0142	0,0142	0,0250	0,0928	−0,4318	0,2856
D	0,0000	0,0000	0,0000	0,0000	0,0000	0,0000	0,0000	0,0000

RECOVERING THE GENERATOR

Here we look in more detail at an issue that arises from the main text: how to recover the generator. First, assume that P(1) is given. Since

$$P(1) = I + \Lambda + \frac{\Lambda^2}{2} + \cdots$$

it is tempting to think that we could use the approximation

$$\Lambda = P(1) - I$$

However, we might be worried that the approximation error would become increasingly severe as we consider horizons of, say, 10 years. The following method ensures that the generator fits exactly with the one-year probabilities (and hence discrepancies over longer time-horizons would then be due to non-homogeneous behaviour of the Markov chain – or even non-Markovian behaviour). If there exists a matrix B such that

$$B^{-1}\Lambda B = D$$

where D is a diagonal matrix of eigenvalues, then we have

$$B^{-1}\exp(\Lambda)B = \exp(D)$$

and therefore

$$P(1) = B\exp(D)B^{-1}$$

Now assume that we have observed P(1) and that it is given as recorded in Table A.

Find B such that $B^{-1}P(1)B$ is a diagonal matrix. We will not display B and its inverse here: what it looks like is somewhat dependent on the software used, but the diagonal matrix should have in its diagonal eigenvalues of P(1) that look some-thing like the first column of Table B.

For short transitions intervals, such as one year, it will typically be the case that the eigenvalues are positive and therefore that we can take logarithms. This is displayed in the second column of Table B below. Let A denote the diagonal matrix obtained by placing the logarithms of the eigenvalues in the diagonal and now obtain an estimate of given by

$$\Lambda = B^{-1}AB.$$

In this example, we obtain the generator from Table B. With this to hand, the computation of, say, 6-month transition probabilities is straightforward: simply compute the exponential of 0.5Λ to obtain the values shown in Table C. Of course, this computation can be performed for any time-horizon desired.

This method normally works for short transition horizons where the structure of the matrix is close to that of a tridiagonal matrix, which makes it likely that there are only strictly positive (real) roots in the characteristic polynomial corresponding to the observed one-year transition matrix.

The procedure currently advocated by CreditMetrics is one in which a least-squares problem is solved, but there are two problems with the approach currently proposed. First, the least-squares estimation is not weighted in any way, which means that errors related to small default intensities are treated with the same loss in the estimation as errors on high transition probabilities. Of course, an error of 0.01 in the estimated default probabilities of an AA-rated firm is much more serious than an error of 0.01 in the estimated default probability of a B-rated firm. Second, the proposed method tends to over-emphasise the short-end observations.

Table A. Observations of P(1)

0,8915	0,0915	0,0111	0,0026	0,0028	0,0003	0,0000	0,0001
0,0082	0,9025	0,0709	0,0117	0,0033	0,0030	0,0001	0,0002
0,0010	0,0279	0,8927	0,0602	0,0111	0,0053	0,0002	0,0015
0,0007	0,0052	0,0623	0,8473	0,0577	0,0182	0,0022	0,0064
0,0005	0,0025	0,0102	0,0667	0,7816	0,0959	0,0125	0,0301
0,0000	0,0019	0,0038	0,0084	0,0463	0,8292	0,0355	0,0749
0,0000	0,0003	0,0115	0,0120	0,0203	0,0695	0,6511	0,2353
0,0000	0,0000	0,0000	0,0000	0,0000	0,0000	0,0000	1,0000

Table B. Eigenvalues and log(eigenvalues)

Eigenvalues	log(eigenvalues)
0,638272	−0,44899
0,718143	−0,33109
0,80392	−0,21826
0,856399	−0,15502
0,883005	−0,12442
0,916026	−0,08771
0,980185	−0,02001
1	0

Table C. Example values of P(0.5)

0,9441	0,0483	0,0049	0,0012	0,0015	0,0001	0,0000	0,0000
0,0043	0,9496	0,0373	0,0056	0,0016	0,0015	0,0000	0,0001
0,0005	0,0147	0,9440	0,0322	0,0055	0,0025	0,0001	0,0006
0,0003	0,0025	0,0333	0,9193	0,0318	0,0090	0,0011	0,0028
0,0002	0,0013	0,0048	0,0368	0,8826	0,0532	0,0067	0,0144
0,0000	0,0010	0,0018	0,0040	0,0256	0,9094	0,0206	0,0376
0,0000	0,0001	0,0064	0,0065	0,0112	0,0401	0,8063	0,1293
0,0000	0,0000	0,0000	0,0000	0,0000	0,0000	0,0000	1,0000

ing time in a state: the time a chain with generator Λ stays in state i is exponentially distributed with mean

$$\frac{1}{\lambda_i}$$

Hence a diagonal element equal to zero indicates an infinite holding time in a state. With the diagonal elements telling us the exact distribution of the time that the chain stays in a certain state, all we then need in order to simulate the chain is knowledge of where it goes when it jumps.

Naturally, the off-diagonal elements tell us this: the probability that the chain jumps from state i to state j, given that it jumps, is given by

$$\frac{\lambda_{ij}}{\lambda_i}$$

This gives a complete description of how to simulate the chain – all we have to specify is a starting state, and the generator will tell us the rest of the story.

Monotone barrier probabilities

To serve its purpose, a rating system must satisfy some "monotonicity requirements", in the sense that lower-rated firms are at a higher risk of defaulting than higher-rated firms. In other words, it should be the case that we have monotone default probabilities:

$$P_{iK}(t) < P_{jK}(t)$$

for all $t > 0$, $i < j$. That is, the risk of default is higher at all time horizons for the lower-rated firm starting in j (remember class 1 is the highest rating in our generic numbering system) than for the higher-rated firm starting in rating class i. This condition is easy to check from the computed probabilities using the formula for the exponential of the generator. In Figures 1 and 2, we illustrate the default probabilities for the seven categories in the JLT (1997) generator matrix. This reveals that the desire for monotonicity is indeed satisfied.

Now we have to ask whether in fact we would like even stricter requirements (eg as proposed in CreditMetrics), as so-called monotone barrier probabilities:

$$\sum_{m \geq k} P_{im}(t) > \sum_{m \geq k} P_{jm}(t)$$

for all $t > 0$, all k, and $i < j$. This requirement says that if we fix a certain "barrier" rating (level k), and consider probabilities of firms ending at a rating of k or worse, then this probability should be lower at all time horizons for the better-rated firm.

This requirement is easy to check from the generator directly (see JLT 1997 for details). The question is whether this is a reasonable requirement? Before insisting that it is, perhaps we should note that it is not satisfied for the JLT-generator. In Figure 3 we consider the probability of ending at or below rating level BBB as a function of time for two different initial rating levels: CCC and B.

Note that after a while the curves cross, and

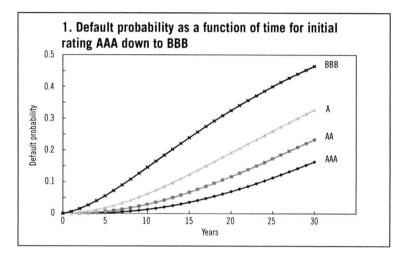

1. Default probability as a function of time for initial rating AAA down to BBB

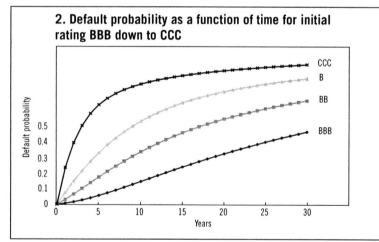

2. Default probability as a function of time for initial rating BBB down to CCC

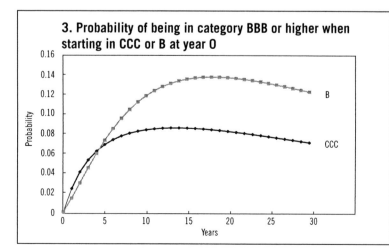

3. Probability of being in category BBB or higher when starting in CCC or B at year 0

that before they cross we have a time horizon for which the lower-rated firm actually has a higher chance of ending at or above level BBB than the higher-rated firm. To understand why this should be so, consider the intensity of firms leaving rating category CCC for BB, versus the intensity of firms leaving category B for BB. While the default intensities are higher for the CCC-rated firms, it may also be the case that certain CCC-rated firms are "do-or-die" type firms. Their very risky nature makes them highly default-prone, but if they succeed they have a significant chance of skipping a few categories on their way to higher ratings.

The fact that this (strict) monotonicity is not satisfied shows up in a different manner when studying forward rate spreads using the empirically-estimated generator, ie when considering spreads that would result when computing prices of defaultable zero-coupon bonds with zero recovery in the event of default and an assumption of risk neutrality. In that case, the forward rate spreads (the spreads in the instantaneous forward rates) between CCC-rated debt and B-rated debt cross at a certain point in time. This would never happen in the case of strictly monotone barrier probabilities. But it may happen even if there are monotone default probabilities. Note, however, that the yield curves will not cross in our example even if the forward spreads do.

The reason for the cross is that the forward rate spread for a zero-recovery defaultable bond is exactly equal to a conditional default intensity, ie default intensities at a certain point in time given survival up to that point in time. If a firm with an initial CCC-rating survives up to a certain time point, then the chance that it will actually have moved up to a higher rating than a firm initially rated B will be so large that it will on average be in better shape! This will show in the conditional survival intensities.

Correlation

Can we address the key question of correlation in a framework based on transition intensities? It turns out that we can in several ways, but as always some are more cumbersome than others.

We will first consider how we can "pair" Markov chains in different ways so as to obtain a model for correlation. To make things as simple as possible while giving the central idea, consider the case of two firms whose rating movements we wish to describe jointly as a Markov chain, and assume that there are only two rating categories for each firm: no default (N) and default (D). We may of course consider the joint

credit movements of these two entities as one big Markov chain whose state space consists of pairs of ratings. The state (N,N), for example, will then describe a state in which both firms have not defaulted. The following generator describes the evolution of two firms with independent migrations:

	(N,N)	(N,D)	(D,N)	(D,D)
(N,N)	$-(\lambda+\gamma)$	γ	λ	0
(N,D)	0	$-\lambda$	0	λ
(D,N)	0	0	$-\gamma$	γ
(D,D)	0	0	0	0

As usual we model default as an absorbing state, so a firm can never return from the state D to the state N, and all the zeros except one in the matrix are due to this assumption. The one zero that is not, is the zero corresponding to the transition from (N,N) to (D,D). The zero here means that the two firms cannot default simultaneously. For Poisson processes (which are generating the uncertainty in continuous-time Markov chains), this amounts to independence.

What we have are two chains, one for Firm 1 in which the default intensity in state N is λ, and one for Firm 2 where the default intensity is γ. Note that our simple example works well for rather small state spaces, but with eight ratings states for each firm we already have to deal with a 64 by 64 matrix. While this can be handled, we would not have to include many more firms in the joint chain before things become intractable. Therefore, the methods we are about to outline can be thought of as reserved for cases of very strong and obvious dependence between firms – a dependence due to direct strong competition, or to one firm being the subsidiary or affiliate of another.

So let us move on and see how dependence could be brought in. Indeed, let us jump to the other extreme, in which the two firms always default at the same time. In this case the generator could be:

	(N,N)	(N,D)	(D,N)	(D,D)
(N,N)	$-(\lambda+\gamma)$	0	0	$\lambda+\gamma$
(N,D)	0	$-\lambda$	0	λ
(D,N)	0	0	$-\gamma$	γ
(D,D)	0	0	0	0

Note that this has typically changed the marginal behaviour of the processes for the individual firms, since now they default with a higher intensity (as they are not only drawn to default by their own default intensity, but also by that of the other firm). If, however, we set γ equal to 0 in row 1 and replace it by λ in row 3, we would have a situation in which both firms would have a default intensity of λ and this would be a way of "coupling" two chains with the same default intensity, while preserving the marginal behaviour. The chain is a little strange as defined above: the entries in rows 2 and 3 will not affect the evolution of firms when they both start in the N category. A slightly less drastic modification is one where the generator is changed to:

	(N,N)	(N,D)	(D,N)	(D,D)
(N,N)	$-(\lambda+\gamma)$	γ	0	λ
(N,D)	0	$-\lambda$	0	λ
(D,N)	0	0	$-\gamma$	γ
(D,D)	0	0	0	0

Here, Firm 1 always triggers the default of Firm 2, but Firm 2 can default without Firm 1 defaulting. This pairing of the two rating processes also changes the marginal behaviour of one of the firms: Firm 2 now has a default intensity of $\lambda + \gamma$, when both firms are solvent, but Firm 1 is still left with the same default intensity of λ regardless of the state of Firm 2.

Can we incorporate dependence into our model while preserving the marginal behaviour of each firm's migration, ie ensure that someone looking only at Firm 1 will see a default intensity of λ, while someone looking at Firm 2 will see an intensity of γ? Indeed we can, and the generator below will accomplish this:

	(N,N)	(N,D)	(D,N)	(D,D)
(N,N)	$-(\lambda+\gamma-\alpha)$	$\gamma-\alpha$	$\lambda-\alpha$	α
(N,D)	0	$-\lambda$	0	λ
(D,N)	0	0	$-\gamma$	γ
(D,D)	0	0	0	0

Note that α should be chosen to be less than both λ and γ, but the higher α is, the more dependence there is.

Here the firms are in a more symmetric kind of relationship. You can extend this to cases with more rating categories. The key thing to remember is that once you have the generator, you obtain the transition probabilities by taking matrix exponentials and this gives you the joint probabilities of all events.

Finally, note that we have focused on default of one firm triggering that of another. An equally interesting scenario could be one in which the default of one firm *helps* the other firm.

Here is a generic way of capturing this:

	(N,N)	(N,D)	(D,N)	(D,D)
(N,N)	$-(\lambda+\gamma)$	γ	λ	0
(N,D)	0	$-(\lambda-\alpha)$	0	$\lambda-\alpha$
(D,N)	0	0	$-(\lambda-\beta)$	$\gamma-\beta$
(D,D)	0	0	0	0

Here, while the two firms are in competition they have default intensities of λ and γ respectively, but when one firm defaults, the default risk of the remaining firm is reduced by α and β respectively.

Even if the rating changes are not announced at the very same date and time, this still offers an interesting approximation that may serve well for risk management purposes. Unfortunately the procedure is rather cumbersome to carry out and it is virtually impossible to include more than a few firms in a large common generator. Therefore, it seems reasonable to reserve the pairing of chains for firms that are very closely and directly related to each other. Given this, the method is easy to use.

Finally, before turning to an alternative way of viewing correlation, consider the approach taken in CreditMetrics. Assume that we are faced with two firms and that one knows the probabilities that the firms will end up in the different categories after a year. Denote these probabilities $(p_1,...,p_K)$ and $(q_1,...,q_K)$ respectively. If the firms were viewed as independent it would of course be an easy task to model joint movements: the probability of Firm 1 ending in state i and Firm 2 ending in state j would then just be $p_i q_j$. But if we view the firms as being correlated we somehow have to model how correlation enters into all joint movements – and it is a major task to assign correlations to all possible joint movements.

The solution in CreditMetrics is to view the vectors $(p_1,...,p_K)$ and $(q_1,...,q_K)$ as arising from quantiles in two separate normal distributions. If the distributions are scaled appropriately (by the asset volatility of the firm) these normal distributions are standard normal distributions. The idea lurking in the background is, of course, a model in which the firms' assets are lognormally distributed, hence log assets are normally distributed, and ratings levels correspond to different levels of log assets. If the firms then have a correlation in asset value given by the parameter ρ, it is straightforward to collect the two standard normal distributions into a two-dimensional normal distribution with correlation ρ; the probabilities of joint rating migrations now can be inferred from this two-dimensional normal distribution.

This approach is a simple way of bringing the correlation in asset value into play. It is not completely consistent from a modelling perspective, in that the assumption in this method is that there is a barrier below which default is triggered (for low values of log assets) and such a boundary is in effect for all time horizons. But if there is a boundary in effect for all maturities, then log assets are not normally distributed, since the distribution of assets in the future has to be computed conditionally upon the default triggering boundary not having been hit. Precise results on the link between asset correlation and default correlation can be found in Zhou (1997).

Finally, it should be noted that if we do have perfect observation of a firm's assets and default occurs when the assets hit a certain boundary, then the Markovian, intensity-based framework for default and rating migration presented here breaks down. However, given imperfect observation of a firm's assets, there is hope of unifying the two approaches (Duffie and Lando, 1998).

The techniques for modelling correlation presented above assume knowledge of some sort of correlation structure between the individual firms. In a portfolio consisting of thousands of bonds and credit-risky securities, the task of maintaining a full covariance matrix is not a small one.

Exogenous factors: integrating credit and market risk

How then should we model correlation? The approach taken for example in Duffie and Singleton (1995) and Lando (1994, 1998) is to introduce correlation by letting default intensities depend on "background" variables. As an example, consider two companies in an industry that are exposed to the same fluctuations in the economy but which are small enough (or in different subsectors of the industry) so that the financial well-being of one firm is not directly linked to the financial well-being of the other. By focusing on the correlation between the firms' default intensities and the industry as a whole, we need only estimate the dependence of each firm on exogenous variables.

Furthermore, if we model firms as correlated through the common dependence on certain variables, but assume that an actual default by one firm does not affect the default intensity of another, then a natural way of integrating market risk and credit risk arises through diversification. We will illustrate this both mathematically in Panel 2, using the continuous-time analysis, and

through an illustrative example in a discrete-time setting that does not require anything but elementary probability theory and a formula for the variance of a random variable. The central idea is that of splitting default risk into two parts: one related to market factors and one that is non-systematic given the evolution of the market factors.

A simple version of the story runs as follows. Consider ten firms whose probabilities of default all depend on the same "background" or "market risk" variable X. In this very simple setup, X can take on one of two values: "good" or "bad", and let us assume that the probability of "good" is 0.8. If X is "good", conditions are good for the firms of the type that we are considering, and the probability of a firm defaulting within a year is 0.1. If X is "bad" then the probability of default within a year is higher and equals 0.5. For a *given* value of X there is independence between individual firm defaults: the default or non-default of a firm does not in any way influence the default of another firm once we know the value of X.

All firms have issued zero-coupon bonds with principal, and for simplicity we assume that there is zero recovery in the event of default. Now consider two different portfolios: Portfolio 1 consists of 10 zero-coupon bond issued by one of the ten firms; Portfolio 2 consists of a single zero-coupon bond from each of the ten companies. It is not surprising that Portfolio 2 is more diversified than Portfolio 1. The interesting point to consider is how Portfolio 2 comes closer to being a function of market risk only. To see what is going on, we first recall a rule for computing the variance of a random variable Y whose joint distribution with the random variable X is known:

$$V(Y) = V\big(E(Y|X)\big) + E\big(V(Y|X)\big)$$

That is, the variance of a random variable can be obtained by first computing its conditional mean and conditional variance given X and then taking the variance of the first and the mean of the second and adding them!

Now let us illustrate this through our example. To calculate the mean payoff of the portfolio consisting of 10 bonds, first condition on whether conditions are "good" or "bad". The mean payoff when conditions are good is 9, since in good conditions the survival probability of the firm is 0.9. If conditions are bad the mean payoff is 5, since the survival probability in that case is 0.5. Now the overall mean payoff is therefore the weighted average of these two mean payoffs and the weight is determined by the probability of

PANEL 2

CONDITIONAL INDEPENDENCE AND DIVERSIFICATION:
THE CONTINUOUS-TIME STORY

Here we describe the mathematical formulation of conditionally non-systematic credit risk, building on results in Lando (1994, 1998). Suppose a situation in which we have a state-variable diffusion process X and defaultable bonds with default intensity given as $\lambda(X_s)$, ie the state variable modulates the default intensity at all times. In the setting of a so-called Cox process, it is possible to construct the default mechanism such that conditionally on the evolution of the state variable – and hence on the intensity – the default process (which starts at 0 and then jumps to 1 when there is a default) is a non-homogeneous Poisson process. For illustrative purposes, in the following we consider a one-year horizon. Define the payoff on a bond

$$Z^i = \begin{cases} 1 & \text{if firm i has no default before year 1} \\ 0 & \text{if firm i does default before year 1} \end{cases}$$

and let G denote the information contained in the evolution of X up to time 1. Then

$$\operatorname{Prob}\left(Z^i = 1 | G\right) = \exp\left(-\int_0^1 \lambda(X_s)ds\right)$$

$$\operatorname{Prob}\left(Z^i = 1\right) = E\exp\left(-\int_0^1 \lambda(X_s)ds\right)$$

Note that conditionally on the evolution of the state variable, the payoff on the corporate bond is a Bernoulli random variable with success probability equal to

$$\exp\left(-\int_0^1 \lambda(X_s)ds\right)$$

and therefore the conditional variance is given by

$$\exp\left(-\int_0^1 \lambda(X_s)ds\right)\left(1 - \exp\left(-\int_0^1 \lambda(X_s)ds\right)\right)$$

Now consider two portfolios: one consisting of 1 unit of a corporate bond and another portfolio consisting of 1/n units of each of n different corporate bonds, whose payoffs are independent *conditionally* on G. We compute total variances for both portfolios using the conditioning rule. We then obtain for the portfolio with 1 bond:

$$V(Z^i) = E\left(V(Z^i | G)\right) + V\left(E(Z^i | G)\right) = E\left(\exp\left(-\int_0^1 \lambda(X_s)ds\right)\left(1 - \exp\left(-\int_0^1 \lambda(X_s)ds\right)\right)\right) + V\left(\exp\left(-\int_0^1 \lambda(X_s)ds\right)\right)$$

Now, for the portfolio with n different bonds each held in a quantity of 1/n:

$$V\left(\frac{1}{n}\sum_{i=1}^n Z^i\right) = \frac{1}{n^2}V\left(\sum_{i=1}^n Z^i\right) = \frac{1}{n^2}E\left(V\left(\sum_{i=1}^n Z^i | G\right)\right) + \frac{1}{n^2}V\left(E\left(\sum_{i=1}^n Z^i | G\right)\right)$$

$$= \frac{1}{n^2}E\left(n\exp\left(-\int_0^1 \lambda(X_s)ds\right)\left(1 - \exp\left(-\int_0^1 \lambda(X_s)ds\right)\right)\right) + \frac{1}{n^2}V\left(n\exp\left(-\int_0^1 \lambda(X_s)ds\right)\right)$$

$$= \frac{1}{n}E\left(\exp\left(-\int_0^1 \lambda(X_s)ds\right)\left(1 - \exp\left(-\int_0^1 \lambda(X_s)ds\right)\right)\right) + V\left(\exp\left(-\int_0^1 \lambda(X_s)ds\right)\right)$$

and this expression converges, as n goes to infinity, towards

$$V\left[\exp\left(-\int_0^1 \lambda(X_s)ds\right)\right]$$

Not only does the variance converge but so does the actual payoff of the portfolio. This means that as n becomes large we have diversified the "conditionally non-systematic" credit risk away and are left only with credit risk that is sensitive to market risk. If we have the usual setup in term structure modelling, with a money market account accumulating wealth at the continuously compounded (short) rate $R(X_s)$, then the well-diversified portfolio of corporate zero coupons should have a price equal to

$$E\left(\exp\left(-\int_0^1 (R + \lambda)(X_s)ds\right)\right)$$

where the expectation is taken under the suitable risk-neutral measure.

good conditions, that is:

$$E(payoff) = 0.8 \cdot 9 + 0.2 \cdot 5 = 8.2$$

We already noted that the mean payoff was 9 when conditions were good and 5 when they were bad. The variance of a random variable which is 9 with probability 0.8 and 5 with probability 0.2 is

$$(9 - 5)^2 \cdot 0.8 \cdot 0.2 = 2.56$$

and this explains the variance of the conditional mean for the one bond portfolio.

The variance of the payoff in good conditions is equal to the variance of a random variable which is 10 with probability 0.9, and 0 with probability 0.1, and this is 9. The variance in bad conditions is similarly computed to 25. The mean of these two variances, using again that good conditions have probability 0.8, is equal to 12.2. The total variance is obtained by adding these two quantities, and we may check the formula by computing the variance of the payoff without thinking about conditioning on whether conditions are good or bad.

The same exercise can be carried through for the second portfolio in which there are 10 bonds, one from each of 10 different firms. The key property to remember when performing the calculation is that when conditioning on "good" or "bad", the payoffs of the bonds are independent. (This is illustrated in more detail in Panel 2, which provides a more technical account of the results.) Hence, conditionally, diversification is working very well. Not surprisingly, the total variance decreases and the dominant factor becomes the variability that is due to variability in overall conditions. The exercise can be continued with larger portfolios, ending up in a situation where one comes as close as desired to a "limit portfolio" that pays off 9 when conditions

Table 2. Portfolio example

	Portfolio 1	Portfolio 2	Limit portfolio
E(payoff)	8,2	8,2	8,2
V(E(payoff|X))	2,56	2,56	2,56
E(V(payoff|X))	12,2	1,22	0
Total variance	14,76	3,78	2,56

are good and 5 when conditions are bad.

In other words, conditionally non-systematic credit risk must be eliminated through diversification while the remaining credit risk can be hedged using "market risk" instruments. The example is summarised in Table 2.

Conclusion

In this chapter, we have attempted to describe the workings of continuous-time transition analysis, with an emphasis on the role of the generator. We have also discussed the issue of modelling correlation in migrations and defaults, and the main point here was to show how the notion of correlation through common dependence on "market factors" gives a convenient way of analysing how a portfolio of credit-risky instruments can be diversified to become a product that can be hedged using securities dealing in market risk. Of course, we will typically not have enough information on defaults to estimate from historical data the sensitivity of default risk to changes in market conditions. But we are still left with a model that can help us "back out" the market's perception of this dependence. Furthermore, once a large portfolio (in terms of the number of different securities held) is in place, the method seems very well suited to provide a picture of credit risk sensitivity to a relatively low-dimensional number of factors.

BIBLIOGRAPHY

Duffie, D., and D. Lando, 1998, "Term Structures of Credit Spreads with Incomplete Accounting Information", Working paper.

Duffie, D., and K. Singleton, 1995, "Modelling Term Structures of Defaultable Bonds", Working paper, Stanford University.

Jarrow, R., D. Lando and S.Turnbull, 1997, "A Markov Model for the Term Structure of Credit Risk Spreads",

Review of Financial Studies, 10(2), pp. 481-523.

Lando, D., 1994, "Three Essays on Contingent Claims Pricing", PhD thesis, Cornell University.

Lando, D., 1998 forthcoming, "On Cox Processes and Credit Risky Securities", *Review of Derivatives Research*.

Zhou, C., 1997, "Default Correlation: An Analytical Result", Working paper, Federal Reserve Board.

REGULATORY TRENDS AND ISSUES IN TAXATION

12

Regulatory Developments and Capital Allocation for Credit Derivatives

Matthew Elderfield*
International Swaps and Derivatives Association

W hile credit derivatives have provided important new risk management tools for financial firms, they have brought headaches for the supervisory community. The new instruments have challenged regulators to review their assumptions about risk and the nature of trading, and have exposed severe weaknesses in the regulatory capital regime. To their credit, the leading regulatory authorities have risen to the challenge and over the past two years they have issued revised capital rules and risk management guidelines to address developments in the market. However, the constraints of European Union law and the Basle rules mean that progress has been painfully slow. As a result, the regulatory capital framework is emerging as a constraint on the use of credit derivatives.

Risk management framework

While regulated institutions often focus on capital standards when addressing regulatory requirements, the regulators themselves put considerable emphasis on risk management. Capital requirements target explicitly only those components of risk that lend themselves readily to quantification. Market risk and credit risk attract a lot of attention, even though experience has shown that substantial losses are more likely to arise from the less quantifiable bits – operational risk. Capital requirements are the ambulance at the bottom of the cliff, but the fence at the top is risk control.

Regulators are now becoming more explicit about the need for good risk management and have published a number of guidelines.[1] These documents provide high-level guidance, emphasising the need for rigorous controls, designed and applied by the regulated institutions. Supervisors pay close regard to a firm's compliance with these standards as part of routine supervision and, in particular, the model recognition process.

Risk management is perhaps not an area where detailed regulatory guidance is to be expected; regulators state the requirement for risk management rather than how it should be done. However, some direct references have been made by those regulators who have published their requirements for credit derivatives, including the Bank of England and SFA in the UK, the Commission Bancaire in France and the Comptroller of the Currency (OCC) and the Board of Governors of the Federal Reserve System in the US.

The Federal Reserve paper (which is addressed to Fed supervisors) clearly states the overall principle to which all the other regulatory bodies implicitly subscribe:

An institution should not enter into credit derivative transactions unless its management has the ability to understand and manage the credit and other risks associated with these instruments in a safe and sound manner. Accordingly, examiners should determine the appropriateness of these instruments on an institution-by-institution basis. Such a determination should take into account management's expertise in evaluating such instruments; the adequacy of relevant policies, including position limits; and the quality of the institution's relevant information systems and internal controls.

* The author is grateful for the assistance of Rose Gibson of the UK Financial Services Authority. However, the views expressed within are those of the author alone, as are any errors or deficiencies.

REGULATORY

DEVELOPMENTS

AND CAPITAL

ALLOCATION

FOR CREDIT

DERIVATIVES

Both the Fed and the OCC refer to other papers they have published on risk management, indicating that they expect a seamless structure, arguably implying that they see no new risks in credit derivatives.

The OCC guidelines were issued in August 1996. The document highlights the necessity for "proper care and due diligence", especially in the light of uncertainties associated with the products: it mentions the relatively underdeveloped nature of valuation techniques, and the fact that capital requirements and accounting standards will "almost certainly lag advances in product development."

The UK guidance (contained in the SFA's Board Notice 414 and the Bank of England's discussion paper *Developing a Supervisory Approach to Credit Approaches*) is more detailed. The Bank of England document states that "in considering appropriate risk management techniques... the Bank's general approach has been to ask in what ways various credit derivative products are similar to longer-established financial products, and in what ways they are different. To the extent that they are similar to other products, we would want to be satisfied that the same rigorous standards of risk management and control were applied to them... To the extent that credit derivatives offer new features, the Bank would also want to be satisfied that rigorous standards of risk management and control had been developed to cater for these features".

Credit derivatives do not involve any new form of risk; they are new combinations of familiar risks, so the Bank's remarks may best be interpreted as referring to risks new to the dealing bank, or to new combinations in a single product.

Risk management issues for total return swaps and for default products are discussed separately. For total return swaps, the Bank suggests procedures should be in place to ensure that the liquidity of the reference asset is verified and monitored when applying trading assumptions in the process of marking to market; there are questions about the management of "rollover risk" (the liquidity/market risk of replacing a hedge), how exposures are monitored when credit risk is acquired indirectly, potential insider-dealing implications of the new products, and the management of basis risk (where a different type or seniority of asset is used either as a hedge, or as a marking proxy).

For credit default products, the Bank highlights the possibility that some credit derivatives may be regarded as insurance.[2] Again, the need is stressed for procedures and controls to be applied as stringently as they are to other products, mentioning particularly credit risk analysis, limits, systems co-ordination and management reporting.

Among the legal/documentation problems discussed by the Bank's paper are the lack of standardised documentation, the effectiveness of dealer polls, and the need for clarity on which party has recourse to the defaulting party. Since the paper was written, the problem of non-standardised documentation has been mitigated by ISDA's production of credit derivatives documentation. ISDA has published a standard long-form confirmation for credit default swaps and is working on documentation for total return swaps, credit spread options and, ultimately, a standard booklet of credit derivatives definitions for use with short-form confirms.[3]

The section of the SFA document discussing internal controls issues has sub-sections covering new product approval, understanding the risks and matching them to the firm's risk appetite, credit approval and review processes, imperfect hedging, and monitoring exposures. Interestingly, the paper stresses the SFA's expectation that firms should be able to perform stress tests and what it calls "reality tests" (see Panel 1).

More informally, Vicki Fitt of the SFA set out her views in an article for *Risk* magazine in July 1997. She emphasised the need for substance rather than form when assessing controls: "Any blue-print of internal controls can only address 'hardware'. How do you encapsulate culture? Hardware – committees with the right names, people with the right titles and reporting lines, reports going to all the right people, containing all the right information – does not itself add value. Culture is about hearts and minds – it's soft stuff that cannot be measured, and can only be judged by looking people in the eyes... the principal 'test' for embarking upon credit derivatives trading should be one of culture, not capital requirements."

This underlines the fact that supervisors are first and foremost interested in the quality of risk management systems and the management culture that underpins them. Clearly, financial firms too take great interest in these issues. However, in the regulatory arena it has been the capital framework that has attracted most attention, due to the very real impact that regulatory capital costs have on firms.

161

REGULATORY
DEVELOPMENTS
AND CAPITAL
ALLOCATION
FOR CREDIT
DERIVATIVES

PANEL 1

EXTRACTS FROM SFA GUIDANCE ON CREDIT DERIVATIVES

Scenario testing

Routine scenario testing should be undertaken in order to aid the measurement and control of risks in "normal" circumstances. In addition, "stress" scenarios should be designed to test the potential for loss under extreme conditions, or to highlight possible risk control problems that may arise. These should include:

❑ abnormal market movements;

❑ periods of inactivity or illiquidity; and

❑ the break-down of key assumptions.

Individual firms will need to devise tests that are meaningful to their particular situations; in each case, the criteria should explicitly identify plausible events or influences to which the firm could be exposed. Of crucial importance in the case of credit derivatives is that the results should be capable of clear interpretation even where, by the very nature of the instruments, the distinction between market risk and credit risk becomes increasingly blurred...[Any] subjective judge-

ments...made in order to price or mark to market... should be routinely reviewed and their potential effect included within the scenario testing.

The results of scenario testing should be regularly communicated to senior management, and to the Board or equivalent body, and should be reflected in the policies and limits set by management.

Reality testing

The essence of reality testing is the comparison of actual trading results with expected outcomes... Any firm that incurs credit risk in its trading activities should ensure that it has a mechanism to test whether, and to what extent, its assumptions have been robust. There should also be a recognised route for the results of reality testing to feed back into the process governing the way in which the firm limits its risk-taking activity.

Source: SFA Board Notice 414

Capital adequacy framework

This section examines the emerging capital adequacy framework for credit derivatives, looking at how the basic principles of EU law and Basle rules are applied, drawing on ISDA's work with British, French, North American and other supervisors. It is important to emphasise that these rules are in a state of flux, as the use of credit derivatives has highlighted fundamental weaknesses in the credit risk capital framework, which has in turn spurred efforts to reform the 1988 Basle Capital rules. The rules described below are therefore the interim capital rules – a case of each supervisor trying to hammer square pegs into round holes as they try to accommodate credit derivatives under the current capital regime as best they can. As will become clear, these rules are still the subject of intense discussion and the final outcome is still unclear at the time of writing; this section is therefore best seen as a report on the state of the debate on credit derivatives capital, rather than a definite description of any final rules.

TRADING BOOK/BANKING BOOK SPLIT

The first key question that is posed in the capital framework is the choice of assignment of a posi-

tion to the trading or banking book. All positions must be subject to either traditional banking book rules based on the 1988 Capital Accord, designed for credit risk on loans and other traditional banking products, or to the trading book framework, embodied in the Capital Adequacy Directive and the 1996 Basle market risk capital rules.[4] Capital requirements are generally more favourable in the latter, but positions must be marked-to-market, held for trading intent and defined as a "financial instrument".

How then do credit derivatives fit into this somewhat artificial regulatory divide? For products such as total return swaps, supervisors easily accepted that they may be eligible for trading book treatment, largely because of their similarity to equity swaps and other instruments already subject to trading book rules. However, the initial instinct of some supervisors – the Bank of England at least – was that credit default transactions were fundamentally similar to bank guarantees and therefore merited banking book treatment in all cases.[5]

The assignment of book is of no simple academic interest; it has a real impact on regulatory capital cost. If a guarantee treatment were adopted, all credit derivative traders (ie protec-

REGULATORY
DEVELOPMENTS
AND CAPITAL
ALLOCATION
FOR CREDIT
DERIVATIVES

Table 1. Key characteristics of credit derivatives and other instruments

	Interest rate swap	Total return swap	Credit default swap	Guarantee
Pricing	Market	Market	Market	Private
Post-default costs	N/A	None	None	Work out participation
Risk management with other derivatives	Yes	Yes	Yes	No
ISDA documentation	Yes	Yes	Yes	No
Marked-to-market	Yes	Yes	Yes	No
Legal structure	Standardised	Standardised	Standardised	Bespoke
Generic risk management use	Yes	Yes	Yes	No - attached to specific obligation
Netting with other derivatives	Yes	Yes	Yes	No

tion sellers) would have to treat positions as full 8% risk weighted charges. Trading book charges, by contrast, can be as low as 0.25%, 1.00% or 1.65%, depending on whether the underlying is of investment grade and on the instrument's residual maturity. Trading book charges are applied to both long and short positions, while short positions do not receive a capital charge in the banking book.

Apart from the stark capital cost objections to a mandatory banking book treatment, this proposed approach is simply at odds with the way in which default swaps are documented, priced and managed. Table 1, taken from ISDA's Bank of England response, makes these points very clearly and highlights the key differences between credit derivatives and guarantees.

In the course of discussions with the Bank of England and other supervisors, it became clear that valuation of credit derivatives was the key issue in the banking book/trading book split. The most important criterion for trading book eligibility is the requirement that positions are marked to market: if a blanket ban on trading book treatment were dropped for credit default swaps, this test would still need to be met. Supervisors queried the ability to mark to market instruments where the underlying reference asset of the credit derivative was itself illiquid and not marked-to-market. The valuation test is important. As we have seen, trading book capital charges tend to be lower than those in the banking book, but the quid pro quo is that any losses on trading book positions hit P&L immediately through marking to market – they are not deferred as under historic cost accounting.

In an effort to assuage supervisory concerns, ISDA looked at valuation questions in some depth in our comment to the Bank of England. We noted that marking to market was straightforward in cases where the underlying reference asset was itself marked-to-market. However, after consultation with members and accountants, we explained that robust valuation techniques may also be applied for other instruments. Where a particular reference asset is not sufficiently traded to establish a mark to market directly, valuation can be derived by looking to comparable instruments of the same issuer, with due account taken for differences in seniority (looking at traded bond prices to help value a loan reference asset default swap, for example). Even if there are no directly analogous instruments to the reference asset issued by the underlying credit in question, comparable instruments issued by similar credit types may be used with appropriate adjustments.

Financial firms can expect close scrutiny of valuation techniques from supervisors, at least in the United Kingdom, and should be prepared for particularly intense review where underlying reference assets are themselves not marked-to-market. Supervisors are particularly conservative in their attitude to loan reference asset credit derivatives, not only because of questions relating to the valuation of the underlying loan but as a result of concerns about these instruments' legal status under EU directives and the possibility for regulatory arbitrage by repackaging loans in order to receive trading book treatment.[6] The position is now becoming clearer and the Bank of England no longer objects to trading book treatment simply because of the name of the instrument – that it is a default swap rather than a total return swap, for instance. However trading book treatment may be denied unless robust valuation techniques are in place.

BANKING BOOK RULES

As we have seen, those credit derivatives that are given banking book treatment receive guarantee-type capital charges.[7] But even though trading book eligibility is possible, some banks will nevertheless assign these instruments to their banking book. This is likely to be the case for end-users of credit derivatives, who either do not have trading books at all (because they have no or de minimis trading activity) or because they are using a credit derivative to hedge an underlying loan position which is itself in the banking book.[8]

Under the guarantee regime, the risk weighting of the guarantor – or in this case credit protection seller – is substituted for that of the underlying asset being hedged. So a bank with an exposure to a corporate weighted at 100% would reduce this to 20% if the position is properly hedged by a credit default swap purchased from a bank or investment firm with a risk weighting of 20%. From the perspective of the credit protection seller, no relief is provided if the credit derivative is retained in the banking book – the seller has now assumed an exposure to a corporate at a 100% risk weighting.

The weaknesses of this treatment are simply those of the current banking book regime in general. Very blunt risk weightings apply to positions and, in the case where protection is purchased from neither a bank nor an investment firm, no relief is provided for the hedge – one 100% risk weighting is substituted by another. Also, under Bank of England rules, the maturity of the underlying position and that of the hedge must match in order to provide capital relief. This question of the treatment of maturity mismatches and other standards for recognising hedges is discussed below.

TRADING BOOK RULES

While credit derivative end-users will likely be subject to banking book charges for their positions, dealers are likely to be covered by trading book rules.[9] These rules are set out in EU law in the Capital Adequacy Directive (and a recently adopted amending directive, the so-called "CAD 2") and under Basle rules in the January 1996 Amendment to the Capital Accord concerning market risk.[10]

These rules provide two alternative approaches to calculating capital charges for market risk: the use of internal value-at-risk (or VAR) models, subject to various supervisory guidelines and approval, or the application of standardised "building block" capital charges. Under the building block regime, positions are assigned either general market risk or specific risk charges, with different capital calculation methods depending on whether the position is a debt or equity instrument or related derivative. (Charges also apply for foreign exchange and commodity risk, which need not concern us here.) General market risk charges are assigned to cover the risk of adverse overall market movements, such as general interest rate changes or equity market-wide price movements. In contrast, specific risk charges cover the risk of adverse movements of individual positions relative to the market as a whole – that ICI bonds or shares fall or rise in value at a different rate than overall UK interest rates or the FTSE 100, for instance.

In the context of credit derivatives, general market risk charges may apply in cases where an instrument is exposed to interest rates, but the main concern is with specific risk requirements for debt positions. These are set at the 0.25%, 1.00% and 1.65% levels described above, so long as the instrument in question is "qualifying" – that it is deemed of investment grade quality by one or more credit rating agencies. Otherwise the normal 8% capital requirements apply.

All this means that trading book charges for qualifying instruments are significantly lower than those in the banking book. For credit derivatives, charges are applied by looking through to the underlying asset and analysing whether or not it meets the qualifying test. This is a straightforward process for bond reference assets, but the treatment is not so clear for loan reference asset instruments. In these cases, the fact that loans tend to be unrated causes problems and supervisors may have to see whether the credit in question has any debt which meets the qualifying test and therefore permits qualifying status for the loan-based instrument. This is a very grey area where practice is still evolving.

When applying specific risk charges, long and short positions may be netted or offset against each other in order to set charges on smaller residual positions. However, most readings of EU law and Basle, and certainly the interpretation of the UK supervisors, is that this is only possible in very limited circumstances. This has led to a major debate about the role of offsets under the current capital regime.

OFFSETS

The offsetting of long and short positions is a widely-accepted feature of capital adequacy rules: regulators have consistently acknowledged the great importance of recognising hedging in prudent risk management by setting charges only on the residual net position. With credit risk, however, offsetting is severely constrained under the current rules. As a result, the capital regime provides a deterrent to risk management and the growth of the credit derivatives market. Firms do not receive capital relief for putting a hedge in place and may even receive an additional capital charge!

REGULATORY

DEVELOPMENTS

AND CAPITAL

ALLOCATION

FOR CREDIT

DERIVATIVES

There are two main problems for offsets under the current rules: the treatment of maturity mismatches and of instrument mismatches. The current specific risk rules (and the UK authorities' interpretation of guarantee rules) require the maturity of an underlying to be matched or exceeded by the hedging instrument in order to receive any capital relief. So a 10-year ICI bond hedged by a nine-year credit default swap would receive no capital relief at all, even though the hedge is in place for 90% of the maturity of the underlying.

There are similarly inflexible rules for instrument mismatches: the underlying reference asset must be exactly the same as the position being hedged in order to qualify for an offset. Slight differences in coupon or seniority invalidate the hedge for capital purposes, as an underlying senior unsecured ICI bond, for instance, may not be offset by a credit default swap on a junior ICI bond. In fact, the hedge is very robust in such a case, as the firm holding the unsecured bond will benefit from the higher recovery rate on this position, while the credit event payment under the swap will be equal to the full principal amount of the bond reduced only by the smaller recovery rate on the junior position.

These standards have highly perverse effects, as firms receive no capital relief at all for prudent hedging activity. While a full offset in the case of a maturity mismatch is not justified (and in some instrument mismatches residual risk would remain because of differences in recovery rates), the rules do not provide for partial capital relief. In fact, the position is even worse than this: at present some EU supervisors feel bound by the CAD to impose capital charges on both the underlying position and the credit derivative hedging that position.[11] This means that firms are actually punished for undertaking prudent hedging activity, as capital charges increase when entering into a hedge. As the supervisors themselves recognise, this is patently absurd. From the perspective of ISDA members dealing in credit derivatives, the capital rules provide a strong disincentive for customers to enter into transactions. The fact that the credit derivatives market has grown as fast as it has despite this significant impediment points to the potential for even more growth if only this anomaly in the rules could be addressed.

These regulations are clearly a major source of concern for ISDA members and we have argued strongly for revisions to the capital framework to accommodate offsets. We have proposed simple rules of thumb concerning seniority/instrument mismatches which would recognise offsets under the standardised rules and have also proposed a simple method to allow partial offsets in the case of maturity mismatches. It is unclear what the prospect is for the adoption of these changes in the short term, as the question of credit derivatives capital has become subsumed into a wider debate about the treatment of credit risk capital.

COUNTERPARTY RISK

Credit derivatives are also subject to counterparty risk charges. As well as the risk relating to the underlying reference asset, there is also a risk to the credit protection buyer that the seller will default and be unable to meet its obligations. And for the seller, there is a risk that the buyer will be unable to pay premiums or otherwise meet its end of the transaction.

Counterparty risk charges apply to OTC derivatives held in either the banking or trading book. However, in the context of credit derivatives, the fact that a guarantee treatment is applied in the banking book means that counterparty risk charges are not, in fact, assessed in this book.[12] The method for establishing counterparty risk charges was set out in the initial 1988 Basle Accord (adopted into EU law in the Solvency Ratio Directive) and has gradually evolved over time to reflect the use of close out netting and to allow a refinement of charges for potential future counterparty exposure. Charges are two-fold. First, a capital requirement is imposed for the current counterparty exposure based on the mark-to-market value of an instrument (or portfolio of instruments after taking account of netting). Secondly, a charge is assessed for potential future counterparty exposure – that is, the risk that future market movements may increase the size of a firm's exposure to its counterparty. These charges are set out in an "add-on" matrix: a series of risk factors applied to the notional principal value of an instrument depending on the maturity of the position and the nature of the underlying risk – interest rate, foreign exchange, equity, precious metal, or commodity, roughly in order of lower to higher charges.[13] Limited recognition of close-out netting is permitted. Current exposure and potential future exposure charges are then summed, with normal banking book risk weightings applied, capped at 50%.

In applying counterparty risk charges to credit derivatives, the only area of debate relates to the potential future exposure "add-on" charge,

165

REGULATORY

DEVELOPMENTS

AND CAPITAL

ALLOCATION

FOR CREDIT

DERIVATIVES

as the mark-to-market value of the credit derivative determines the current exposure charge. The difficulty in determining the appropriate add-on relates to the fact that credit derivatives were not considered when establishing the add-on matrix, and different supervisors have different views as to which add-ons are most appropriate. In the US, for example, equity add-ons are imposed for investment grade reference assets and commodity add-ons for all other positions. However, in the UK, equity add-ons apply across the board at the time of writing, with the prospect that interest rate add-ons will be introduced for investment grade positions. The debate is continuing about the asymmetry of risk in regard to credit derivatives: in case of counterparty default the credit protection buyer has a lot more to lose than the protection seller under some structures.[14] In future this may be reflected by differentiated charges and sellers of credit default swaps may not have counterparty risk charges when all premiums are known and received. However, like the rest of the credit derivatives capital regime, the position is still in flux and firms must look at the prevailing local rules carefully.

BASKETS, CREDIT-LINKED NOTES AND STRUCTURED PRODUCTS

While we have seen the basic capital position for credit default swaps and total return swaps, there are other types of credit derivative structures that pose further complications for supervisors in terms of their capital treatment.

There has been intense debate in the UK and France about the treatment of basket products, instruments where protection may be bought on a basket of names, with a credit event payment provided on the first of these to default. In effect there is no single reference asset upon which to assess appropriate capital charges. While an accurate view of the risk of these instruments requires an assessment of the correlation between the names in the basket and the joint probability of default, the current capital rules cannot cater for this level of sophistication. The supervisors' initial view was simply to assess charges based on the riskiest single name in the basket. However, the British and French regulatory authorities have concluded that this method probably underestimates the risk. They have proposed a much tougher approach: assessing charges with respect to each name in the basket. This has prompted deep concern in the industry, as the charges in this case dramatically overstate

the risk and are inconsistent with the logic of the current capital accord. The outcome of this debate is unknown at the time of writing.

Credit-linked notes pose similar issues: there is a risk both to the issuer of the note and to the underlying reference asset determining the instrument's cashflow. Again, an analysis of joint probability of default is warranted but cannot be accommodated under the current regime. Accordingly, capital charges are assessed with respect to both the reference credit and the issuer (in the trading book specific risk charges apply to both, for example). This treatment has been less debated than that of baskets and seems likely to continue.

Finally, it should be noted that credit derivatives are increasingly being used in structured transactions, often in a manner similar to securitisation. This poses real difficulties for supervisors and it is hard to generalise about the capital treatment, as a case-by-case assessment is made in light of the specifics of the deal and the prevailing rules for straightforward securitisation. However, the recent JP Morgan "BISTRO" structure, involving the use of credit derivatives to hedge and eliminate regulatory capital charges for loan positions, is perhaps the most innovative so far, and highlights the advantages of using these instruments rather than normal securitisation.

MODELS

The regulatory capital regime now provides for internal models to calculate capital charges in certain circumstances. While subject to supervisory criteria, and constrained in the manner in which they may be applied to a firm's full range of risks, they are powerful tools for overcoming many of the weaknesses of the current rules.

The Basle regime and, shortly, EU law[15] provide firms with the ability to employ internal value-at-risk models to calculate trading book capital charges. Initially, the regulatory regime only provided for the use of these models for general market risk charges but a further revision was made in September 1997 to allow VAR modelling of specific risk rather than the application of standardised charges. This is an important development. Modelling will allow firms to calculate charges (within the constraints of the supervisor's parameters[16]) more accurately for individual instruments, and will permit recognition of offsets even in the cases of maturity and instrument mismatches, as these can be assessed directly within the context of the modelling process. Firms that use credit derivatives have a

REGULATORY
DEVELOPMENTS
AND CAPITAL
ALLOCATION
FOR CREDIT
DERIVATIVES

PANEL 2

LATEST DEVELOPMENTS IN THE UK, FRANCE AND GERMANY

As this chapter was being prepared, the picture on credit derivatives capital was further clarified with the publication of interim rules by the French Commission Bancaire in May 1998 and the release, in July 1998, of both updated standards by the British FSA and draft rules by the German Federal Supervisory Banking Authority.

These actions show the extent to which supervisors are trying to respond to industry concerns within the constraints of current EU law and Basle guidelines. For example, both the French and British rules now find a way with the rules to permit partial capital relief (a 70% risk weighting) for banking book positions in the case of maturity mismatches. Similarly, the FSA has dropped its insistence on double charges for trading book positions in cases of mismatches and the French and German authorities are considering whether or not to follow suit. Also, all the supervisors seem to have adopted a more flexible stance on the range of credit derivatives eligible for trading book treatment, dropping restrictions on loan-referenced products.

With these steps by the three EU supervisors, it now appears that as much progress as possible has been made at the national level. The focus of attention thus firmly shifts to Basle and Brussels and the question of how EU and international standards can be updated. Here the timetable is very unclear, with debate continuing as to whether a short-term "fix" for credit derivatives should be contemplated, or whether a full-scale reform of the 1988 Basle framework for credit risk should be the goal. Clearer signs should emerge from the Basle Committee as to the approach to be taken, but it will take quite some time before a more rational capital regime that recognises hedging and prudent portfolio management of risk is adopted. The credit derivatives capital debate is by no means over...

strong incentive to develop specific risk modelling capability in order to receive more appropriate regulatory capital charges.

Some supervisors may permit relatively simple, "no-frills" models to be employed just to address credit derivative offsets, rather than requiring full-blown, sophisticated specific risk models for all positions. The advantage of this approach is that simplified modelling techniques will be more accessible, more quickly, to a wider universe of banks. A more rational, and prudent, capital treatment can be achieved without waiting to develop full specific risk modelling. The scope for employing such simplified modelling methods is still uncertain in many jurisdictions, but firms should consider approaching their local authorities to see whether it will be permitted, at least on an interim basis, before moving to full specific risk modelling.

BEYOND CREDIT DERIVATIVES: CREDIT RISK CAPITAL REFORM

The scope for specific risk modelling in the trading book does not address all the problems posed in accommodating credit derivatives into the current capital regime: models may not, for example, be applied to banking book positions or for counterparty risk charges. Inappropriate standardised rules still apply in these areas.

The shortcomings of the current credit risk capital rules are numerous and well known: the blunt risk weighting categories, the static 8% risk charge, the lack of term structure, the blunt add-ons for potential future exposure, the lack of portfolio diversification recognition and so on. There is now a ground swell of opinion within the financial industry – shared by many supervisors – that the time has come for a full-scale reform of the 1988 credit risk capital standards. ISDA has published proposals for an "evolutionary models-based approach" to credit risk capital which would permit the use of portfolio or simplified models to calculate credit risk capital charges.[17]

It is this broader reform effort that holds out the best hope for a sensible, coherent capital regime for credit derivatives. But comprehensive changes to the current regime will take years to complete, involving extensive quantitative analysis and consultation before final rules are published, never mind implemented. The industry must continue to pursue a dual-track approach, seeking the best interim capital rules possible within the constraints of the current regime, while urging faster progress on more comprehensive reform of the overall Basle framework.

REGULATORY
DEVELOPMENTS
AND CAPITAL
ALLOCATION
FOR CREDIT
DERIVATIVES

Conclusion

The capital framework outlined above must be intensely frustrating to the credit derivatives practitioner, and the pace of change discouragingly slow. But progress is gradually being made. Not only are the supervisory authorities revising their interim capital rules, but much more importantly, the advent of credit derivatives is changing the whole mindset behind credit risk management and trading. Supervisors are tackling the need to reform the 1988 Basle Capital Accord more quickly than would have seemed possible even one year ago because of the issues posed by these important new instruments. Credit derivatives have shown the importance of portfolio diversification and hedging in the real world, making reform not just theoretically desirable, but a pressing necessity. Credit derivatives are not only making an important contribution to the development of the financial markets and risk management practice, but also to the debate about the way in which banks hold capital against risk. This in itself is no small achievement.

1 *See the Basle Committee on Banking Supervision and Technical Committee of the International Organisation of Securities Commissions,* Risk Management Guidelines for Derivatives *(July 1994) and Group of Thirty,* Derivatives: Practices and Principles *(July 1993).*

2 *ISDA has obtained a legal opinion clarifying that credit derivatives should not be deemed insurance in most cases.*

3 *Documentation issues are also discussed in Chapter 2, Panel 3 and Panel 7.*

4 *In addition, counterparty risk charges apply to OTC derivatives held in either book, although not to credit derivatives treated as guarantees; see below.*

5 *This was the position taken in the Bank's consultation document of November 1996, but was abandoned and is not followed by any other supervisor as far as ISDA is aware.*

6 *Untraded loans are almost certainly prohibited from trading book treatment by the trading book definition of the Capital Adequacy Directive, due to its cross reference to a list of specified "financial instruments" in the Investment Services Directive. However, analysis by ISDA, LIBA and the BBA points to the eligibility of loan-reference asset credit derivatives.*

7 *This is the case for the rules that have been published so far in the UK, US, France and Canada.*

8 *As a general principle, capital rules dictate that hedges should apply the capital regime of the underlying position.*

9 *Again, subject to meeting the trading book eligibility test - above all with relation to valuation; see above.*

10 *See Elderfield, M., (1996) "OTC Derivatives and the EC Capital Adequacy Directive" in* Swaps and Off-Exchange Derivatives Trading: Law and Regulation *for a full description of the CAD standardised rules.*

11 *Non-EU supervisors apparently do not feel bound in this way by the Basle framework. Federal Reserve rules only provide full offsets when instrument and maturity matching is in place, but do not punish hedging: rather than applying capital charges on both underlying and hedge as in the UK, the Fed only sets charges on one of the two sides of the deal. Thus, while banks are not rewarded for partial hedges they are at least not punished for them. The US banking agencies also are less prescriptive about maturity mismatches in the banking book and will grant guarantee treatment even when mismatches occur - within reason and subject to supervisory discretion.*

12 *If they were, firms would be even further punished for entering into banking book hedges as only limited relief would be provided under the guarantee rules with a new, additive, charge introduced for counterparty risk.*

13 *These rules are clearly flawed in their blunt assessment of potential future exposure - charges are equal for Nikkei and S&P500 positions, even though the latter is less volatile - and in their inexact recognition of netting. The PFE regime is therefore clearly another area for debate concerning credit risk capital reform.*

14 *This point is well explained in the French Commission Bancaire's consultation paper on credit derivatives capital treatment (Credit Derivatives: Issues for Discussion on Interim Prudential Treatment, June 1997).*

15 *Under "CAD 2".*

16 *A 10-day holding period, 99% confidence interval, one-year observation period, multiplication factor of three applied to the model out-put, plus other standards. See Basle January 1996.*

17 *ISDA, "Credit Risk and Regulatory Capital", (March 1998). A copy of this paper is available on ISDA's website: www.isda.org and a summary is available in* Risk, *April 1998, pp. 25-9.*

13

US Federal Income Tax Consequences of Credit Derivatives Transactions

David Z. Nirenberg and Steven L. Kopp
Orrick, Herrington & Sutcliffe LLP

redit derivatives, including total return swaps, default swaps and credit-linked notes, have begun to play an increasingly important role in the capital markets. They are used for a myriad of purposes – some tax-motivated, others not – but whatever the participant's motivation, these transactions raise serious, and sometimes difficult, tax issues.

In a total return swap, a total return receiver is in the same economic/cashflow position as a person who makes a 100% leveraged purchase of the reference security. In analysing such a transaction it is necessary to determine whether it will be taxed according to its form, as a notional principal contract (the formal tax name for a swap), or recharacterised as a leveraged purchase of the reference security.

A default swap provides a protection buyer with protection against a default on a reference security (or a credit event with respect to a reference obligor). In analysing this transaction it is necessary to determine whether it will be respected as a notional principal contract or recharacterised as a put option or guarantee.

A credit-linked note is a security that mimics the performance of a debt instrument issued by a reference obligor. In analysing some of these transactions it is necessary to determine whether the security will be characterised as a debt instrument for tax purposes or some other sort of financial instrument and, if characterised as a debt instrument, whether certain rules for contingent payment debt instruments will apply.

This chapter discusses the US federal income tax characterisations of total return swaps, default swaps and credit-linked notes and the consequences of participating in these transactions under the likely (and certain alternative)

characterisations. Special concerns for non-US participants are discussed throughout as well. In particular, Panel 4 provides a summary of the US federal income and withholding tax rules applicable to non-US participants in credit derivative transactions.[1]

Total return swaps

A total return swap is a bilateral financial contract between the "total return receiver" and the "total return payer". The "total return receiver" pays a periodic amount that is determined by applying a floating-rate interest index to a notional principal balance. In return, the total return payer pays an amount equal to the total return of a reference debt security of the same notional principal balance, which return includes all of the interest, fees and other cashflows paid on a reference debt security of the same notional principal balance, plus any increase (or less any

---

1 *Caution should be exercised in reviewing conclusions reached herein with any particular transaction in mind; the consequences for any particular person of participating in a transaction will depend not only on the terms of the particular transaction, but also on that person's circumstances. Certain classes of investors may be subject to special rules. For ease of presentation, unless otherwise indicated, the discussion herein applies to accrual method, US domestic C corporations that are not banks, thrifts, regulated investment companies, insurance companies, real estate investment trusts or dealers in securities or commodities and that do not hold their positions as part of a straddle, hedge, integrated or conversion transaction or other than as a capital asset.*

The discussion herein is correct at July 15, 1998 and, like all tax matters, is subject to change. Except where otherwise indicated or where the context otherwise requires, references herein to sections are references to the Internal Revenue Code of 1986 (the "Code") or the Treasury regulations thereunder.

US FEDERAL
INCOME TAX
CONSEQUENCES
OF CREDIT
DERIVATIVES
TRANSACTIONS

decline) in the value of the reference security (the "change-in-value payment"). The change-in-value payment is usually paid only at maturity, but is sometimes made periodically. Thus, the total return receiver's economic (cashflow) position is similar (ignoring counterparty default risk) to a 100% leveraged purchase of the reference debt security.

All payments made pursuant to the swap are made in cash and may be netted. The swap is documented on standard ISDA (International Swaps and Derivatives Association) documents. The total return payer is not required to own the reference security. For ease of discussion it is assumed that the reference security is a fully taxable, dollar-denominated, actively traded bond issued by a US domestic corporation. The consequences of using a commercial loan made by a US domestic bank as a reference security are also discussed where the tax treatment would materially differ. It is also assumed that (i) the total return swap is not "off-market" when entered into and, thus, no upfront payment is made for entering into the swap; and (ii) the term of the swap is significantly less than the remaining term to maturity of the reference security.[2] Total return swaps are used in a variety of transactions to achieve a variety of goals. They are often used, for example, effectively to sell a debt instrument where an actual sale would be prohibited – eg where the buyer would not be a permitted assignee under the terms of the debt instrument. Where the sale of the reference security is not actually prohibited, a total return swap, nonetheless, may be preferable to a sale where the seller does not wish the borrower to know that it has disposed of the reference security.

In addition, a total return swap is sometimes used to achieve off-balance-sheet financing of a reference security. In such a case, the would-be borrower (the total return receiver) sells the reference security to a purchaser and at the same time enters into a total return swap with the purchaser (the total return payer) under which the would-be borrower receives the total return on that security. The two transactions taken together are economically equivalent to the seller retaining ownership of the reference security and borrowing from the purchaser what would be the proceeds of the sale of the security.

CHARACTERISATION AS A NOTIONAL PRINCIPAL CONTRACT

The swap regulations (Treasury Regulations §1.446-3) define a notional principal contract as:

> a financial instrument that provides for the payment of amounts by one party to another at specified intervals calculated by reference to a specified index upon a notional principal amount in exchange for specified consideration or a promise to pay similar amounts.

For this purpose, a specified index includes an index based on "objective financial information", which itself is defined in section 1.446-3(c)(4)(ii) as:

> any current, objectively determinable financial or economic information that is not within the control of any of the parties to the contract and is not unique to one of the parties' circumstances (such as one party's dividends, profits, or the value of its stock).

Section 1.446-3(c)(1)(i) lists examples of notional principal contracts, including interest rate swaps, interest rate caps and floors, currency swaps, basis swaps, commodity swaps, equity swaps and equity index swaps. The regulation specifically excludes collars, which are sometimes treated as two separate contracts, a floor and a cap. The swap regulations also exclude contracts that would be treated as indebtedness under general tax principles, futures, forward contracts and options.[3]

The definition of "notional principal contract" is extremely broad and a total return swap fits squarely within it. Payments by the total return receiver are made periodically with reference to a notional amount, are based on objective financial information not in the control of the relevant parties and are made in exchange for a promise to pay similar amounts by the total return payer.

---

2 *A total return swap with change-in-value payments made solely at maturity and a term equal to the remaining term to maturity of the reference security would be substantially similar to a default swap, discussed below.*

3 *Further, without regard to the swap regulations, under general tax principles, a financial contract may be characterised for tax purposes consistent with the economic substance of the transaction, notwithstanding the form of the transaction or the label attached to it by the parties. See, for example, Helvering v F & L Lazarus & Co, 308 US 252 (1939). In extremely general terms, a transaction may be characterised as indebtedness if one party makes a payment to the other in return for the other party's promise to (a) return that original amount on demand or by a specified date in the future and (b) make additional payments (periodically or upon repayment) that are effectively for the use of that money and reflect the time value thereof.*

171

US FEDERAL
INCOME TAX
CONSEQUENCES
OF CREDIT
DERIVATIVES
TRANSACTIONS

PANEL 1

SWAP TAX ACCOUNTING

In very general terms, there are three types of payments that may arise on a notional principal contract – "periodic payments", which are treated as ordinary income (or deductions) when accrued, "non-periodic payments", which are taken into account in a manner that reflects the economic substance of the swap, and termination payments, which are generally treated as payments made in connection with the disposition of the swap.

Periodic payments are defined as payments that are: (i) payable at intervals of one year or less during the entire term of the swap, (ii) based on a specified index, and (iii) based on a single notional principal amount (or a variable notional amount that varies in the same proportion as the notional principal amount that measures the other party's payments). Non-periodic payments are defined as payments that are neither periodic payments nor termination payments. Termination payments are defined as payments made or received to extinguish or assign all or a portion of the rights under a notional principal contract.

Where periodic and/or non-periodic payments are made in both directions on a notional principal contract, the payments are netted and only the net amount is included in, or deducted from, gross income.

Further, although total return swaps, as defined above, are not listed among the contracts specifically described as notional principal contracts in section 1.446-3(c), equity swaps are included. An equity swap is, essentially, a total return swap where the reference security is a share of stock.[4] Although there are differences between these two types of reference securities (debt instruments provide for creditor rights and a fixed maturity date), these differences should not result in different characterisations. Moreover, in Notice 98-5, Example 3, by providing an example of a transaction to which certain new foreign tax credit rules will apply, the Internal Revenue Service (the "Service" or the "IRS") assumed (albeit without analysis) that a total return swap is a notional principal contract.

Nevertheless, as indicated above, the swap regulations specifically exclude options, futures, forward contracts and debt instruments ("excluded instruments") from the definition of notional principal contract. Thus, classification of an instrument as an excluded instrument will pre-empt classification as a notional principal contract. Accordingly, it is necessary to determine that a contract in the form of a notional principal contract will not be characterised under general tax principles as an excluded instrument or as some other type of financial contract (or a combination of several other instruments) not consistent with its characterisation as a notional principal contract.[5] Where the reference security is an actively traded debt instrument and the total return payer does not own the reference security, a total return swap does not sufficiently resemble any other financial contract (or combination of contracts) to cause such a swap to be recharacterised as other than a notional principal contract. (The potential recharacterisation of a total return swap, where the total return payer holds – or is required to hold – the reference security on behalf of the total return receiver, or where the reference security is not actively traded, is discussed below.)

TAXATION OF NOTIONAL PRINCIPAL CONTRACTS

Assuming that a total return swap is a notional principal contract, the periodic payments (other than any periodic change-in-value payments) for each tax year are treated as ordinary income when accrued. In general, all taxpayers, regardless of their method of accounting, must recognise the rateable daily portion of a periodic payment for the taxable year to which that portion relates. Where payments are made in both directions on a

---

4 *Although equity swaps are specifically included in section 1.446-3(c)(1)(i)'s non-exclusive list of notional principal contracts, they are not described therein. They are described, however, under the proposed section 1.1092(d)-2(d).*

5 *Although, under general tax principles, bifurcation of a financial instrument is the exception rather than the rule, the rules treating a collar as constituting two notional principal contracts and the rules treating certain off-market swaps as constituting an on-market swap and a loan seem to support the view that "bifurcation" or "deconstruction" may be appropriate in selected circumstances. For a typical total return swap, however, bifurcation seems unlikely, except perhaps into an interest rate swap and a cash-settled forward sale contract on the reference security. Such a recharacterisation may have few consequences, except to ensure that the final payment is capital gain or loss. See footnote 15, below.*

US FEDERAL
INCOME TAX
CONSEQUENCES
OF CREDIT
DERIVATIVES
TRANSACTIONS

notional principal contract, the payments are netted and only the net amount is included in, or deducted from, gross income.[6] Although not explicitly addressed by the swap regulations, it is generally believed that periodic swap payments are ordinary in character. The Service adopted this position in PLR 9824026 (June 12, 1998) and PLR 9730007 (April 10, 1997).

Where any change-in-value payment is made solely at the maturity of the total return swap, the timing of the related inclusion in, or deduction from, income is not entirely certain. The payment should be treated as a non-periodic payment which, under section 1.446-3(f), is taken into account "in a manner that reflects the economic substance of the [swap]".[7] While "economic substance" is subject to differing interpretations, the economic substance of a total return swap should require that the payment at maturity be taken into account in the year when it was made because any "built-in" gain or loss existing at any earlier time may be eliminated by further changes in value of the reference security prior to the maturity of the swap.[8] Further, the change-in-value payment on a total return swap resembles the settlement of a cash-settled forward contract, which, under general tax principles, is treated as an exchange on the settlement date, which, in the case of a swap, is its maturity date. Of course, in the light of the inherent ambiguity in the nature of the "economic substance" of a transaction, it is impossible to rule out the possibility of the IRS asserting that the final payment must be included in some other manner.[9] The Service might, for example, take the position that any payment at maturity that reflects the increase in value of the reference security attributable to the accretion of

---

6 *Sections 1.446-3(d) and (e).*

7 *Section 1.446-3(f)(2)(i).*

8 *Taxpayers routinely defer income in swaps, which often have a one-time final change-in-value payment. While some of these transactions have been thought of as abusive on other grounds, the current deductibility of periodic payments and the deferral of income with respect to truly contingent pay-outs has not been so viewed. For example, under HR 3170 (the "Kennelly Bill"), which was introduced recently in Congress, where non-periodic payments on an equity swap reflect the income arising from sales of reference equities made prior to the payment of the non-periodic payment, the recipient would be taxed in a manner that reflects (in terms of character and, indirectly, timing) the taxpayer's indirect economic ownership of the reference equities and its indirect interest in such sales. Importantly, however, the Kennelly Bill would not defer deductions for periodic payments accrued, nor accelerate (nor change the character of) non-periodic payments accrued that reflect the income the holder would have earned had it held the reference equities directly. Nevertheless, the statement in the text assumes that the amount of the payment is determined at the time payment is required to be made. Where the amount of the payment is calculable prior to maturity, the payment may be attributable to an earlier period – cf sections 1.1275-4(b)(9)(ii) and 1.1275-4(c)(4)(iii) (in very general terms, where a contingent payment is fixed more than six months prior to payment, the present value of the payment is accrued immediately upon becoming fixed).*

9 *Section 1.446-3(e)(2)(ii) provides a quasi-mark-to-market rule specifically for periodic payments where a payment interval straddles two tax years. The apparent intentional omission of a similar rule with respect to non-periodic payments should (in the absence of an amendment to the regulations) prevent the application of such a rule without some compelling economic argument. Any such argument could hardly be compelling in light of the fact that under general tax principles no amount of income or deduction accrues with respect to a contingent liability, until that con-*

tingency is resolved. Section 1.1275-4, which provides rules for contingent payment debt instruments ("CPDIs"), would probably fail (without an amendment to the swap regulations) as a basis for an argument that the economic substance of the transaction compels the earlier inclusion of the non-periodic payment. First, those regulations effectively separate out of a CPDI a forward contract or option and thus create a hypothetical non-contingent bond, the income on which may be accelerated. This makes sense where the instrument being taxed is a debt instrument itself; here, however, there is no debt instrument. Further, under section 1.1275-4, income accrues at a rate based on a hypothetical borrowing rate for the borrower on a non-contingent bond and not based on any party's actual expectations for contingent payments. That would hardly suggest that accruing income based on the value of, or expected payment on, a contingent payment is appropriate. More importantly, although section 1.1275-4 modifies general tax principles for certain CPDIs, it does not by its terms (or in the preambles to the various versions) purport to reflect economic substance. It just provides a particular method for accruing income on certain CPDIs. Finally, the fact that the IRS took 10 years and went through three different approaches before finalising section 1.1275-4 hardly suggests that the method contained therein for accruing income on CPDIs is the compelling method for transactions not even contemplated by the regulations.

Under section 475(a), notional principal contracts held by a dealer in securities (or other financial contracts) that are not identified as held for investment are required to be marked-to-market at the end of each year and gain or loss on the mark is generally ordinary. Where an investor holds a reference security and a total return swap as part of a hedging transaction within the meaning of section 1.1221-2(b) (but not as part of an integrated transaction to which section 1.1275-6 applies), the rules of section 1.446-4(e)(6) would apply (provided section 475(a) does not apply). Under those rules, if the reference security is disposed of while the swap is retained, then the built-in gain or loss on the total return swap may be required to be marked-to-market on the date the holder disposes of the reference security.

173

US FEDERAL
INCOME TAX
CONSEQUENCES
OF CREDIT
DERIVATIVES
TRANSACTIONS

original issue discount on that security is required to be spread out over the life of the swap. A similar rule may apply to market discount and premium. In the absence of any amendment to the swap regulations, it is unlikely that any general requirement by the Service to mark-to-market the built-in gain or loss on the swap would be sustained.

The character (as capital or ordinary) of any change-in-value payment, whether periodic or at maturity, is not indicated in the swap regulations and the commentators have a range of views.[10] The uncertainty arises from the fact that capital gain or loss treatment requires a "sale or exchange" of the total return swap (assuming it is held as a capital asset) or, in the absence of a sale or exchange, a statutory provision specifically providing for capital treatment. Under general tax principles, specifically the so-called "extinguishment doctrine", payments made pursuant to the terms of, or to terminate, a contract are not treated as arising from a sale or exchange.[11] While a party's rights in a swap may be a capital asset, payments pursuant to the swap do not arise from a sale or exchange. Thus, unless one can conclude that a statutory constructive sale or exchange treatment applies, change-in-value payments will be treated as ordinary income or expense.

Section 1234A characterises the "cancellation, lapse, expiration or other termination" of a right or obligation with respect to property as constructive sales. As change-in-value payments are made at the scheduled termination of the swap (or periodically over its life) and not in connection with an early extinguishment of the swap, they should be either periodic or non-periodic payments and not "termination" payments under the swap regulations.[12] Although not certain, it appears that the Service has historically assumed that a payment that is not a termination payment under the swap regulations is not a cancellation or termination (or other similar) payment under section 1234A. Compare section 1.446-3(h), which uses the phrase "gain or loss" with respect to the income from termination payments, with section 1.446-3(d), which uses the phrase "net income or net deduction" with respect to the income from periodic and non-periodic payments. In addition, the preamble to the swap regulations states: "Nothing in the regulations supports characterizing either periodic or nonperiodic payments as attributable to the settlement, exercise, cancellation, lapse, expiration, or other termination of forward or option contracts."[13] If the change-in-value payment is not a

termination payment, section 1234A would not provide constructive sale or exchange treatment and, lacking a sale or exchange, the change-in-value payment would be ordinary in character. It is possible, however, that section 1234A operates independently of the swap regulations and that the change-in-value payment, because it is made at the time when the swap terminates (in common parlance) or, in the case of a periodic change-in-value payment, partially terminates, is a "termination" or "expiration" payment under section 1234A.[14]

In PLR 9730007 (April 10, 1997), the Service ruled that all periodic change-in-value payments (including final periodic payments) are ordinary in character. In PLR 9824026 (March 12, 1998), the Service confirmed this and extended its rationale to up-front non-periodic payments as well. Accordingly, it seems that the Services's position is that all change-in-value payments are ordinary.

---

10 *See New York State Bar Association (Tax Section), "Report on Notional Principal Contract Character and Timing Issues". See also Kevin Dolan and Carolyn Dupuy (1995), "Equity Derivatives: Principles and Practices", 15* Va Tax Review *161, 194; Edward D Kleinbard (1995), "The US Taxation of Equity Derivative Instruments",* The Handbook of Equity Derivatives *(Irwin Professional Publishing) pp. 569–74; Daniel P Breen and John N Bush, 1993, "A Practical Guide to Tax Issues Associated with New Equity Derivative Investments by Individuals",* USC Law Center Tax Institute *pp. 8-19 to 8-24; NY State Bar Association (1992),* Report on Proposed Regulations on Methods of Accounting for Notional Principal Contracts *(March 2).*

11 *Under the "extinguishment doctrine" there is no sale or exchange where the property is not transferred to another person, but rather is extinguished by the event itself. See, for example, Fairbanks v United States, 306 US 436 (1939) (under prior law, gain on the redemption of a corporate bond is ordinary income). This doctrine also extends to payments made (not pursuant to the terms of a contract) to terminate a contract. See Leh v Commissioner, 260 F.2d 489 (9th Cir. 1958).*

12 *See Panel 1 for a discussion of periodic, non-periodic and termination payments.*

13 *T.D. 8491, 58 F.R. 53125. See also PLR. 9730007 (April 10, 1997) and PLR 9824026 (March 12, 1998) (neither periodic nor non-periodic payments are treated as termination payments on notional principal contracts).*

14 *The interplay between sections 1234A and 582(c) is unclear. See footnote 38, below and accompanying text. Thus, the gain or loss on a termination payment might be capital under section 1234A even though the gain or loss from a sale of the reference security would be ordinary under section 582(c). (Banks and certain other financial institutions have ordinary income from the sale of debt instruments, even if held as capital assets).*

US FEDERAL

INCOME TAX

CONSEQUENCES

OF CREDIT

DERIVATIVES

TRANSACTIONS

PANEL 2

TREATMENT OF FEES

Where the reference security of a total return swap is a bank loan, the treatment of any payment that is in respect of a one-time borrower-paid fee is uncertain. (Fees that are paid as a number of basis points per annum should be included in, or deducted from, ordinary income when accrued.) A one-time payment might be viewed as a periodic payment, as a component of the total return index, and thus similarly be includable in, or deductible from, ordinary income when accrued. Alternatively, such a payment may be viewed as a non-periodic payment that must be included "in a manner that reflects the economic substance of the contract". If treated as a non-periodic payment, the timing of the related income inclusion or deduction may depend on whether the payment is viewed substantively as a fee for services or as a payment in respect of an offset to the issue price of the reference security. If viewed as a fee for services it may arguably be includable immediately in income in the hands of the total return receiver but amortisable on a straight-line basis in the hands of the total return payer. If viewed as a payment in respect of an offset to the issue price of the reference security it may be includable by the total return receiver and deductible by the total return payer, in each case over the life of the swap under a constant yield method (but where *de minimis* in amount the inclusion arguably may be deferred until the termination of the swap).

The maturity of certain total return swaps may be accelerated in the event of a default on the reference security. If the right to accelerate the swap is exercised the acceleration may be treated as the extinguishment of the swap and, consequently, the payment may be viewed as a termination payment.[15]

Where the total return payer owns the reference security and the total return swap requires the sale of that particular security on its termination, basing the swap payments on the proceeds of that sale, then (assuming that the total return swap is not initially recharacterised as a sale of the reference security, as discussed below) arguably the change-in-value payment should be treated as an adjustment to the proceeds of the sale. In that case, no separate gain or loss (which, if it were present, could cause character mismatch) would be recognised in respect of the swap. Instead, the change-in-value payment will eliminate the loss or gain on the sale of the reference security.[16]

If the payment made or received at the maturity of the total return swap is ordinary in character, it may be offset *economically* with capital gain or loss on the seller's long position in the reference security; ordinary income, however, may not be offset *effectively* for tax purposes by capital loss.[17]

Payments received on a notional principal contract are sourced at the residence of the recipient. Thus, payments made to a total return payer or receiver that is not a US person (and not engaged in a US trade or business) would be foreign source income and, thus, may be paid free of US federal withholding tax. (See Panel 4 for an overview of the US federal income and withholding tax rules that apply to non-US persons.)

IS THE REFERENCE SECURITY TRANSFERRED?
It is a basic tenet of tax law that the party who has the benefits and burdens associated with the ownership of property will be treated as the owner of that property for tax purposes. Moreover, it is frequently said that the substance, not the form, of the arrangement is controlling for tax purposes.[18] Where a total return payer

15 *Similarly, the fact that the final payment on a default swap (described below) is made upon the occurrence of a credit event, rather than at final maturity, increases the likelihood that the payment will be treated as a termination payment. Another possible ground for capital gain or loss treatment is treating a total return swap as two contracts, an interest rate swap, the payments on which generally would be ordinary income or deduction, and a cash settlement forward contract, payments on which generally would be capital gain or loss. See Estate of Israel v Comm'r, 108 TC No 13 (April 1, 1997). But see PLR 9730007 (April 10, 1997) (although a notional principal contract is economically similar to a series of cash-settled forward contracts, it is, nevertheless, a single indivisible financial instrument). See also PLR 9824026 (same).*

16 *Where the term of the total return swap equals the remaining life of the reference security, consideration should be given to whether the two positions may be integrated and treated as a synthetic debt instrument under section 1.1275-6.*

17 *The two positions in the reference security will likely be a straddle. See Panel 3.*

18 *See, for example, Helvering v F & R Lazarus & Co, 308 US 252 (1939).*

175

US FEDERAL
INCOME TAX
CONSEQUENCES
OF CREDIT
DERIVATIVES
TRANSACTIONS

PANEL 3

STRADDLES

Two offsetting positions in actively traded property will generally constitute a "straddle" under section 1092. Thus, if a total return payer offsets its long position in a reference security with a total return swap, its two positions will constitute a straddle. (A less likely possibility is that if a protection buyer offsets its long position in a reference security with a default swap, its two positions will constitute a straddle.) Generally, any loss on the disposition of one leg of a straddle is deferred except to the extent that the loss exceeds the unrecognised gain in the offsetting leg. However, this rule applies only to losses allowable under section 165 ("Losses", which include capital losses) and therefore should not apply to deductions for periodic and possibly even non-periodic payments made under the swap because they are allowed under section 162 ("Trade or Business Expenses"), rather than under section 165 (assuming they are treated as ordinary deductions and not capital losses under section 1234A). "Interest and carrying charges" allocable to a leg of a straddle are subject to capitalisation (instead of current deduction) under section 263(g). These amounts presumably would include interest on debt incurred to acquire the reference security but should not include the periodic and non-periodic payments made under the terms of the swap itself.

In very general terms, a taxpayer's holding period for positions in a straddle is tolled. Thus, any payments under the straddle that are treated as capital gain or loss, and, if the taxpayer disposes of either of the two positions constituting the straddle, any gain or loss on disposition, will generally be short-term gain or loss.

A total return swap and a reference security should not constitute a straddle if the reference security is not of a type that is actively traded within the meaning of section 1092 and the regulations thereunder. Under those regulations, however, "actively traded" is defined quite broadly and includes many securities that are not actively traded in common parlance.

---

owns the reference security, a total return swap has the effect of shifting at least some of the benefits and burdens of ownership of the reference security to the total return receiver. Thus, the issue arises of whether the swap effects a transfer of ownership.[19] (The total return payer's long position in a reference security and its position in the same security under a total return swap generally will constitute a "straddle". See Panel 3 for a discussion of straddles.)

The two factors generally believed to be central to the determination of tax ownership of property are: (i) the opportunity for profit and the risk of loss from the property and (ii) the control over disposition of the property.[20] Thus, it is fairly clear that, with respect to an actively traded security, the total return payer will not be considered to have disposed of its ownership of the reference security unless, ironically, it is legally or practically required to continue to hold the reference security on behalf of the total return receiver.

This conclusion is supported by Notice 98-5, Example 3, which (in describing a transaction deemed abusive on other grounds) treats a total return swap written by the holder of the reference security as a notional principal contract and not a sale of the reference security. Further,

implicit in certain proposed regulations concerning straddles is the conclusion that the ownership of "actively traded" stock and the selling of a related equity swap (a total return swap on the equity) is not a transfer of the reference security.[21] Finally, section 1259, which treats the holder of certain appreciated positions in certain securities as having constructively sold the position (so as to recognise gain, but not loss) if the holder has entered into certain other positions that substantially eliminate both the risk of loss and opportunity for gain, makes it clear that the offsetting of a long position in a reference security with a short position in the same security through an equity swap is not generally treated as

---

19 *If the term of the swap is shorter than the maturity of the reference security, the recharacterisation would be as a transfer of tax ownership of the reference security coupled with a forward contract to sell the security back to the original seller (the total return payer) on the maturity of the swap at the then market price.*

20 *For an explanation of this point with full citations, see Nirenberg and Kopp (1997), "Credit Derivatives: Tax Treatment of Total Return Swaps, Default Swaps, and Credit Linked notes", 87 Journal of Taxation, No. 2 (August).*

21 *Proposed Treasury Regulation Section 1.1092(d)-2(d), Example.*

US FEDERAL

INCOME TAX

CONSEQUENCES

OF CREDIT

DERIVATIVES

TRANSACTIONS

a sale of the reference security. (Section 1259 does not affect the treatment of the counterparty and thus would not cause the counterparty – here, the total return receiver – to be treated as constructively acquiring the appreciated position.)[22]

Although the historical precedents for ignoring the transfer of the economic benefits of owning securities have generally involved publicly traded securities,[23] one should feel relatively comfortable extending these precedents to (a) actively traded bank loans (even though, other than for certain tax purposes, they are generally not thought of as securities) and (b) non-publicly traded securities, such as securities transferred in the so-called Rule 144A market, provided the market for such securities has some liquidity.

Although the matter is less certain, the answer should be the same where the market for the reference security is not liquid, as is true for many bank loans (again, provided the total return payer is not required, actually or effectively, to hold the reference security). As indicated above, the ability of the total return payer to dispose of the reference security is a significant indicator of ownership and it is not necessary for the title owner of an asset to have more than a significant ownership interest in the asset.[24] Thus, as long as the total return payer has a true ability to dispose of the reference security there should be no transfer of tax ownership.

22 *TD 8491, 58 FR 53125. See also PLR 8818010 (where a taxpayer has established currency swaps, "the establishment of the reverse swap positions will not be a realisation event because [the] taxpayer has not extinguished its positions under the currency swap agreements").*

23 *Although the securities were not described as being publicly traded and the conclusions were not conditioned on that status, it was apparent from the factual contexts that the securities were in fact publicly traded.*

24 *The total return payer's right to vote the asset is a further indicator of the total return payer's ownership of the reference security. The relative weight to give this factor has not received much attention in the authorities dealing with traded securities and is thus uncertain. The factor may be of greater weight in the case of a bank loan than, for example, for a publicly traded bond, because the opportunities to vote for such things as covenant waivers arise more frequently with bank loans.*

25 *On the other hand, the treatment of the transaction as a sale of the reference security is not a foregone conclusion. The total return payer retains title to, and thus voting rights with respect to, the reference security and the total return receiver still bears the credit risk of the total return payer, two features that distinguish total return swaps from sales of reference securities.*

Where there is no market for the reference security, or the total return payer is effectively required to hold the reference security on behalf of the total return receiver, there is a substantial risk that the total return swap will be treated as a transfer of tax ownership because the total return payer will have neither the right to appreciation and the risk of loss nor the practical ability to transfer the reference security. Thus, the total return payer may not have retained sufficient indicia of ownership to retain ownership for tax purposes and thus may be viewed as a mere nominee holder on behalf of the total return receiver.[25]

The total return payer may be effectively required to hold the reference security, for example, (a) where the total return payer is a trust and the governing documents of the trust prohibit the disposition of the reference security; (b) where the total return payer pledges the reference security as collateral for its obligations under the total return swap; (c) where the reference security is unique and it would either be practically impossible to determine its fair market value at the maturity of the swap unless the total return payer owned it (so as to be able to solicit actual bids) or the total return receiver could demand physical settlement; or (d) where the total return payer agrees to exercise the voting rights of the reference security according to the total return receiver's instructions.

Further, where the total return payer acquired the reference security from the total return receiver, the transaction may be recharacterised as a loan. There, the total return payer may never have had the economic ownership of the reference security, as the sale and the total return swap would have essentially no effect on the total return payer's position.

CONSEQUENCES OF RECHARACTERISATION
If a total return swap is recharacterised as a transfer of tax ownership of the reference security, the consequences for the total return receiver and the total return payer will differ.

Total return receiver's perspective
If a total return swap is recharacterised as a transfer of the tax ownership of the reference security, the total return receiver should be treated as owning the security and having borrowed the purchase price from the total return payer. Under this analysis, interest and original issue discount on the reference security would be included in the total return receiver's income

US FEDERAL
INCOME TAX
CONSEQUENCES
OF CREDIT
DERIVATIVES
TRANSACTIONS

(rather than the total return payer's) as it accrues. The gross amount of periodic payments owed by the total return receiver would be treated as interest payments that would generally be deductible as accrued (subject to any limitations on deductibility provided in the Code).[26] On the maturity of the swap, the total return receiver would be treated as reselling the reference security to the total return payer and would have capital gain or loss, except to the extent of the accrued market discount (which would be ordinary). For a bank, all of the gain or loss would be ordinary income under section 582(c).

The recharacterisation of notional principal contract expense as interest expense may have other secondary, but significant, consequences. For example, income on the reference security would be debt-financed income in the hands of a pension plan or other tax-exempt investor that is subject to tax on unrelated business taxable income. Further, interest expense is subject to allocation under section 861 and the regulations thereunder (and thus may affect, *inter alia*, a holder's foreign tax credit) but the expense from a total return swap, although not certain, may not be subject to such allocation.

If the total return receiver is not a US person, payments made on the swap that are treated as interest on the reference security may be subject to a 30% withholding tax under sections 871(a)(1) and 1441 or sections 881(a)(1) and 1442 unless that interest is treated as "portfolio interest" under sections 871(h) or 881(c). With a limited exception for interest on debt originally sold to non-US persons, portfolio interest does not include interest on loans made in bearer form, which would include many bank loans. Further, if the total return receiver is a foreign bank and the reference security is a bank loan, consideration should be given to section 881(c)(3)(A) (and the legislative history thereof), which provides that interest received by a foreign bank under a loan agreement made in the ordinary course of its trade or business is not portfolio interest. In addition, in determining whether a foreign person is engaged in a US trade or business, the activities of the total return payer may be attributable to the total return receiver.

Total return payer's perspective

If a total return swap is recharacterised as a transfer of tax ownership of the reference security, the total return payer would be considered to have sold the reference security and agreed to repurchase it at a market price. Any built-in gain attributable to the reference security would be recognised, but any loss would presumably be deferred under the wash sale rules.[27] Periodic payments (other than change-in-value payments) made to the total return payer would be interest income and, subject to the application of the wash sale rules, the total return payer would be considered to have acquired the reference security anew on the maturity of the swap at a price equal to the value of the reference security used in computing the final payment under the swap.[28] (Where periodic change-in-value payments are made, the total return payer presumably would be treated as having reacquired and immediately resold the reference security.) Where the total return payer is a non-US person, payments to it treated as interest may be subject to a 30% withholding tax unless the interest qualifies as portfolio interest, which generally requires: (a) a determination that the swap is in registered form

---

26 *A discussion of the various limitations on the deductibility of interest expense is beyond the scope of this chapter but would include, for example, section 1277 (a portion of the interest expense on an obligation incurred to purchase market discount bonds is deferred until recognition of the related market discount). Further, with respect to a bank, section 265(b) disallows a portion of all interest expense, including interest on debt not directly used to purchase tax-exempt obligations, to the extent such interest expense is allocated (under a formula) to tax-exempt interest.*

27 *Section 1091(a). The wash sale rules apply to contracts entered into within 30 days of the sale of a security to acquire securities substantially identical to the securities sold. There does not appear to be any exception for contracts to acquire, for forward delivery, the identical securities at market prices. The wash sale rules only apply to sales of stocks or "securities", which is not defined in section 1091 or the regulations thereunder. The Service has taken the position that all evidences of indebtedness are "securities" for purposes of section 1091 (see GCM 39551 (August 26, 1986)), but there is little direct authority for that position. In any event, it seems highly likely that any intermediate or long-term debt instrument issued in the capital markets will be treated as a security for purposes of section 1091. The issue is less clear for other debt instruments.*

28 *Under section 1091(d), the basis of the newly-acquired reference security would be the basis of the reference security immediately before the swap, increased or decreased, as the case may be, by the difference, if any, between the price at which the new reference security is deemed acquired and the price at which the "old" reference security was deemed to have been disposed. Under section 1223(4) and section 1.1223-1(d), the holding period of the reference securities for the period prior to the swap is tacked onto the holding period of the reference securities deemed to have been acquired at the maturity of the swap.*

US FEDERAL

INCOME TAX

CONSEQUENCES

OF CREDIT

DERIVATIVES

TRANSACTIONS

and (b) the total return payer to provide an Internal Revenue Service Form W-8 to the total return receiver.

Default swaps

A default swap (which some market participants refer to as a "credit swap") is a bilateral financial contract in which the "protection buyer" pays a periodic amount that is a fixed number of basis points applied to a notional principal amount, and the "protection seller" pays the decline in value below par of a reference security of the same notional amount if, depending on the terms of the particular swap, (a) there is a default on the reference security or (b) a "reference obligor" (typically, the issuer or guarantor of the reference security) is subject to a "credit event" during the term of the swap.

Although the definition of "credit event" varies from swap to swap, it typically includes the bankruptcy or insolvency of a reference obligor or the reference obligor's failure to make payments on any of its obligations when due. In order to ensure that only material credit events trigger payment under a default swap, the occurrence of a credit event often also requires a significant price deterioration of the reference security. The amount by which the reference security is considered to decline, and thus the amount the protection seller is required to pay, is usually based on the average trading price for the post-default security determined by a poll of several dealers.

In certain situations, a default swap may provide for physical settlement – that is, the protection seller may require the protection buyer to deliver the reference securities to the protection seller in exchange for their par amount. In other situations (swaps with "binary settlement"), in lieu of the payment being made based on the actual decline in value of the reference security, the final payment is based on a predetermined assumed recovery rate, generally a percentage of

---

29 *The taxation of notional principal contracts is summarised in Panel 1 (Swap Tax Accounting) and in the discussion of total return swaps above. Where the default swap is held as a hedge of the reference security, consideration should be given to whether section 1.446-4 (hedging transactions) applies. Under that regulation, periodic payments may be deductible against ordinary income when made, even if the default swap is characterised as other than a notional principal contract.*

30 *Section 1.446-3(c)(2)(i).*

31 *See Panel 1 (Swap Tax Accounting) and footnote 10 and accompanying text, above.*

the notional principal amount. Default swaps are typically documented on standard ISDA documents and the protection buyer is generally not required to own the reference security.

Except where otherwise indicated, the following discussion assumes that the reference security is a fully taxable, dollar-denominated, actively traded bond of a domestic C corporation. Where the tax treatment would materially differ, the consequences of using a commercial loan made by a domestic bank are also discussed. For the purposes of this discussion it is also assumed that the default swap is not "off-market" when entered into and, thus, no up-front payment is made for entering into the swap.

Default swaps are used for a variety of purposes. Protection sellers that are banks, for example, use default swaps as substitutes for letters of credit or committed standby liquidity or credit facilities. Sometimes, a market participant with an investment portfolio that is heavily concentrated will rebalance it by purchasing protection on loans (or securities) that it owns and selling protection on loans (or securities) to which it is under-exposed. Selling protection is also used as a substitute for an investment in the debt of the reference obligor. If the periodic payments equal the spread over the risk-free rate for the reference obligor's actual debt obligations, a default swap permits a protection seller effectively to earn that spread without the need to actually develop a lending relationship with the reference obligor or to fund an actual loan to it.

CHARACTERISATION OF DEFAULT SWAPS
Although the tax characterisation of default swaps is not settled, the better view is that most should be characterised as notional principal contracts. A default swap neatly fits the definition of notional principal contract in that it is a financial instrument in which payments by one party, the protection buyer, are paid at specified intervals based on a specified index applied to a notional amount.[29] (A specified index includes a fixed rate.)[30] Thus, periodic payments under a default swap should be includable in, or deductible from, ordinary income when accrued. As is the case with the final payment on a total return swap, the character of the payment made upon a credit event is uncertain. It depends, in large measure, on whether the payment is treated as a non-periodic payment (in which case it is likely to be ordinary income or loss) or a termination payment (in which case its character is uncertain).[31] Although the final payment on a

179

US FEDERAL
INCOME TAX
CONSEQUENCES
OF CREDIT
DERIVATIVES
TRANSACTIONS

default swap appears to be a termination payment – the default swap expires upon that final payment – the payment is made pursuant to the contract and not to terminate it (other than in accordance with its terms). Thus, as with total return swaps, the nature of the final payment, and thus the character of the gain or loss, is uncertain.

Although most default swaps should be characterised as notional principal contracts, there is some risk that any particular default swap may be recharacterised as some other type of financial instrument. As discussed above, a financial instrument that meets the definition of notional principal contract nonetheless may be recharacterised as some other sort of financial contract if it would be characterised under general tax principles as, or would economically represent, an excluded instrument or some other specific type of financial instrument. Default swaps in some respects are similar to put options and credit guarantees and there is a risk that they may be recharacterised as such.[32] The degree of that risk depends, in part, on the default swap's specific terms, including: (a) physical or cash settlement; (b) whether it is triggered solely by a default on the reference obligation or any credit event of a reference obligor; or (c) binary or fair market value based settlement.

IS A DEFAULT SWAP A PUT OPTION?
A default swap, particularly one that is required to be settled physically, economically resembles a put option held by the protection buyer, which is exercisable only in the case of a credit event.[33] Thus, if an option that is subject to a condition precedent is treated as an option for tax purposes, a default swap could be recharacterised as an option.

There is authority for the proposition that, to be an option, a contract must provide the holder with an unconditional power of exercise and thus an option that is subject to a condition precedent is not an option for tax purposes.[34] In light of this authority, the risk that a cash-settled default swap would be recharacterised as an option is somewhat limited. Nonetheless, the risk of recharacterisation is not trivial. The authorities on contingent options generally analysed options that lasted for a specified period of time but the exercise of which is subject to conditions precedent (in some cases in the control of the option writer). In a default swap, the condition precedent, the credit event, is of a substantially different nature from the conditions

precedent dealt with by the various authorities. It is not a condition whose occurrence starts the option period (as in the relevant authorities); it is the element of the option that causes the option to be exercised. Thus, the authorities discussing contingent options are in some measure distinguishable. In light of the novelty of default swaps and the swap regulations' specific exclusion of options from the definition of notional principal contract, one cannot rule out the possibility that the Service would seek to characterise default swaps as options. As noted at footnote 33, the risk is greater in the case of a default swap that provides for physical settlement and less for a swap that provides for a binary cash settlement.

CONSEQUENCES OF RECHARACTERISATION
If a default swap is treated as a put option for tax purposes, the protection buyer would be treated as a holder of the option and the protection seller would be treated as the writer of the option. Generally, premiums paid or received on an option (here, the periodic payments made by the protection buyer) are not immediately deducted from, or included in, income. Instead, the premium paid or received is capitalised and taken into account upon the sale, exercise or lapse of the option. This rule applies not only where the premium is paid at the inception of

---

32 *Further, it is impossible to rule out the possibility that the Service would take the position that a default swap is something else entirely, perhaps just a contract for which no specific rules apply. Besides the other uncertainties such a position would create, it would make uncertain the treatment of the income in the hands of investors, such as pension plans and foreigners, for whom the nature of the income determines its taxability.*

33 *The requirement of a physical settlement for a default swap makes it look more like an option and less like a notional principal contract because: (a) typical notional principal contracts are cash settled and (b) the payment by the protection seller of the par amount of the reference security appears to be the payment of the notional principal amount – thus making it not "notional". On the other hand, a requirement of cash settlement does not prevent a swap from being characterised as an option. See section 1234(c)(2) (treatment of cash settlement options). A binary settlement default swap does not resemble a conventional cash settled option since its settlement amount does not change with changes in the value of the reference security and, thus, is less likely to be recharacterised as an option.*

34 *See, for example, Old Harbor Native Corp v Comm'r, 104 TC 191 (1995); Saviano v Comm'r, 80 TC 955 (1983), aff'd, 765 F.2d 643 (7th Cir 1985). See also Saunders v United States, 450 F.2d 1047 (9th Cir 1971).*

180

**US FEDERAL
INCOME TAX
CONSEQUENCES
OF CREDIT
DERIVATIVES
TRANSACTIONS**

35 *See Koch v Comm'r, 67 TC 71 (1976), acq, 1980-2 CB 1;
Virginia Iron Coal & Coke v Comm'r, 37 BTA 195, aff'd, 99
F.2d 919 (4th Cir. 1938), cert denied, 307 US 630 (1939).*

*If the protection buyer acquires the reference security
on the same day as it enters into the default swap and the
swap is recharacterised as a put option, then depending on
the facts of the particular transaction, section 1233(c)
might apply. In that event, at the expiration of the default
swap, the option premium would be added to the protection buyer's basis in the reference security, rather than
being immediately recognised as a loss.*

36 *Section 1234(a); see also section 1233(b). The option is
treated as sold on the day it is cash settled or lapses. See section 1234(c) and the legislative history thereto and section
1234(a)(2); see also Revenue Ruling 88-31, 1988-1 CB 302.
It appears that the capital gain or loss will be long term if
the option had been held for the long-term holding period
(idem). In general, if the option holder also owns (or later
acquires) the reference security, any capital gain or loss on
the reference security will be short-term if the security had
not been held for more than one year before the acquisition
of the option or for more than one year after the disposition or lapse of the option. Section 1233(b).*

*The foregoing discussion (and that in footnote 37 and,
in each case, in the accompanying text) assumes that the
reference security would be "property", which for purposes
of sections 1233(b) and 1234(b) (but apparently not for
section 1234(a)) would require the reference security to be
a "security" for purposes of section 1233(e)(2)(A) and section 1234(b)(2)(B). There is little authority defining "security" for these purposes. Presumably, any intermediate or
long-term debt instrument issued in the capital markets
will be a security for this purpose. The same is probably
true for other debt instruments, such as bank loans, but the
matter is less clear.*

37 *Section 1234(b); section 1234A; see also Revenue Ruling
88-31, 1988 1 CB 302. Any capital gain or loss recognised
by the writer on any "closing transaction" (which would
not include any exercise or lapse of the option) will also
automatically be short-term under section 1234(b)(1).
Under section 1234A, capital treatment (but not automatic
short-term treatment) apparently would apply even if the
reference security were not a "security" (see footnote 36,
above).*

38 *Prior to its partial recodification in section 1271, former
section 1232(a)(2)(A) provided that "on the sale or
exchange of [certain] bonds or other evidences of . . .
indebtedness . . . held by the taxpayer for more than six
months, any gain realized shall . . . be considered gain
from the sale of a capital asset held for more than 6
months." Notwithstanding that language, the regulations
under section 1232 provided that gain would not be capital
gain if section 582(c) applied. See section 1.1232-
3(a)(1)(iii). Cf section 1.1234-1(a)(2) (where section 1231
would have applied to an actual sale of property subject to
an option, treatment of a loss as capital under section
1234(a) is trumped by section 1231, which treats certain
losses that would otherwise be capital losses as ordinary);
section 1.582-1(d) (notwithstanding section 1233, gain or
loss from the short sale of a debt instrument is not treated
as gain or loss from the sale of a capital asset).*

the option but also where the option premium is
paid periodically over the term of the option, as
is true for the default swap.[35] The gain or loss on
the sale, cash settlement or lapse of the option
will be capital for both the holder (here, the protection buyer)[36] and the writer (here, the protection seller).[37] Thus, from the protection buyer's
perspective, characterisation of a default swap as
an option has the effect of: (a) deferring the
deduction of the periodic payments made under
the swap and, if there is no credit event, convert-
ing that deduction into a capital loss; and (b) if
there is a credit event, making it clear that any
gain recognised in respect of any payment
received from the protection seller is capital
gain. From the protection seller's perspective,
the effect is (a) to defer the recognition of the
income from the periodic payments and convert
it to capital gain, but (b) if there is a credit event,
to make it clear that the payment made at the
maturity of the swap gives rise to a capital loss.

The interplay between sections 1234 (and
1234A) on the one hand and section 582(c) on
the other hand is not certain. Section 1234(a)
provides that gain or loss with respect to an
option will have the same character as the property to which the option relates. Section 1234A
provides that gain or loss with respect to personal property that is a capital asset in the hands
of the taxpayer will be treated as gain or loss
from the sale of a capital asset. Section 582(c)
provides that gain or loss on the sale of a debt
instrument by a bank is ordinary. It does not,
however, expressly provide that such a debt
instrument is not a capital asset in the hands of a
bank. Accordingly, where a bank holds debt
instruments as capital assets, gain or loss with
respect to an option on a debt instrument
arguably would be capital under sections 1234(a)
or 1234A. Nevertheless, based on the policy
behind section 582(c) (and on the resolution of
the interplay between section 582(c) and other
Code sections that generally require capital gain
or loss treatment), for a protection buyer or
seller that is a bank, ordinary gain or loss treatment should prevail.[38]

IS A DEFAULT SWAP A GUARANTEE?
Where the protection buyer owns the reference
security, a default swap resembles a guarantee –
in the event of a default on the reference security,
the protection seller effectively makes the protection buyer whole. Accordingly, there is some risk
that the Service could seek to characterise such a
swap, for tax purposes, as a guarantee. Such a

US FEDERAL
INCOME TAX
CONSEQUENCES
OF CREDIT
DERIVATIVES
TRANSACTIONS

characterisation generally should not be sustained. Default swaps are different from guarantees in at least one material way – the protection buyer is not required to own the reference security; thus, the protection buyer might be paid even though it suffered no loss. Default swaps that provide for binary settlement may be further distinguished from guarantees. Even where the protection buyer holds the reference security, the protection seller will pay an amount that is determined without reference to the protection buyer's loss. Further, although contracts that are considered to be guarantees come in a myriad of varieties, one can identify certain additional characteristics of default swaps that differ from the typical financial guarantee. First, payment on many default swaps is triggered by a credit event with the respect to the reference obligor, even if the reference security itself is not in default. Secondly, with respect to many default swaps, no final payment is made on a default swap unless the fair market value of the reference security declines more than a specified amount, but if the threshold is passed, the entire assumed loss is paid (including the threshold amount).[39] Finally, the protection seller has no right of subrogation or reimbursement against the reference obligor.

The risk of recharacterisation as a guarantee will be somewhat greater if the default swap requires the protection buyer to hold the reference security (whether explicitly or effectively, for example, by requiring physical settlement – that is, requiring the protection buyer on the occurrence of a credit event to deliver the reference security to the protection seller in return for a payment of par from the protection seller). In such a case, one of the features that distinguishes a default swap from a guarantee would be eliminated. The risk would be greater still if, in addition, the term of the swap is substantially coextensive with the remaining life of the reference security. In such a case, the default swap would then effectively protect against the actual losses realised by the buyer (provided, of course, that the payment on the default swap was triggered by a credit event with respect to the reference security – not the reference obligor generally). Contracts that protect a person from actual realised losses in a security have been characterised for tax purposes as guarantees.

CONSEQUENCES OF RECHARACTERISATION

The consequences of writing or acquiring a guarantee and paying or receiving payments thereunder are not settled and are beyond the scope of

this chapter.[40] Nonetheless, it generally appears that: (a) all periodic payments would be includable in gross income by the protection seller and deductible by the protection buyer when accrued; (b) in the hands of the protection buyer, the payment made in the case of a credit event would be treated as either an amount realised on the sale of the reference security or as a payment of principal thereon[41] (in both cases effectively offsetting the capital loss on the protection buyer's long position in the reference security); and (c) in the hands of the protection seller, the payment made on the occurrence of a credit event would be an ordinary deduction.[42] Further, if a default swap is recharacterised as a guarantee (or some other unspecified type of financial contract), income from the swap would not benefit from the rules that exclude income on a notional principal contract from unrelated business taxable income in the hands of a pension plan or other tax-exempt investor or the rules treating such income as sourced outside the US and, thus, not subject to withholding tax in the hands of a foreign investor.

If a default swap is determined to be a guarantee, a second question arises – is it insurance? Depending on its terms, it might be. The rules relating to insurance are beyond the scope of this chapter but, in exceedingly general terms, the two elements of insurance are risk shifting and risk distribution.[43] To the extent that the final payment on a default swap is tied to the protec-

39 *In contrast, with a guarantee, except for a deductible (or other retained first loss exposure), there is no threshold loss that is a condition precedent to payment. The threshold in a default swap, however, does not have the same effect as a guarantee's deductible because, with a guarantee, the loss relating to the deductible is never paid.*

40 *For an in-depth discussion, see David S Miller "The Federal Income Tax Consequences of Guarantees: a Comprehensive Framework for Analysis", 48 The Tax Lawyer 103 (Fall 1994).*

41 *Cf Revenue Ruling 76-78, 1976-1 CB 25 ("proceeds of insurance . . . representing maturing interest on defaulted obligations of a state or political subdivision thereof are excludable from . . . gross income [as if they were payments from the obligor]"); Sections 1.861-2(a)(5), 1.862-1(a)(5) (source of interest paid under guarantee is same as the source of the guaranteed interest).*

42 *Of course, there is the possibility that a credit guarantee itself may be recharacterised as a cash-settled put option, the principal consequence of which is to convert the protection seller's loss into a capital loss. See Miller, "The Federal Income Tax Consequences of Guarantees", footnote 40, above.*

43 *See Helvering v LeGierse, 312 US 531 (1941).*

US FEDERAL

INCOME TAX

CONSEQUENCES

OF CREDIT

DERIVATIVES

TRANSACTIONS

OVERVIEW OF US FEDERAL INCOME TAXATION OF NON-US PERSONS

Non-resident aliens and foreign corporations are subject to net income taxation in the US (at the rates applicable to US persons) on income that is effectively connected to a trade or business in the US. In general, undertaking any regular, continuous and substantial business activity in the United States will cause a non-US person to be engaged in a business in the US. Accordingly, any income generated will effectively be connected income and subject to net income taxation in the US.

Notwithstanding the general rule, trading in securities or commodities (and, under recently proposed regulations, notional principal contracts and certain other derivatives) for one's own account (and other activities "closely related thereto") will not cause a non-US person to be considered to be engaged in a US trade or business. Bank loans may not constitute "securities" for this purpose and even if they were considered to be "securities", acquiring interests in bank loans arguably may not constitute "trading" (it might be viewed as part of a lending business, for example). Thus, a business of acquiring interests in bank loans might arguably cause a non-US person to be engaged in a US trade or business if that person undertakes regular, continuous and substantial activities in the US.

Non-US persons not engaged in a US trade or business are subject to a 30% withholding tax on the gross amount of "fixed or determinable annual or periodical" income ("FDAP income") arising from sources within the US. Most passive income, including interest and dividends, is FDAP income.

Gain from the sale of property, however, is not FDAP income. (Income from the exercise or lapse of an option is treated as arising from the sale of property and thus is also not FDAP income.) Income on a notional principal contract is generally sourced by the residence of the recipient and thus income on such contracts received by a non-US person is considered to arise from sources outside the US. Thus, such income may be paid free of withholding tax.

Under an exception to the general rule, "portfolio interest" is not subject to the 30% withholding tax. Portfolio interest includes: (a) interest on debt instruments in registered (rather than bearer) form, provided that the holder complies with certain certification and identification requirements and (b) interest on debt instruments in bearer form, provided they are targeted to non-US persons in the original offering. Interest will not qualify as portfolio interest, however, if (a) the lender and borrower are considered related, (b) the interest is certain contingent interest or the (c) interest is "received by a bank on ... a loan agreement ..."

Applying these general rules to credit derivatives we find that:

❑ Payments made on total return swaps and default swaps may be made free of US federal withholding tax provided such swaps are respected as notional principal contracts. Under certain proposed regulations, entering into credit derivative transactions generally will not cause a non-US person to be engaged in a US trade or business.

❑ If a total return swap is recharacterised as the

---

tion buyer's actual loss on a particular security, then the swap has the effect of shifting the risk of loss to the protection seller. To the extent the protection seller sells protection on various reference obligors to various protection buyers, then the risk of loss on any particular reference security is effectively distributed among those purchasers.

The principal consequences of the recharacterisation of default swaps as insurance are: (a) for an insurance company, periodic payments would be treated as insurance premiums (rather than investment income) and reserves for losses

44 *See section 831(a); Section 301.7701-2(b)(4); Revenue Ruling 83-132, 1983-2 CB 270.*

may be established in respect of the swaps; (b) for a special purpose entity that has a trade or business of selling default protection, the entity may be treated as an insurance company and thus be subject to the corporate income tax even if it is a partnership under general tax principles;[44] and (c) a foreign insurer that is the protection seller under a default swap written other than in connection with a US trade or business may be subject to a 4% excise tax.[45]

Credit-linked notes

There are two types of credit derivative securities that are colloquially referred to as credit-linked notes – the securities issued in

183

US FEDERAL
INCOME TAX
CONSEQUENCES
OF CREDIT
DERIVATIVES
TRANSACTIONS

leveraged purchase of the reference security by the total return receiver, then a total return receiver that is a non-US person will receive payments in respect of interest on the reference security free of US federal withholding tax only if interest on the reference security would qualify as portfolio interest. Because many commercial loans, most mortgages, and other consumer loans are in bearer form (but not issued in offerings targeted to non-US investors) interest on them would not be portfolio interest. If the total return payer is a non-US person, the periodic payments it receives, which would be treated as interest, would be payable free of withholding tax if: (a) the swap is treated as issued in registered form, (b) the total return payer complies (or is deemed to comply) with the certification and identification requirements applicable to holders of registered debt instruments, and (c) the total return payer is not a bank or the payments received on the swap are not considered to arise under a "loan agreement".

❏ If a total return swap is recharacterised as the leveraged purchase of the reference security, then the activities of the total return-payer in the US might be attributed to the total return receiver. Although it is generally unlikely, in certain circumstances such an attribution might cause a total return receiver that is a non-US person to be engaged in a US trade or business. This is most likely to be the case if the reference security is arguably not a "security", such as a mortgage, bank loan or consumer receivable and the swap relates to a pool of such loans that is not fixed in composition.

❏ If a default swap is recharacterised as a put option, then payments made to a non-US person, whether the protection seller or the protection buyer, would generally be payable free of withholding tax.

❏ If a default swap is recharacterised as a guarantee, then the periodic payments made to a protection seller that is a non-US person would not benefit from the rule that treats income on notional principal contracts as arising from sources outside the US. Thus, such income may be subject to the 30% withholding tax if the obligor on the reference security is a US person. As payments made under a guarantee are treated as if they represented the guaranteed payments, if the protection buyer is a non-US person payments made to it that are in respect of principal would be payable free of withholding tax. Payments in respect of interest would be free of withholding tax if interest paid directly by the obligor would have qualified as portfolio interest.

❏ If a default swap is recharacterised as insurance then periodic payments made to a protection seller that is a non-US person will be subject to a 4% tax on insurance premiums received with respect to US persons or US risks.

❏ The tax treatment of credit-linked notes depends on whether they are respected as indebtedness or treated as an equity interest in the issuer. If respected as indebtedness, interest payments on such notes would generally qualify as portfolio interest (assuming the usual requirements were met). If such notes were treated as indirect interests in the Issuer's assets and liabilities, the withholding tax consequences would depend on the characterisation of those assets and liabilities. If the notes were treated as equity interests in a non-US corporation, payments of interest generally would be treated as dividends arising from sources outside the US and would not be subject to US Federal withholding tax.

"all-certificates transactions" and "true credit-linked notes". Credit-linked notes are used for the same purposes as total return swaps and default swaps but, because they are in the form of pass-through securities or debt instruments, they are more appealing to certain investors that have regulatory or other constraints on entering into credit derivative transactions directly.

"ALL-CERTIFICATES" TRANSACTIONS
Despite their name, in an "all-certificates" transaction, credit-linked notes take the form of certificates (the "certificates") of beneficial interest (equity interests) in a trust (the "trust") and not notes or any other form of debt. The trust typi-

cally holds a highly rated, fixed- or floating-rate debt instrument (the "collateral asset") and is the protection seller under a default swap (of the type described above). The principal amount of the certificate is the principal amount of the collateral asset. The notional principal balance of the default swap equals the actual principal balance from time to time of the collateral asset and the default swap's term to maturity equals the maturity of the collateral asset. There is typically only one class of certificates in the trust and all distributions on the certificates are made pro rata. The trust engages in no transactions other than acquir-

45 *See section 4371.*

US FEDERAL
INCOME TAX
CONSEQUENCES
OF CREDIT
DERIVATIVES
TRANSACTIONS

PANEL 5

NOTE AND CERTIFICATE TRANSACTIONS

Certain trusts issuing credit-linked certificates issue notes as well. The notes are entitled to a fixed or floating rate of interest and a fixed principal amount in all events, even on the occurrence of a credit event with respect to the reference obligor. Thus, the note's payment terms are not formally linked to the creditworthiness of the reference obligor. However, whereas payments on the notes are senior to payments on the certificates, they are subordinate to payments due the protection buyer on the default swap. Thus, on the occurrence of a credit event where the payment due the protection buyer under the default swap

exceeds the "overcollateralisation" provided by the certificates, the holders of the notes would suffer a loss. (In that event, the certificate holders would suffer a complete loss.) These transactions typically involve highly-rated reference obligors and significant overcollateralisation. Accordingly, the notes are generally treated as conventional debt instruments for tax purposes. The tax consequences of an investment in these notes is similar to that of true credit-linked notes that are not "contingent payment debt instruments" (discussed in footnotes 49–53 and accompanying text).

ing the collateral asset and entering into the default swap. The trust is liquidated upon the final maturity of the collateral asset (or earlier in the event of a default on the collateral asset or a credit event under the default swap). As a creditor of the trust, the protection buyer under the default swap is senior to the holders of the certificates (which are treated as equity holders).

Economically, a certificate resembles a synthetic debt instrument of the reference obligor (hence the use of the term "credit-linked note" despite the form of the transaction), with a principal amount (and maturity) equal to the principal amount (and maturity) of the certificate. That is, assuming no default with respect to the collateral asset, the periodic distributions on the certificate – the combination of the interest payments on the collateral asset and the periodic payments received on the default swap – will equal (or slightly exceed) the interest payments made on comparable debt instruments issued by the reference obligor and, in the absence of a credit event, the par amount of the certificate will be paid at maturity. If there is a credit event with respect to the reference obligor, the holder of the certificate will be entitled to the liquidation proceeds of the collateral asset reduced by the payment made to the protection buyer, the net amount of which is expected to approximate the expected recovery value of the reference security.

46 *For a discussion of the qualification of grantor trusts and the taxation of their owners, see James M Peaslee and David Z Nirenberg (1994),* The Federal Income Taxation of Mortgage-Backed Securities, *(revised edition) Irwin Professional Publishing), pp. 5-13.*

CHARACTERISATION OF CERTIFICATES IN ALL-CERTIFICATES TRANSACTIONS

The trusts that issue credit-linked certificates are generally structured to qualify as "grantor trusts" for federal income tax purposes. For virtually all federal income tax purposes grantor trusts are ignored and each owner of a certificate of beneficial interest in such a trust is treated as if it directly owned its proportionate share of the assets of the trust and was directly liable for its proportionate share of the obligations of the trust.[46] Thus, each holder of a certificate will be treated as if it owned its proportionate share of he collateral asset and had written its proportionate share of the default swap. The collateral asset will generally be a debt instrument for tax purposes. The default swap will be taxed as described above.

In any particular case, consideration ought to be given to whether the collateral asset and the default swap together may be viewed as a "conversion transaction" or an "integrated transaction". Under section 1258(c), a conversion transaction includes, among others, any transaction from which substantially all of the taxpayer's expected return is attributable to the time value of the taxpayer's net investment in such transaction and which is (a) a straddle or (b) marketed as producing capital gains. In such a case, a portion of any gain that would otherwise be a capital gain if the certificate is sold or the default swap is terminated may be treated as ordinary income. In very general terms, the amount treated as ordinary income would not exceed the amount of interest that would have accrued on the taxpayer's net investment in the transaction at a rate

185

US FEDERAL
INCOME TAX
CONSEQUENCES
OF CREDIT
DERIVATIVES
TRANSACTIONS

equal to 120% of the "applicable Federal rate" (a rate determined by the Service based on the yields of Treasury securities).

As only gain is recharacterised as ordinary, taxpayers are permitted to net certain capital losses and gains from a conversion transaction and thus reduce the amount of capital gain that may be recharacterised as ordinary income. Netting is permitted, however, only if the transaction is identified as a conversion transaction on the taxpayer's books and records on or prior to the date on which the conversion transaction is entered into and when certain other conditions are met. Further, under regulations that have been mandated but have not yet been issued, the amount of capital gain recharacterised as ordinary income will be reduced by ordinary income received in the transaction, presumably including the interest income earned on the collateral assets.

In very general terms, under §1.1275-6, a debt instrument and certain other financial contracts may be integrated and treated as a single, synthetic debt instrument if the synthetic debt instrument would have the same maturity as that of the underlying debt instrument and cashflows that resemble a conventional fixed- or floating-rate debt instrument or that can otherwise be taxed under the rules for accruing original issue discount. In such a case, the certificate would be treated for most tax purposes as a newly issued debt synthetic debt instrument.

TRUE CREDIT-LINKED NOTES

There is a wide variety of true credit-linked notes. For the purposes of this discussion, however, a credit-linked note will mean a debt instrument, the full repayment of the principal of which depends on the non-occurrence of a default of a reference obligor. More fully, such a note is a security that is issued by a party unrelated to a reference obligor, is in form of a debt instrument, pays a fixed (or floating) rate of interest and, in the absence of a credit event either (a) with respect to a reference obligor generally or (b) on a specified reference security, has a fixed maturity date on which the par amount of the security is repaid. In the event of a default by a reference obligor or on the reference security, however, the maturity is accelerated and the amount required to be repaid is limited to a sum computed with reference to the trading value (sometimes the recovery value) of a specified reference security issued by the reference obligor. (Sometimes, the final payment in the case of a credit event is a binary payment – that is, a fixed percentage of par.)

Credit-linked notes are issued either by (a) real and substantial operating companies or (b) in some cases by a special purpose vehicle (an "SPV") that is itself the protection seller under a default swap with respect to the same reference obligor and that holds some other collateral assets, the cashflow on which is used to make debt service payments on the credit-linked notes. (The collateral assets are generally high-quality, asset-backed, corporate or governmental securities, the interest payments on which, when added to the periodic payments made by the protection buyer on the default swap, will be sufficient to pay interest on the credit-linked notes.)

TAXATION OF TRUE CREDIT-LINKED NOTES

The first issue is whether a credit-linked note is a debt instrument for tax purposes. The traditional definition of a debt instrument – an unqualified obligation to pay a sum certain on demand or prior to a fixed maturity date along with additional payments to compensate for the use of money – requires that the principal amount of the note be a *sum certain*.[47] Thus, under the traditional analysis, a debt instrument the principal payment on which is wholly contingent would be subject to a substantial risk of recharacterisation as something other than a single debt instrument.

Nonetheless, it is not a foregone conclusion that a credit-linked note is not a single debt instrument. Recently, the IRS has implicitly recognised that debt instruments that have contingent principal may in fact be considered debt for tax purposes. See, for example, section 1.1275-4(b)(4)(vi), Example 1 (contingent payment rules for debt instruments applied to a bond the principal of which could either be increased without limit or could be reduced by 35% in the event of certain contingencies) and section 1.1275-6(h), Example 6 (a bond the principal of which could be increased or decreased by 50% depending on certain contingencies was treated as a debt instrument). In each of these examples, when fixed interest payments were taken into account, the total amount of the non-contingent payments, including interest, exceeded the issue price of the debt instrument. Thus, with respect to those examples (but not with credit-linked notes) it could be argued that

---

47 *See, for example, Gilbert v Comm'r, 248 F2d 399 (2d Cir. 1957).*

US FEDERAL
INCOME TAX
CONSEQUENCES
OF CREDIT
DERIVATIVES
TRANSACTIONS

since an amount equal to the original principal amount would be paid in all events, a sum certain was required to be repaid.

For a US SPV, if a credit-linked note were not respected as debt, it would generally be characterised as an indirect ownership interest in the SPV's assets or as an equity interest in the SPV. If the SPV were a grantor trust or partnership, recharacterisation of the notes as equity interests in the SPV would lead to the treatment of the notes as indirect interests in the SPV's assets as well. In either such case, holders of the credit-linked notes would be taxed in a manner similar to that of holders of certificates in an all-certificates transaction.

For a foreign SPV, if a credit-linked note is not respected as debt it would generally be treated as stock (and, possibly, voting stock) in the issuer. The issuer would generally be a "passive foreign investment company" (a "PFIC") for US federal income tax purposes. Special unfavourable rules apply to a US shareholder in a PFIC unless the investor makes a so-called QEF ("qualified electing fund") election. If a QEF election is made, the US holder will be required to include its *pro rata* share of the issuer's ordinary income and net capital gains (not reduced by any prior year losses) in income (as ordinary income and long-terms capital gain, respectively) for each taxable year and pay tax thereon even if such income and gain is not distributed to it. Such holder is not subject to tax a second time when the cash attributable to such income is distributed. If US persons owning 10% or more of the equity in the issuer together own 50% or more of such equity, the issuer will be a "controlled foreign corporation" (a "CFC"). A US shareholder in a CFC is taxable on its share of a CFC's income whether or

not it is distributed (but is not subject to tax a second time when cash attributed to such income is distributed). Non-US persons holding credit-linked notes generally would not be subject to tax in the US as the dividends on a foreign corporation's stock are not treated as arising from US sources (unless the SPV is considered to be engaged in a trade or business in the US).

Although it is far from certain, it is more likely that the note will be treated as indebtedness if the issuer of the credit-linked note is not an SPV and is not the protection seller under a default swap. Such a note is debt in form and does not, in substance, more closely resemble equity in the issuer rather than debt. Accordingly, the note should not be recharacterised as an equity interest. Although, economically, a credit-linked note resembles an investment unit consisting of a debt instrument and a default swap (the protection seller of which is the holder of the credit-linked note), there is no clear authority for such a position from the IRS. As, in this scenario, the issuer of the credit-linked note is not itself a protection seller under a default swap, no conduit analysis of the type described in the immediately preceding paragraph should be sustained – that is, the issuer of the credit-linked note does not have any assets that the IRS could argue are held on behalf of the holders of the credit-linked notes.

Assuming that a credit-linked note is a debt instrument, the timing and character of income in the hands of an investor will depend on whether the credit-linked note is a contingent payment debt instrument ("CPDI") within the meaning of section 1.1275-4(a). With limited exceptions, a CPDI is any debt instrument that provides for one or more contingent payments. For this purpose, a payment is not considered contingent solely because it is subject to a contingency whose likelihood of occurrence is remote.[48] Arguably, then, a credit-linked note will be considered a CPDI only if the likelihood of a credit event with respect to the reference obligor (or on the reference security) is greater than "remote". The regulations do not provide any guidance regarding the meaning of "remote". Where the reference obligor is an obligor with a high credit rating or where the credit-linked note has a short maturity, the argument that the possibility of a credit event during the term of the note is "remote" is strengthened.[49]

Where a credit-linked note is not a CPDI, interest on the note will be ordinary interest income for the holder, and ordinary interest expense to the issuer, as it accrues. If there is a

---

48 *Section 1.1275-4(a)(5) (remoteness of occurrence is tested as of the issue date); see also section 1.1275-2(b).*

49 *A payment is not considered contingent solely on account of the possibility of impairment by "insolvency, default, or similar circumstances". Section 1.1275-4(a)(3). Although the situation is not certain, this provision probably refers only to the insolvency and so forth of the issuer of the debt instrument in question. This rule is unlikely to cause credit-linked notes generally to be characterised as other than CPDIs. On the other hand, where the issuer of the credit-linked note is an SPV and a credit event would cause it to be unable to make payments on its notes (for example, because the SPV is the protection seller under a default swap with respect to the same reference security, which is senior to the notes), a strong argument can be made (assuming that the note is respected as debt) that the failure to pay the full par amount of the notes is on account of "insolvency, default or similar circumstances".*

US FEDERAL
INCOME TAX
CONSEQUENCES
OF CREDIT
DERIVATIVES
TRANSACTIONS

credit event and less than the full principal amount of the note is repaid, the issuer would probably be considered to have cancellation of indebtedness income, which is ordinary.[50] The character of the holder's loss is unclear. As discussed earlier, unless a specific Code provision applies, capital loss treatment only applies to sales or exchanges.[51] Arguably, if the issuer is a corporation, the note would be treated as a worthless security and, thus, the loss would be a capital loss for the holder under 165(g).[52] If the note is not a worthless security, then arguably it is a bad debt under section 166; in that case, if the holder is a corporation it will be entitled to an ordinary deduction for the loss. If the holder is not a corporation, then the loss generally will be a short-term capital loss.[53]

If a credit-linked note is treated as a CPDI, different rules apply. Although the rules generally applicable to CPDIs are exceedingly complex, as applied to typical credit-linked notes, they may be summarised as follows.

First, the issuer determines the issuer's assumed yield. That is generally the yield the issuer would have been required to pay (taking account of the issuer's credit quality and general market conditions) had it issued a conventional (non-credit-linked) fixed-rate debt instrument with a term equal to that of the credit-linked note.[54] Then the issuer determines the credit-linked note's projected payment schedule.[55] That schedule, despite its name, is not a schedule of expected payments. Instead, the schedule consists of all non-contingent payments, such as interest, and a number for the contingent payment, the principal payment, which forces the original yield on the instrument to be the issuer's assumed yield.[56] Over time, the holder (even if otherwise a cash method taxpayer) accrues original issue discount (interest) at a rate equal to the issuer's assumed yield. In general, the excess of the actual interest payments made on the note over the original issue discount accrued on the note (at the assumed yield) would be treated as a return of capital.[57] If there is no credit event over the entire term of the note and the entire principal amount is paid at maturity, the excess of the amount received by the investor over the "projected" amount would be treated as additional interest income (or, for the issuer, expense). The effect of this approach – determining periodic income (or deduction) based on the assumed yield – is that the portion of the interest on the note that reflects compensation for taking the credit risk of the reference obligor is not included in income by the holder (or deducted by the issuer) until maturity.

Under special rules for CPDIs, if there is a credit event and less than par is repaid, the loss will be treated as an ordinary loss in an amount up to the amount of interest previously included in income and the balance will be a capital loss.[58] All gain on the sale of a CPDI is treated as interest income.[59]

There is an alternative approach that has some merit. The above description assumes that peri-

---

50 *If the issuer of the credit-linked note owns the reference security it may recognise a capital loss on the sale of that security that would not directly offset the ordinary cancellation of indebtedness income arising on the credit-linked note.*

51 *Section 1234A (discussed at footnotes 12–14 above and accompanying text) would not provide a basis for capital treatment; by its terms it does not apply to the retirement of a debt instrument.*

52 *Under section 165(g)(2)(c) only debt instruments issued by corporations or governmental entities may be considered worthless securities.*

53 *Section 166(d)(1)(B).*

54 *Section 1.1275-4(b)(4)(i)(A). If the issuer could hedge its exposure to the contingent payments so as to create, from its own perspective, a synthetic, non-contingent debt instrument, the assumed yield will be the yield on that synthetic debt instrument.*

55 *This schedule is determined once, upon the issuance of the note, and is binding on all holders of the note unless unreasonable. Sections 1.1275-4(b)(3)(ii), 4(b)(4)(iv) and (v).*

56 *More technically, the schedule consists of all non-contingent payments and the forward price of any "market-based" contingent payment and the "expected value", as of the issue date, of any non-market-based contingent payments. Section 1.1275-4(b)(4)(ii). If, as is likely, the yield based on that schedule does not match the issuer's assumed yield, the amounts of the contingent payments are adjusted in a manner that forces the yield under the adjusted schedule to equal the issuer's assumed yield. (Where there are both market-based and non-market based payments, the non-market based payments are adjusted first.) Section 1.1275-4(b)(ii)(C).*

57 *That is, all payments on the instrument under a projected payment schedule are considered to be included in the instrument's stated redemption price at maturity and original issue discount is accrued at the original yield to maturity determined under that payment schedule. Section 1.1275-4(b)(3)(iii); section 1.1275-4(b)(5).*

58 *Section 1.1275-4(b)(6)(iii) and (b)(8)(ii).*

59 *See section 1.1275-4(b)(8)(i).*

US FEDERAL
INCOME TAX
CONSEQUENCES
OF CREDIT
DERIVATIVES
TRANSACTIONS

odic payments of interest on a credit-linked note are treated as non-contingent. This is not certain. Arguably, like the principal payment, they are contingent on the non-occurrence of a credit event. If treated as contingent, then, the projected schedule arguably might project interest payments at the assumed yield and full repayment of principal.[60] In that situation, the excess of actual interest payments over those on the schedule would be additional interest income. The effect of this approach would be to require inclusion in income (allow a deduction) of the entire interest payment on the note over the life of the note, including that portion that reflects economically compensation paid to investors for taking the credit risk of the reference obligor.

If a holder acquires a credit-linked note in the secondary market it continues to accrue original issue discount based on the original assumed yield (that is, the projected payment schedule does not change) regardless of intervening events (including the deterioration in the credit quality of the reference obligor).[61] Special rules apply, however, to any market discount or premium with which a CPDI is acquired in the secondary market. In very general terms, market discount or premium is allocated between two separate components: the portion arising from changes in interest rates and the like and the portion attributable to changes in the credit quality of the reference obligor. The former is taken into account over the life of the note and the latter, upon its maturity.

Conclusions

Although no authoritative guidance discusses the characterisation of contracts with terms substantially the same as a total return swap, a default swap, or a credit-linked note, certain conclusions can be drawn from the available authorities.
❑ A total return swap on an actively traded debt instrument will be treated, for federal income tax purposes, as a notional principal contract. Accordingly, periodic payments (other than periodic change-in-value payments, if any) made pursuant to a total return swap will generally give rise, when accrued, to ordinary income or an ordinary deduction. The same should be true with respect to the gain or loss recognised in connection with any change-in-value payment on

a total return swap (whether made periodically or at the maturity of swap) but while this result reflects the view expressed in private letter rulings by the Service, it is not entirely certain.

Where the total return payer owns the reference security (but is not required to do so) and the reference security is an actively traded debt instrument, the issuance of the total return swap should not have the effect of transferring the tax ownership of the reference security to the total return receiver. Where the reference security is not actively traded or the total return payer is actually or effectively required to hold the reference security on behalf of the total return receiver, the risk of recharacterisation of the transaction as a leveraged purchase of the reference security by the total return receiver is increased. Such a recharacterisation would cause the total return payer to recognise any built-in gain inherent in the long position in the reference security. It also would have a number of other (secondary) consequences for both the total return payer and the total return receiver that will depend on their particular circumstances but, in general, will not necessarily be either advantageous or adverse.
❑ A default swap (particularly one requiring cash settlement) whose reference security is a debt instrument that is not owned by the protection buyer, should be treated for federal income tax purposes as a notional principal contract. There is some possibility, however, that a default swap will be recharacterised as a put option or a guarantee. Where the default swap may be physically settled or where the protection buyer is actually or effectively required to hold the reference security, the risk of recharacterisation is greater.

The most significant consequence of recharacterisation of a default swap as a put option is that the periodic payments made by the protection buyer and received by the protection seller would be capitalised and, thus, not be immediately deductible by the protection buyer and not immediately includable in income by the protection seller. Gain or loss on the triggering of the default swap or, if there is no credit event, the loss to the protection buyer and the gain to the protection seller arising from the capitalised periodic payments, generally would be capital gain or loss.

If a default swap is recharacterised as a guarantee (or some other unspecified type of financial contract), income from the swap would not benefit from the rules that exclude income on a

---

60 *See sections 1.1275-4(b)(4)(ii)(C) and 4(b)(4)(v)(B) (projected payment schedule should not cause frontloading or backloading of interest).*

61 *See section 1.1275-4(b)(9).*

US FEDERAL
INCOME TAX
CONSEQUENCES
OF CREDIT
DERIVATIVES
TRANSACTIONS

notional principal contract from unrelated business taxable income in the hands of a pension plan or other tax-exempt investor, or the rules treating such income as sourced outside the US in the hands of a foreign investor.

❑ In an "all-certificates" transaction, the holder of a credit-linked note (which, despite its name, takes the form of a certificate of beneficial interest in a trust) generally is treated as owning an indirect interest in a collateral asset and being the protection seller under a default swap.

❑ The tax consequences for a holder of a true credit-linked note depend on whether the note is a "contingent payment debt instrument" ("CPDI"). If not, all interest on the note is included in income as it accrues, including the portion that represents compensation for accepting the credit risk of the reference obligor. In the case of a note that is a CPDI, while the situation is not certain, it appears that only the portion of the interest that reflects the issuer's borrowing cost, excluding compensation for accepting the credit risk of the reference obligor, is taken into income as it accrues. The balance is treated as additional interest income at maturity.

❑ Where a participant in a credit derivative transaction has a position in the reference security (other than through its participation in the transaction), consideration should be given to whether the two positions may be integrated and treated as a single, synthetic debt instrument under section 1.1275-6 and, if not, whether the two positions constitute a straddle or conversion transaction.

INDEX